ADOPTION OF CHILDREN
IN SCOTLAND

AUSTRALIA
LBC Information Services
Sydney

CANADA AND THE USA
Carswell
Toronto

NEW ZEALAND
Brooker's
Auckland

SINGAPORE AND MALAYSIA
Thomson Information (S.E. Asia)
Singapore

ADOPTION OF CHILDREN IN SCOTLAND

by

Peter G. B. McNeill, Q.C., M.A., LL.B., Ph.D.

THIRD EDITION

EDINBURGH
GREEN/Sweet & Maxwell
1998

First published 1982
Second edition 1986
Third edition 1998

Published in 1998 by W. Green & Son Limited
21 Alva Street
Edinburgh EH2 4PS

Typeset by Hewer Text Limited
Edinburgh

Printed in Great Britain by Redwood Books
Trowbridge, Wiltshire

No natural forests were destroyed to make this product;
only farmed timber was used and replanted

A CIP catalogue record of this book is available from the British
Library

ISBN 0 414 01134 1

To

M.F.M.

PREFACE TO THIRD EDITION

This third edition has been occasioned primarily by the bringing into force of the Children (Scotland) Act 1995. The new provisions relating to adoption are to be found in Part III of and Schedule 2 to that Act. These provisions amend the Adoption (Scotland) Act 1978. The first major change is to vary the terms of section 6: now the court must have regard to the need to safeguard the welfare of the child "throughout his life" (in place of "throughout his childhood") and the welfare of the child is "the paramount consideration" (in place of "the first consideration"). The 1995 Act (section 97) also permits a step-parent who is married to the natural parent of the child to present a petition for adoption alone without the necessity of a joint application along with the parent of the child. Apart from these major alterations and some less fundamental changes created by the schedules to the 1995 Act, the 1978 Act remains substantially in force.

New sheriff court rules which relate to adoption are now contained in Act of Sederunt (Child Care and Maintenance Rules) 1997, Chapters 1 and 2 (Parts I to V). The corresponding rules of the Court of Session are Rules of the Court of Session 1994, Chapter 67.

I have taken into account other legislative changes and decisions that have been made since 1986; and I have pruned some of the text in the second edition.

Generally, the effect of the changes in the recent legislation is to create a more elaborate procedure for adoptions. This trend takes place at a time when about 95 per cent of the petitions for adoption are granted unopposed; and when the number of petitions which are presented continues to fall. The Scottish statistics over the years illustrate this: "the total number of applications has decreased by 40 per cent from 942 in 1985 to 555 in 1995 (*Statistical Bulletin, Social Work Series*, July 1997, page 3). In addition, in recent years, there have been about 60 applications to free a child for adoption each year.

The trend of the reported cases over the last decade or more shows two developments. There have been about half a dozen Inner House cases which have set out authoritatively the correct approach to several aspects of adoption procedure. On the other hand, there has been a welter of over-reporting of adoption cases. These reports are often duplicated in different law reports and journals. They are usually single judge decisions which proceed on their own facts: they are not authoritative and most disclose no point of principle. Indeed, the Court of Appeal has said "that the task of the court in determining an adoption application was to be performed not by applying a test based on other cases, but by having regard to all the statutory considerations (*H* (also cited as *A (A Minor) (Adoption Application: non patrial*) [1996] 4 All E.R. 600). Similarly, it was observed that a party focused too much on judgments in earlier proceedings and insufficiently upon the sheriff's judgment which was under review (*K and K, Petitioners*, Sheriff Principal Risk, Aberdeen Sheriff Court, February 8, 1994, unreported). One result of this over-reporting is that it encourages some practitioners to refer to these cases to little purpose and with increasing delay.

(For the future, a new adoption Bill exists. It provides for the replacement and amendment of the (English) Adoption Act 1976 and for a few, but significant, alterations to the Adoption (Scotland) Act 1978. It is not known when this Bill will be proceeded with.)

I would like to acknowledge with thanks the assistance and encouragement that I have received in a variety of ways from Lord Rodger of Earlsferry, Lord President of the Court of Session, the Clerks of the Court of Session, the staff of the Sheriff Clerks Office, Edinburgh (and in particular Miss Alison Williams and Mr Douglas Watt), the staff of Advocates' Library, Mr Peter Gillam, solicitor, Edinburgh, Mrs Janys Scott, advocate, Sheriff Daphne Robertson, Edinburgh, the staff of the Registrar General for Scotland, Dr Ian Grant and the staff of the Keeper of Records, Susan Sills of British Agencies for Adoption and Fostering (BAAF), Scotland, and Mr Michael Stevens, Social Works Services Group, Edinburgh, and to Mrs Elanor Bower McGarry and Miss Karen F. Taylor of W. Green & Son Ltd.

Again Sheriff D. B. Smith has read the typescript and made many helpful suggestions. And as before, I must acknowledge the help given by my wife: without her assistance this edition would not have appeared.

Edinburgh   P. G. B. McN.
August 1998

PREFACE TO FIRST EDITION

Adoption of children was introduced into Scotland over 50 years ago: yet there is no Scottish textbook on the subject such as there is in England in the form of J. F. Gosling, *Adoption of Children* (9th ed.), Oyez Practice Notes. It is hoped that the present work will go some way towards filling the gap in Scotland. The book arose out of lectures which were given to the panel of curators *ad litem* in Glasgow Sheriff Court and to a conference of solicitors; and it has been expanded to include additional aspects of procedure in the sheriff court where all but a tiny handful of petitions are presented. The result may be of interest to those who are professionally involved in adoption in or out of court and also to lay people.

I have only dealt with the extant law, that is, chiefly the residue of the 1958 Act together with those parts of the 1975 Act which relate to adoption and have been brought into force in Scotland. At the same time, I have included references to the corresponding provisions of the 1978 Act which prospectively consolidates the Scottish law of adoption. I have taken into account the changes in the law which came into force on 15 February 1982 and which are contained in the Children Act 1975 (Scotland) (Commencement No. 3) Order 1982 (S.I. 1982 No. 33) and Adoption Agencies (Scotland) Regulations 1982 (S.I. 1982 No. 34). I have also noted the prospective changes effected by the British Nationality Act 1981 in so far as they affect the adoption of children.

In 1930 there were 339 adoption petitions in the sheriff courts of Scotland; in the late 1960s there were over 2000; and in the late 1970s there were about 1600 and decreasing. In England the decline is even more marked. The recent fall in numbers is probably due to several causes: the increase in use of contraception, the greater resort to abortion and the fact that more unmarried mothers are willing to bring up their children themselves in a moral and economic climate which is less harsh than formerly. The figures come from the Civil Judicial Statistics and the Reports of the Registrar General for Scotland.

For lay people and the profession also an ideal outline of adoption procedure before and after the case comes into court is to be found in *Adopting a Child* (1981), a booklet of the British Agencies for Adoption and Fostering, 11 Southwark Street, London SE1 1RQ: (01) 407 8800. The booklet also contains a list of adoption agencies throughout Britain with their addresses and telephone numbers. The addresses and telephone numbers of the courts and the Keeper of the Records of Scotland which respectively hold the more recent and older adoption processes can be found in the telephone directories. Local authorities also produce their own leaflets directed to those inquiring about adoption, for example, *Thinking about Adoption?* which is produced by Strathclyde Regional Council.

Glasgow   P. G. B. McN.
1 February 1982

PREFACE TO SECOND EDITION

At the time of the first edition of this book, some of the provisions of the Children Act 1975 which related to adoption in Scotland had already been brought into force. The remaining adoption provisions were brought into force in 1984, and at the same time the Adoption (Scotland) Act 1978 came into force, thereby repealing and re-enacting the adoption provisions of the 1975 Act and consolidating them with such parts of the Adoption Acts of 1958, 1960, 1964 and 1968 as were still in force. Thus in Scotland, there is in the Adoption (Scotland) Act 1978 a consolidated statute dealing with adoption; but between the passing of the act and its commencement, some parts have been amended, such as the provisions relating to nationality; and some other parts of the law of adoption are to be found outside the 1978 Act, such as section 53 of the 1975 Act which empowers the court in an adoption petition to treat the petition as if it were an application for custody.

(In England the adoption law has also been consolidated in the same way—in the Adoption Act 1976; but in England that consolidating statute has not been brought into force; and the law has to be found in the unrepealed parts of the Adoption Acts of 1958, 1960, 1964 and 1968 and Part I of the Children Act 1975.)

The principal change which has now been brought into force is the new procedure of freeing a child for adoption, whereby the question of the agreements of the natural parents may be disposed of in advance of any actual adoption. In addition, the statute and the rules of court have made hearings compulsory in all cases, even where there is no dispute, whereas, formerly, in undisputed matters no hearings were required unless the court felt that a hearing was necessary. Also, whereas formerly the court was only concerned with one officer—the curator *ad litem*—there is now, in addition, the new reporting officer. In the past, the court relied upon a single report: now the legislation provides for nine types of report. New regional panels of curators *ad litem* and reporting officers have been created; and the fees of these officers in most cases is borne by the local authority and not the petitioners as was the case formerly.

The terms of the adoption rules of the sheriff court and the Court of Session were at one time the same, and thereafter substantially identical: now, in form they are significantly different, but despite these verbal differences, the total information which will be given to each court will in substance be the same. Indeed, generally, the changes brought about by the 1978 Act and the subordinate legislation are more apparent than real. There has been no significant change in the conditions precedent nor in the merits; and even the agreements of the natural parent and the consent of the child in a freeing application are the same in a freeing application as in a petition for adoption, but with some elaboration in procedure: thus, the duties of the reporting officer merely provide a more elaborate method of establishing the agreement of the natural parents which, formerly, was executed in most cases before a justice of the peace.

The size and nature of the problem of adoptions can to some extent be illustrated by reference to the statistics. For the last few years the number of adoptions which have been granted are of the order of 1600 per year. In court, the proportion of parent and step-parent adoptions on the one hand and non relative adoptions on the other hand is about equal; and the total of them is well over 90% of the whole number. Almost all adoption petitions are presented in the sheriff court: only a tiny number are presented in the Court of Session. (It is unlikely that petitions to free a child for adoption will show any difference.) Surprisingly, almost all appeals from the decision of the sheriff are made to the Court of Session rather than to the sheriff principal. Almost all petitions for adoption are by married couples rather than by a single person. And probably most significant of all, almost every adoption is unopposed most throughout the proceedings and the rest eventually. In these cases, if the court is otherwise satisfied that all the requirements have been met it will, no doubt, grant the adoption order after the hearing.

I have taken into account the further implementation of the 1975 Act, section 53 of which allows the court in an adoption petition to deal with custody instead of adoption, and the modifications of the regional panel of curators *ad litem* and reporting officers. The Law Reform (Parent and Child) (Scotland) Act 1986 received the Royal Assent on 26 March 1986; but the Act shall only come into force on such day as the Secretary of State may appoint by order made by statutory instrument.

Edinburgh　　　　　　　　　　　　　　　　　　　　P. G. B. McN.
9 May 1986

CONTENTS

TABLE OF CASES

TABLE OF STATUTES

TABLE OF STATUTORY INSTRUMENTS

LIST OF ABBREVIATIONS

A.S. 1959   Act of Sederunt (Adoption of Children) 1959
A.S. 1997   Act of Sederunt (Child Care and Maintenance Rules) 1997
R.C.   Rules of the Court of Session 1965
RCS   Rules of the Court of Session 1994
1926 Act   Adoption of Children Act 1926
1930 Act   Adoption of Children (Scotland) Act 1930
1950 Act   Adoption Act 1950
1958 Act   Adoption Act 1958
1968 Act   Social Work (Scotland) Act 1969
1975 Act   Children Act 1975
1976 Act   Adoption Act 1976
1978 Act   Adoption (Scotland) Act 1978
1995 Act   Children (Scotland) Act 1995

CHAPTER 1

ADOPTION

Adoption Defined

Adoption is the legal process whereby a new status of parent and child is **1.01** created by the order of a court[1] between an adult and a child, whether they are related to each other or not. The statutory definition of an adoption order is "an order vesting the parental responsibilities and parental rights in relation to a child in the adopters, made on their application by an authorised court".[2] Notwithstanding the procedure of Roman law for adoption, and the former Scottish practice of legitimation by Church or state,[3] the law of Scotland has never recognised any private contract of adoption; and attempts to achieve adoption in this way have been regarded by the courts as unenforceable.[4] Adoption in Scotland and England is the creature of the legislation of the last half century.

Adoption Legislation

Adoption was introduced into England and Wales by the Adoption of **1.02** Children Act 1926, and into Scotland by the Adoption of Children (Scotland) Act 1930. Subsequent amendments and the consolidation Acts of 1950 and 1958 were Great Britain measures—although in many respects there were quite separate Scottish and English provisions contained within each statute. The Children Act 1975 added to the complication in respect that not only was it a Great Britain measure, but it also dealt with both adoption and custody of children. In addition, the parts of the 1975 Act which had been brought into force had been enacted piecemeal in both countries and large and significant parts of the Act—such as the power to make a custody order in an adoption application: sections 37 (England) and 53 (Scotland) constituted an important part of the report of the Houghton Committee which preceded the legislation—had only been brought into force on April 1, 1986.[5] Formerly, until the end of 1984 it was necessary to refer to the residue of the 1958 Act and to such parts of the 1975 Act (as were Scottish and as

---

[1] *J and J v. C's Tutor*, 1948 S.C. 636 at 641.
[2] 1978 Act, s. 12(1).
[3] Green's *Encyclopaedia of the Laws of Scotland* (1926 and 1929), i, 134 and viii, 32.
[4] *Kerrigan v. Hall* (1901) 4 F. 10.
[5] Children Act 1975 (Scotland) (Commencement No. 6) Order 1985 (S.I. 1985 No. 1557), para. 3: in England, s. 37 (as amended by the Health and Social Services and Social Security Adjudications Act 1983, s. 9 and Sched. 2, para. 23) came into force on December 1, 1985: Children Act 1975 and Domestic Proceedings and Magistrates' Courts Act 1978 (Commencement) Order 1985 (S.I. 1985 No. 779), reg. 2(1) and Sched. 1.

related to adoption) as well as the 1960 Act, the 1964 Act and the 1968 Act.

The fragmented state of the law came to an end in Scotland only in 1984 when the Adoption (Scotland) Act 1978 was brought into force.[6] In England and Wales the corresponding consolidating statute, the Adoption Act 1976, has also been brought into force.[7] The (Scottish) 1978 Act has been amended in minor respects over the years since 1984[8]: and the Children (Scotland) Act 1995[9] has introduced significant changes, the most fundamental of which is the amendment of section 6.[10] The provisions of the 1995 Act, which amended the 1978 Act, have different commencement dates.[11] A few of the provisions came into force on December 12, 1996, but only for the purpose of enabling directions, rules or regulations to be made under those provisions "so as to come into force on or after 1st April 1997".[12] Apart from the insertion from April 1, 1998 of a new section 51A (which deals with adoption allowances) and the non-enforcement of a minor amendment in section 2 of the Trusts (Scotland) Act 1921, the provisions of the Children (Scotland) Act 1995 in so far as not already in force came into force on April 1, 1997.[13]

1.03   The Scottish procedural rules which govern petitions presented in the Court of Session are contained in Act of Sederunt (Rules of the Court of Session) 1994,[14] Chap. 67. The rules are printed in Appendix 1 of this book. The corresponding sheriff court rules are contained in Act of Sederunt (Child Care and Maintenance Rules) 1997,[15] Chap. 1 and Pts I to IV of Chap. 2, which also appear in Appendix 1. The current regulations governing adoption agencies approved under the 1978 Act[16] came into force on April 1, 1995.[17]

1.04   There are differences in adoption between the laws applying in Scotland and in England and Wales. The procedural provisions are

---

[6] Adoption (Scotland) Act 1978 Commencement Order 1984 (S.I. 1984 No. 1050), para. 3.

[7] ss. 58A and 74 on May 27, 1984; Children Act 1975 and Adoption Act 1976 Commencement Order 1983 (S.I. 1983 No. 1946), and the remaining provisions of the 1976 Act on January 1, 1988; Adoption Act 1976 (Commencement No. 2) Order 1987 (S.I. 1987 No. 1242), but with the amendments specified in that commencement order.

[8] These are noted in Append. 1.

[9] Pt III and Sched. 2.

[10] See para. 8.24, below.

[11] Children (Scotland) Act 1995 (Commencement No. 1) Order 1995 (S.I. 1995 No. 2787); Children (Scotland) Act 1995 (Commencement No. 2 and Transitional Provisions) Order 1996 (S.I. 1996 No. 2203); Children (Scotland) Act 1995 (Commencement No. 3) Order 1996 (S.I. 1996 No. 3201).

[12] Children (Scotland) Act 1995 (Commencement No. 3) Order 1996 (S.I. 1996 No. 3201), para. 3(1)–(6). S. 101 is one of the "suspended" provisions which empowers the Secretary of State to make provision by regulations *inter alia* for the establishment of panels of persons from whom curators *ad litem* and reporting officers may be appointed. Accordingly, the current 1984 Regulations will apply in the meantime; see K. McK. Norrie, *Children (Scotland) Act 1995* (1995 W. Green and Son Ltd), note to s. 101. See paras 7.04 and 14.02, below.

[13] Children (Scotland) Act 1995 (Commencement No. 3) Order 1996 (S.I. 1996 No. 3201), para. 3(7)(a) and (b).

[14] S.I. 1994 No. 1443. Hereinafter RCS.

[15] S.I. 1997 No. 291. Hereinafter A.S. 1997.

[16] As modified by the 1995 Act, s. 98(1) and Sched. 2, paras 1–5.

[17] Adoption Agencies (Scotland) Regulations 1996 (S.I. 1996 No. 3266).

quite distinct and are contained in separate statutory instruments applicable to each of the courts of each country.[18] However, many of the important provisions in the statutes are expressed in the same language. In this respect Lord President Clyde said in *AB and CB v. X's Curator*:

> "In a matter of this kind it would be unfortunate if the Courts of these two countries arrived at different constructions of the same statutory provision equally applicable to both, and I see no reason in the present case for reaching a different interpretation from that arrived at in England."[19]

Yet the impression may be had from some of the statutory provisions and certain dicta of the judges that in England there is or was a bias against adoption and in favour of contact (formerly custody), particularly in relation to adoptions by a parent and a step-parent. Thus, there was a provision, which did not apply to Scotland, that where the application is by a married couple who consisted of a parent and a step-parent of the child, "the court shall dismiss the application if it considers the matter would be better dealt with under section 42 (orders for custody, etc.) of the Matrimonial Causes Act 1973".[20] This provision did not allow the court in an adoption petition to grant a custody (now residence) order; such an alternative remedy had been in force in England and Wales since 1985 and in Scotland since 1986,[21] but has been repealed.[22] Further, the "well and firmly" expressed observations of the judges in *Re B*,[23] which included the phrase "the statutory guillotine", were expressed in a case in which there was a protesting parent—which is not a common situation—and it was in the same context in that case at page 145 that Bagnall J. said:

> "The disadvantages of adoption are perhaps too obvious to be stated. It is an irrevocable step constituting a change of status and also involving not only cutting the child off from his father as a matter of law, but also from grandparents and any other relevant members of the father's family. The child is thereby deprived of any opportunity, as he grows up in later life, to decide whether he wishes to maintain a contact with his father."

Those remarks can at most only apply to an adoption by a parent **1.05** and a step-parent with a still-protesting father, and no doubt depend on the facts of the particular case; and although the remarks just quoted cannot be regarded as an unqualified and general statement of the law, they may be taken as such even to the extent of dissuading potential adopters from embarking on proceedings or solicitors from so advising a client. Yet there has never been any suggestion that in matters other

---

[18] In the High Court and county courts, Adoption Rules 1984 (S.I. 1984 No. 265), and the magistrates' courts, Magistrates' Courts (Adoption) Rules 1984 (S.I. 1984 No. 611).
[19] 1963 S.C. 124 at 135.
[20] 1975 Act, s. 10(3), repealed by the Family Law Act 1996, ss. 66, 67 and Sched. 10.
[21] 1975 Act, ss. 37 and 53.
[22] See para. 1.16, below.
[23] [1975] Fam. 127.

than procedure there is any difference in the law between the two countries: indeed, appeals to the House of Lords from both countries appear to have equal acceptance.[24]

Adoption Order and Other Orders

1.06   The legislation dealing with adoption provides for several different kinds of order.

1.07   (a) An *adoption order* is the most common: the overwhelming majority of petitions seek an adoption order, and the present book is almost wholly concerned with them. Briefly, an adoption order is appropriate where the child is in Scotland and (generally) where the petitioners are domiciled in Scotland or elsewhere in the United Kingdom or the Channel Islands or the Isle of Man, and in most cases have their usual residence in Scotland or England.[25]

1.08   (b) A *freeing order*, which was introduced by legislation which came into force in 1984,[26] may only be sought by an adoption agency. A petition to free a child deals with the agreement of the natural parents in advance of an adoption petition: the subsequent petition for adoption deals with the remainder of the matters in issue. If this procedure is used, in the following adoption process, it is unnecessary to deal again with the agreement of the natural parent. Before the final adoption order is granted the natural parent may seek to revoke the freeing order.[27] In most cases there will be no freeing order in force before the adoption petition is presented.

1.09   (c) An *interim order* is an alternative to an adoption order: it is not an adoption order, but merely an interim order giving parental responsibility and parental rights to the petitioner for a period of up to two years by way of a probationary period. Thereafter the court may grant or refuse an adoption order.[28] Before an interim order can be made there must be the agreement of the natural parents (or their agreement must have been dispensed with) and where the child was not placed with the applicant by an adoption agency, notice must have been given to the local authority; but the other matters do not apply until the time of granting the adoption order. Although an interim order may be made for a fixed period, with or without conditions, the court could, if the interests of the child demanded it, vary the conditions or bring the order to an earlier end, on the motion of parties, or *ex proprio motu*. Since an interim order vests in the petitioners parental responsibility and parental rights in relation to the child, they are entitled to have an extract decree[29] for the purposes of

---

[24] *cf. Re W* [1971] A.C. 682; *A v. B and C*, 1971 S.C. (H.L.) 129; *Re D* [1977] A.C. 602, all of which cases were decided on the law as it stood before s. 10(3) was in force. See also paras 8.32 and 9.04, below.
[25] *cf. Re W* [1962] Ch. 918; Append. 2, 6.
[26] 1978 Act s. 18; see para. 5.21, below.
[27] See para. 5.26, below.
[28] 1978 Act, s. 25. See para. 8.23, below; Append. 2, 5.
[29] See para. 11.05, below.

schooling, income tax, state benefits or medical services as well as to vindicate the right to parental responsibility and parental rights against anyone seeking to resist it. In order to preserve confidentiality, the interlocutor need not mention the word "adoption", or one interlocutor can postpone determination of the petition for adoption, and the other can grant parental responsibility and parental rights.[30] Where an interim order has been made at the statutory hearing,[31] the circumstances of the case will determine whether there should be a continued hearing to consider the grant of a full adoption order.

(d) An *order to adopt a child abroad* (formerly referred to as a *provisional* **1.10** *adoption order*[32]) is appropriate where the petitioners are usually resident in Scotland, but are not domiciled in England or Wales or Scotland, and where an authorised court is satisfied that they intend to take the child out of the country with the intention of adopting the child under the law of or within the country in which the petitioners are domiciled.[33] Petitions to adopt a child abroad are most common in courts within whose jurisdiction there are substantial numbers of servicemen of visiting forces. Except under the authority of an order to adopt a child abroad it is not lawful for any person to take or send a child who is a British subject or a citizen of the Republic of Ireland out of Great Britain to any place outside the United Kingdom, the Channel Islands and the Isle of Man with a view to the adoption of the child by any person not being a parent or guardian or relative of the child.[34] The order authorises the petitioners to remove the child out of the country for the purpose of adoption. The order only vests in the applicant the parental rights and duties relating to the child,[35] but it does not create the relationship of adoptive parent and child[36]; and there is no change brought about in relation to succession or citizenship.[37] As will be noted,[38] a longer period of care and possession of the child by the petitioners is necessary in a petition to adopt a child abroad than an adoption petition. Otherwise, the provisions of the legislation apply equally to petitions to adopt a child abroad and an adoption petition.[39] The style of the petition in the two cases is substantially similar[40]; but the petitioners must adduce evidence of the law of adoption in the country in which the child is domiciled.[41] The form of the order to be transmitted to the Registrar General for Scotland will also be the same as in an adoption order, but with such variations as the case requires.[42]

---

[30] See Append. 2, 5. Confidentiality is discussed later; see para. 5.03, below.
[31] See para. 8.77, below.
[32] 1958 Act, s. 53.
[33] 1978 Act, s. 49.
[34] 1978 Act, s. 50(1); *cf.* Interpretation Act 1978, s. 5 and Sched. 1.
[35] 1978 Act, s. 49(1).
[36] *Re M* [1965] Ch. 203 at 210, *per* Buckley J.
[37] 1978 Act, s. 38.
[38] See para. 3.05, below: the child must be at least 32 instead of 19 weeks old; and the child must have its home with the petitioners for 26 instead of 13 weeks: 1978 Act, s. 49(2).
[39] 1978 Act, s. 49(2).
[40] A.S. 1997, r. 2.21(1) and Form 11 or 12 (RCS, r. 67.22 and Form 67.22).
[41] A.S. 1997, r. 2.22 (RCS, r. 67.27).
[42] 1978 Act, s. 49(3). See Append. 2, 7.

1.11   (e) *Convention adoption orders* were introduced in substance, but not by
that name, by the 1968 Act: in that Act they were merely referred to as
"adoption orders",[43] which nomenclature served to show that what are
now called "Convention adoption orders"[44] are with certain variations the
same as adoption orders: a Convention adoption order is an adoption order
made in accordance with section 17(1).[45] The purpose of the 1968 Act was
to implement the Hague Convention on the Adoption of Children,[46] hence
the name Convention adoption order. These provisions have been in force
since October 23, 1978.[47] A Convention adoption order can only be granted
by the Court of Session, for which provision has been made in the Rules of
the Court of Session, rr. 67.33 to 67.41. An application is appropriate where
there is a foreign element in relation to the child or the petitioners—apart
from domicile, which is not relevant[48]: indeed the provisions are an
alternative to the case where the petitioners are domiciled in the United
Kingdom, the Channel Islands or the Isle of Man. The court may make a
Convention adoption order where:

   (i) the petitioners
      (a) (1) are nationals of the United Kingdom or a Convention
              country, and
          (2) are habitually resident in Great Britain; or
      (b) (1) are United Kingdom nationals, and
          (2) are habitually resident in British territory or a Conven-
              tion country; and
   (ii) the child
      (a) is a national of the United Kingdom or a Convention
          country, and
          (1) habitually resides in British territory or a Convention
              country, but
          (2) is not a United Kingdom national living in British
              territory if both petitioners are; and
          (3) must not be or have been married.[49]

1.12   Those conditions must be satisfied both at the time that the application
is made and when the order is made.

1.13   The 1978 Act also covers adoptions which have been made outwith the
United Kingdom. These are of two categories.

1.14   (i) *Convention adoption* means an overseas adoption—but restricted to
adoptions of a description designated by the Convention Adoption (Miscellaneous Provisions) (Scotland) Order 1978[50] and made under section 53(1)
of the 1978 Act as an adoption regulated by the Convention.[51]

---

[43] 1968 Act, s. 1(1).
[44] 1978 Act, s. 17.
[45] 1978 Act, s. 65(1).
[46] Cmnd. 2613 (1965).
[47] 1975 Act, s. 24 and the Children Act 1975 (Scotland) (Commencement No. 2) Order
1978 (S.I. 1978 No. 1440); 1978 Act, s. 17.
[48] 1978 Act, ss. 14(2)(b) and 15(2)(b).
[49] 1978 Act, s. 17.
[50] S.I. 1978 No. 1441.
[51] 1978 Act, s. 65(1).

(ii) *Overseas adoption* means an adoption of such a description as the **1.15**
Secretary of State may by order specify.[52] The first order to be made
designated several Commonwealth countries and United Kingdom dependent territories as well as other countries and states.[53] Overseas
adoptions form a wider group than Convention adoptions. There are
provisions for recognising overseas adoptions,[54] and for the annulment of
Convention adoptions.[55] Further, where an overseas adoption of a child
who was born in Great Britain is recognised here, the Registrar General
for Scotland will, if he is satisfied that the order relates to an entry in the
Register of Births, record the adoption in the Adopted Children Register.[56] In the first six years of their creation, an average of 23 overseas
adoptions per year have been recorded by the Registrar General for
Scotland; in 1995 five overseas adoptions were recorded.[57]

(f) *Parental responsibility and parental rights* arise in adoption proce- **1.16**
dure in several ways.

> (i) Formerly in England and Wales, but not in Scotland, in step-
> parent adoptions, the court had to dismiss the application for
> adoption, if it considered that the matter "would be better dealt
> with" under section 42 of the Matrimonial Causes Act 1973 (which
> deals with orders for custody)[58];
> (ii) in a petition to adopt a child abroad, the order of the court vests
> in the petitioner the parental rights and duties relating to the child[59];
> (iii) in a petition for adoption the court may make an interim order
> "giving parental responsibilities and parental rights to the peti-
> tioners"[60]; and
> (iv) the present position is that in considering whether to make an
> adoption order or a freeing order, the court must have regard to the
> welfare of the child concerned as its paramount consideration and
> shall not make the order in question unless it considers that it would
> be better for the child that it should do so than it should not.[61] The
> former provisions had a greater bias in favour of residence (now
> custody) rather than adoption.[62] Now, there is no duty on the court

---

[52] 1978 Act, s. 65(2).
[53] Adoption (Designation of Overseas Adoptions) Order 1973 (S.I. 1973 No. 119); the
Republic of China was added in 1995: Adoption (Designation of Overseas Adoptions)
(Variation) (Scotland) Order 1995 (S.I. 1995 No. 1614), para. 2; *Re H (An Infant)*
[1973] C.L.Y. 2167.
[54] 1978 Act, s. 53(1).
[55] 1978 Act, s. 47.
[56] 1978 Act, s. 45 and Sched. 1, para. 1(2).
[57] Report on the Registrar General for Scotland, 1978: Annual Report of Registrar
General for Scotland (No. 142, 1996), p. 137.
[58] 1975 Act, s. 10(3) (1976 Act, s. 14(3)).
[59] 1978 Act, s. 49; see para. 1.10(d), above.
[60] 1978 Act, s. 25(1) as amended by the 1995 Act, s. 89(1) and Sched. 2, para. 17; see
para. 1.08, above.
[61] 1978 Act, s. 24(3): see para. 8.36, below.
[62] 1975 Act, s. 37 in England and Wales (repealed by the Children Act 1989) and s. 53(1) in
Scotland (repealed by the 1995 Act from November 1, 1996; Children (Scotland) Act 1995
(Commencement No. 2 and Transitional Provisions) Order 1996 (S.I. 1996 No. 2203),
art. 3(3) and Sched.; but the 1995 Act adds a new s. 51(5) which appears to refer to ss. 52 and
53 "of this Act").

to consider residence as an alternative to adoption.[63] However, in complying with its duties to promote the welfare of the child, an adoption agency (but not a court) is required, before making any arrangements for the adoption of a child, to consider whether adoption is likely best to meet the needs of the child or whether there is some better, practicable alternative. If it concludes that there is such an alternative it must not proceed to make those arrangements.[64]

1.17   In England, in a case under the former section 37(1) of the 1975 Act, it was held that the court had to be satisfied that the child's welfare could be better served by making a custodianship order than by an adoption order. If the factors were evenly balanced, the court could not be satisfied that it would be better for the child's welfare to make a custodianship order.[65]

1.18   It has now been enacted, following upon various decisions,[66] that where a child has been adopted or freed for adoption, the natural parent of the child cannot seek an order relating to parental responsibilities and associated matters under section 11 of the 1995 Act.[67]

Effect of Adoption Orders and Other Orders

1.19   It has been the purpose of the legislation dealing with adoption to put, as far as it is possible, the adopted child into the same position in law in relation to his adoptive parents as he would be with natural parents. In relation to the 1926 Act, Lord Atkin observed:

> "that the Act does not put the adopter and the child into the position of natural parent and child for all purposes. But, as to the matters enumerated in sub-s. 1, custody, maintenance and education, it does in the plainest language transfer from the natural parent to the adopter the whole of the rights and obligations that flow from parenthood; and places the child in the same position as though he were the lawful natural child of the adopter".[68]

And Vaisey J. said:

> "normally, an adoption presupposes a complete and final separation between the child and its natural parents. The child looks thenceforth to the adopters as its parents, and the natural parents, relinquishing all their parental rights and duties, step as it were for ever out of the picture of the child's life".[69]

---

[63] These former rules were dealt with in McNeill, *Adoption of Children in Scotland* (2nd ed., 1986, W. Green & Son Ltd), para. 1.03(f)(i) and (iv).

[64] 1978 Act, s. 6A.

[65] *Re LW (A Minor) (Adoption or Custodianship)* [1991] F.C.R. 867. The corresponding provision in Scotland was the 1975 Act, s. 53.

[66] *Beagley v. Beagley*, 1984 S.C. (H.L.) 69; *Borders Regional Council v. M*, 1986 S.C. 63; *Grampian Regional Council v. D*, 1995 S.L.T. 519.

[67] 1995 Act, s. 11(4)(a) and (b).

[68] *Coventry Corporation v. Surrey County Council* [1935] A.C. 199 at 205.

[69] *Re DX* [1949] Ch. 320, a single-judge decision in an interlocutory application.

The making of the order vests the parental responsibilities and parental **1.20** rights relating to a child in the adopters.[70] The former parents have no locus to seek parental responsibilities and parental rights relating to the child[71]; but the making of an adoption order does not exclude the right of others, such as grandparents of the child, to seek parental responsibilities and parental rights relating to the child.[72]

In one case where there were concurrent actions for adoption by petitioners and for custody by the grandparents in respect of the same children, the grandparents were allowed to appear in the hearing as parties to the petition for adoption, thus obviating the need to hear the evidence twice over in two separate processes in order to reach a decision as to how the competing claims should be resolved.[73]

The change in the status of a child which occurs on the making of an **1.21** adoption order has several aspects.

(1) Legitimation

A child who is the subject of an adoption order shall be treated in law **1.22**

    (a) where the adopters are a married couple, as if
      (i) he had been born a legitimate child of the marriage (whether or not he was in fact born after the marriage was consummated); and
      (ii) he were not the child of any other person other than the adopters;
    (b) where the adoption order is made by virtue of section 15(1)(aa) (that is, where a step-parent applies for an adoption order but the natural parent does not) as if
      (i) he has been born as a legitimate child of the marriage between the adopter and the natural parent to whom the adopter is married (whether or not he was in fact born after the marriage was consummated); and
      (ii) he were not the child of any other person other than the adopter and that natural parent; and
    (c) in any other case, as if
      (i) he had been born as a legitimate child of the adopter; and
      (ii) he were not the child of any other person other than the adopter.[74]

However, where a child has been adopted by one of his natural parents **1.23** as sole adoptive parent, and the adopter thereafter marries the other natural parent, these provisions do not affect any enactment or rule of law whereby, by virtue of the marriage, the child is rendered the legitimate child of both natural parents.[75] Further, where the unmarried

---

[70] 1978 Act, s. 12(1).
[71] See para. 1.18, above.
[72] *AB and CD, Petitioners*, 1992 S.L.T. 1064.
[73] *ibid.*
[74] 1978 Act, s. 39(1) as substituted by the 1995 Act, s. 93(3).
[75] 1978 Act, s. 39(2).

parents of a child, one of whom has adopted him in Scotland, have subsequently married each other, the court by which the adoption order was made may, on the application of any of the parties concerned, revoke that order.[76]

(2) Adopted Children Register

1.24   Every adoption order must contain a direction to the Registrar General for Scotland to make an entry in the Adopted Children Register recording the adoption, which will include the date and place of birth as determined by the court and the names and surname of the child.[77] The granting of an adoption order and the making of an entry by the Registrar in the Adopted Children Register are not affected by the marking of an appeal in the adoption process: that only arises if the adoption order were quashed in the appeal and the appellate court gives directions to the Registrar to cancel the entry.[78] Generally, as far as the child is concerned, the Adopted Children Register takes the place of the Register of Births and an extract relating to him would be of an entry in the Adopted Children Register. Thus, for example, in an application for a passport, an adopted person is not required to disclose his former names.

1.25   Formerly, for approximately the last 60 years, adoptions by a parent and a step-parent were effected by a petition at the instance of both spouses: the effect of an adoption order was that the natural parent surrendered his, or more often her, sole rights toward the child, and both petitioners became equal adoptive parents. Presently, in "step-adoptions", an adoption order may be made on the application of one person, the step-parent, of the appropriate age,[79] not being a person in any of the three situations,

> (i)   whose spouse cannot be found;
> (ii) where the spouses have separated and are living apart and the separation is likely to be permanent; or
> (iii) his spouse is by reason of ill health, whether physical or mental, incapable of making an application for adoption.[80]

1.26   Where an adoption order is made under these provisions, its making does not operate to extinguish the parental responsibilities and parental rights which immediately before the making of the order were vested in the natural parent to whom the adopter is married.[81] It is submitted that in a step-adoption the spouses would have an option to proceed under the new

---

[76] 1978 Act, s. 46. A style of petition for revocation of an adoption order appears in Append. 2, 22.

[77] 1978 Act, s. 45(9) and Sched. I, para. 1.

[78] 1978 Act, s. 45, Sched. I, para. 4(3).

[79] At the age of 18 in the case of the husband or the wife in a petition by a married couple, and 21 in all other cases: 1978 Act, ss. 14 and 15.

[80] 1978 Act, s. 15(1)(aa).

[81] 1978 Act, s. 12(3A); but *cf.* the effect of such an adoption on the status conferred on the child by virtue of the new s. 39(1): see para. 1.17, above.

provisions, or to proceed with a joint petition by both of them. The petition of the step-parent would have as a production an extract of an entry of the birth of the child (which will be sealed up with the process). When the adoption order has been granted, it will contain a direction to the Registrar General to cause the entry in that register to be marked with the word "Adopted". However, there is a doubt as to whether the spouse married to the adopter will be entitled to rely on an extract of an entry of the birth; and the child would have two certificates—one of adoption and one of birth.[82] Problems may arise where each spouse has children of whom the other spouse is not the parent: presumably they would then proceed with a joint adoption as a married couple under section 14 of the 1978 Act.

(3) Forbidden Degrees

The provisions relating to legitimation on adoption do not apply in **1.27** determining the prohibited degrees of consanguinity and affinity in respect of the law relating to marriage, or in respect of the crime of incest, except that, on the making of an adoption order, the adopter and the child are deemed, in all time coming, to be within the said prohibited degrees in respect of the law relating to marriage.[83] In *H.M. Advocate v. RM*, which was a decision on the now-repealed analogous provision which had excluded reference to the law of incest,[84] it was held that sexual intercourse between a man and his adopted daughter is not a crime by the law of Scotland. By statute, in the crime of incest the relationship by consanguinity is equiparated to relationship by adoption and extends to adoptive and former adoptive parents and adoptive and former adoptive children.[85]

(4) Domicile

The new status of parent and child which is created by an adoption **1.28** order "must be validly created by the law of the domicile of the adopting parent. You do not look to the domicile of the child: for that has no separate domicile of its own. It takes its parents' domicile. You look to the parents' domicile only".[86] In Scotland, since 1991, a girl and a boy can acquire an independent domicile at the date when she or he attains the age of 16.[87] By statute, the domicile of a child (which includes an adopted child) who is incapable of having an independent domicile and whose parents are living apart may have the domicile of his mother.[88] It is submitted that if there exists a foreign adoption (other than the adoption orders widely defined in the legislation[89]) which is not a decree of the court of the domicile of the adopters, it will not be recognised in Scotland, and if the adopters wish to have an adoption order which will receive

---

[82] See paras 11.03, 11.04, below.
[83] 1978 Act, s. 41.
[84] 1969 J.C. 52; 1958 Act, s. 13(3).
[85] Criminal Law (Consolidation) (Scotland) Act 1995, s. 1.
[86] *Re Valentine's Settlement* [1965] Ch. 831 at 842, *per* Lord Denning.
[87] Age of Legal Capacity (Scotland) Act 1991, s. 7.
[88] Domicile and Matrimonial Proceedings Act 1973, s. 4.
[89] 1978 Act, s. 39(1) as substituted by the 1995 Act, s. 97(1).

international recognition,[90] they must start again with a Scottish or British adoption. It has been held that in deciding whether the court should make an adoption order, the question whether the order will be recognised abroad is not decisive.[91]

(5) Citizenship

1.29   Where an adoption order is made in respect of a child who is not a British citizen, then, if the adopter, or in the case of a joint application one adopter, is a British citizen, the child becomes a British citizen as from the date of the order[92] but the status of legitimacy conferred by adoption[93] does not apply for the purposes of any provision of

  (a) the British Nationality Act 1981;
  (b) the Immigration Act 1971;
  (c) any instrument having effect under an enactment within these two statutes; or
  (d) any other law for the time being in force which determines British citizenship, British Dependent Territories citizenship or British Overseas citizenship.[94]

1.30   This provision does not affect the nationality of persons who are adopted by persons who are not citizens of the United Kingdom and Colonies. Generally, even if a British child is adopted by an alien, he will remain British.

(6) Parent and Child

1.31   As has been indicated, the adoptive parent has vested in him the parental responsibilities and parental rights relating to the adopted child. As in the case of a natural parent, he will have the child living with him; he will be bound to aliment the child; and he will have to ensure the education of the child and give such advice and guidance as a parent should.[95] Generally, the duties between the natural parent and the child in these respects are extinguished.[96]

(7) Succession, etc.

1.32   For all purposes relating to

  (i) the succession to a deceased person (whether testate or intestate), and
  (ii) the disposal of property by virtue of any *inter vivos* deed,

---

[90] *Re Valentine's Settlement* [1965] Ch. 831 at 842, *per* Lord Denning; Anton, *Private International Law* (2nd ed., 1990, W. Green & Son Ltd), pp. 506–507; *cf. Re Y (Minors) (Adoption: jurisdiction)* [1985] 3 All E.R. 83, *per* Sheldon J. However, in practice the foreign decree may not be valueless: if there is a foreign decree of adoption which is not recognised in Scotland, and there is in the foreign process an agreement of a parent, that agreement may be used in the Scottish process.
[91] *Re B* [1967] 3 All E.R. 629, *per* Goff J.
[92] British Nationality Act 1981, s. 1(5) and (6).
[93] See para. 1.17, above.
[94] 1978 Act, s. 41(2).
[95] *cf.* 1995 Act, s. 2(1).
[96] 1978 Act, s. 12(3) and (4).

an adopted person must be treated as the child of the adopter, and not as the child of any other person.[97] However, where the adopter has died before the commencement of that Act the adopted person shall be treated for the purposes of succession to the estate of a natural parent who dies after August 3, 1966, as the child of that parent.[98] It has been held that it is irrelevant whether the adoption order had been made before or after the execution of the deed under which the children were to benefit, and that children adopted under an overseas adoption were to be treated in the same way as any other adopted child.[99] However, titles of honour are not affected; and where the terms of any deed provide that any property or interest in property shall devolve along with a title, honour or dignity, these provisions shall not prevent that property or interest so devolving.[1] A few minor rights are preserved to the child notwithstanding the adoption order, such as entitlement to a pension and funeral benefit.[2] These provisions appear to be unaffected by the introduction of the procedure whereby the parent of a child who is married to the step-parent of the child need not be a party to a petition for adoption which is at the instance of the step-parent alone.[3]

(8) Title to Sue

An adoptive child has the same title to sue as a natural child and by **1.33** statute a right to claim damages in respect of the death of his adoptive parents and vice versa.[4]

It is provided in terms that a parental responsibilities order of a local **1.34** authority assuming parental rights shall terminate when the child becomes the subject of an adoption order or when a freeing order or an adoption abroad is made in respect of the child.[5]

Generally, the provisions as to the effect of an adoption order on the **1.35** status of an adopted child apply to:

  (i) an adoption order under the 1978 Act, s. 65(1)[6];
 (ii) an adoption order under the 1975 Act, the 1958 Act, the 1950 Act or any enactment repealed by the 1950 Act;
(iii) an order effecting an adoption made in England and Wales, Northern Ireland, the Isle of Man or any of the Channel Islands;
 (iv) an "overseas adoption" as defined in the 1978 Act, s. 65(2); or
  (v) any other adoption recognised by the law of Scotland.[7]

---

[97] Succession (Scotland) Act 1964, s. 23(1).
[98] Law Reform (Miscellaneous Provisions) (Scotland) Act 1966, s. 5.
[99] *Salvesen's Trs, Petitioners*, 1993 S.C. 14.
[1] Succession (Scotland) Act 1964, ss. 23(3) and 37.
[2] 1978 Act, ss. 42 and 43.
[3] See paras 11.03, 11.04, below.
[4] Damages (Scotland) Act 1976, s. 1 and Sched. 1, para. 1(b); 1978 Act, s. 39(1).
[5] 1995 Act, s. 86(6)(b).
[6] 1978 Act, s. 38(1).
[7] 1978 Act, s. 38(1) and the Succession (Scotland) Act 1964, s. 23(5). Recognition of foreign decrees of adoption has been discussed at para. 1.28, above.

1.36   To be recognised, an adoption order "must be validly created by the law of the domicile of the adopting parent".[8]

1.37   The provisions do not apply to the orders which are in essence orders conferring parental responsibilities and parental rights, that is to say, an interim order[9] and an order to adopt a child abroad[10]; nor do they apply to an order following an adoption application which is treated by the court as if it were an application for parental responsibilities and parental rights.[11]

1.38   Where an order freeing a child for adoption is made, the parental rights and duties relating to the child vest in the adoption agency, and the former rights and duties between the child and his natural parents are extinguished.[12] To that extent only, a freeing order has the same effect as an adoption order.

1.39   An adoption order which has been properly made subsists until a successful appeal has been taken against it. The mere marking of an appeal does not suspend the operation of the order nor modify the obligation that is placed on the Registrar General to make an entry regarding the adoption in the Adopted Children Register.[13]

---

[8] *Re Valentine's Settlement* [1965] Ch. 831 at 842, *per* Lord Denning.
[9] 1978 Act, s. 25.
[10] 1978 Act, s. 49.
[11] 1975 Act, s. 53 has been repealed; see para. 1.16(f), above; see also 1995 Act, s. 11(7) and K. McK. Norrie, *Children (Scotland) Act 1995* (1995, W. Green & Son Ltd), note to Sched. 2, para. 16.
[12] 1978 Act, ss. 12(2), (3) and 18(5); see para. 5.24, below.
[13] See para. 13.04, below.

CHAPTER 2

WHO MAY ADOPT

General

An adoption order may only be sought by two classes of petitioner: **2.01**

    (a) a married couple[1]; or
    (b) a single person.[2]

However, that single person must not be married, or if married the court must be satisfied that his spouse cannot be found, or is separated, or is incapable of making an application for an adoption order, or, since the 1995 Act came into force, is a person who is married to the natural parent of the child.[3] Presumably, if in the course of proceedings by a married couple, they were divorced from each other the petition would be thereby rendered incompetent, unless one of the petitioners dropped from the action.

The same provisions apply to Convention adoptions, and are applied to an order to adopt abroad.[4] If petitioners are otherwise eligible to adopt a child, their relationship to the child does not by itself render them ineligible, except in so far as that relationship does not enure to the benefit of the child. To assert that a particular relationship such as grandparent and grandchild or step-parent and step-child should inhibit the granting of an adoption order would be not only to do violence to the rule that each case must be decided on its merits, but also to fly in the face of the law. The statutory provisions envisage adoptions by relatives, which term "means a grandparent, brother, sister, uncle or aunt, whether of the full blood or half-blood or by affinity and includes, where the child is illegitimate, the father of the child and any person where he is not a parent within the meaning of this Act, and any person who would be a relative within the meaning of this definition if the father were such a parent"[5]; and the court must have regard to "all the circumstances",[6] of which the relationship between the child and the petitioner is only one. Decisions in particular cases have indicated a variety of unexceptionable relationships between adopters and children (many of which are now commonplace) including adoption

---

[1] 1978 Act, s. 14(1).
[2] 1978 Act, s. 15(1).
[3] See para. 2.02, below.
[4] 1978 Act, s. 49(2).
[5] 1978 Act, s. 65(1).
[6] 1978 Act, s. 6; *cf. Re W* [1971] A.C. 682 at 699, when Lord Hailsham referred to "the totality of the circumstances".

(a) by two spouses of a child who has already been adopted by one of the spouses[7];

(b) by one parent of his or her illegitimate child whose parents are not married[8];

(c) by both natural parents now married to each other of their own illegitimate child whose parents are not married born to the female petitioner during the subsistence of a former marriage[9];

(d) by a husband and wife of the legitimate child of the wife by a former marriage[10];

(e) by a mother of an illegitimate child whose parents are not married and her husband who was not the father of the child[11];

(f) by the grandparents of a grandchild.[12]

However, in other cases the court refused to grant adoption orders in petitions

(a) by a married man living in adultery with a married woman of their illegitimate child whose parents are not married, because to grant the order would be contrary to public policy[13];

(b) in one case, by married parents of their own legitimated child.[14] However, in a later uncontested case, such an order was granted. The child had been legitimated by the subsequent marriage of his parents, but the petitioners had opinion of counsel to the effect that the child could not benefit under a trust unless he had the status of an adopted child.[15]

Matrimonial Status of Petitioners

2.02   Different rules apply depending on whether the petitioners are married or not.

(a) In the case of an application made by a married couple
  (i) at least one of them must be domiciled in a part of the United Kingdom, or the Channel Islands or the Isle of Man; or
  (ii) the application is for a Convention adoption order.[16] Convention adoption orders have been discussed earlier[17]; or

---

[7] A.S. (Adoption of Children) 1984 (S.I. 1984 No. 1013), r. 25, which rule was not re-enacted in the current rules.

[8] *D, Petitioner*, 1938 S.C. 223; *H and H, Petitioners*, 1948 S.L.T. (Sh.Ct.) 37; 1978 Act, s. 46.

[9] *B and B, Petitioners*, 1936 S.C. 256; *H and H, Petitioners*, 1948 S.L.T. (Sh.Ct.) 37.

[10] *I and I, Petitioners*, 1947 S.C. 485.

[11] *B and B, Petitioners*, 1932 S.L.T. (Sh.Ct.) 37.

[12] *F and HF, Petitioners*, 1949 S.L.T. (Sh.Ct.) 48; *CD, Petitioners*, 1963 S.L.T. (Sh.Ct.) 7, where the court refused to pronounce an adoption order on other grounds; *cf. AB, Petitioners* (1962) 78 Sh.Ct. Rep. 148; and in England: *Re W* [1980] 10 Fam. 190; [1981] C.L.Y. 1751.

[13] *JS, Petitioner*, 1950 S.L.T. (Sh.Ct.) 3.

[14] *M and M, Petitioners*, 1950 S.L.T. (Sh.Ct.) 3; *cf.* 1978 Act, s. 46(1).

[15] *E and E, Petitioners*, Sheriff Smith, Cupar Sh.Ct. (AC 11/93), November 29, 1993, unreported. Clearly, the acquisition of a significant estate would be for the welfare of the child; see para. 8.24, below.

[16] 1978 Act, s. 14(1).

[17] See para. 1.11, above.

      (iii) both of them were habitually resident in a part of the United Kingdom, or the Channel Islands or the Isle of Man throughout the period of one year which ends with the date of the application.

  (b) In the case of an application by a single person[18] an adoption order may be made

      (i) where that person is not married, and

         (1) is not a parent, there is no specialty,

         (2) is a parent, the adoption can be made only if

            (a) the other natural parent cannot be found, or

            (b) there is some other reason justifying the exclusion of the natural parent (which reason must be recorded by the court)[19]; or

      (ii) where that person is married to a person

         (1) who is the natural parent of the child; and

         (2) in whom are vested parental responsibilities and parental rights in relation to the child[20]; or

      (iii) where that person, not being a person who may make an application as the spouse of a natural parent, is married and

         (1) his spouse cannot be found, or

         (2) the spouses have separated and are living apart and the separation is likely to be permanent, or

         (3) his spouse is incapable of making an application by reason of ill health, whether physical or mental,[21] then the adoption order can be made[22]; and

      (iv) (1) the person must be domiciled in the United Kingdom or in the Channel Islands or the Isle of Man, or

         (2) the application must be for a Convention adoption order[23]; or

         (3) the applicant was habitually resident in a part of the United Kingdom, or the Channel Islands or the Isle of Man throughout the period of one year which ends with the date of the application.

Age of the Petitioner

The age at which a petitioner may be an adopter has varied **2.93** throughout the history of adoptions in Scotland.[24] Under the Adoption (Scotland) Act 1978 a petitioner must have attained the

---

[18] See paras 3.04, 8.13, below.

[19] 1978 Act, s. 15(3).

[20] 1978 Act, s. 15(1)(aa).

[21] 1978 Act, s. 15(1).

[22] An adoption petition may be competently presented, but an order cannot competently be granted in respect of a sole spouse, unless the case comes within these exceptions: *M, Petitioner*, Edinburgh Sh.Ct. (E/17 and E/18), June 14, 1988, unreported.

[23] 1978 Act, s. 15(2).

[24] Adoption of Children (Scotland) Act 1930, s. 2; Adoption of Children (Regulation) Act 1939, ss. 8, 15(1); Adoption Act 1950, s. 2; Adoption Act 1958, s. 2(1); Children Act 1975, ss. 10, 11; Adoption (Scotland) Act 1978, s. 14 (as amended by the Children Act 1989, s. 88(2) and Sched. 10, para. 33) and s. 15.

age of 21, except in the case of a petition by a married couple where
the husband or the wife is the father or the mother and has attained
the age of 18.[25] Thus, although persons may marry at 16 and have
children, and are able to vote at 18, they cannot adopt a child—even
their own child—until the petitioner who is the parent of the child is 18
and the other petitioner is 21. There is no upper age limit for a
petitioner at which a petition would be incompetent; but since 1966
the court must have a report on the considerations arising from the
difference in age between the petitioners and the child if such difference
is more or less than the normal difference between parents and their
children.[26] No doubt any considerable difference between the age of
the petitioners and the child would be taken into account; but in
many cases where such differences exist the child has been with the
petitioners for a long time and no matter what happens in the adoption
proceedings is likely to remain in the care and possession of the
petitioners.

Occasionally, attempts have been made by adoption agencies, in effect,
to ration the demand for adoptive parents by imposing an age limit on
them and arbitrarily excluding them from consideration. Such unqualified
policies have no legal foundation and are contrary to the duty incumbent
on an adoption agency under section 6 of the 1978 Act to have regard to
"all the circumstances". "Grandparent adoptions" are discussed elsewhere.[27]

Domicile

2.04   In each case the domicile in the United Kingdom, the Channel Islands
or the Isle of Man of the petitioner where there is only one, and of one of
them where there are two, is an overriding condition of granting the
adoption order.[28] If neither petitioner is so domiciled, then according to
an English decision on the former United Kingdom provisions relating to
domicile,[29] it would be incompetent to grant an adoption order: only a
provisional adoption order under section 53 of the Adoption Act 1958
(now an order to adopt a child abroad), could competently be granted.[30]
In addition it is now competent to apply for a Convention adoption
order.[31] Under the former law it had been held that the ordinary
residence of the petitioners need not be within Great Britain,[32] and
the present requirements do not appear to render that situation impossible.[33] Recognition of foreign decrees of adoption is discussed
elsewhere.[34]

---

[25] 1978 Act, s. 14; *cf. H, Petitioner*, 1960 S.L.T. (Sh.Ct.) 3.
[26] A.S. 1997, r. 2.21(3)(p) (RCS, r. 67.24(2)(q)); see para. 8.35, below.
[27] See para. 2.01, above; see para. 4.07, below.
[28] 1978 Act, ss. 14(2)(a) and 15(2)(a).
[29] 1958 Act, s. 1(1).
[30] *Re R* [1962] 3 All E.R. 238.
[31] 1978 Act, ss. 14(2)(b) and 15(2)(b).
[32] *Re W* [1962] Ch. 918.
[33] See para. 8.35, below.
[34] See para. 1.28, above.

"Authorised Court"

Formerly the criterion for jurisdiction was the residence of the child[35]; **2.05** now, generally, if the child is in Scotland when the application is made the authorised courts are

(a) the Court of Session;
(b) the sheriff court of the sheriffdom (not merely the sheriff court district[36]) within which the child is resident.[37]

In the case of an application for an adoption order or for an order **2.06** freeing a child for adoption, where the child is not in Great Britain, or for a Convention adoption order, then the authorised court is the Court of Session.[38] These rules are not affected by E.U. rules on jurisdiction.[39] Presumably, the rule that the child must be present at the time that the petition is presented does not extend to a requirement that the child should also reside in Scotland at the time of granting the order: the former provisions[40] to that effect have been repealed.[41] However, after the authorised court has been ascertained, the child must at all times immediately preceding the date of the order have had his home with the petitioners or one of them: that phrase is the obverse of the petitioners having the care and possession of the child.[42] It would appear to be incompetent to prorogate the jurisdiction of a court other than the authorised court.[43] The power to transfer a cause from one sheriff court to another[44] would no doubt be applicable to adoption procedure also.[45]

Transfer and Remit of Cause

The sheriff may, on cause shown, transfer any cause to another sheriff **2.07** court[46]; and an interlocutor transferring a cause may, with leave of the sheriff, be appealed to the sheriff principal, but is not subject to appeal to the Court of Session.[47] The sheriff may remit an adoption petition (but a freeing application is not mentioned in the section) to the Court of Session,[48] but there is no appeal against such an interlocutor.[49] The

---

[35] *e.g.* 1930 Act, s. 8(1).

[36] But the sheriff has a discretion whether to grant warrant to cite a defender who is resident in another district: Macphail, *Sheriff Court Practice* (1988, W. Green & Son Ltd), para. 6-02: *Tait v. Johnston* (1891) 18 R. 606; *Davidson v. Davidson* (1891) 18 R. 884.

[37] 1978 Act, s. 56(2).

[38] 1978 Act, s. 56(3) and (4).

[39] Civil Jurisdiction and Judgments Act 1982, s. 2(2) and Sched. 1, art. 1 shall not apply to "the status or legal capacity of natural persons".

[40] 1958 Act, s. 1(5); *cf. X v. Y*, 1954 S.L.T. (Sh.Ct.) 86.

[41] 1975 Act, s. 108 and Sched. 4, Pt IV; Children Act 1975 (Scotland) (Commencement No. 1) Order 1977 (S.I. 1977 No. 227), para. 3 and Sched. 1.

[42] 1978 Act, s. 13.

[43] *G and G, Petitioners, S and S, Petitioners* and *R and R, Petitioners*, Edinburgh Sh.Ct. (E50/85, E49/85 and E51/85), unreported.

[44] Act of Sederunt (Sheriff Court Ordinary Cause Rules) 1993 (S.I. 1993 No. 1956), r. 26.1.

[45] See para. 5.02.

[46] Act of Sederunt (Sheriff Court Ordinary Cause Rules) 1993 (S.I. 1993 No. 1956), r. 26.1(1).

[47] Act of Sederunt (Sheriff Court Ordinary Cause Rules) 1993, r. 26.1(8).

[48] Sheriff Courts (Scotland) Act 1971, s. 37(2A); *T, Petitioner*, 1996 S.C.L.R. 897.

[49] *ibid.* s. 37(3).

Court of Session may, in relation to an action before it which could competently have been brought before a sheriff, remit the action at its own instance or on the application of any of the parties to the action to the sheriff within whose jurisdiction the action could have been brought where, in the opinion of the court, the nature of the action makes it appropriate to do so.[50]

Health of Petitioner

2.08   There is no statutory requirement that prospective adopters be of good health. The former requirement to have a medical report on the health of the petitioner has not been re-enacted in the sheriff court rules[51]: now, as in the Court of Session, there must be a medical report on the health of the child, but only when the child was not placed by an adoption agency.[52] In addition the Court of Session rules still require a medical certificate on the health of the petitioner except where the petitioner is a parent of the child.[53] There is no reason why the lack of good health in a petitioner should of itself preclude the granting of an adoption order: it is merely one of the circumstances to which the court shall have regard, "the paramount consideration" being given to the need to promote the welfare of the child "throughout his life".[54] In *G and C, Petitioners*[55] an adoption order was refused because of the possible danger of infection of the child by the female petitioner who was suffering from a chronic tuberculosis condition. The circumstances of the case might require other medical evidence about a petitioner or a parent who was not a petitioner, for example, as to the mental condition of a parent who has seriously ill-treated the child[56]; or who is incapable of giving his agreement[57]; or is incapable of making an application for an adoption order or falls to be excluded from an application.[58]

---

[50] Law Reform (Miscellaneous Provisions) (Scotland) Act 1985, s. 14; RCS, r. 32.1.
[51] A.S. (Adoption of Children) 1984 (S.I. 1984 No. 1013), r. 16(3)(c).
[52] A.S. 1997, r. 2.21(2)(c) (RCS, r. 67.23(2)(d)); see paras 3.10, 5.14, below.
[53] RCS, r. 67.23(2)(e).
[54] 1978 Act, s. 6.
[55] 1949 S.L.T. (Sh.Ct.) 60.
[56] 1978 Act, s. 16(2)(d).
[57] 1978 Act, s. 16(2)(a).
[58] 1978 Act, s. 15(1)(b)(iii) and 15(3)(b).

CHAPTER 3

THE CHILD

Child Defined

(a) Since 1969 only a child who has not attained the age of 18 can be **3.01** adopted.[1] However, since 1997 an adoption order may be made in relation to a person who has attained the age of 18 if the application was made before such attainment.[2] A child can only be adopted after it is at least 19 weeks old (and 32 weeks old where the petition is to adopt the child abroad[3]) and has had his home with the petitioners at all times during the 13 weeks preceding the making of the order[4] (and 26 weeks where the petition is to adopt the child abroad[5]). Where the child is not being adopted by a parent, step-parent or relative or is not being placed for adoption by an adoption agency, the child must be at least 12 months old and at all times during the 12 months preceding the making of the order have had his home with the petitioners or one of them.[6]

(b) A child who is or has been married cannot be adopted.[7]   **3.02**

(c) Since 1991 a child of or over 12 and not yet 18 must consent to the **3.03** making of the adoption order, except that where the court is satisfied that the minor is incapable of giving his consent, then it may dispense with that consent.[8] This is the only ground for dispensing with the consent of the minor, whereas there are several grounds for dispensing with the agreement of the parent.[9] The *punctum temporis* for dispensing with consent is the making of the adoption order, not the lodging of the petition,[10] but presumably where a child has attained the age of 18 and the application was made before he attained 18, his consent could still be given. In England and Wales the consent of the child is not required. Apart from the question of such formal consent to the making of an adoption order, in

---

[1] 1978 Act, s. 65(1); *cf. M, Petitioner*, 1953 S.C. 227.
[2] 1978 Act, s. 12(1).
[3] 1978 Act, s. 49(2).
[4] 1978 Act, s. 13(1); *e.g. O and O, Petitioners*, Edinburgh Sh.Ct. (E54/85), unreported, where the child had been found abandoned in Delhi and had been given into the guardianship of the petitioners by the Indian courts.
[5] 1978 Act, s. 49(2).
[6] 1978 Act, s. 13(2).
[7] 1978 Act, s. 12(5).
[8] 1978 Act, ss. 12(8) (adoption) and 18(8) (freeing); Age of Legal Capacity (Scotland) Act 1991, ss. 2(3)(a) and 11(2).
[9] See para. 10.11, below.
[10] 1978 Act, s. 12(8).

reaching any decision relating to the adoption of the child the court must so far as is reasonably practicable ascertain the wishes and feelings of the child regarding the decision and give due consideration to them, having regard to the age and understanding of the child and having regard to his views (if he wishes to express them), taking into account his age and maturity.[11] In sheriff court cases the curator *ad litem* must report to the court on these matters[12] but this is not presently so required in the Court of Session.[13] In addition the local authority or the adoption agency must investigate and report on "matters relevant to the operation of section 6"[14] which would include the welfare of the child.

3.04   (d) Until 1958 an adoption order could not be made in respect of a child who was a female where the sole applicant was a male unless there were special circumstances "which justify as an exceptional measure the making of an adoption order".[15] In one case, which was decided while that section was in force, a policeman and his wife received a one-month-old female child into their care and possession with the intention of applying for an adoption order. On the death of his wife, the policeman went to reside with his wife's mother who looked after the child. He applied for an adoption order, and it was held, after hearing evidence, that in the special circumstances the adoption order should be granted.[16] That provision of the Adoption Act 1958 has been repealed[17] and it has not been re-enacted. However, notwithstanding the repeal of that subsection, in the case of a sole male petitioner who is seeking to adopt a female child the welfare of the child would still be a very important consideration in the decision whether to grant the adoption order, as would be the case of a sole male seeking to adopt a male child in so far as it affected the welfare of the child.[18]

Care and Possession

3.05   (a) Generally, before a child can be adopted it must have been continuously in the care and possession of the petitioner. Before 1978 the *de facto* custody which the petitioners had of the child which they intended to adopt was called "care and possession". It was essential that before an adoption order could be granted the child should have been continuously in the care and possession of the petitioners for at least three months preceding the date of the order.[19] The phrase "care and possession" is still used in some aspects of the new law,[20] but in the provisions dealing with the child being with the petitioners, the child must have "had

---

[11] 1978 Act, s. 6.

[12] A.S. 1997, r. 2.26(2)(u) (RCS, r. 67.24(2)(bb)); see para. 8.37, below.

[13] RCS, r. 67.24(2)(s).

[14] 1978 Act, ss. 22, 23; see para. 8.56, below.

[15] 1958 Act, s. 2(3).

[16] *H, Petitioner*, 1960 S.L.T. (Sh.Ct.) 3.

[17] 1975 Act, s. 108 and Sched. 4, Pt IV, and the Children Act 1975 (Scotland) (Commencement No. 1) Order 1977 (S.I. 1977 No. 227), art. 3 and Sched. 1.

[18] This is discussed at para. 8.24 below.

[19] 1958 Act, s. 3(1).

[20] *e.g.* 1978 Act, s. 30(1).

his home with" the petitioners for a probationary period.[21] The two phrases are different views of the same thing—from the point of view of the child, and of the petitioners. Accordingly, the former law is applicable to the child having his home with the petitioners. Using the new, later terminology, the present position is:

(1) generally, before a child can be adopted he must have at all times during the preceding 13 weeks had his home with the petitioners or one of them, and the child must be at least 19 weeks old immediately preceding the making of the order[22];

(2) in the case of a petition to adopt a child abroad the period is 26 weeks and the child must be 32 weeks old[23]; and

(3) in the case of a child which has been placed for a purpose other than adoption the period is 12 months.[24]

Formerly, where one of the petitioners was a parent they did not need to give notice to the local authority of the intention to adopt the child, whereas in other cases the petitioners had to give such notice.[25] Now the positions have been reversed and are made more elaborate: if the child was not placed by an adoption agency, the petitioner must give notice to the local authority within whose area he has his home of his intention to apply for an adoption order.[26] On receipt of such notice, the local authority must investigate and report on the matter.[27] (Previously, where arrangements were made by a registered adoption society for the adoption of a child by an adopter resident in Great Britain, no application to the court could be made until after the period of care and possession had expired.[28]) Until the Children (Scotland) Act 1995 came into force, the giving of notice to the local authority brought into play the provisions relating to a protected child.[29] While an adoption petition is pending where the parent or guardian has agreed to the making of the adoption order (whether or not he knows the identity of the applicant), the parent or guardian is not entitled, against the will of the person with whom the child has his home, to remove the child from the custody of that person except with the leave of the court.[30] A similar provision exists where the adopters have provided a home for the child for more than five years.[31]

(b) The former provisions which applied have been modified in the case **3.06** where an application for an adoption order was made jointly by spouses

---

[21] 1978 Act, s. 13.
[22] 1978 Act, s. 13(1).
[23] 1978 Act, s. 13(2).
[24] 1978 Act, s. 49(2). *e.g. O and O, Petitioners*, Edinburgh Sh.Ct. (E54/85), unreported.
[25] 1958 Act, s. 3(2).
[26] 1978 Act, s. 22(1).
[27] 1978 Act, s. 22(2).
[28] Adoption of Children (Regulations) Act 1939, s. 6(2).
[29] 1978 Act, s. 32, repealed by the 1995 Act, Sched. 2, para. 21: *cf. D v. F*, 1994 S.C.L.R. 417 at 423E.
[30] 1978 Act, s. 27. This is discussed at para. 5.13, below.
[31] 1978 Act, s. 28. This is discussed at para. 5.13, below.

who were not, or one of whom was not, ordinarily resident in Great Britain.[32] The situation is now governed by the generality of section 13 of the 1995 Act. This aspect is discussed later.[33]

3.07   (c) The fact of care and possession has been held to have been satisfied where the child was a nurse in residence in hospital,[34] a child was in hospital as a patient,[35] but not where a child was serving in the RAF. In that case there were other reasons for refusing the adoption order.[36] However, the requirements were satisfied where a regular soldier spent his leaves with his family in the house of the female petitioner's parents.[37] Now the child will require to have his home with the applicants, or one of them, at all times during the appropriate period.[38]

In England, "home" had a statutory definition. The Children Act 1975[39] provides that in the Act, unless the context otherwise provides, references to the person with whom a child has had his home refer to the person who, disregarding absence of the child at a hospital or boarding school and any other temporary absence, has actual custody of the child. The existence of care and possession is a question of fact. Obviously, the child will have had his home with the petitioners and that situation will not alter merely because the child or a petitioner is out of the home for schooling or employment or the like. A further requirement has been added: the court must be satisfied that sufficient opportunities to see the child with the petitioners or the petitioner in their home environment have been afforded to the adoption agency which placed the child and to the local authority in other cases.[40]

3.08   (d) As has been noted, the *terminus ad quem* in the running of the period of care and possession is the granting of the adoption order not the lodging of the petition. It may be, however, that at the time when the curator *ad litem* visits the home of the petitioners, such a short time will have elapsed from the beginning of the period of care and possession that no satisfactory report can be made. The curator *ad litem* may then wish to make a later visit to the home, or the court may deal with any outstanding matters arising from the care and possession by interviewing the petitioners. On the other hand, in many cases, the child has been in the care and possession of the petitioners for considerably longer than the minimum period long before the petition has been lodged.

3.09   (e) Apart from the case of a petition for a Convention adoption order, the domicile and nationality of the child do not matter.

---

[32] 1958 Act, s. 12(3).
[33] See para. 8.35, below.
[34] *A, Petitioners*, 1953 S.L.T. (Sh.Ct.) 45.
[35] *G, Petitioner*, 1955 S.L.T. (Sh.Ct.) 27.
[36] *M, Petitioner*, 1953 S.C. 227, also cited as *S, Petitioner*, 1953 S.L.T. 220; see also *F, Petitioners*, 1955 S.L.T. (Sh.Ct.) 12.
[37] *A, Petitioners*, 1958 S.L.T. (Sh.Ct.) 61.
[38] 1978 Act, s. 13.
[39] 1975 Act, s. 87(3).
[40] 1978 Act, s. 13(3).

Child Coming from Abroad

Apart from the cases of Convention adoption orders, Convention **3.10**
adoptions and overseas adoptions, there is the fairly common situation
where the child, who is the subject of an adoption petition in Scotland, has
been brought from a country outside Scotland, England, Wales, Northern
Ireland, the Isle of Man or any of the Channel Islands. The child may have
come to Scotland following upon a form of adoption granted in the
country of the child's origin, or the child may have entered the country as
a visitor with or without a parent, or may have been born in Scotland of a
foreign national. If the requirements of the Scottish adoption law have
been complied with, there is no reason why the adoption should not be
granted. Problems may arise, however, if the placement was illegal or if the
sole purpose of the proposed adoption was to acquire British nationality
or the like.[41]

Health of the Child

There is no requirement that the child be of good health at the time of **3.11**
adoption. At the earlier stage of placement for adoption by an adoption
agency there must be a report on the child's medical condition.[42] In the
Court of Session, and now in the sheriff court, on presentation of the
petition for adoption, where the child was not placed for adoption by an
adoption agency, the petitioners must lodge three copies of a medical
report showing the physical and mental health of the child.[43] The
regulations[44] merely provide that no child shall be placed by an adoption
agency in the care and possession of a person proposing to adopt him until
the agency has "obtained a report prepared within the previous 12 months
by a fully registered medical practitioner as to the health of the child". It
would appear that one reason for requiring such a report is to safeguard
the interests of the proposed adopters. No doubt the nature of any medical
condition which the child may suffer from—such as a condition which
required special medical attention on the part of the petitioners, or of the
former parents[45]—would be a matter which the court would have to take
into account in considering the welfare of the child; and if such a condition
came to the knowledge of the court, it would undertake such further
inquiries as seemed necessary. Pre-existing ill health which only becomes
apparent subsequently is not a ground for reduction of the adoption
order[46]; and there is no provision for cancellation of an adoption order.[47]
In *M and M v. Glasgow Corporation*,[48] where there was supervening
manifestation of brain damage to a child which had been caused at

---

[41] These matters are dealt with later; see para. 8.24, below.
[42] Adoption Agencies (Scotland) Regulations 1996 (S.I. 1996 No. 3266), para. 9(1)(b).
[43] A.S. 1997, r. 2.22(2)(c); (RCS, r. 67.22(2)(d)).
[44] Adoption Agencies (Scotland) Regulations 1996 (S.I. 1996 No. 3266), para. 9(1)(b).
[45] *B and B, Petitioners*, 1996 S.C.L.R. 874; see para. 8.32, below.
[46] *J and J v. C's Tutor*, 1948, S.C. 636.
[47] *Skinner v. Carter* [1948] Ch. 387 at 395, *per* Lord Greene M.R.; *Re B (Adoption Order: jurisdiction to set aside)* [1995] Fam. 237; see also para. 13.03b, below.
[48] 1976 S.L.T. (Sh.Ct.) 45.

birth, it was held that a local authority which had placed the child with the pursuers had been under a duty to take reasonable care to avoid placing for adoption a child who was medically unsuitable.

Foundling

3.12   It is not an impediment to the adoption of a child that the child is a foundling. If the parents cannot be found their agreement can be dispensed with on that ground.[49] No doubt the petitioners can lodge any police report as to the circumstances of the finding of the child and the efforts made, for example by local inquiry, advertisement in the press and on television or the like, to trace the parents. In these circumstances the child is usually given an artificial name. In one case the child was given as its first name the Christian name of the matron of the home to which the child had been taken by the police, and as its surname the name of the street in which the child had been found. Similarly, in the case of a child found abandoned in Delhi, in which situation the authorities did not issue a birth certificate, the date and circumstances of the birth were attested by an affidavit of the person responsible for the care of the child and who had been appointed as guardian by the High Court of Delhi.[50] If need be, the court must determine the probable date and country of birth of the child.[51] If the correct place and time of birth of the child emerge later, these particulars can be entered in the Adopted Children Register by amendment or rectification.[52] Amendment of the registers is discussed later.[53]

Subsequent Adoptions

3.13   A child who has formerly been adopted may be adopted again.[54] In that case it is the agreement of the adoptive parents—not the natural parents— to the making of the adoption order that is required.[55] Instead of an extract of an entry in the Register of Births an extract of an entry in the Adopted Children Register will be produced when the petition is lodged. A second adoption was refused where the sheriff-substitute was of the opinion that it was designed to meet the situation where a headstrong child was rebelling against her adoptive mother.[56] In terms of section 24 of the Adoption (Scotland) Act 1978, where the petitioner has made a previous application for a British adoption order in respect of the same child, the court must not proceed to determine an application for an adoption order in relation to that child where the previous application has been refused by any court unless:

> (a) in refusing the previous application the court directed that section 24 should not apply; or

---

[49] 1978 Act, s. 16(2)(a).
[50] *C and C, Petitioners*, Edinburgh Sh.Ct. (E77/85), July 1985, unreported.
[51] 1978 Act, s. 45, Sched. 1, para. 1(3).
[52] 1978 Act, s. 45, Sched. 1, para. 4
[53] See para. 12.01, below.
[54] 1978 Act, s. 12(7).
[55] *E and E, Petitioners*, 1939 S.C. 165 (where the earlier adoption order had been made in England); *Re M* [1941] W.N. 244.
[56] *B, Petitioner*, 1952 S.L.T. (Sh.Ct.) 48.

(b) it appears to the court that because of a change in circumstances or for any other reason it is proper to proceed with the application.[57]

These restrictions on the making of a subsequent application do not apply where the earlier petition was withdrawn. Where the earlier petition was refused it would appear to be necessary to produce the process in that earlier petition or otherwise prove the former circumstances. The process in a petition which was not granted does not require to be sealed up,[58] and accordingly there will be no difficulty in producing the process.

---

[57] 1978 Act, s. 24. See para. 11.02, below.
[58] See para. 11.05, below.

CHAPTER 4

PLACEMENT OF A CHILD FOR ADOPTION

Parent Adopting own Child

4.01 Generally, placement of a child for adoption may arise in two ways:

(a) where a relative of that child is the proposed adopter;
(b) otherwise, only an adoption agency may make arrangements for the adoption of a child, or place a child for adoption.[1]

4.02 "Parent" is defined as meaning (whether or not they have been married to each other)

(i) the mother of the child where she has parental responsibilities or parental rights in relation to him;
(ii) the father of the child where he has such responsibilities or rights; and
(iii) both of his parents where both have such responsibilities or rights.[2]

4.03 Presumably, a step-parent is merely a person who is married to a mother or a father of the child.

4.04 In this context, "relative" is defined as a grandparent, brother, sister, uncle or aunt, whether of the full blood or half-blood or by affinity. It includes, where the child's parents were not married to each other, the father of the child "where he is not a parent within the meaning of this Act, and any person who would be a relative within the meaning of this definition if the father were such a parent".[3] The class of relatives cannot be enlarged to include remoter relatives, such as great-aunts[4]; and it would appear that a testamentary placement would be illegal.[5] But the making of a supervision requirement (under section 70 of the Children (Scotland) Act 1995) by a children's hearing which, in respect that it provides as to where he is to reside, facilitates his being placed for adoption by an adoption agency, does not constitute the making of such arrangement.[6]

---

[1] 1978 Act, s. 11(1). The section envisages that where the adopter is a relative of the child, a person other than an adoption agency may "make arrangements for the adoption of a child". But it is almost unheard of for such a person to be involved: the proposed adoption proceeds without anyone other than the adopters making the arrangements.

[2] 1978 Act, s. 65(1) as inserted by the 1995 Act, s. 98(1) and Sched. 2, para. 29(a)(v).

[3] 1978 Act, s. 65(1) as amended by the 1995 Act, s. 98(1) and Sched. 2, para. 29(a)(vi).

[4] Nor a great-uncle: *Re C (Minors) (Adoption by a Relative)* (1989) 133 S.J. 20.

[5] 1984 S.L.T. (News) 73.

[6] 1978 Act, s. 65(3).

These provisions only relate to placement for adoption. If a child had **4.05** been placed with persons for a purpose other than adoption,[7] such as for fostering, these persons could later seek to adopt the child without breaching these rules, but as in the case of other adoptions which do not involve placement by an adoption agency, the petitioners must intimate to the local authority their intention to adopt.[8] These provisions not only prohibit placements contrary to their terms but impose criminal sanctions of imprisonment not exceeding three months or a fine not exceeding level 5 on the standard scale (£5,000) or both[9]; and where a person is convicted of such a contravention, the court may deal with the care of the child.[10]

A substantial group of these adoptions in most courts is the one **4.06** where the child is a natural child of one of the petitioners. The commonest situation is where a mother seeks to adopt her own child along with her new husband on marriage or on remarriage after divorce or widowhood. In addition, where a natural parent is married to a step-parent, the step-parent alone may present a petition for adoption of the child and the natural parent need not conjoin in the petition.[11] Occasionally, the petition is presented by the natural father and the stepmother of the child.[12] In Scotland this group of petitions has amounted to almost half of adoptions.[13] Usually, such cases present little difficulty where the natural father has died (in that case his agreement to the making of the adoption order is not required) or where the natural father gives his agreement or his agreement is dispensed with by the court. On the other hand, in the much rarer case, where, for example, after divorce the child resides with the natural mother who has been awarded custody of the child and the natural father has been granted access, now contact, with the child and has kept in touch with the child, "it is quite wrong to use the adoption law to extinguish the relationship between the protesting father and the child, unless there is some really serious factor which justifies the use of the statutory guillotine"[14]; "an adoption order (which is irrevocable) should not be used to deal with practical questions concerning custody, or care and control of the child, or access to the child. These can, and should be flexibly dealt with by the court exercising matrimonial jurisdiction".[15] The provisions whereby in a petition for an adoption order the court may direct that the application be treated as if it were made for the custody of the

---

[7] 1978 Act, s. 13(1).

[8] 1978 Act, s. 22.

[9] 1978 Act, s. 11(3).

[10] 1978 Act, ss. 11(5) and 26: but s. 26 appears to have been repealed: 1995 Act, s. 105(5) and Sched. 5; see n. 18, below.

[11] See para. 2.02, above.

[12] *e.g. H and H, Petitioners*, Edinburgh Sh.Ct. (E72/85 and E73/85), unreported.

[13] First Report on the Children Act 1975 (March 7, 1980).

[14] *Re B* [1975] Fam. 127 at 143.

[15] *Re D* [1977] A.C. 602 at 627, *per* Lord Wilberforce.

[16] The 1975 Act, s. 53 was repealed by the 1995 Act, s. 105(4) and Sched. 4, para. 26(6). See para. 1.04, above.

child, discussed earlier, have been repealed.[16] The 1995 Act introduced a new provision which may be regarded as a less rigorous substitute for the former provision. In considering whether to make an adoption order or a freeing order, the court shall regard the welfare of the child as the paramount consideration and shall not make such an order unless it considers that it would be better for the child that it should not.[17] However, as has been observed, "the minimum intervention principle is of little strength and cannot be used to justify keeping the child in a position of long-term fostering rather than being adopted, for the security given by the latter will always be a strong consideration and can easily outweigh the minimum intervention principle".[18]

Other Relatives Adopting a Child: Adoption by Grandparents

4.07   Another small but significant group of cases is where the child to be adopted is related to the petitioners but is not a child of the petitioners. A common relationship is that of grandparent and grandchild. The situation often happens where the mother of the child has died or has abandoned the child or for some reason—such as extreme youth or shiftlessness—is unable or unwilling to look after the child properly.[19] Cases have also arisen where a married couple do not wish to keep their child and are quite content that it be adopted by an aunt or other relative. The constant practice of the courts over the years is sufficient authority for the competent illustration of adoption by grandparents or other relatives.[20] However, there are differing views on the desirability of such adoptions, particularly adoption by a grandparent. One of the objections put forward is that it would conceal from the child that the adoptive parents are not his true parents. However, that objection has sufficient answer in the former practice: in *A, Petitioner*[21] the court required that the child was made acquainted with the whole circumstances set forth in the petition. In addition, the present statutory requirements make it mandatory that the child should, if he is a minor, consent to the making of the adoption order. In any event the court must ascertain the wishes and feelings of the child and the curator *ad litem* must report on these matters as well: this is discussed elsewhere.[22]

It is said that such adoption orders should only be made in the special circumstances of a given case, as there may be no final separation between the child and its natural mother.[23] It is also said that such adoptions distort the natural family relationship, and in the case of adoption by grandparents often result in the adoptive parents being somewhat older

[17] 1978 Act, s. 24(3) as substituted by the 1995 Act, s. 98(1) and Sched. 2, para. 16.
[18] Professor Kenneth McK. Norrie, *Children (Scotland) Act 1995*, commentary to Sched. 2, para. 16.
[19] *e.g. L and L, Petitioners*, 1965 S.L.T. (Sh.Ct.) 66; *Re W* [1980] 10 Fam. Law 190; [1981] C.L.Y. 1751, a decision of the Court of Appeal, where the grandparents were in their middle sixties and the child was seven.
[20] See para. 2.01, above.
[21] 1936 S.C. 255.
[22] See para. 8.47, below.
[23] *Re DX* [1949] Ch. 320, a single-judge decision; *cf. CD, Petitioners*, 1963 S.L.T. (Sh.Ct.) 7.

than would be the case with natural parents. These considerations are often not capable of exact proof and are only part of the whole circumstances which must be taken into account.[24] The curator *ad litem* and the court are frequently faced not with a choice between a good adoption and a less good adoption, but between the adoption which is before the court and no adoption at all. In most cases of adoptions of this kind the granting of the order does give legal approval to a *de facto* family; and whether the adoption order is granted or not, the child is almost certain to remain in the same family without the benefits which adoption can confer.

It is doubtful whether the court should *ex proprio motu* seek to counsel the petitioners to drop a petition for adoption which is otherwise in order merely because the petitioners stand in a particular relationship to the child. Indeed if the petitioners were not dissuaded and the court refused to grant the order on that ground, it would be difficult to formulate findings in fact and reasons to support such a decision, unless the proposed adoption was not in the interests of the child, as in *H and H, Petitioners*[25] where the separation of the natural parents was not final; but in *LH and LH, Petitioners*[26] the separation of the natural parents was final. There does not need to be a "compelling reason" before an adoption order can be granted.[27] In *H and H, Petitioners*,[28] which was a step-parent adoption in which the natural father had "washed his hands" of the child, the sheriff had dismissed the petition. The court allowed the appeal, and at its own hand dispensed with the consent of the natural father and granted the prayer of the petition. In the course of its opinion the court said:

> "On the merits of the petition and upon the question of whether discretion should be exercised to dispense with the father's consent, we are satisfied that the sheriff misdirected himself in the approach which he took. From his note it is clear that he had no regard to the advice of the curator to the effect that the proposed adoption was consistent with the child's welfare. He appears further to have given undue weight to the custody order without fully appreciating its limitations as a means of safeguarding the child's position in an established home, and the effect upon a child at the beginning of a school life of bearing a name different from that of the persons who to all in the locality would appear to be her mother and father. In addition, notwithstanding the competency of the application and in spite of the fact that the father had 'washed his hands' of his daughter, the sheriff has, it seems, questioned the propriety of adoption by a parent and a step-parent and has been influenced in that view by a working paper and the report of a departmental committee which he mentions in his note. In the result he refused both the motion and the crave because no 'compelling reason' for adoption by the petitioners had yet been shown. The true question in all such cases which is relevant to both the merits of an

[24] See paras 2.01 and 2.03, above and para. 8.24, below.
[25] 1951 S.L.T. (Sh.Ct.) 17.
[26] 1951 S.L.T. (Sh.Ct.) 46.
[27] See the opinion of the court in *H and H, Petitioners*, 1976 S.L.T. 80 at 83.
[28] 1976 S.L.T. 80.

application and to the motion to dispense with consent, is whether the making of an order or refusing to make it is more likely to enure to the welfare of the child (see *AB v. CD*, 1970 S.C. 268, the opinion of Lord President Clyde at p. 269). What is required is a balancing of advantages and disadvantages from the point of view of the welfare of the child. What is not required is a search for a compelling reason to grant the order, the propriety of which the court chooses to question upon the ground that the order is sought by a parent and step-parent of a legitimate child whose other parent is still alive."

4.08　　In one case the court granted an adoption order in favour of grandparents subject to the undertaking of the natural father to pay a weekly sum into the hands of the children's officer for disbursement to the child in the event of need.[29]

4.09　　If a placement is effected in a manner contrary to section 11 of the 1978 Act, the statute provides that certain criminal sanctions may follow, but it does not prohibit the adoption, whereas, in other areas, such a prohibition is expressly stated.[30] If an adoption is arranged abroad, there is no placement until there is physical contact between the child and the proposed adopters.[31] In one case, just after the child was born in Scotland to a mother who was a citizen of the Republic of Ireland, the mother and one adoptive parent went to Ireland where the mother handed over the child to that parent: the mother remained in Ireland and the adoptive parent took the child back to Scotland to live with him and his wife.[32] In the latter case, the sheriff took the view that the manner of placement of the child was one of the circumstances which had to be taken into account in terms of section 6 of the Adoption (Scotland) Act 1978, and in an appeal on that aspect of the decision it was observed that the sheriff could not be faulted.[33] This approach had also been adopted in an earlier case.[34]

Surrogacy Agreements

4.10　　In proceedings for the adoption of a child who was the subject of a surrogacy agreement between the petitioners and the natural mother, the natural mother would have to agree to the making of the order or her

---

[29] *GD, Petitioners*, 1950 S.L.T. (Sh.Ct.) 34.

[30] 1978 Act, ss. 12(8), 15(2), 16(1), 22(1) and 51 read in conjunction with s. 24(2).

[31] *Re A (Adoption: Placement)* [1988] 1 W.L.R. 229, *per* Lincoln J.

[32] *D and D v. F*, Sheriff McNeill, Edinburgh Sh.Ct. (E92/92), May 5, 1993, unreported; and (I.H.), 1994 S.C.L.R. 417.

[33] *D and D v. F*, Sheriff McNeill, Edinburgh Sh.Ct. (E92/92), May 5, 1993, unreported at pp. 35–41 where it is also pointed out that the English decisions on the effect of s. 11 are of limited application to Scotland, because the (English) Adoption Act 1976 has an additional s. 11(1)(b) which is absent in the Scottish Act—a point not taken on appeal: 1994 S.C.L.R. 417 at 423F; irregular placements were considered in *Re C* [1991] 1 F.C.R. 337; *Re ZHH* [1993] 1 Fam. 83; *Re an Adoption Application* [1992] 1 F.L.R. 341; *Re A* [1988] 1 W.L.R. 229; Re K *(A Minor) (Wardship: Adoption)* [1991] 1 F.L.R. 57; *Re Adoption Application (Adoption of Non-patrial)* [1992] 1 W.L.R. 596 per Hollings J.; *Re Adoption Application (Non-patrial: breach of procedure)* [1993] Fam. 125, D.C.; *Re an Adoption Application* [1992] 1 F.L.R. 341.

[34] *SS, Petitioners*, 1953 S.L.T. (Sh.Ct.) 29 at 30: but the rubric of that case is not warranted by the decision of the sheriff.

agreement would have to be dispensed with in the normal way. The agreement of any father who is a parent as defined in the statute would have to be disposed in the same way.[35]

Other Private Adoptions Prohibited

Before February 15, 1982 it was competent for an individual— **4.11** including non-relatives of the child—to assist in the placing of the child: such persons might be doctors, nurses or merely friends. The number of such placements was tiny. The advantages were probably only greater speed and simplicity as compared with the more sophis-ticated apparatus which is available when an adoption agency is involved. The disadvantages were that the advice and support which can arise from the professionalism and experience of the trained staff of an adoption agency was not available to the parties. From 1982 the law has prohibited such private placements except where the proposed adopter is a relative of the child.[36] Since 1985 there is no doubt that where a children's hearing makes a supervision requirement, which, in respect that it provides where the child is to reside, and thereby facilitates his being placed for adoption by an adoption agency, that requirement does not constitute an arrangement which is struck at by sections 11 and 65(3) of the 1978 Act.[37]

ADOPTION SOCIETIES AND ADOPTION AGENCIES

An adoption agency is either a local authority, that is, a council **4.12** constituted under section 2 of the Local Government etc. (Scotland) Act 1994[38] (replacing the former regional or islands councils) or an approved adoption society[39] (replacing the former registered adoption society[40]). The corresponding bodies in England and Wales may be included in these definitions if the Adoption Act 1976 is to be regarded as being in force for these purposes.[41]

Adoptions within the family are usually arranged privately by an **4.13** individual, such as the natural mother, without the intervention of an adoption society. An adoption society is defined as a body of persons

---

[35] See *C and C v. S*, 1996 S.C.L.R. 837. The financial aspect of surrogacy agreements is considered later; see para. 8.21, below.

[36] 1958 Act, s. 29(1)(a) as amended by the 1975 Act, s. 28 (1978 Act, s. 11(1); Children Act 1975 (Scotland) (Commencement No. 3) Order 1982 (S.I. No. 33), para. 3). The current provision is the 1978 Act, s. 11(1).

[37] Law Reform (Miscellaneous Provisions) (Scotland) Act 1985, ss. 27 and 60(3)(a) reversing the opinion expressed in *R v. Children's Hearing for Borders Region*, 1984 S.L.T. 65. That was a decision on the former provision contained in the 1958 Act, s. 29(1); *cf.* the 1995 Act, s. 73(4) and (5).

[38] 1978 Act, s. 65(1).

[39] 1958 Act, s. 1(4).

[40] 1958 Act, s. 57(1) before amendment by the 1975 Act, Sched. 3, para. 21(3) and S.I. 1982 No. 33.

[41] 1978 Act, s. 65(1) which refers to the 1976 Act, s. 12. A list of adoption agencies in England and Scotland—with their addresses and telephone numbers—is contained in the booklet *Adopting a Child* produced by the British Agencies for Adoption and Fostering.

whose functions consist of or include the making of arrangements for the adoption of children. The body of persons may be incorporated or unincorporated.[42] Since 1984 there have been provisions for the setting up of local authority adoption services[43]; and in this scheme the local authority and the approved adoption societies may be referred to as adoption agencies.[44] Since 1982 it has been unlawful for a person other than an adoption agency to make arrangements for the adoption of a child or to place a child for adoption unless the proposed adopter is a parent, step-parent or relative of the child,[45] or the child has been placed with him by a children's hearing.[46] In one case in which applicants for an adoption order had obtained the child not from an adoption society but from a foster-mother who was registered with the local authority as such, it was held that the application should be granted, but the sheriff-substitute observed that such an arrangement was irregular and would normally lead to the refusal of the application and "incurs the liability of having the application refused".[47] But non-compliance with the statutory provisions in this respect would provide no ground for reducing the adoption orders.[48]

Although it is unlawful for a person other than an adoption agency to place a child for adoption or to make arrangements for the adoption of a child, it is lawful to adopt a child who has been placed with the petitioners for a purpose other than adoption, for example, for fostering; but in such cases the period of care and possession must be 12 months.[49] In the case of placements by adoption agencies, the number of potential adopters greatly outweighs the number of available children: yet a substantial number of children do not find adoptive homes usually because they are much older or because they are handicapped. In one case, adopters with four boys of their own adopted a girl with Down's syndrome when the girl's parents could not face bringing her up themselves.[50] There is no objection to an adoption agency advertising for adopters and describing the child, subject to the strict requirements of confidentiality.[51]

---

[42] 1978 Act, s. 65(1).
[43] 1978 Act, s. 1(1).
[44] 1978 Act, s. 1(4).
[45] 1978 Act, s. 11.
[46] See para. 4.11, above.
[47] *SS, Petitioners*, 1853 S.L.T. (Sh.Ct.) 29.
[48] *J and J v. C's Tutor*, 1948 S.C. 636 at 644.
[49] 1978 Act, s. 13(2).
[50] *K and K, Petitioners*, Edinburgh Sh.Ct. (E63/85), September 21, 1983, unreported.
[51] See para. 5.03, below.

CHAPTER 5

PETITION FOR ADOPTION; PETITION TO FREE
A CHILD FOR ADOPTION

A JUDICIAL PROCESS

Adoption in Scotland, as in England, is effected not by an administrative **5.01** process but by a judicial process. That process is *sui generis*.[1] The process is effected by a petition—not an initial writ or summons.

Since almost all petitions for adoption and petitions to free a child for **5.02** adoption and other associated procedures are at first instance disposed of in the sheriff court, reference in this book has been made to the sheriff court procedure which is contained in the Act of Sederunt (Child Care and Maintenance Rules) 1997, Chaps 1 and 2[2] as the leading provisions, with corresponding references to Court of Session procedure (which is contained in the Rules of Court, Chap. 67). The legislation envisages that there may be different statutory provisions for different circumstances.[3] Just as there are different rules in England and Wales for the High Court and the county court on the one hand and the magistrates' court on the other hand,[4] so in Scotland there are different rules in the Court of Session and the sheriff court. Within the limits of that legislation the court has considerable freedom to adopt the procedure which is most appropriate to the circumstances of the case.[5] However, such flexibility would not permit an incompetent procedure, such as allowing a person who was not a party (for example, the unmarried father who does not claim to be the father of a child in a freeing petition in respect of that child) into the proceedings, or allowing parties to be represented by unqualified persons.[6]

> "Where a new and special jurisdiction is given to any Court the exercise of it must be regulated entirely by the conditiohs of the statute under which it is conferred, and that in the general case remedies which might have been competent in an ordinary civil

---

[1] *J and J v. C's Tutor*, 1948 S.C. 636 at 642, *per* Lord President Cooper; approved in the House of Lords in Scottish and English appeals: *A v. B and C*, 1971 S.C. (H.L.) 129 at 141; *Re D* [1977] A.C. 602 at 626.

[2] S.I. 1997 No. 291.

[3] 1978 Act, s. 60(5).

[4] Adoption Rules 1984 (S.I. 1984 No. 265) and Magistrates' Courts (Adoption) Rules 1984 (S.I. 1984 No. 611).

[5] *cf. A v. B and C*, 1971 S.C. (H.L.) 129 at 135, *per* Lord President Clyde in the Inner House.

[6] See para. 5.10, below.

process are not to be presumed or inferred to be given by the particular statute. . . . But, on the other hand, I imagine that where a well-known and recognised jurisdiction is invoked by the Legislature for the purpose of carrying out a series of provisions which are important for the public without any specific form of process being prescribed, the presumption is that the ordinary forms of that Court are to be observed in carrying out the provisions, and, indeed, generally that the Court has been adopted and chosen and selected because it is seen to be advisable that the ordinary rules of such Court and the forms of its procedure shall be applied to give effect to the provisions of the legislative Act."[7]

The various modes of inquiry are discussed later.[8]

Confidentiality

5.03   Unlike most other judicial proceedings, which have for centuries been open to the public, adoption proceedings are strictly confidential. Briefly, this confidentiality has several aspects.

(a) The petitioners in a petition for adoption may keep their identity from any person who has agreed to the granting of an adoption order.[9]
(b) Where an adoption agency which proposes to apply for an order freeing a child for adoption wishes to prevent the address of the child being disclosed to any person whose agreement or consent is required, the agency may apply to the sheriff clerk for a serial number to be assigned for that purpose.[10] Unless the adoption agency adopts this procedure, the address of the child must appear in the petition.[11]
(c) All proceedings are, in general, conducted in private[12] and, unless the court otherwise directs, all documents lodged in process may only be open to the court, the curator *ad litem*, the reporting officer, the parties (and presumably their solicitors or counsel) and the clerk of court unless the court otherwise directs.[13] Employees of petitioners' solicitors would be entitled to see the papers in so far as their duties required them to. The authors of reports made in terms of sections 22 and 23 of the 1978 Act are not entitled to see the process. In reports, opinions of the court, law reports[14] and other documents, the circumstances of a case should only be referred to in a way that does not identify the parties.[15] The same precautions

---

[7] *Magistrates of Portobello v. Magistrates of Edinburgh* (1882) 10 R. 130, *per* Lord Justice-Clerk Moncrieff; *Central Regional Council v. B*, 1985 S.L.T. 413.
[8] See Chap. 6, below.
[9] A.S. 1997, r. 2.24 (RCS, r. 67.20); see para. 5.10, below.
[10] A.S. 1997, r. 2.5(3) (there appears to be no corresponding provision in the Rules of Court).
[11] A.S. 1997, r. 1.2(3) and Form 1.
[12] 1978 Act, s. 57.
[13] A.S. 1997, r. 2.30 (RCS, r. 67.3).
[14] Opinions of the judges can be consulted in the act book in the sheriff court and in the opinion department in the Court of Session.
[15] A party in prison should be designed by reference to his home address: *C and C, Petitioners*, Glasgow Sh.Ct., February 18, 1982, unreported; Practice Note, July 23, 1952 (*Parliament House Book*, para. C2000).

should be taken in correspondence between parties and others; and files and computer records relating to adoptions should be kept secure. It would be a breach of that confidentiality for solicitors to mention the names of the petitioners or the child in an adoption petition in a newspaper advertisement which sought the whereabouts of the natural father. In one case, records of a social work department which had been obtained for the purposes of adoption proceedings, but which related to the medical condition of the child and mother, were recovered by a party in a civil litigation.[16]

(d) In novel provisions which apply not only to adoption procedure but also to other litigations involving children, where the child wishes to express a view, the sheriff is empowered to direct that a written record of the views of the child shall be sealed in an envelope, be available to the sheriff only, not be opened by any person other than a sheriff and not form part of the process.[17]

(e) After the adoption order has been granted and communicated to the Registrar General for Scotland, the process must be sealed up and not be made accessible to any person for 100 years except in certain circumstances, including the attainment by the adopted child of the age of 16 years.[18] It is thought that the process could not be opened up even to the judge or clerk of the court which granted the order—any more than anyone else: they would have to seek the authority of the custodier of the record. The clerk of court will require to have a secure place to keep the processes while they are pending and after they have been sealed up. In England it has been held under the Adoption Agencies Regulations 1976[19] that where the social services committee of a local authority were dealing with reports prepared in connection with making arrangements for a child's adoption before any petition had been presented in court, the information in the reports might in very limited circumstances be divulged to all members of the local authority, including elected members. The utmost care must be taken to prevent the unnecessary dissemination within the council of details relating to the child, to its natural parents, to any foster or adoptive parents and of sources of information.[20] The corresponding Scottish provision would appear to have the same effect.[21] That decision has no direct bearing on adoption proceedings in court; thus the curator *ad litem* and reporting officer who are appointed personally may not reveal any matters—even to other servants of the adoption agency with whom they happen to be employed.[22] In one case the court refused the request of the guardian *ad litem* in English access proceedings by

---

[16] *Parks v. Tayside Regional Council*, 1989 S.L.T. 345, and the cases there cited.

[17] See para. 8.47, below: it is difficult to imagine circumstances where it would be appropriate or conducive to a fair consideration, at first instance or on appeal, of all the circumstances of the case.

[18] A.S. 1997, r. 2.33(2)(a) (RCS, r. 67.32(2)(a)); see para. 11.09, below.

[19] S.I. 1976 No. 1796.

[20] *Birmingham City District Council v. O* [1983] A.C. 578.

[21] Adoption Agencies (Scotland) Regulations 1996 (S.I. 1996 No. 3266), reg. 23.

[22] See para. 7.04, below.

a natural father of the child which was the subject of adoption proceedings in Scotland to have a sight of the report of the curator *ad litem* in the adoption proceedings.[23]

Avoidance of Delay

5.04　There are consistent dicta about the dangers of delay in dealing with adoption petitions.[24] Delay may act as a circumstance in itself so as to make it virtually impossible to alter the status quo, but now an adoption order may be made in relation to a person who has attained the age of 18 if the application was made before such attainment.[25] Delays can occur at almost every stage in the proceedings—with the solicitor, between receiving instructions and presenting the petition or before presentation when the matter is with the adoption agency; in court, in the provision of a report by the local authority under section 22 of the Adoption (Scotland) Act 1978, between the remit to the curator *ad litem* and reporting officer and the return of the reports, between receipt of the reports and consideration of them by the court, in finding a diet for interview or proof; and in appeals, especially where a sist has been granted to allow a party to apply for legal aid.

The current legislation has grappled with some of these problems. Thus, in proceedings in which the question arises as to whether the court is satisfied that a parent agrees to the making of an adoption order or that his agreement should be dispensed with, the court is required to draw up a timetable specifying periods within which certain steps must be taken in relation to these proceedings, and to give such directions as it considers appropriate for the purpose of ensuring that the timetable is adhered to.[26] Generally, the authors of reports must report in writing within four weeks from the date of the interlocutor appointing them.[27]

No doubt the need for expedition would be a consideration in refusing to grant a sist. In one case the court declined to sist the adoption proceedings which were before it to await the outcome of the investigations of the Ombudsman into the care of the child while the child was with the local authority in England.[28] In most cases the court would not sist adoption proceedings to await the outcome of proceedings in other courts, particularly if the adoption proceedings would supersede the other proceedings—such as an action for custody[29] or (formerly) proceedings for the assumption of parental rights. However, in cases where there are concurrent proceedings in relation to the same child for adoption and for parental rights by grandparents of the child, there should be a single hearing in the same sheriff court so that the sheriff does not have to hear

---

[23] *P and P, Petitioners*, Edinburgh Sh.Ct. (E46/84), September 13, 1984, unreported.

[24] *e.g. A v. B and C*, 1971 S.C. (H.L.) 129 at 144, *per* Lord Guest.

[25] 1978 Act, s. 12(1).

[26] 1978 Act, s. 25A; A.S. 1997, r. 2.4 (*cf.* RCS, rr. 67.11(1)(t), 67.11(2)(i), 67.14(5)(g), 67.24(1)(l) and 67.24(2)(x)).

[27] A.S. 1997, r. 2.8(2) (freeing), r. 2.26(2) (revocation) and r. 2.21(5) (adoption); and the same rule applies to the other non-adoption reports, *e.g.* 2.53(1) (human embryology).

[28] *P and P, Petitioners*, Edinburgh Sh.Ct. (E46/84), September 13, 1984, unreported.

[29] *Borders Regional Council v. M*, 1986 S.L.T. 222.

the evidence twice in two separate processes.[30] Sisting of adoption proceedings should be avoided, even for reasons such as an application for legal aid. However, in some cases a sist may be necessary—as where an adoption petition was sisted to await the outcome of another litigation which would decide whether the unmarried father had parental rights.[31] Even after an appeal has been heard and advised, the appeal court may remit the case back to the lower court for a proof or a rehearing or for the sheriff to make further findings in fact.[32] In a few cases the period between the decision of the sheriff and that of the appeal court has been two years.[33]

In relation to the duties on all parties to avoid delay, it was said in a judgment of the Inner House, **5.05**

> "It is essential, especially in a small court where judicial resources are already under pressure for other reasons, that the sheriff should be given at the outset a carefully considered forecast of the time which the proof is expected to take. With the benefit of that information arrangements can and should be made for the sheriff to be released from other duties so that he can give priority to the case without interruption and until it has been completed by the issuing of his interlocutor."[34]

These directions were adopted in the conduct of a proof in one petition for adoption. The petitioners relied on several medical reports on the child, which reports had been previously prepared for care proceedings in England. The authors of the reports were senior doctors in England. The parties agreed a timetable for the doctors to fly up from England. At the proof the solicitor for the petitioners limited his examination of each medical witness to asking him to identify his report and to confirm that the matters stated in the report still represented his view. Thus, it was left to the solicitor for the respondents to limit his cross-examination to the matters in the report which he was challenging.[35] In another Outer House case, it was said, "The agreement of parties to accept these **5.06**

---

[30] *AB and CD, Petitioners*, 1992 S.C.L.R. 274; see para. 6.11, below.

[31] *M v. S*, Edinburgh Sh.Ct. (E48/95), September 1, 1996, unreported; in *S v. M*, Sheriff Stoddart, Edinburgh Sh.Ct. (CA1031/94), unreported, an action for parental rights by an unmarried father in respect of the same child, the pursuer enrolled a motion asking the court to allow him to have the right to agree to the making of an adoption order, and to dispense with intimation on the mother who was the petitioner in an action for adoption. After hearing counsel, both motions were granted. As a result, the unmarried father became a person to whom the petitioner became obliged to intimate the hearing, but the petitioner had no way of knowing that the motion had been granted. There was also a third associated action (for access) by this unmarried father: the action failed before the sheriff, the sheriff principal, in the Outer House, in the Inner House (1995 S.C.L.R. 902) and in the House of Lords (1997 S.C.L.R. 281). Thereafter, the adoption order was granted unopposed.

[32] *AB v. CD*, 1970 S.C. 268; *Re F (R)* [1970] 1 Q.B. 385; *Strathclyde Regional Council v. A*, 1993 G.W.D. 9-585; *Lothian Regional Council v. A*, 1992 S.L.T. 858 at 862–863.

[33] *A v. W and W*, Glasgow Sh.Ct., November 29, 1978, unreported; *A v. A and A*, Glasgow Sh.Ct., November 4, 1980, unreported; *Q and Q v. O*, Inner House, October 16, 1992, unreported.

[34] *Lothian Regional Council v. A*, 1992 S.L.T. 858 at 861–862.

[35] *N v. W*, Sheriff McNeill, Edinburgh Sh.Ct., July 28, 1995, unreported.

findings as fact for the purposes of the petition before me greatly reduced my task and, more importantly, put me in the position to decide the issues before me much more speedily than could otherwise have been possible."[36] It respectfully appears that such a procedure should be adopted in relation to most documentary evidence—especially since hearsay to any extent is now admissible.[37] Further, there is a dictum of Lord Reid in the House of Lords made 25 years ago on unnecessary medical evidence which, in view of the conduct of some recent cases, can be repeated with profit:

> "In a case like this I think that a judge is well able to estimate the probable effect of uprooting a child of tender years and transferring it from adopting parents, with whom it is happy, to its natural parents, of whom it has no recollection. In unusual cases medical evidence may be helpful, but I should be sorry to see any general tendency to call medical evidence in these cases."[38]

5.07   In petitions for adoption in the Outer House, the court commended the agreement by the parties of the findings in fact made by the sheriff in related access proceedings.[39] More general and more forceful observations were made in 1992:

> "there is a heavy responsibility on the parties' representatives to exercise all reasonable economy and restraint in their presentation of the evidence and in their submissions to the court".[40]

Procedure by Petition

5.08   All applications for an adoption order, or to free a child for adoption or to adopt a child abroad, are in the form prescribed in the Rules of Court,[41] with such variations as the circumstances require. In the case of a petition to free a child for adoption there is a difference between the rules of the Court of Session and the rules of the sheriff court in the procedure at this stage. In the sheriff court at the time of lodging a simple petition in terms of Form 1, there must also be lodged a report of the adoption agency which deals with 12 numbered items treating substantially the same matters.[42] In the Court of Session there is no prescribed form of petition: the petition is one referred to in rule 67.9(1), but the petition must either include averments in relation to, or refer to a report or other documents produced which deal with the 13 items set forth in lettered paragraphs.[43] It may be that the most convenient course in Court of Session petitions would be to proceed by reference to the report of the adoption agency. This would achieve greater congruence of the procedures of the two jurisdictions and any other documents may be lodged as productions.

---

[36] *AB and CD, Petitioners*, Lord McCluskey, *The Scotsman*, March 20, 1987.
[37] Civil Evidence (Scotland) Act 1988, s. 2.
[38] *A v. B and C*, 1971 S.C. (H.L.) 129 at 142.
[39] *AB and CD v. GH*, Lord McCluskey, July 4, 1986, unreported.
[40] *Lothian Regional Council v. A*, 1992 S.L.T. 858 at 862.
[41] A.S. 1997, r. 1.2(3) (RCS, r. 1.4).
[42] A.S. 1997, r. 2.5(2)(b).
[43] RCS, r. 67.9(2).

The concurrent regulations which govern adoption agencies provide that where a petition to free a child for adoption is made to a court the adoption agency shall provide a report to the court dealing generally with "such information on the background and circumstances of the child, his family and (where appropriate) the persons proposing to adopt him as they have been able to discover" in accordance with the regulations and any other matters relevant to the operation of section 6 of the 1978 Act as read with section 6A.[44] If the petition is commenced by one spouse and it is desired that the other spouse should also be a party to the action, he can, no doubt, be sisted as an additional petitioner. In the overwhelming number of cases, only one child is being adopted at a time; in cases where several children are being adopted by the same adoptive parents simultaneously, it is submitted that it is the better course and the normal practice to have one petition for each child.[45] In cases where there were two petitions to free children who had the same mother, but who had different fathers—one who was married to the mother and the other who was not—separate proofs were allowed.[46]

Jurisdiction: "Authorised Court"

In the Court of Session the petition should be presented in the Outer House.[47] In respect of an application for an order relating to a child, generally, jurisdiction is determined by reference to an "authorised court".[48] Where the child is in Scotland, the authorised court is either the Court of Session, or the sheriff court of the sheriffdom (not merely sheriff court district[49]) in which the child is; but the Court of Session has privative jurisdiction

5.09

> (a) in a petition for adoption, or a petition to free a child, where the child is not in Great Britain when the application is made[50] and
> (b) in a petition for a Convention adoption order[51];

and where there is an application to return a child taken away in cases where its removal is restricted and there is pending a petition for adoption or a petition to free a child, the authorised court is the one before which

---

[44] Adoption Agencies (Scotland) Act Regulations 1996 (S.I. 1996 No. 3266), reg. 22. Before making an application for an order to free a child for adoption, or before placing or securing the placing of a child for adoption, the adoption agency is required, as far as it has been able to discover as far as is appropriate to the proceeding, to ascertain the particulars relating to the child, each parent and guardian and each prospective adopter as set out in the regulations: regs 8, 9 and Sched. 2.

[45] The arguments for and against single and multiple petitions were noted at McNeill, *Adoption of Children in Scotland* (2nd ed.), para. 5.05.

[46] *Lothian Regional Council v. W*, Sheriff McNeill, Edinburgh Sh.Ct. (E19/91), May 27, 1991, unreported: *Lothian Regional Council v. W*, Sheriff McNeill, Edinburgh Sh.Ct. (E20/91), May 27, 1991, unreported.

[47] RCS, r. 14.2(h).

[48] 1978 Act, s. 56. The Civil Jurisdiction and Judgments Act 1982 does not apply to "the status or legal capacity of natural persons": s. 1(3) and Sched. 1, Art. 1.

[49] See also Macphail, *Sheriff Court Practice* (1988, W. Green & Son Ltd), para. 2-03; see para. 2.05, above.

[50] 1978 Act, s. 56(3).

[51] 1978 Act, s. 56(4).

the petition is pending.[52] A petition in the Court of Session is presented in the Outer House.[53] However, the overwhelming number of petitions are for adoption or to free a child for adoption where the child is in Scotland; and all but a tiny number are raised in the sheriff court—no doubt, for reasons of economy. Since 1980 in the case of any action in the sheriff court in relation to the custody or adoption of a child, the sheriff may, of his own accord, at any stage of the action remit the action to the Court of Session,[54] and the Court of Session may in relation to any action before it which could competently have been brought before a sheriff, remit that action (at its own instance or on the application of any of the parties to the action) to the sheriff within whose jurisdiction the action could have been brought, where, in the opinion of the court, the nature of the action makes it appropriate to do so.[55]

Serial Number: Legal Aid

5.10   If the petitioner in an adoption petition or a petition to adopt a child abroad, does not want his identity disclosed to any person whose agreement to the order is required, he may before presenting the petition apply to the clerk of court for a serial number to be assigned to him; and the record of the serial number is treated as confidential and is open only to the court[56]; this provision affects the document signifying the agreement of that person.[57] In a freeing application, where an adoption agency wishes to prevent the address of the child being disclosed to any person whose agreement to the making of an adoption order or consent to the making of an application for adoption is required, the agency may apply to the sheriff clerk for a serial number to be assigned for that purpose[58]; but in other cases the date of birth and address of the child must appear in the petition.[59] There is no provision as there is in England that this information should be withheld from the respondent: on the contrary, all documents must be available to the parties.[60]

If legal aid has been granted, the words "assisted person" should follow the name of the assisted person in every step of process in the proceeding to which he is a party.[61]

---

[52] 1978 Act, s. 56(5).

[53] Expressly in respect of petitions for adoption, petitions to adopt a child abroad and petitions for a Convention adoption order: RCS, rr. 67.72 and 67.36 and Form 67.72; and impliedly in a petition to free a child for adoption: RCS, rr. 4.1, 14.2(h) and 14.4 and Form 14.4 and notes to these rules.

[54] Sheriff Court (Scotland) Act 1971, s. 37(2A); *cf.* Act of Sederunt (Sheriff Court Ordinary Cause Rules) 1993 (S.I. 1993 No. 1956) r. 26 and RCS, r. 32.1.

[55] Law Reform (Miscellaneous Provisions) (Scotland) Act 1985, s. 14.

[56] A.S. 1997, r. 2.24 (RCS, r. 67.20).

[57] A.S. 1997, r. 2.24 (RCS, r. 67.20(3)).

[58] A.S. 1997, r. 2.5(3) (there appears to be no corresponding provision in the Rules of Court). This is a new sheriff court provision which came into force in 1997, but there is no provision for a register of serial numbers and related matters as there is in petitions for adoption: A.S. 1997, r. 2.24.

[59] A.S. 1997, r. 2.5 and Form 1.

[60] A.S. 1997, r. 2.12 (freeing) and r. 2.30 (adoption) (RCS, r. 67.3 (all causes)); Magistrates' Courts (Adoption) Rules 1984 (S.I. 1984 No. 611), r. 27(4); *Re M* [1973] 1 Q.B. 108 at 125; *cf.* Adoption Rules 1984 (S.I. 1984 No. 265), rr. 14 and 53.

[61] Act of Sedurunt (Legal Aid Rules) 1987 (S.I. 1987 No. 492), r. 3(1).

Solicitors: Fee of Curator *ad Litem* and Reporting Officer

It is trite law that the only persons who can appear in an action in **5.11** court are the parties and their legal representatives, that is to say, solicitor or counsel. If the party is a juristic person such as a local authority or an adoption agency they cannot appear by themselves but can only be represented by solicitor or counsel or "other person having rights of audience",[62] not by one of their servants, unless that servant is a law agent with a current practising certificate. This rule includes all the procedural aspects of the case, including the presentation of papers to the court offices.[63] In certain circumstances it may also constitute a criminal offence for a person who is not a solicitor or advocate to prepare documents.[64]

Only solicitors who have a place of business in Edinburgh may borrow a Court of Session process, and only a solicitor or his authorised clerk can borrow a sheriff court process.[65] The general provisions relating to borrowing a process in the Court of Session[66] refer to all processes whereas those relating to the sheriff court[67] relate only to ordinary actions. In adoption petitions it is provided that unless the court otherwise directs "all documents lodged in process, including the reports of the curator *ad litem* and the reporting officer, shall be open only to the Court, the curator *ad litem* and the reporting officer and the parties".[68] In terms of that provision or at common law, the process is usually borrowed by the curator *ad litem* (or he is given a copy by the sheriff clerk) to enable him to furnish his report—it is difficult to see how parties could properly conduct the case unless they were able to borrow the process. This is especially true at certain stages of the case, as where a party wishes to consider the terms of the petition of which he has only received notice,[69] or the terms of the report of the curator *ad litem* or other document, or the terms of any interlocutor, especially an interlocutor making or refusing an adoption order. The need to borrow would also be essential where copies of the process would be necessary as where there are correspondents or where counsel has been instructed. If a potential respondent is not to be regarded as a party, he may have access to the documents by direction of the court. The clerk of court would, no doubt, be particularly vigilant to see that only these persons have access to the process, and if he is in doubt he can consult the court.

If the adopters have a legal aid certificate or if they put their solicitor in funds—at least to the extent of the fee of the curator *ad litem* and the reporting officer—considerable delays can be avoided in waiting for

---

[62] *Equity and Law Life Assurance Society v. Tritonia Ltd*, 1943 S.C. (H.L.) 88; *Scottish Gas Board v. Alexander*, 1963 S.L.T. (Sh.Ct.) 27; *B and B, Petitioners*, Edinburgh Sh.Ct. (E92/83), February 1984, unreported.

[63] *Rush v. Fife Regional Council*, 1984 S.L.T. 391.

[64] Solicitors (Scotland) Act 1980, ss. 31 and 32.

[65] Act of Sederunt (Sheriff Court Ordinary Court Rules) 1993 (S.I. 1993 No. 1956), r. 11.3 (RCS, rr. 4.11 and 4.12).

[66] RCS, r. 4.11.

[67] Sheriff Courts (Scotland) Act 1907, s. 39.

[68] A.S. 1997, r. 2.12 (freeing) and r. 2.30 (adoption) (RCS, r. 67.3).

[69] A.S. 1997, r. 2.11 (freeing) and r. 2.28 (adoption) (RCS, rr. 67.13 and 67.25).

settlement of that fee. In ordinary actions in the Court of Session[70] and in the sheriff court,[71] where the appointment of a reporter is made on the motion of a party, that party is responsible in the first instance for the fees and outlays of the reporter, and where the court makes the appointment, on its own motion, that responsibility is on the pursuer or minuter. There is no reason in principle why the same rule should not also apply to expenses of the report of a curator *ad litem* and reporting officer in an adoption process in the Court of Session or the sheriff court, under the wide powers of the court to deal with expenses in adoption matters.[72]

Effect of Petition or Notice to Local Authority on Care and Possession of the Child

5.12   The legislation deals with the right of the adopters or the prospective adopters or others to maintain their care and possession of a child awaiting adoption.

(1) Where
(a) an adoption agency has placed a child with a person with a view to his being adopted by the person and
(b) the consent of each parent or guardian of the child has been duly obtained in accordance with the regulations[73] to that placement (whether or not in knowledge of the person)
any such parent or guardian shall not be entitled to remove the child from the care and possession of the person without the leave of the adoption agency or the court.[74]
(2) Where a petition is pending in respect of a child made by the person with whom the child has had his home for the five years preceding the petition, then no person is entitled, against the will of the petitioner to remove the child from his care and possession, except with leave of the court, or under the authority conferred by any enactment, or on the arrest of the child.[75]
(3) Where a prospective adopter gives notice in writing to the local authority within whose area he has his home of his intention to adopt a child who has had his home with him for the preceding five years, then no person is entitled against his will to remove the child from his care and possession except with leave of the court, or under authority conferred by any enactment, or on the arrest of the child.[76]

5.13   It is a criminal offence to contravene these provisions, with liability to imprisonment for a term not exceeding three months or to a fine not exceeding level 5 on the standard scale (£5,000) or both.[77] The rights of the

---

[70] RCS, r. 42.15.
[71] A.S. 1997, r. 33.21(2).
[72] A.S. 1997, r. 2.2 (RCS, r. 67.7).
[73] 1978 Act, s. 27(2).
[74] 1978 Act, s. 27(1).
[75] 1978 Act, s. 28(1).
[76] 1978 Act, s. 28(2).
[77] 1978 Act, ss. 27(3) and 28(7).

local authority to recover a child from the care and possession of an adopter or a prospective adopter are enforced with leave of the court.[78] Where the leave of the court is required in these situations, the application is made by minute (or note) lodged in the adoption petition process.[79] The former provisions relating to protected children have been repealed.[80] If, in relation to a child, the parent had not agreed to the making of the adoption order, and the application was not for a freeing order and the child had not had his home with the applicants for five years the placement of the child with prospective adopters by a mother would have no legal effect; presumably, the mother could seek to have the child back at any time. If the prospective adopters agreed to return the child, there would be no problem; but if the adopters resisted the claim of the mother, it seems she could only proceed by an action for residence or contact or other order by a separate action.[81]

Probable Cost

It is not possible to say precisely what the probable cost of an adoption petition would be to the adopters. Generally, there are three elements in that cost. **5.14**

> (a) The dues of court are laid down in the Acts of Sederunt. These amount to £45 and are exigible when the petition is lodged. Further dues may be exigible in respect of additional steps in process, such as fixing a proof £25, for each day of proof £57 and for enrolling a motion £23.[82]
>
> (b) The solicitor is entitled to charge his fees and outlays in respect of the work which he carries out. Where the petition is straightforward and is unopposed—as is the case in most petitions—the solicitor's standard rate would be relatively modest. Where there is opposition involving hearings or an appeal, especially an appeal to the Court of Session, it would be considerably more.[83]
>
> (c) The fee of the curator *ad litem* and reporting officer, unless these officers are appointed from the local authority panel of curators *ad litem* and reporting officers, in which case the local authority are obliged to pay.[84] The standard fee in respect of a joint appointment is presently £91 with extra fees in case of difficulty; but if the charges of the curator *ad litem* and reporting officer were to be made according to professional levels the fee would be very much more

---

[78] 1978 Act, ss. 28(3) and 30(2).

[79] A.S. 1997, r. 2.36(1) (RCS, r. 67.28); procedure is by minute in relation to ss. 27, 28, 29 and 30: see Append. 2.

[80] 1995 Act, s. 98(1) and Sched. 2, para. 21.

[81] 1995 Act, s. 11 (which replaced the corresponding provisions of the Law Reform (Parent and Child) (Scotland) Act 1986).

[82] Sheriff Court Fees Order 1997 (S.I. 1997 No. 687).

[83] See Chap. 14, below.

[84] Curators ad litem and Reporting Officers (Panels) (Scotland) Regulations 1984 (S.I. 1984 No. 566); Curators ad litem and Reporting Officers (Panels) (Scotland) Amendment Regulations 1985 (S.I. 1985 No. 1556). There is no liability on the local authority to pay these amounts if the adoption order is not made: r. 10(c). The amendment came into force on April 1, 1986: but see paras 7.04 and 14.01, below.

than that figure.[85] The petitioners should ascertain, in advance, what the fee is and who is liable to pay it. (Similarly, the curator *ad litem* and reporting officer should make the same inquiries in advance, whether he is to look to the local authority or the petitioners for his fee.)

5.15   A party is always entitled to conduct his own case, including an adoption case. However, there are serious qualifications to that general rule, which are partly legal and partly practical. In a petition to free a child for adoption, the petition can only be presented by an adoption agency and both local authorities and adoption societies are corporate bodies who can only appear and even lodge papers through a solicitor or advocate: any other form of representation is incompetent.[86] In a petition for adoption or in a minute (or note) to revoke a freeing order, the petitioner is a natural person who may sign writs, lodge papers and appear by himself, or who may do these things through a solicitor or advocate: again, any other form of representation is incompetent. If there is any question of fee, gain or reward, such actings by unqualified persons may amount to a criminal offence.[87] It is most inadvisable for petitioners to act without a solicitor and attempt to do the work themselves. Any savings will almost inevitably be outweighed by the difficulties, delays and extra expense which may arise, often unexpectedly, even in the apparently most straightforward cases.

One example will suffice. In several cases the application of the maxim *pater est quem nuptiae demonstrant* arises. A lawyer will appreciate at once that the question has arisen and that he has the skill to deal with it; the layman may not even appreciate that it exists.

If the petitioners are of reasonable means, the legal expenses of an adoption would normally be regarded as a small price to pay to ensure the expeditious and successful conclusion of a procedure whose end is the security of the child in a new home for the remainder of his childhood. If the petitioners are of limited means, they may be entitled to legal aid with or without a contribution by them towards the cost of the proceedings. Generally, where there is a legal aid certificate, the whole of their expenses is borne by the legal aid fund; but in the event of a party being found liable in the expenses of the proceedings, he may be liable to pay the expenses of his opponent, unless his liability for these expenses is assessed by the court at some lesser figure or at nil. His liability will not exceed the amount (if any) which in the opinion of the court is a reasonable one for him to pay, having regard to all the circumstances, including the means and conduct in connection with the dispute of all the parties.[88] In an opposed petition, where the solicitor's fee will be greater (because of the larger amount of work to be done) the question of legal aid becomes more important.[89]

---

[85] *e.g.* guide to fees for advocates preparing reports in cases involving children.

[86] *Equity and Law Assurance Society v. Tritonia Ltd*, 1943 S.C. (H.L.) 88; *Scottish Gas Board v. Alexander*, 1963 S.L.T. (Sh.Ct.) 27; *Rush v. Fife Regional Council*, 1984 S.L.T. 391.

[87] Solicitors (Scotland) Act 1980, s. 32.

[88] Legal Aid (Scotland) Act 1986, s. 18(2).

[89] See Stoddart, *The Law and Practice of Legal Aid in Scotland* (2nd ed., 1985, W. Green & Son Ltd), Chap. 9.

Since 1991 a person under the age of 16 has legal capacity to instruct a **5.16**
solicitor in any civil matter, where that person has a general understanding of what it means to do so; and a person of 12 years or more
is presumed to have sufficient age and maturity to have such understanding.[90]

FORM OF PETITION

There are separate styles or modifications of styles of petition for each **5.17**
kind of adoption order[91]:

(a) petition for adoption,[92] which is by far the most common;

(b) petition for adoption abroad[93];

(c) petition for a Convention adoption order[94];

(d) petition to free a child for adoption.[95] In this case, in the Court
of Session, no style is prescribed, but the rules provide that the
petition in these cases shall include averments about, or refer to, a
report or other documents produced which deal with the sundry
matters enumerated in the rules.[96] In the Court of Session, the
general rules governing petitions are disapplied in adoption procedure[97]; and

(e) minute (or, in the Court of Session, note) to revoke an order
freeing a child for adoption in the process of the original petition.[98]
Again, in the Court of Session, no special style is prescribed but
the general rules relating to petitions are applied to notes with
the exception that the note is not intimated on the walls or in the
minute book or advertised.[99] The general rules prescribe that a
narrative or statement of facts in articulate numbered paragraphs
setting forth the grounds of the note shall precede the prayer.[1] Such
applications are not common. There was one example in 1988 when
minutes in respect of five children were dealt with at a conjoined
proof.[2]

---

[90] Age of Legal Capacity (Scotland) 1991, s. 2(4A).

[91] A.S. 1997, r. 2.5 and Form 1 (freeing), r. 2.15 and Form 8 (revocation) and r. 2.21 and
Forms 11 (adoption) and 12 (adoption of child abroad) (RCS, r. 67.8 and 67.9 (freeing),
r. 67.14 (revocation), r. 67.22 and Form 67.22 (adoption) and r. 67.27 (adoption of child
abroad)).

[92] A.S. 1997, Form 11 (RCS, Form 67.22).

[93] A.S. 1997, Form 12 (RCS, Form 67.22).

[94] RCS, r. 67.35 and Form 67.22.

[95] A.S. 1997, Form 1.

[96] RCS, r. 67.9(2).

[97] Previously these disapplications were separately enumerated: RCS, r. 220(2) (freeing),
r. 222(2) (adoption), r. 223(2) (adoption of children abroad) and r. 230B (Convention
adoption orders); now there is one general provision: RCS, r. 67.2. Notwithstanding that
disapplication, answers are competent in a note (a minute in the sheriff court) to revoke a
freeing order: RCS, r. 67.15(1) and A.S. 1997, r. 2.15(3); see para. 5.26, below.

[98] A.S. 1997, Form 8.

[99] RCS, r. 67.2.

[1] RCS, r. 67.2.

[2] *M v. Strathclyde Regional Council*, Sheriff Stoddart, Paisley Sh.Ct., December 20, 1991,
unreported.

5.18   In all cases the matters which are set forth in numbered paragraphs should present little difficulty. These matters, averments, facts or circumstances—as they are variously called— are what the court has to be satisfied upon, either by reference to the reports before it, or by proof.[3] After the averments there follows the prayer of the petition in which the petitioner craves the court to do certain things—such as to dispense with the intimations (where that is appropriate), to grant an adoption order, or an order to adopt abroad or a Convention adoption order as the case may be, and to direct the Registrar General for Scotland to make the appropriate entries in the registers. The prayer is the appropriate place to state the name by which the child will be known after the adoption order has been granted. The part of the prayer which craves the court "to pronounce such other or further orders or directions upon such matters, including the expenses of this petition as the court may think fit", would entitle the court to grant an interim order, or to appoint a particular form of inquiry. The petition is signed[4] by counsel or the solicitor or by the parties. Even where the child has been placed by an adoption agency, only the parties or their legal representatives can sign.[5] There is no place in adoption procedure for lodging a caveat[6]—that is, a document lodged in court by a party who is apprehensive that legal proceedings will be taken against him. A writ or warrant may not be issued until he has had an opportunity to be heard: the persons entitled to notice of a hearing are those who are specified in the rules.

Productions

5.19   The productions to be lodged include:

> (a) extract of the entry in the Register of Births (but not an abbreviated certificate of birth which only discloses the name of the child, the place and date of birth) relating to the child[7]; or, in the case of a subsequent petition, an extract of an entry in the Adopted Children Register; and, in the case where the adoption order in the former petition had been refused, the process in that former case. If there is no birth certificate, as is sometimes the case in India or Pakistan, the birth will require to be proved by other evidence[8];
>
> (b) in the case of a joint petition by spouses, the extract of an entry in the Register of Marriages relating to the petitioners[9]; and, presumably also, in the case of a petition by one of two spouses[10];
>
> (c) a medical certificate as to the health of the petitioner is now no longer required.[11] However, in the Court of Session and now in the

---

[3] See Chap. 6, below.

[4] A.S. 1997, Forms 1, 8, 11, 12 (RCS, r. 4.2).

[5] See para. 5.07, above.

[6] *cf. Wards v. Kelvin Tank Services Ltd*, 1984 S.L.T. (Sh.Ct.) 39.

[7] 1978 Act, s. 45 and Sched. 1, para. 1(4); A.S. 1997, r. 2.21(2)(a) (RCS, r. 67.22(2)(a) (adoption) and r. 67.27(2)(a) (adoption of child abroad)).

[8] *C and C, Petitioners*, Edinburgh Sh.Ct. (E77/85), July 1985, unreported.

[9] A.S. 1997, r. 2.21(2)(b) (RCS, r. 67.22(2)(b)).

[10] 1978 Act, s. 15(1)(aa) or (b).

[11] See A.S. (Adoption of Children) 1984 (S.I. 1984 No. 1013), r. 16(3)(c).

sheriff court[12] three copies of a medical report are required on the health of the child, but only when the child was not placed by an adoption agency. The matters to be reported upon are "the physical and mental health of the child (including any special needs) and his emotional, behavioural and educational development". The report should be reasonably up to date: but the health of the child is not the *de quo* of the proceedings, as it is in a petition for the appointment of a curator *bonis* where the certificates should not be more than one month old.[13] In any event in adoption procedure the curator *ad litem* would on the visit to the home no doubt notice and report on any obvious ill health of the petitioners;

(d) a report on the suitability of the petitioners and on any other matters relevant to the operation of section 6 of the 1978 Act (which deals with the duty to promote the welfare of the child) made by the local authority under section 22 where the child was not placed by an adoption agency,[14] and by the adoption agency under section 23 in other cases[15]; any other document founded upon by the petitioner in support of the petition.[16] For example, where the natural parent has died the death certificate should be produced, or where a petitioner has been divorced the extract decree of divorce should be produced;

(e) the consent of the child, and the agreement of the natural parents[17] and, where the child has been freed for adoption, the order of the court which freed the child[18];

(f) if the child has not been placed by an adoption agency, the acknowledgment by the local authority of the notice by the petitioners to that authority of their intention to apply for an adoption order. In sheriff court practice such notice is normally given before the petition has been presented, but in the Court of Session, on presentation of the petition, the court must make an order requiring the petitioners to give notice to the adoption agency or the local authority as the case may be. The statute envisages the notice being given before the petition has been presented.[19] The notice must be in writing[20] and may be given by post[21];

(g) in the case of a petition for an order to adopt a child abroad, in addition to the requirements already mentioned, the petitioner must adduce evidence of the law of adoption in the country in which he is domiciled; and the court may accept as evidence of that law an affidavit sworn by a person who is

---

[12] A.S. 1997, r. 2.21(2)(c) (RCS, r. 67.22(2)(d)).

[13] Green's *Encyclopaedia of Styles*, v. 387, n. 1.

[14] 1978 Act s. 22; see para. 8.70, below.

[15] 1978 Act, s. 23; see para. 8.70, below.

[16] A.S. 1997, r. 2.21(2)(g) (there appears to be no corresponding provision in the Rules of Court).

[17] A.S. 1997, rr. 2.26(1)(a) and 2.26(2)(b) (RCS, rr. 67.24(1)(c) and 67.26(2)(a)).

[18] A.S. 1997, r. 2.21(2)(f) (RCS, r. 67.22(2)(f)).

[19] RCS, r. 67.23; 1978 Act, s. 22.

[20] 1978 Act, s. 65(1).

[21] 1978 Act, s. 62. Intimation of a diet of hearing, however, would appear to be a judicial intimation to which the Citation Amendment (Scotland) Act 1882, s. 3 applies: that section applies to any civil action or proceeding in any court.

> (i) conversant with it and practises or has practised as a barrister or advocate in that country, or
> (ii) a duly accredited representative of the government of that country in the United Kingdom[22];
>
> (h) in the case of a petition for a Convention adoption order, the petitioners must lodge documentary evidence relative to *inter alia* the nationality of the petitioners or of the child and of consents[23];
> (i) where a litigant is an assisted person, the legal aid certificate or emergency certificate issued to him should be lodged by him when he enters the process.[24]

EVIDENTIAL VALUE OF DOCUMENTS

5.20   The evidential value of the documents which are used in evidence in an adoption process varies depending on the character of the document and the statutory provisions regulating the matter.

5.21   (a) United Kingdom judicial and vital records are generally accepted without proof, not only as to the truth of the facts contained in them but also as to the identity of the persons mentioned in them.[25]

5.22   (b) Certain foreign vital records have at least an equal privilege in terms of section 1 of the Evidence (Foreign and Colonial Documents) Act 1933, and section 5 of the Oaths and Evidence (Overseas Authorities and Countries) Act 1963; and orders in council have been made under this legislation covering about 50 countries, an up-to-date list of which can be found in the latest edition of *Index to Government Orders* (HMSO) under the title "Evidence".[26]

5.23   (c) Where the documents which have to be lodged are in a foreign language, the principals should be accompanied by translated copies which can be spoken to and identified by the person translating them and stating the name of the foreign language and the qualification of the translator.[27]

5.24   (d) The rules provide that the consent of a child or the agreement of a parent or the agreement of a parent to an adoption by a step-parent to whom the parent is married, if given in writing, shall be in Form 4, 13 or 14 as appropriate and such form duly executed shall be sufficient evidence of such consent or agreement.[28] Despite the peremptory words of that rule, the statute provides that these consents and agreements "may" be given in

---

[22] A.S. 1997, r. 2.22 (RCS, r. 67.27).

[23] RCS, r. 67.37.

[24] Act of Sederunt (Civil Legal Aid Rules) 1987 (S.I. 1987 No. 492), r. 3(1).

[25] See A. G. Walker & N. M. L. Walker, *The Law of Evidence in Scotland* (1964, William Hodge & Co. Ltd), pp. 232–233 and Civil Evidence (Scotland) Act 1988, ss. 2 and 6.

[26] See Append. 4, below. These two Acts are not affected by the Civil Evidence (Scotland) Act 1988, s. 10(3)(d) and (e).

[27] The former R.C. 230L has not been re-enacted: but the provision appears to be trite.

[28] 1978 Act, s. 55 and A.S. 1997, r. 2.23(1) (RCS, r. 67.5 and Forms 67.5A–67.5F).

writing. It is submitted that if consents and agreements are not executed in terms of the rules, the effect is that they do not have the privileged quality given by the legislation, and a petitioner could rely on other writings,[29] and even on an oral statement made in court which may be recorded in an interlocutor. Where a serial number has been assigned to an applicant any form of agreement must not contain the name and designation of the petitioner but must refer to him by means of the serial number assigned to him and must specify the year in which and by which court such serial number has been assigned.[30]

A form of consent or agreement executed outwith the United King- **5.25** dom shall be sufficient evidence of such consent or agreement if it is witnessed

> (1) where the person who executes the form is serving in Her Majesty's Forces by an officer holding a commission in any of those forces; or
> (2) in other cases, by a British consular official, or any person for the time being authorised by the law of the country in which the form is executed to administer an oath for any judicial or legal purpose.[31]

If the British consular officer is unable to act as a local reporting officer, **5.26** the court could appoint a Scottish reporting officer to carry out the duty of procuring the form of agreement of the mother by correspondence (together with translations in the local language) with a view to execution of the form specified in these rules for agreements made outside the United Kingdom. A sufficient time would be allowed for a reply. No doubt, if there were no reply, or if the parent could not be found, the petitioner could seek to dispense with the agreement of the mother.

Interlocutors

Normally each stage in the course of an adoption process is effected by **5.27** an interlocutor of the court which is partly an executive order and partly a minute of the proceedings. Thus, for example, it will be necessary to pronounce an interlocutor

> (a) to appoint a curator *ad litem* and a reporting officer[32];
> (b) on receipt by the court of the reports of the curator *ad litem* and reporting officer, to order a diet of hearing to be fixed and if appropriate to ordain the petitioners to serve a notice in terms of Form 7[33] on any of the persons mentioned in the Act of Sederunt, para. 2.28 (these are enumerated below[34]);
> (c) subsequently, as the situation demands, as for example, after a hearing, to record who was present, what documents were produced,

---

[29] 1978 Act, s. 55(1).
[30] A.S. 1997, r. 2.5(3) (freeing) and r. 2.24(4) (adoption) (RCS, r. 67.20 (adoption): so far there are no provisions for freeing).
[31] A.S. 1997, r. 2.23(2) (RCS, r. 67.27.(3)).
[32] A.S. 1997, r. 2.25 (RCS, r. 67.23(1)(b) and (c)).
[33] RCS, Form 67.25.
[34] See para. 5.43, below.

what concessions were made, what facts were found to be proved, or to appoint further inquiry, or to make avizandum, or to grant the prayer of the petition.

5.28   In *A v. B and C*[35] the absence of any reference by the sheriff to the date of a step in procedure became apparent in the House of Lords and had to be cleared up by means of a certificate by the sheriff clerk: "If the judge interviews any party, it is desirable that this should be recorded in his judgment."[36] In the case of a petition by one natural parent alone, the statute provides explicitly that the reason for excluding the other natural parent must be recorded by the court.[37] If a particular fact is contested or in doubt it may be desirable to make a finding in fact after such inquiry as may appear necessary. Where the area of dispute is wide or where issues of credibility are important, the court may wish to proceed by way of proof as in an ordinary civil action and make findings in fact and findings in law with a note setting forth the grounds of the court's decision.[38] Proof by witnesses is discussed later.[39]

FREEING FOR ADOPTION

5.29   Since 1984 it has been open to an adoption agency which is a local authority[40] (but not a private person) to proceed not by way of a petition for adoption in which all aspects of the matter are disposed of at the one time, but to seek an order merely disposing of the agreement of the natural parents in advance, without there being any adoption of the child before the court. This procedure is called freeing a child for adoption.[41] Generally, the provisions relating to the freeing of a child are identical to those parts of an adoption petition which deal with the agreement of the natural parents. Two exceptions are the status of the unmarried father of the child,[42] and, where it is sought, to dispense with the agreement of the natural parent. In a petition to free a child for adoption the child must be in the care of the adoption agency[43] otherwise both processes of freeing

---

[35] 1971 S.C. (H.L.) 129.

[36] *per* Lord Guest at p. 142.

[37] 1978 Act, s. 15(3).

[38] *cf. B and B v. B*, Sheriff Principal Risk, Aberdeen Sh.Ct., March 30, 1994, unreported; A.S. 1997, r. 2.29 (RCS, r. 67.6) and in the sheriff court, Act of Sederunt (Sheriff Court Ordinary Cause Rules) 1993 (S.I. 1993 No. 1956), r. 12(2)(a).

[39] See para. 6.09, below.

[40] This limitation was introduced by the 1995 Act, s. 9(1) and Sched. 2, para. 11. The earlier name for this procedure was "relinquishment", which is a more accurate description of the original intention of this innovation: the mother would *relinquish* the child for adoption at an earlier stage. This aspect of the new procedure has been provided for in s. 18(1)(a) where the parent may agree to the making of the adoption order; and in that situation it is not necessary that the child has been placed for adoption nor for the court to be satisfied that the child will be placed for adoption. However, in practice, the majority of petitions to free a child for adoption have related to older children who have been with their mothers for some years and have a non-agreeing parent—usually in the situation where formerly the local authority would have sought to assume the parental rights over the child under the Social Work (Scotland) Act 1968, s. 16 (now repealed by the 1995 Act, s. 105(5) and Sched. 5).

[41] 1978 Act, s. 18; 1985 S.L.T. (News) 1.

[42] 1978 Act, s. 18(7).

[43] 1978 Act, s. 18(1).

and adoption are effected by a petition. The conditions precedent—such as jurisdiction—are the same.[44] The court remits the question of the parental agreement and the welfare of the child to a curator *ad litem* and a reporting officer.[45] On receipt of the reports the court must appoint a hearing[46]; the specification of the grounds for dispensing with the agreement of the parent[47] and the consent of the child are the same as in a petition for adoption.[48] A reporting officer may be appointed in advance of the lodging of the petition, but only on cause shown,[49] for example, that the natural parent is about to go abroad. The attitude of any person who is not or has not been married to the mother of the child and does not have any parental responsibilities or parental rights in relation to the child claiming to be the father of the child has to be considered. Before making an order, the court must satisfy itself that

> (a) he has no intention of applying for, or, if he did so apply, it is likely that he would be refused, an order under section 11 of the Children (Scotland) Act 1995 (orders in relation to parental responsibilities and parental rights); and
> (b) he has no intention of entering into an agreement with the mother under section 4(1) of that Act (acquisition by natural father by agreement of such responsibilities and rights), or, if he has such an intention, that no agreement under that subsection is likely to be made.[50]

A person in the situation of claiming to be the father is entitled to **5.30** receive intimation of the diet of hearing[51] whereas, in a petition for adoption, such a person is not entitled to receive that intimation. The subsection does not specify what results should follow from the court's being satisfied on these matters but it seems that the existence of these matters would be part of the circumstances to which the court must have regard in terms of section 6 of the 1978 Act. Thus, a situation where such a father, who had not kept up with the family over the years, would be far different from that of a father who had lived in family with the mother and child for a significant period.[52] It is now provided that in considering whether to make an adoption order or a freeing order the court must have regard to the welfare of the child concerned as its paramount consideration and shall not make the order unless it considers that it would be better for the child that it should do so than it should not.[53]

---

[44] 1978 Act, ss. 12(1) and 18(1).

[45] A.S. 1997, rr. 2.7 and 2.25 (RCS, rr. 67.10, 67.23(1)(b) and (c)). In some cases the remit to these officers is not mandatory: see para. 7.01, below.

[46] A.S. 1997, rr. 2.11 and 2.28 (RCS, rr. 67.13 and 67.25).

[47] 1978 Act, ss. 16(2) and 18(1)(b).

[48] 1978 Act, ss. 12(8) and 18(8).

[49] 1978 Act, s. 58(3); A.S. 1997, rr. 2.7(3) and 2.25(4) (RCS, rr. 67.10(3) and 67.23(3)).

[50] 1978 Act, s. 18(7).

[51] A.S. 1997, r. 2.11(2)(b) (RCS, r. 67.13(3)(aa)).

[52] *Lothian Regional Council v. S*, Sheriff Principal Nicholson, Edinburgh Sh.Ct., February 14, 1991, where the former s. 18(7) was considered.

[53] 1978 Act, s. 24(3) as inserted by the 1995 Act, s. 98(1) and Sched. 2, para. 16; see para. 1.16(f)(iv), above.

5.31   From past experience of petitions for adoption, it would appear that this situation would arise only on very rare occasions. The court must also satisfy itself in relation to each parent or guardian of the child who can be found that he has been given an opportunity of making, if he so wishes, a declaration that he prefers not to be involved in future questions concerning the adoption of the child. Any such declaration must be recorded by the court.[54] Where a freeing application is made with the consent of the natural parent, there need not be an actual adoption in prospect[55] but if the adoption agency seeking the order applies for the agreement of the natural parent to be dispensed with, then the court must be satisfied that the child has already been placed for adoption or that it is likely that the child will be placed for adoption.[56] In a case where the sheriff had not made a finding on this point, the sheriff principal refused the appeal, but observed that he would have continued the appeal to allow the applicants, if so advised, to lead evidence as to the likelihood of the child being placed for adoption.[57] Also, if dispensation of agreement is sought, the child must be in the care of the adoption agency.[58]

5.32   Against the possible advantages of proceeding first by way of a petition to free a child for adoption, consideration should be give to the duplication of expense in having two petitions with the consequent delay. In cases where the ground of dispensing with the agreement of a natural parent is that it is unreasonably withheld, it would be more difficult to hold that where there was no actual adoptive family in being the natural parent was withholding agreement unreasonably.

Effect of Freeing for Adoption

5.33   Where the order freeing a child for adoption has been made, the parental rights and duties relating to the child vest in the adoption agency[59] and the parental rights and duties of the natural parents are extinguished "as if the order were an adoption order and the agency were the adopters". Formerly, it was competent for a local authority to use other statutory powers and resolve that the relevant parental rights and duties with respect to any child shall vest in them or in a voluntary organisation: this provision has been repealed.[60] Where a court making an order freeing a child for adoption who is subject to a supervision requirement is satisfied that, in consequence of its doing so, compulsory measures of supervision in respect of the child are no longer necessary, it may determine that the child shall forthwith cease to be subject to that requirement.[61]

---

[54] 1978 Act, s. 18(6).
[55] 1978 Act, s. 18(2)(a).
[56] 1978 Act, s. 18(3).
[57] *Grampian Regional Council v. X*, 1994 G.W.D. 10-579.
[58] 1978 Act, s. 18(2)(b).
[59] 1978 Act, s. 18(5).
[60] 1968 Act, s. 16 repealed by the 1995 Act, s. 105(5) and Sched. 5.
[61] 1978 Act, s. 18(9) inserted by the 1995 Act, s. 98(1) and Sched. 2, para. 11.

The application to free a child for adoption is made by a petition in the **5.34** sheriff court or in the Outer House of the Court of Session. The petition must be in the form appearing in the rules.[62]

Revocation of Freeing Order

Further procedure at the instance of the parent may be initiated to **5.35** revoke an order under section 18.[63] This is begun by a minute (or note) in the original process granting the order under section 18.[64] Presumably, one or both parents can seek the revocation.[65]

If an application to revoke an order under section 18 is dismissed, the **5.36** parent may in certain limited circumstances make a further application.

The application to revoke an order under section 18 may be made **5.37**

(a) where the parent has agreed to the order under section 18[66]; or
(b) where the agreement of the parent has been dispensed with.[67]

The application must be made after 12 months of the making of the order under section 18,[68] an adoption order must not have been made in respect of the child and the child must not have his home with a person with whom he has been placed for adoption.[69] The parent craves the court to revoke the order under section 18 "on the ground that he wishes to resume parental responsibilities and rights".[70] The effect of a pending application to revoke an order under section 18 is to prevent the adoption agency which has the parental responsibilities and parental rights from placing the child for adoption without the leave of the court.[71] The effect of a revocation of an order under section 18 is that the court must, by an order under section 11 of the Children (Scotland) Act 1995, determine on whom are to be imposed the parental responsibilities, and to whom are to be given the parental rights, in relation to the child.[72-73]

In England, it has been held that the court has no jurisdiction to make **5.38** an interim care order in favour of the local authority if it decided to revoke the freeing order.[74]

---

[62] A.S. 1997, r. 2.5(1) and Form 1 (RCS, r. 67.8).

[63] 1978 Act, s. 20.

[64] A.S. 1997, r. 2.15(1) and Form 8 (RCS, r. 7.14(1)). An example of a revocation, which is not common, was heard in a sheriff court case, then the minutes by each parent in respect of five children were conjoined for proof: Paisley Sh.Ct. (A42/88 to A46/88), December 20, 1991, unreported.

[65] *cf.* 1978 Act, s. 20(3); Interpretation Act 1978, s. 6.

[66] 1978 Act, s. 18(1)(a).

[67] 1978 Act, s. 18(1)(b).

[68] 1978 Act, s. 20.

[69] 1978 Act, s. 20(1).

[70] A.S. 1997, Form 8.

[71] 1978 Act, s. 20(2).

[72-73] 1978 Act, s. 20(3).

[74] *G (A Minor: freeing order)* [1996] 2 F.C.R. 761, C.A.

Further Applications to Revoke Freeing Order

5.39   If an application to revoke an order under section 18 of the 1978 Act is dismissed, the scope for further applications is restricted. An application can be made by "the former parent" who is defined as a person who has declared that he prefers not to be involved in future questions concerning the adoption of the child.[75] The former parent cannot make a further application to revoke an order under section 18 if the original application was "dismissed on the ground that to allow it would contravene the principle embodied in section 6".[76] This reference to section 6 is presumably to that part of section 6 which obliges the court to have regard to all the circumstances, the paramount consideration being given to the need to safeguard and promote the welfare of the child throughout his life.

5.40   In the same circumstances, the adoption agency is released from the duty of complying with the duty of giving the former parent notice of the making of an adoption order (if and when made), and meanwhile giving the former parent notice whenever the child is placed for adoption, or ceases to have his home with a person with whom he had been placed for adoption.[77]

5.41   However, there is a relaxation of these severe limitations on the right of a former parent to make a further application to revoke an order under section 18: namely, in the provisions of section 20(4), where the court which dismisses the application gives leave to make a further application. However, such leave must not be given unless it appears to the court that because of a change of circumstances, or for any other reason, it is proper to allow the further application to be made.[78] These words echo the provisions of section 24 in relation to a further application for an adoption order where the earlier one had been refused.

Procedure where Freeing Order is in Force

5.42   As has been noted, the freeing process deals with that part of the adoption process which relates to the agreement of the natural parent. Where the order freeing the child has been made in respect of every person whose agreement or consent to the making of the order is required to be given and remains unrevoked, and later a petition for adoption is presented in respect of the same child, there is no need to deal with these agreements again. The later petition for adoption need only deal with the merits, and a hearing may be fixed by the court[79] but it seems that in most cases a hearing will not be necessary, as was the law before the 1997 Rules came into force.[80] Apart from these matters there is, in general, no difference in the procedural requirements in dealing with the merits.

---

[75]   1978 Act, ss. 18(6) and 19(1).
[76]   1978 Act, s. 20(4)(a).
[77]   1978 Act, s. 20(4)(b).
[78]   1978 Act, s. 20(5).
[79]   A.S. 1997, r. 2.28(2). In the Court of Session, presumably if neither a reporting officer nor a curator *ad litem* is appointed: RCS, r. 67.23(1)(b) and (c), there will be no reports to receive and no hearing will be required: RCS, r. 67.25(1).
[80]   1978 Act, s. 59(2), A.S. 8, 22 (R.C. 220 (10), (11), (12), 222 (11), (12), (13)).

Intimation

In a petition to free a child for adoption, a petition for adoption and a **5.43**
petition for adoption abroad there is no intimation of the petition on
potential respondents. In the Court of Session there is an express
provision which excludes from adoption petitions the normal rules
appointing intimation of other classes of petitions.[81] Although the prayer
set forth in the style of petition does crave the court "to dispense with
intimation and order notice of this petition to be served on such persons if
any as the court may think proper",[82] in practice neither intimation nor
service is in use. However, at a later stage, after the sundry reports have
been lodged, the court fixes a hearing and then appoints the petitioners to
intimate the diet of hearing[83] on the classes of persons specified in the
rules. In a petition for adoption,[84] a petition to adopt a child abroad[85] and
a petition for a Convention adoption,[86] intimation of the hearing

(a) must be made to every person who can be found and whose
agreement (in the case of a parent or guardian) or consent (in the
case of a child who is a minor) to the making of the adoption order is
required to be given or dispensed with; and
(b) the sheriff may, if he considers it appropriate, order intimation
on
(1) any person or body
(i) having the rights and powers of a parent of the child, or
(ii) having the custody or care of the child, or
(2) a local authority having the child committed to its care by
virtue of section 11 (court orders relating to parental responsibilities, etc.), 54 (reference to the principal reporter by court) or
86 (parental responsibilities order) of the 1995 Act or section 5
(appointment of guardians), 8 (orders with respect to children)
or 31 (care and supervision orders) of the Children Act 1989[87];
(3) any person liable by virtue of any order or agreement to
contribute to the maintenance of the child;
(4) the local authority to whom the petitioner has given notice
of his intention to apply for an adoption order; or
(5) any other person or body who in the opinion of the court ought
to be served with notice of the hearing.[88] It is thought that such
service should not be used unless there is a significant connection
between that person and the adoption or that his knowledge of the
adoption may affect the result, as for example, where the father of
the child was married to the mother of the child during the currency
of the petition for adoption[89] or where grandparents of the child

---

[81] RCS, r. 67.1.
[82] A.S. 1997, Form 11 (RCS, Form 67.22).
[83] A.S. 1997, rr. 2.11 and 2.88 (RCS, rr. 67.13 and 67.25).
[84] A.S. 1997, r. 2.28(3)(a) (RCS, r. 67.23).
[85] A.S. 1997, r. 2.28(3)(b) (RCS, r. 67.27).
[86] RCS, r. 67.28.
[87] A.S. 1997, r. 2.28(4)(d) (*cf.* RCS, r. 67.25(2)(b)(ii)).
[88] *A v. B and C*, 1971 S.C. (H.L.) 129; Adoption, Sheriff McNeill, Edinburgh Sh.Ct. (E72/
92), January 21, 1993, unreported.
[89] *AB and CD, Petitioners*, 1992 S.C.L.R. 274.

who was the subject of a petition for adoption had raised a concurrent action for a residence order in relation to the same child.[90] In one petition for adoption in Scotland of a child who was a citizen of the Republic of Ireland,[91] the sheriff ordained intimation on the Secretary of State in terms of the then rule 22(3)(d)—now rule 2.28(4)(d). It is thought that there the sheriff relied on an English case[92] which proceeded on a provision in the English rules[93] which was not part of the Scottish rules. In any event, the Secretary of State did not seek to intervene at the hearing. In Scotland the court could ordain the petitioner to serve notice of the hearing on the Secretary of State as a person who in its opinion ought to be served with such notice. If the unmarried father of the child does not come within the category of a parent who has parental responsibilities and parental rights, or of a guardian of the child by deed or will, his agreement to the making of an adoption is not required. Accordingly, he is not a person to whom the hearing should be intimated and a reporting officer should not approach an unmarried father to seek his agreement.[94] However, in a petition to free a child for adoption, the position of the unmarried father is different.[95]

5.44   In a petition to free a child for adoption, intimation must be made to every person who can be found and whose agreement or consent to the making of the order freeing the child for adoption is required to be given or dispensed with.[96] In the case of a child whose father is not married to the mother, intimation must be made to any person whose whereabouts are known to him and who claims to be the father of the child but is not his guardian and in respect of whom no order relating to parental responsibilities has been made.[97] These are the only classes of persons on whom the diet of hearing must be intimated: there is no provision, as there is in a petition for adoption, whereby the sheriff may ordain the petitioner to intimate to other persons.[98]

5.45   Where a serial number has been assigned to the petitioner by the clerk of court, in order to prevent disclosure of the identity of the petitioner the

---

[90] *A and B v. C*, 1987 G.W.D. 8-241.

[91] *D v. F*, Sheriff Craik, Edinburgh Sh.Ct., March 18, 1993; later stages of this case were an interlocutor after proof dated May 5, 1993, unreported, and an appeal reported at 1994 S.C.L.R. 417.

[92] *Re W (A Minor)* [1986] Fam. 54.

[93] Adoption Rules 1984 (S.I. 1984 No. 265), r. 15(3), which provides that "the court may at any time direct that any other person or body, save in the county court, be made a respondent in the process". It may be that, in Scotland, the court could order service of intimation of the hearing on the Secretary of State.

[94] *A and B v. C*, 1991 G.W.D. 38-2298 (in Scotland); *Re L (A Minor) (Adoption Procedure)* [1991] 1 F.L.R. 171 (in England and Wales).

[95] *A and B v. C*, 1987, G.W.D. 8-241.

[96] A.S. 1997, r. 2.11(2)(a) (RCS, r. 67.13(3)).

[97] A.S. 1997, r. 2.11(2)(b): this provision was introduced in the 1997 Rules, although there is no corresponding Rule of Court, but it is submitted that such intimation would be made under the rule which requires intimation to any other person or body who in the opinion of the court ought to be served with such a notice: RCS, r. 67.13.(2)(b)(ii).

[98] A.S. 1997, r. 2.28(4); but in the Court of Session a wider class of persons may receive intimation of the diet: RCS, r. 67.13.(2)(b)(ii).

intimation of the diet of hearing should be identified by reference to the serial number and the year.[99]

Answers to the petition are not competent. In the Court of Session the **5.46** requirement for answers has been expressly excluded in petitions for adoption, for adoption abroad, and to free a child[1] (but in one case the lord ordinary used power under the then current rules to dispense from the rules in advance to order answers[2]); and answers are impliedly excluded in sheriff court procedure.[3] However, in a minute (or note) to revoke a freeing order, intimation of the process on the petitioners in the original petition to free the child and on other persons is required; and the sheriff court rules provide for answers.[4] Subsidiary procedures governing the whereabouts of the child during the adoption process and procedure dealing with amendment and revocation of adoption orders are discussed later.[5] The statutory hearing only deals with the agreements and consents. Other aspects of the case require to be proved, and that proof may take several forms.

---

[99] "For that purpose": A.S. 1997, r. 2.5.(3) (freeing); and "For all purposes connected with the petition": A.S. 1997, r. 2.24 (adoption) (RCS, r. 67.20(1) adoption; there is no corresponding Rule of Court for freeing).

[1] RCS, r. 67.2.

[2] *AB and CD, Petitioners, The Scotsman,* March 20, 1987, reported on a later point: 1987 S.C.L.R. 398; *cf.* Act of Sederunt (Rules of Court, Consolidation and Amendment) 1965 (S.I. 1965 No. 321), preamble, para. (3), which provision was not re-enacted in the current rules.

[3] A.S. 1997, r. 2.15(3). In one appeal, the sheriff principal thought that, in the case he was considering, there should have been an order for answers and that the specification which is appropriate to a former assumption of parental rights as mentioned in *Central Regional Council v B,* 1985 S.L.T. 413 should apply equally to an application to free a child: *Lothian Regional Council v. R,* 1988 G.W.D. 28-1172. It is respectfully thought that such procedures are at variance with the rules and the forms appended to them.

[4] A.S. 1997, r. 2.15(3) (RCS, r. 67.15 impliedly).

[5] See Chap. 12, below.

CHAPTER 6

PROOF

Statutory Provisions

6.01 The legislation refers to "the facts stated in the petition",[1] and to "the facts and circumstances averred in the petition".[2] The court has to be satisfied that the matters averred in the petition have been established. The provisions envisage that many of these matters may be established by the production of documents—as has already been indicated[3]; and generally these facts are vouched by reports of the curator *ad litem*, the reporting officer and of the local authority or the adoption agency. Apart from proof by means of documents and these reports, proof may be by interview before the judge[4]; by oral evidence at the statutory hearings[5] or at a proof[6]; or by the report of a reporter which would take the place of a proof. In *A v. B and C*[7] such a procedure was adopted by consent of parties and with approval of the appeal court. Hearsay evidence is now admissible[8] and corroboration is no longer required.[9]

Reports

6.02 The normal and most comprehensive mode of verification of the averments in the petition is the report or reports made to the court. One of the two main innovations in the Adoption (Scotland) Act 1978 was the increase in the number of reports. Formerly, there was a single report from the curator *ad litem*: now there are nine varieties of report. These reports may be classified according to the type of procedure:

    (a) in a petition to free a child
        (i) report of the adoption agency on the proposed adoption proceedings including the prospects for adoption,[10]
        (ii) report of the reporting officer,[11]

---

[1] A.S. 1997, rr. 2.8(2)(b) and 2.26(2)(c).
[2] RCS, rr. 67.11(1)(a) and 67.24(1)(a).
[3] See para. 5.19, above.
[4] See para. 6.04, below.
[5] A.S. 1997, rr. 2.11, 2.18 and 2.28 (RCS, rr. 67.13, 67.15 and 67.25).
[6] A.S. 1997, r. 2.11(4) (freeing) and 2.29 (adoption) (RCS, r. 67.6 (all causes)).
[7] 1971 S.C. (H.L.) 129.
[8] Civil Evidence (Scotland) Act 1988, s. 2.
[9] Civil Evidence (Scotland) Act 1988, s. 1.
[10] A.S. 1997, r. 2.5(2)(b) (RCS, r. 67.11(1) where these matters are dealt with by the reporting officer): Adoption Agencies (Scotland) Regulations 1996 (S.I. 1996 No. 3266), reg. 22.
[11] A.S. 1997, r. 2.8(1) (RCS, r. 67.11(1)).

(iii) report of the curator *ad litem*[12];

(b) in a minute (or note) to revoke an order freeing a child
    (iv) report of the curator *ad litem*[13];

(c) in a petition for adoption, or a petition to adopt a child abroad
    (v) report of the reporting officer,[14]
    (vi) report of the curator *ad litem*,[15]
    (vii) report of the local authority where the child had not been placed by an adoption agency,[16] or
    (viii) report of the adoption agency where the child had been placed by the adoption agency,[17]
    (ix) report under regulation 22.[18]

In the legislation there is a difference of emphasis between the sheriff court and the Court of Session in respect that the matters to be reported upon are distributed differently among those whose duty it is to report to the court. However, in both jurisdictions the primacy of the curator *ad litem* as officer on whom the duty of safeguarding the welfare of the child is placed has been maintained.[19]

It may be that in the case of an interim order or where an additional **6.03** petitioner is sisted, the court would require a supplementary report dealing with the up-to-date circumstances. The curator *ad litem* and the reports to the court are discussed in greater detail later[20]; at this stage it is sufficient to note that the court may, if it is not satisfied by the verification of the statements provided by the documents lodged or by the reports, cause further investigation.[21] A common step would be to interview the petitioners or the curator *ad litem* in chambers. Where there are important matters in doubt or in dispute it would be appropriate to seek evidence beyond the report of the curator *ad litem*.[22]

Interview by the Court

In the straightforward case the petition is normally granted without an **6.04** interview. However, it is quite common for the court to interview the curator *ad litem* alone to supplement the report or to discuss some difficulty; such interview may be at the instance of the court or the

---

[12] A.S. 1997, r. 2.8(2) (RCS, r. 67.11(2)).

[13] A.S. 1997, R. 2.16 (RCS, r. 67.14(5)).

[14] A.S. 1997, R. 2.26(1) (RCS, r. 67.24(1)).

[15] A.S. 1997, r. 2.26(2) (RCS, r. 67.24(1)). In a petition for a Convention adoption order, the same provisions are applied: RCS, r. 67.34.

[16] 1978 Act, s. 22.

[17] 1978 Act, s. 23.

[18] Adoption Agencies (Scotland) Regulations 1996 (S.I. 1996 No. 3266), reg. 22.

[19] 1978 Act, s. 58(1)(a); A.S. 1997, r. 2.8(2)(a) (freeing), r. 2.16(1)(b) (revoking) and r. 2.26(2)(a) (adoption) (RCS, rr. 67.11(2)(a), 67.14(2)(b) and 67.24(2)(a)).

[20] See Chaps 7 and 8, below.

[21] A.S. 1997, r. 2.11(4) (freeing) and r. 2.29 (adoption) (RCS, r. 67.6 (applies to all causes)).

[22] *cf. C v. D*, 1968 S.L.T. (Sh.Ct.) 39; *AB and CB v. X's Curator*, 1963 S.C. 124; *AB v. CD* 1970 S.C. 268.

curator *ad litem.* Similarly, the court may wish to interview the author of any of the reports. Also, if the court feels that the gravity of the matter should be further brought home to the petitioners—especially where the child is not related to the petitioners—it may be desirable to speak to the petitioners. In other cases the circumstances may indicate the necessity of an interview where, for example, the court feels that it may refuse the petition, and that the parties should be given an opportunity to be heard.[23] The necessity for an interview will normally become apparent after consideration of the report of the curator *ad litem* but in some cases an earlier interview may be appropriate, as where questions of competency or jurisdiction arise. The court would normally appoint an interview by interlocutor and the diet would be intimated to the parties and their solicitors by the clerk of court. Depending on the circumstances of the case or the matters in dispute, the court would probably wish to interview, usually with their solicitor being present, the petitioners, the child and the natural parent. All the interviews are held privately. However, as parties the petitioners may wish to be present throughout, and if any information is acquired outwith the presence of the petitioners they should, where appropriate, be given an opportunity to challenge it—as where, for example, in a petition for the adoption of a female child the male petitioner had a recent conviction for assault with intent to ravish. At an interview, the judge will normally ask the parties being interviewed about the matters which he has in mind, but there is no reason why the parties' solicitor or counsel should not examine them before or after the court. Generally, although the interview may be conducted informally round a table, the parties and witnesses should be put on oath and the sheriff should take notes to enable him to formulate findings in fact, and also for the use of the appellate courts.[24]

Statutory Hearing

6.05   Since 1984 the statutory provisions relating to the agreement of the natural parents to the making of an adoption order have become more elaborate.[25] In a petition to free a child for adoption or a petition for adoption where the child has not been freed for adoption in an earlier freeing petition, the natural parent who wishes to agree to the making of the adoption order will normally do so in the prescribed form in the presence of the reporting officer.[26] When the report of the reporting officer on these matters has been lodged in court, along with the report of the curator *ad litem* the court must, in cases where the child is not free for adoption,[27] appoint a hearing of which the natural parent—and other persons entitled to appear—shall receive intimation. The purpose of the hearing is to deal with agreements and consents, not with the merits of the adoption. At the hearing a compearing natural parent may be heard; but

---

[23] A.S. 1997, r. 2.29 (*cf.* RCS, r. 67.25(2)(b)(iii); *T, Petitioner,* 1996 S.C.L.R. 897; Dobie, *Sheriff Court Practice,* p. 547).
[24] *cf. A v. B and C,* 1971 S.C. (H.L.) 129 at 144, *per* Lord Wilberforce.
[25] 1978 Act, ss. 58(1)(b), 59; A.S. 1997, rr. 2.8(1) and 2.26(1) (RCS, rr. 67.11(1) and 67.24.(1)).
[26] A.S. 1997, r. 2.6 (freeing) and r. 2.23 (adoption) (RCS, r. 67.5 (all causes)).
[27] 1978 Act, s. 59(2); A.S. 1997, r. 2.28 (RCS, r. 67.25); see para. 5.34, above.

at that hearing, only in about one or two cases in 100, does the natural parent appear or is represented by a solicitor in order to continue to refuse to agree to the making of the adoption order. Accordingly, in all but a tiny number of cases the petitioners or their solicitor require to be present at the hearing in the absence of any contradictor merely to move the court to grant the adoption order. In the few cases where the natural parent (or other person entitled to be heard) does appear and wishes to be heard, the court may hear him, or order a further diet to be fixed at which he may be heard; and at such diets evidence given shall be given in the presence of the petitioner or his solicitor.[28] In practice, where the agreement of a natural parent is in issue, it would normally not be practicable to hear evidence at this statutory hearing, because at that stage the parties would have no certain knowledge of what matters were still in dispute and they would have had no time to instruct a shorthand writer to prepare a case, or to apply for legal aid.[29] Further, the court would still have to decide what form of inquiry was to take place.

At the hearing—or before—the petitioner must lodge the execution of **6.06** service. If the agreement of the natural parent has been given and has not been withdrawn and if the sheriff is satisfied on the merits, he would normally grant the order. If the natural parent does not agree, and does not appear at the hearing, the court may properly on the information contained in the reports dispense with the agreement of the natural parent. The form of intimation of a diet of hearing includes the words, "If you do not attend this hearing the court may make an order as noted above".[30] This might be more readily done when the ground for dispensing with the agreement is that the natural parent cannot be found or is incapable of giving his agreement. In other cases, for example where the ground relied upon by the petitioner is that the agreement is unreasonably withheld, the court may wish to make further inquiry, perhaps from the petitioners there and then, or by calling for further reports or by having a proof.[31] If the natural parent compears and does not agree to the making of the adoption order, it will almost always be necessary to appoint a proof to resolve the differences between the parties.

Report of a Reporter

Where, after the statutory reports have been lodged, there are matters **6.07** still unresolved, resort has been had to the report of a reporter. In *A v. B*[32] there was before the Court of Session a petition for the custody of a child in respect of which there was also a petition for adoption in Falkirk Sheriff

---

[28] A.S. 1997, r. 2.28. In the Court of Session, a hearing is necessary if there are reports (RCS, r. 67.25(2)(a)), but reports may not be necessary: thus a reporting officer is not necessary if the child if free for adoption and is under 12 years of age, and a curator *ad litem* is only necessary where it appears desirable in order to safeguard the interests of the child: RCS, r. 67.23(1)(b) and (c)).

[29] These observations in the text were approved in *M v. S*, Sheriff Principal Risk, Banff Sh.Ct., May 18, 1994, unreported.

[30] A.S. 1997, Form 7 (RCS, Form 67.25 is less stark in its terms).

[31] *cf.* A.S. 1997, r. 2.11(4) (freeing) and r. 2.29 (adoption) (RCS, r. 67.6 (all causes)).

[32] 1955 S.C. 378.

Court. The Court of Session had the process in the sheriff court action transmitted to the Court of Session. After hearing argument in the petition for custody on the question of further procedure, Lord President Clyde said, with the agreement of the other members of the court:

> "The sole question for us at this stage is the form which the inquiry should take, since both sides recognise that an inquiry is essential for the determination of the question in the case. We have heard a full argument on the matter and have reached the conclusion that the proper course in the circumstances is to remit to a member of the Bar to report to this Court. The alternative would have been a proof, either before a member of this Court or before some other tribunal. A proof, even held *in camera*, might not have preserved that anonymity of the adopting parents which it is one of the prime objects of the Adoption Act to preserve, since at a proof the parties are entitled to be present and among the parties the adopting parents are included. Moreover, as I have indicated, adoption proceedings have already been commenced in the Sheriff Court at Falkirk. The sheriff-substitute has meantime of consent continued consideration of this petition as the present proceedings were being commenced in the Court of Session, but we have had the process transmitted here, and included in it is a report by a curator *ad litem* appointed in this sheriff court process. It seems to me that it would be most unsatisfactory to have the issues raised between the parties determined partly by a proof and partly by a report by a curator, which is confidential but which might well have a bearing on the ultimate decision in the petition before us."[33]

6.08   In *X v. Y*[34] the sheriff-substitute quoted that passage and used the procedure in an adoption petition: "I have remitted the present issues to a reporter. The reporter will have available to him the report of the curator *ad litem* and of course, the parties will be entitled to be heard on the report when it is available." The same sheriff-substitute (A. M. Prain) adopted the same course in a later petition for adoption but of consent. On appeal[35] the procedure of a report by a reporter was expressly approved by the Inner House and in the House of Lords. In the Inner House Lord President Clyde said:

> "It is indeed in applications of this sort a perfectly proper way of ascertaining the situation, and where, as here, the petitioners exercised their right to remain anonymous, no doubt in the interest of the child himself, ascertainment of the situation almost necessarily can only be achieved by a remit to a reporter. In any event, the anonymity of the parties is a well-recognised feature of applications such as the present, where the court is required to take such care to avoid publicity regarding the circumstances of an adoption."[36]

---

[33] 1955 S.C. 378 at 379.
[34] 1967 S.L.T. (Sh.Ct.) 87 at 88.
[35] *A v. B and C*, 1971 S.C. (H.L.) 129.
[36] 1971 S.C. (H.L.) 129 at 135.

In the Lords, Lord Reid said:

> "In this case there were reports by a curator *ad litem* and a reporter. That appears to me to be a proper procedure. I agree with Lord President Cooper when he said in *J. & J. v. C.'s Tutor* (at p. 642) that 'adoption proceedings are *sui generis*, uniquely devised to effectuate a new statutory institution, and incapable of being forcibly compressed into any of our pre-existing categories of forms of action'. These reports were carefully and skilfully prepared. A reporter who sees the parties in an informal way has perhaps a better opportunity to form a correct impression than a judge who sees them for a short time in the unaccustomed atmosphere of a court. So I would attach great weight to their conclusions."[37]

The reasoning of Lord Reid does no violence to the right of a party to see the process.[38] Wherever possible all reports and documents should not refer to the child or the parties by name, but should refer to them as "the child", "the male petitioner", "the natural father" and the like.

Proof by Witnesses

Where there is a fundamental and substantial challenge of the aver- **6.09** ments in the petition or of the statements in the reports or where the interviews with the parties disclose irreconcilable differences on matters of substance, the court may *ex proprio motu* or on the motion of parties allow a proof which proceeds in the manner of an ordinary action and thereafter make findings in fact and in law. This course was adopted in *AB and CB v. X's Curator*.[39] In *A v. B and C*[40] Lord Guest referred to such a procedure without criticism:

> "It may be that, if a formal proof takes place and findings in fact are made by the Sheriff-substitute, these findings, unless altered by the Inner House, would be sacrosanct in this House: see the Court of Session Act 1825, section 40."[41]

Nowadays, proof by witnesses is the normal procedure.[42] In *AB and CB v. X's Curator*[43] the sheriff-substitute heard the evidence of the respective parties and their witnesses on separate days. This course may result in a sense of injustice in that one of the purposes of proceeding by way of proof is to resolve questions of credibility and that would be

---

[37] 1971 S.C. (H.L.) 129 at 141.

[38] A.S. 1997, r. 2.12 (freeing) and r. 2.30 (adoption) (RCS, r. 67.3 (all causes)).

[39] 1963 S.C. 124 at 125. A similar view was exposed in relation to a question of access: it was held that a court should not depart from the recognised procedure of determining disputed questions of access by proof in open court, even with the consent of the parties: *Macdonald v. Macdonald*, 1985 S.L.T. 194.

[40] 1971 S.C. (H.L.) 129.

[41] *ibid.* at 142.

[42] And was approved in *M v. S*, Sheriff Principal Risk, Banff Sh.Ct., May 18, 1994, unreported; and in *Strathclyde Regional Council v. C*, Sheriff Principal Caplan, Paisley Sh.Ct., December 16, 1987, unreported.

[43] 1963 S.C. 124.

more difficult if the parties were not present throughout each other's case. This would be all the more so if the parties already knew each other's identity so that there was no confidentiality to preserve. Further, in terms of the legislation all documents must be open to, *inter alia*, "the parties".[44] No doubt the circumstances of the case would determine the form which the proof took.

In *AB v. CD*[45] where the sheriff-substitute did not hold a proof but interviewed the parties separately and decided that the natural mother was not withholding her consent unreasonably, it was held on appeal that the sheriff-substitute ought to have taken into consideration the welfare of the child, and the case was remitted to him to hold a proof. Lord Cameron was of the opinion that in such a situation a proof was not inevitable.[46] In *C v. D*[47] the sheriff principal had adopted a similar course. In England, in *Re B*[48] one of the judges expressed concern that "though there were disputes of primary fact, the justices had made no specific findings in fact". Presumably, in such cases the court would apply the civil standard of proof, namely, a balance of probabilities.

6.10   The petitioners are entitled to be present at the proof, but need not attend if, for example, they have no knowledge of the matters which are the subject of the proof, such as whether the natural parent is withholding his agreement unreasonably. Where three children, brothers and sisters, were being adopted by different petitioners, but where the petitioners were represented by the same solicitor and both natural parents were opposing all the petitions, parties agreed by joint minute in each process that the evidence in one proof would be the evidence in the two succeeding proofs, with separate interlocutors in each case.[49] The sheriff should hear parties on each of the petitions separately and then issue the appropriate interlocutor in each case.[50] The parties would be entitled to call the authors of the reports as witnesses.[51]

6.11   In a case in which two brothers were the subject of petitions for adoption in Greenock Sheriff Court at the instance of petitioners, and also the subject of an action for custody at the instance of the grand-parents of the children in Glasgow Sheriff Court, it was held that the sheriff in Greenock had power to proceed by way of a hearing. Since the children had already been freed for adoption there was no power to order a hearing under paragraph 22 but there was power to do so under paragraph 23.[52] There was also power to make such ancillary orders as

---

[44] A.S. 1997, r. 2.12 (freeing) and r. 2.30 (adoption) (RCS, r. 67.3 (all causes)).
[45] 1970 S.C. 268.
[46] *cf. Re C* [1981] C.L.Y. 1752.
[47] 1968 S.L.T. (Sh.Ct.) 39.
[48] [1975] Fam. 127 at 144.
[49] *R v. O; G v. O; S v. O*, Edinburgh Sh.Ct. (E49/85 and E51/85), unreported; *AB and CB, Petitioners*, Lord Abernethy, September 6, 1996, unreported. English decisions about separate hearings do not assist, because they turn on special rules: *C (A Minor)* [1985] 7 C.L. 505b; *cf.* Magistrates' Courts (Adoption) Rules 1984 (S.I. 1984 No. 611), r. 27(4)(b).
[50] *AB v. CB*, 1985 S.L.T. 514 at 516, *per* Lord Justice-Clerk Wheatley.
[51] See para. 7.03, below.
[52] Act of Sederunt (Adoption of Children) 1984 (S.I. 1984 No. 1013).

might be necessary to enable that hearing to take place. It was also held that the sheriff did not have to hear the evidence twice over in two separate processes in order to reach his decision as to how the competing claims should be resolved.[53] The "hearing" would no doubt take the form of a proof as has been discussed above.

---

[53] *AB and CD, Petitioners*, 1992 S.C.L.R. 274. A similar approach was adopted in England: *G v. G (Children: concurrent applications)* [1993] Fam. 253.

CHAPTER 7

CURATOR *AD LITEM* AND REPORTING OFFICER

CURATOR *AD LITEM* AND REPORTING OFFICER:
APPOINTMENT BY THE COURT

7.01 The Adoption (Scotland) Act 1978 and the Children (Scotland) Act 1995 have introduced arrangements of increasing elaboration for investigating the circumstances of adoption cases.[1] Generally, that investigation is entrusted to two officers, the curator *ad litem* and the reporting officer. The provisions relating to the appointment of a curator *ad litem* and a reporting officer (which is generally done after the lodging of the petition or minute or note) differ slightly between the rules of the sheriff court and of the Court of Session and also between the different kinds of application.

(1) In a petition to free a child for adoption,
 (a) in the sheriff court, the court must appoint a curator *ad litem* and a reporting officer[2];
 (b) in the Court of Session, a reporting officer must be appointed, but a curator *ad litem*[3] need only be appointed "where it appears desirable in order to safeguard the interests of the child"[4];
(2) in a petition for adoption and a petition to adopt a child abroad and, in the Court of Session, a petition for a Convention adoption order,[5]
 (a) in the sheriff court, the court must appoint a curator *ad litem* and a reporting officer,[6] but where the child has been freed for adoption the reporting officer need not be appointed[7];
 (b) in the Court of Session, the court must appoint a reporting officer, "unless the child is free for adoption and is under the age of 12 years",[8] and must appoint a curator *ad litem* "where it appears desirable in order to safeguard the interests of the child"[9];

---

[1] See McNeill, *Adoption of Children in Scotland* (2nd ed.), para. 7.01.
[2] A.S. 1997, r. 2.7.
[3] RCS, r. 67.10(1)(a).
[4] RCS, r. 67.10(1)(b).
[5] RCS, r. 67.34.
[6] A.S. 1997, r. 2.25.
[7] A.S. 1997, r. 2.25(2): it seems that the words, "save for the purposes specified in r. 2.26(1)(a)" have been inserted in error.
[8] RCS, r. 67.23(1)(b).
[9] RCS, r. 67.23(1)(c).

(3) in revocation of a freeing order,
    (a) in a minute in the sheriff court, the court may appoint a curator *ad litem*[10];
    (b) in a note in the Court of Session the court must appoint a curator *ad litem* "where it appears desirable in order to safeguard the interests of the child".[11]

It is difficult to see how the interests of the child—especially a young child—could be safeguarded without the appointment of a curator *ad litem*. This has been the law and practice for the last 60 years or more that adoption has been part of our law. The interjection of an independent officer of the court is necessary because the child cannot look to his natural parents or to the petitioners to safeguard his welfare because they may have an interest which is contrary to his. The curator *ad litem* in that situation can report to the court with complete independence on the circumstances which persuade him that the interests of the child have been safeguarded. The appointment of the curator *ad litem* and the reporting officer for the purpose of witnessing agreements to adoption and performing such other duties as the Rules of Court may prescribe,[12] is made by the court after the lodging of the petition. (The court may on cause shown appoint a reporting officer before the petition has been lodged[13].) The appointment is effected by an interlocutor or interlocutors of the court; and at the same time the court instructs these officers to investigate and report to the court in terms of the legislation.[14] The interlocutor requires the curator *ad litem* to report in writing to the sheriff within four weeks from the date of the interlocutor, or within such other period as the sheriff in his discretion may allow.[15] These provisions are designed to obviate the real danger of delay—which has been judicially deprecated.[16] If the curator *ad litem* or the reporting officer requires an extension of the time he can come back to the court and state his reasons for the extension. It may be that the additional information which the curator *ad litem* or the reporting officer seeks time to collect is, in the view of the court, not necessary. It is desirable to bring to the attention of the curator *ad litem* by a note appended to the interlocutor appointing him, or otherwise warning him, that he should not take up the appointment if his employment by an adoption agency is incompatible with his acting, and reminding him that his report should only refer to the parties in the report in such a way that they cannot be identified.

---

[10] A.S. 1997, r. 2.16.

[11] RCS, r. 67.14(2)(b).

[12] A.S. 1997, r. 2.7 (freeing), r. 2.16(1) (revocation) and r. 2.25 (adoption) (RCS, r. 67.10 (freeing), r. 67.14 (revocation) and r. 67.23 (adoption)).

[13] A.S. 1997, r. 2.7(3) (RCS, r. 67.10(3)) (freeing) and A.S. 1997, r. 2.25 (RCS, r. 67.23(3)) (adoption).

[14] See Append. 2.2.

[15] A.S. 1997, r. 2.8(1) and (2) (freeing), r. 2.16(1) (revocation) and r. 2.26(1) and (2) (adoption). (In the Court of Session the reports are to be prepared within such period as the court may specify: RCS, rr. 67.11(1)(u), 67.11(2)(i) (freeing), r. 67.14(5)(g) (revocation) and rr. 67.24(1)(l) and 67.24(2)(x) (adoption).)

[16] *e.g. A v. B and C* 1971 S.C. (H.L.) 129, *per* Lord Simon at 147–148.

7.02   It may be that the natural mother whose agreement is in question is a minor. In *AB and CB v. X's Curator*[17] Lord President Clyde observed:

> "The Sheriff-substitute has raised a subsidiary point as to whether in all applications for adoption where the mother of the child is a minor, a curator *ad litem* should be appointed to the mother. I see no necessity for any general rule to this effect, and there may well be many cases in which such a step would be quite unnecessary. It is obviously unnecessary where the mother is legitimate and her father or mother is alive. But, even in other cases, it would rarely be necessary to make such an appointment. Where such an appointment seems necessary, the special need for it would be disclosed by the circumstances described by the curator *ad litem* to the child who is appointed under section 11(4) of the Act."[18]

7.03   It would appear that in the execution of his duty of safeguarding the interests of the child before the court the curator *ad litem* may regard it as necessary to be present or to be represented at the hearing of any proof. However, there is no reported sheriff court case of this, and it would be necessary for the court as a matter of course to intimate such hearings to the curator *ad litem* but this has not generally been done. There is now provision in the Court of Session for appearance or representation of the curator *ad litem* at the hearing, if required by the court.[19]

Who may be a Curator *ad Litem* or Reporting Officer: Statutory Panel

7.04   In practice, the curator *ad litem* is usually a solicitor (or in the Court of Session, an advocate) or a person with social work training. It is usual in the smaller sheriff courts to have one or two curators *ad litem* whereas in the larger courts a panel of curators *ad litem* is necessary. Some sheriffs take the view that since as soon as an adoption petition comes into court, the problem ceases to be a social one and becomes a legal one, it is more appropriate to have a curator *ad litem* with a legal background rather than a social work background because the court has to ensure that the legal requirements have been complied with. For example, one problem which arises from time to time and which may not be appreciated by a non-lawyer is expressed in the maxim *pater est quem nuptiae demonstrant.* Where there is a panel of curators *ad litem* it is common to swear each in at the time of his appointment to perform faithfully the duties of the office in all petitions in which he may be appointed by the sheriff.[20] The curator *ad litem* will be appointed by interlocutor in the cases in which he is to act.[21]

Since 1984, in addition to any informal list of curators *ad litem* that existed in the sheriff courts, panels of curators *ad litem* and reporting

---

[17] 1963 S.C. 124.
[18] *ibid.* at 137.
[19] RCS, r. 67.13(4)(a) (freeing) and r. 67.25(4)(b) and (c) (adoption).
[20] Append. 2.1.
[21] Append. 2.2.

officers[22] for the purposes of petitions for adoption, to free a child for adoption, to adopt a child abroad and to revoke a freeing order[23] have been set up in the area of each local authority, that is, a "council constituted under section 2 of the Local Government etc. (Scotland) Act 1994",[24] (replacing the former regional or islands councils). The members of the panels are appointed by the local authority after consultation with the sheriff principal.[25] The local authority may determine the standard of qualification or experience which should be attained by persons who may be appointed and such determination must be made after consultation with the sheriff principal.[26] One exceptional circumstance which may arise in a significant number of cases is that there may be a potential conflict between the independence of the curator *ad litem* and reporting officer—who are independent officers of the court—and the status of a member of the panel who may be an actual or recent employee of the local authority or adoption society. Thus by statute, a person who is employed

(a) by the adoption agency which placed the child;
(b) by the adoption agency which presented the petition to free the child; and
(c) by the adoption agency which has parental rights and duties in relation to the child in an application to revoke a freeing order,

must not be appointed to act as a curator *ad litem* or a reporting officer for the purposes of the application.[27] The court may feel that to ensure complete independence of these officers, the prohibition should extend also

(d) in the case of an application where the child was not placed by an adoption agency, to those employed by the local authority which is required to furnish a report in terms of section 22;
(e) to a person who is a reporter or is connected with a children's hearing which has been dealing with the child; or
(f) to a person who is employed by the solicitor acting in the case.

The court may also feel that these restrictions should apply to persons who have been recently employed in these capacities.

Since 1986 the local authority must defray the expenses incurred by a **7.05** member of the statutory panel established for their area and must pay him such fees and allowances as they think fit in the case of an application

---

[22] 1978 Act, s. 65(1) as amended by the Local Government etc. (Scotland) Act 1994, s. 180(1) and Sched. 13, para. 112(3).
[23] 1975 Act, s. 103; 1978 Act, s. 66 and Sched. 3, para. 17; Health and Social Services and Social Security Adjudications Act 1983, s. 9 and Sched. 2, para. 28; Curators *ad litem* and Reporting Officers (Panels) (Scotland) Regulations 1984 (S.I. 1984 No. 566) as amended by Curators *ad litem* and Reporting Officers (Panels) (Scotland) Amendment Regulations 1985 (S.I. 1985 No. 1556), para. 3. The corresponding s. 101 of the 1995 Act has not yet been brought into force. Presumably the old legislation and the existing panels remain in force.
[24] 1975 Act, s. 103(a)(i) to be replaced by the 1995 Act, s. 101; see the previous footnote.
[25] S.I. 1984 No. 566, para. 3(2).
[26] S.I. 1984 No. 566, para. 6.
[27] 1978 Act, s. 58(2).

(a) to free a child for adoption;
(b) to revoke a freeing order;
(c) to adopt a child; and
(d) to adopt a child abroad.

There is an unusual qualification in cases (c) and (d) where if the child was not placed by an adoption agency: then the local authority will not be liable in these sums if the court does not grant the order—if that is the correct interpretation of the phrase, "which is made by a court".[28] This provision may have undesirable effects. A curator *ad litem* or a reporting officer may be unwilling to act in such cases where there is a possibility that he will receive no remuneration from the local authority. If the adoption petition is refused (or overturned on appeal), the petitioners may be unexpectedly saddled with these fees and the court may be unwilling to choose a curator *ad litem* or reporting officer from the local authority panel if his fee is to be in doubt. The court may always appoint as curator *ad litem* and reporting officer someone who is not a member of the local authority panel.[29] In that case, the party, not the local authority, is liable for the fee of the curator *ad litem* and the reporting officer.[30]

Although a curator *ad litem* or a reporting officer may be a servant of an adoption agency, he is bound by the same strict duty of confidentiality as any other officer, and in relation to adoption proceedings in court he is not entitled to impart any information in his hands to any person, including any member of the local authority or adoption society unless the disclosure of such information is necessary for the proper discharge of his duties.[31] The position is different under the regulations governing the placement of children by adoption agencies where duties are placed not on an individual but on a corporate body such as a local authority or an adoption society.[32]

Personal Appointment

7.06   The court can only appoint as a curator *ad litem* or a reporting officer an individual person, not a body of persons.[33] This is implied in the Act of Sederunt.[34] Further, it is not open to the curator *ad litem* or the reporting officer to delegate his functions to another person, *delegatus non potest delegare*: his oath and appointment relate to him personally. The report of the curator *ad litem* or the reporting officer must generally be made from his own investigations, not on the investigations of someone else. Apart from the principle, it would be impossible for the curator *ad litem* or the reporting officer to be interviewed by the court on a matter in his report if

---

[28] S.I. 1984 No. 566, para. 10(c); see para. 14.01, below.
[29] 1975 Act, s. 103(1); A.S. 1997, r. 2.7(3) (freeing), r. 2.16 (revocation, where the panel is not referred to) and r. 2.25(3) (adoption) (RCS, r. 67.4).
[30] The amount of and liability for fees are discussed at para. 14.01, below.
[31] A.S. 1997, r. 2.12 (freeing) and r. 2.30 (adoption) (RCS, r. 67.3).
[32] Adoption Agencies (Scotland) Regulations 1996 (S.I. 1996 No. 3266), reg. 9.
[33] 1978 Act, s. 58.
[34] A.S. 1997, r. 2.7 (freeing) and r. 2.51 (adoption) (RCS, rr. 67.10 and 67.23).

he had not investigated it himself. If the curator *ad litem* or the reporting officer is in any doubt he should indicate the state of his inquiries and the court can decide if further verification is necessary. The curator *ad litem* should always differentiate between facts observed by him and information obtained by him from other persons,[35] such as doctors who have examined the child or petitioners, or social workers who have been visiting the family of the petitioners. The position is different in the case of reports which must be provided by an adoption agency or a local authority[36] where there is no personal appointment and the duty of reporting is put on juristic persons. In these reports the person making the report should identify himself in the body of the report in case the court requires to interview that person.[37] In cases where the parents of the child are resident in a foreign country, a member of the consular service in that country may be willing to act as a reporting officer. If that is not possible, the reporting officer appointed by the Scottish court can carry out the duties by correspondence.[38]

---

[35] *Z v. Z*, 1954 S.L.T. (Sh.Ct.) 47.
[36] 1978 Act, ss. 22, 23; see para. 8.72, below.
[37] See Append. 3, Nos 3, 7.
[38] *H and H, Petitioners*, Sheriff McNeill, Edinburgh Sh.Ct. (E11/91), unreported; see para. 10.02, below.

CHAPTER 8

REPORTS: STATUTORY HEARING

General Observations

8.01 In the normal case, the matters which have to be established before an order can be granted, are verified by the reports which have been enumerated earlier.[1] Apart from the conditions precedent, two general matters must be dealt with:

(a) the agreement of every parent; and
(b) the merits, including the welfare of the child.

8.02 However, the procedure of the Court of Session differs from that of the sheriff court in that the matters in the petition which require to be verified in the reports are differently distributed between the reports.[2] There are further procedural differences between the courts of Scotland and the courts of England and Wales, and between the High Court and County Court on the one hand and the Magistrates' Court on the other hand.[3] Notwithstanding these differences, the sum of the matters which are reported upon to the court in each jurisdiction is substantially the same. For the present purpose, to avoid duplication, the commonest procedure—a petition for adoption—and the commonest forum—the sheriff court—have been taken as the leading exemplar, but with reference to the variations in the Court of Session and to variations in a petition to free a child, a petition to adopt a child abroad and a petition for a Convention order. In all cases the reports must be made according to the statutory requirements which are discussed below but the person making the report must always have in mind the continuing need to proceed with expedition. He should not spend undue time trying to ascertain facts which appear to be incapable of being ascertained. It is sufficient that he reports on "what steps he has found himself able to take" in dealing with the point: "it is clear that the curator *ad litem* cannot be faulted if he prepares a report which, to the best of his ability, deals with all the items which are prescribed for him by the relevant rules".[4] The court can decide on what further inquiries (if any) should be made. If the judge is not satisfied with the information which the curator *ad litem* has provided for him, "he should call for more information

---

[1] See para. 6.02, above.
[2] *cf.* 1978 Act, s. 60(5).
[3] Adoption Rules 1984 (S.I. 1984 No. 265); Magistrates' Courts (Adoption) Rules 1984 (S.I. 1984 No. 611).
[4] *T, Petitioner*, 1996 S.C.L.R. 897 at 906E.

before he makes his decision".[5] In a case where the curator *ad litem* felt that "his integrity and efficiency had been criticised without his being given an opportunity to answer these criticisms before they were put in writing by the Lord Ordinary", the court granted leave to the curator *ad litem* to be represented by counsel at the hearing of the appeal.[6]

The curator *ad litem* should not go beyond his duty to investigate and report. It is no part of his duty, for example, to seek to counsel the petitioners towards a particular course—such as encouraging them to drop the petition, or to seek some alternative remedy such as residence—but he should state the facts as he has found them and give his opinion as is required by the legislation. The Inner House has held that a reporting officer should not approach the unmarried father of a child who is the subject of an adoption petition and ask him if he is prepared to agree to the making of the proposed adoption order.[7]

A report which is merely a copy of departmental files is of little value to the court. The report requires the application of the judgment of the reporter in the selection of the material which he uses and the opinion that he comes to. In most cases and with most topics all that will be necessary is a brief statement that the facts are in order: only if there is a difficulty will there need to be any elaboration. Obviously if anything appears to be amiss, the report would draw the attention of the court to it and the court can decide on the appropriate action. If the report discloses a variance with the averments in the petition, no doubt the solicitor can deal with this by amendment or otherwise—such as seeking to challenge the statement in the report by other evidence. The court is not, of course, bound by the terms of the report but the court must have regard to the advice of the curator *ad litem* as, for example, to the effect that the proposed adoption is consistent with the welfare of the child.[8] The court may wish to interview the curator *ad litem* or the reporting officer on additional matters or to amplify some part of his report.

STATUTORY REQUIREMENTS

The form of the reports will obviously be determined by the list of matters on which the curator *ad litem* must report in terms of the legislation.[9] Some courts provide the curator *ad litem*, the reporting officer, the adoption agency and the local authority with a *pro forma* report which can be adapted to the circumstances of each case.[10] It would seem logical to have the report in numbered paragraphs which correspond with the numbered paragraphs in the legislation.[11] The report should be preceded by a separate page which begins with any interlocutor of the **8.03**

[5] A.S. 1997, r. 2.29 (RCS, r. 67.6); *T, Petitioner*, 1996 S.C.L.R. 897 at 906.
[6] *T, Petitioner*, 1996 S.C.L.R. 897 at 906E.
[7] *A and B v. C*, 1987 G.W.D. 8-241.
[8] *H and H, Petitioners*, 1976 S.L.T. 80 at 83.
[9] 1978 Act, ss. 22(3), 23; A.S. 1997, r. 2.8 (freeing), r. 2.16 (revocation) and r. 2.26 (adoption) (RCS, rr. 67.11, 67.14 and 67.24).
[10] A style of report appears in Append. 3.
[11] A.S. 1997, r. 2.8(1) and (2) (freeing), r. 2.16 (revocation) and r. 2.26 (adoption) (RCS, rr. 67.11, 67.14 and 67.24).

court which authorises it and be followed by the instance (which contains the designation of the petitioners and the child and the serial number (if any) and the register number of the case). The report proper should begin on a separate page headed by the serial number (if any) and the register number of the case: the number or numbers will link the separate front page with the body of the report. In this way, if the report requires to be seen by some other party, the top sheet can be removed and complete confidentiality maintained. The writer of the report should refer to the persons involved as "the child", "the natural parent", "the male petitioner" and the like, rather than refer to them by name, and should not refer to them in any way whereby the parties or the child may be identified. However, if a party—such as a compearing natural father—seeks to see the process, it would seem difficult to resist a motion to that effect, in view of the terms of the Act of Sederunt.[12] The position in England is different.[13] Where adopters are seeking to adopt more than one child at the same time, the proper course is to have a separate petition for each child[14]: similarly, it is submitted that there should be a separate report for each child in the case of a report by the curator *ad litem* and the reporting officer—even though in some cases, such as where the children are brothers and sisters of the same household, the reports may be almost identical.

CONTENT OF THE REPORTS

8.04   Briefly, in the sheriff court, in most cases, the same person will normally be appointed as both the reporting officer and the curator *ad litem*.[15]

> (a) The reporting officer witnesses the consent to the making of an application for an order freeing a child for adoption of each parent or guardian and the agreement of each parent or guardian to the making of an adoption order and reports on the aspects of the case which are set out in the rules.[16] Where a parent states to the reporting officer that he will not agree to the making of the order, the reporting officer should merely report that fact: he has no duty to consider the grounds for dispensing with agreement;
> (b) the curator *ad litem*
>> (i) reports on whether the interests of the child have been safeguarded,
>> (ii) generally ascertains the truth of the averments in the petition, and
>> (iii) deals *seriatim* with the particular matters specified in the rules[17];

---

[12] A.S. 1997, r. 2.30 (1) (RCS, r. 67.3); but see *A v. B and C*, 1971 S.C. (H.L.) 129 at 135–136, *per* Lord President Clyde.

[13] *Re G* [1963] 2 Q.B. 73 at 97, *per* Donovan L.J.; *Re PA* [1971] 1 W.L.R. 1530.

[14] *cf*. para. 5.08, above.

[15] 1978 Act, s. 58(2); A.S. 1997, r. 2.7(1) (freeing) and r. 2.25(1) (adoption).

[16] 1978 Act, s. 58(1)(b); A.S. 1997, r. 2.8 (freeing) and r. 2.26 (adoption) (RCS, rr. 67.11 and 67.24).

[17] 1978 Act, s. 58(1)(a); A.S. 1997, r. 2.28(2) (freeing) and r. 2.26(2) (adoption) (RCS, rr. 67.11(2) and 67.24(2)).

(c) the local authority, where the placement was not made by an adoption agency,[18] and the adoption agency, where the placement was by an adoption agency,[19] must report on

    (i) the petitioners,

    (ii) the child, and

    (iii) in a placement not made by an adoption agency whether there was any contravention of section 11 of the 1978 Act, which relates to illegal placements.

There is also an obligation on the adoption agency to produce to the **8.05** court not only a report in terms of section 23 but also a report in terms of the regulations "giving such information . . . as it had been able to discover in accordance with these Regulations".[20]

Report of Curator *ad Litem*: Circumstances of the Petitioner; Criminal Convictions

The character of the petitioner is a matter which often gives rise to **8.06** difficulty when the curator *ad litem* is dealing with the circumstances of the petitioner under this general provision and also more particularly under the later provision relating to his personality.[21] This difficulty usually relates to the petitioner's bad, and especially criminal, character. There is no authority in the adoption legislation or in the appointment of a curator *ad litem* which would justify the curator *ad litem* as a matter of course seeking to know the contents of any criminal records kept by the police: those are for most purposes confidential. Nor is any greater right of inquiry into the criminal background of a petitioner conferred on a curator *ad litem* by the Rehabilitation of Offenders Act 1974. Indeed, the purposes of that Act are quite the reverse; one of its purposes is "to penalise the unauthorised disclosure" of certain convictions of rehabilitated offenders. True, the Act provides for the rehabilitation of certain persons but these provisions have limitations, and shall not "affect the determination of any issue, or prevent the admission or requirement of any evidence relating to a person's previous convictions or to circumstances ancillary thereto . . . in any proceedings relating to adoption".[22] However, it would seem that that provision would not authorise the routine inquiries which are undertaken long before "any proceedings relating to adoption" by some local authorities into the criminal records of those applying to become adopters or other members of the applicant's household.

The 1996 Regulations[23] provide that an adoption agency shall not place or secure the placement of a child in the care of any person until

---

[18] 1978 Act, s. 22.

[19] 1978 Act, s. 23.

[20] Adoption Agencies (Scotland) Regulations 1996 (S.I. 1996 No. 3266), regs 2(1), 8(a) and Sched. 2, Pt I and para. 9(1)(a) and Sched. 2, para. 14(f).

[21] A.S. 1997, r. 2.26(2)(s) (RCS, r. 67.24(2)(r)).

[22] s. 7(2)(c); *cf. Lincoln County Council v. R-J, The Times,* February 1998.

[23] Adoption Agencies (Scotland) Regulations 1996 (S.I. 1996 No. 3266), regs 8, 9 and Sched. 2, Pt IV, para. 14. The Adoption Agencies (Scotland) Regulations 1984 (S.I. 1984 No. 983) revoked on April 1, 1997: Children (Scotland) Act 1995 etc. (Revocations and Savings) (Scotland) Regulations 1997 (S.I. 1997 No. 691), reg. 1(2) and Sched.

the agency has so far as is reasonably practicable ascertained whether the prospective adopter has been convicted of an offence against children. Where a child has not been placed by an adoption agency, there is no such requirement. However, if a curator *ad litem* receives information that a petitioner has what the curator considers to be significant criminal convictions—especially if they involve children—he should include that information in his report to the court. Thereafter, the court can decide what other inquiry should be made: for example, the court can procure extract convictions from the appropriate court, or interview the petitioner. Most trivial convictions—such as minor road traffic matters—can have little bearing on the suitability of a petitioner to be a parent but the situation may be very different if the convictions relate to more serious offences. In England and Wales, a person would be disqualified from adopting (or fostering) a child if he, or a person over the age of 18 within his household, had a criminal conviction for or had been cautioned in respect of or had admitted a serious sexual offence or any offence of violence above the level of common assault.[24]

In one unreported case, where the petitioners and the child lived in rather crowded conditions in the house of the mother of the female petitioner, the male petitioner had a conviction for assault with intent to ravish in respect of which he was sentenced to three years' imprisonment. The offence had occurred at about the time that the former marriage of the male petitioner was in difficulty. He continued to assert his innocence—which assertion was apparently accepted by his new wife who was the female petitioner and whose female child was the child whose adoption was sought. That petition was withdrawn for other reasons. However, the existence of a conviction for an offence of this nature would be most relevant to the welfare of the child, even if, as was likely, the child would remain in the household of the petitioners whether or not an adoption order was granted. If the petition had proceeded and the adoption order had been granted in favour of both petitioners and if difficulties had arisen, then the male petitioner would have had parental rights enabling him to have control of the child; whereas if the adoption order were not granted the natural mother alone would have the parental rights and could lawfully remove the child from the household at the first sign of danger.

However, in a single-judge decision in an appeal from the decision of the justices, it was held that, although the male petitioner's conviction for indecent assault on a six-year-old girl 15 years before was a grave matter, particularly when the court was concerned with the adoption of a female infant, nevertheless, it would be wrong to hold that it must always and necessarily be detrimental to a child to be adopted by a man with this particular stain on his record and that, in the present case, the court ought not to interfere with the decision of the justices.[25] In a case where the petitioners were the grandparents of the child and where the male

---

[24] Children and Young Persons: Children (Protection from Offenders) (Miscellaneous Amendments) Regulations 1997 (S.I. 1997 No. 2308); *Lincoln County Council v. R-J, The Times*, February 1998. There appears to be no corresponding regulation in Scotland.
[25] *Re G (DM)* [1962] 1 W.L.R. 730.

petitioner was also the father of a child by an incestuous relationship with the mother of the child, the order was granted. Again, a petitioner who is a persistent offender may be so often in custody that his ability to provide properly for the child is called in question; or it may be thought that he may lead the child into a life of crime. Each case must depend on its own circumstances. It may very well be, for example, that the child has been with the petitioner for such a long time that it appears that his ability to look after the child is well substantiated notwithstanding his way of life. In other cases, there may be room for considering that an interim order should be made to see if the petitioner's good behaviour is maintained. By statute, in any civil proceedings—which would include adoption proceedings—the fact that a person has been convicted of an offence by or before any court in the United Kingdom or by a court-martial there or elsewhere shall be admissible evidence for the purpose of proving, where to do so is relevant to an issue in those proceedings, that he committed that offence, whether he was so convicted upon a plea of guilty or otherwise and whether or not he is a party to the civil proceedings.[26] If the conviction is proved the person shall be taken to have committed the offence unless the contrary is proved.[27]

Sundry Paragraphs of the Report of Curator *ad Litem*

The 21 numbered paragraphs lettered (a) to (u) in rule 2.26(2) of the Act **8.07** of Sederunt (Child Care and Maintenance Rules) 1997,[28] which apply to a petition for adoption in the sheriff court, and which set forth the detailed questions and matters upon which the curator *ad litem* must report, are not wholly systematic. In this chapter, the paragraphs are discussed *seriatim*. In some instances—for example, in the question of the welfare of the child in paragraph (l)—the commentary goes some way beyond the strict terms of the paragraph. This course has been adopted in order to draw together in one place any matters related to the subject-matter of the paragraph and to avoid the necessity of repeating it when considering the other reports.[29] Of course, the person reporting should, if need be, report on relevant matters which go beyond the numbered paragraphs. Rule 2.26(2) is a preamble which directs that the curator *ad litem* have regard to the welfare of the child as his paramount duty. The succeeding paragraphs are as follows.

(a) Generally Safeguard the Interests of the Child Whose Adoption is the Subject of the Petition

As has been noted, the primary function of the curator *ad litem* is to **8.08** look after the interests of the child, because the child being under age has either no capacity or only a limited capacity; and because the child, unlike children in family, cannot rely on his natural parent nor the adoptive parents (the petitioners) to act as curators because potentially there is a

---

[26] Law Reform (Miscellaneous Provisions) (Scotland) Act 1968, s. 10(1).
[27] *ibid*, s. 10(2).
[28] A.S. 1997, r. 2.26(2) (RCS, r. 67.24(2)).
[29] See para. 6.02, above.

conflict of interests between them and the child. No doubt if the whole circumstances as set out in the remaining paragraphs of the report so indicate, the curator *ad litem* would be able to report that in his opinion the interests of the child have been safeguarded. It is difficult to conceive of a situation where the curator was not of that opinion but was not also of the opinion that the adoption was likely to safeguard and promote the welfare of the child throughout his life as set forth in paragraph (l).

(b) Where the Child in Respect of Whom an Adoption Order is Sought is Over the Age of 12 Years,[30] Witness any Consent to the Order Executed by him in the United Kingdom

(c) Whether the Facts Stated in the Petition are Correct and if they are not, Establish the True Facts

8.09   If the statements are true the curator *ad litem* should say so: if they are not, he should report what is not true and also state what the truth is. In that situation the petitioners or their representatives can deal with the contradiction by amending the petition or leading further evidence or lodging further productions. Similarly, if the curator *ad litem* is in doubt about a matter—such as whether the child was sufficiently mature to be able to express his wishes and feelings regarding the proposed adoption—her should report his doubt to the court which can make such other inquiry as seems appropriate, including an interview with the curator *ad litem*. In one case an error appearing in the birth certificate of the child was corrected before the sheriff granted the petition.[31] Obviously this paragraph will be qualified by circumstances. Some matters cannot be established, or cannot be established without undue expense or delay. In that situation the curator *ad litem* should report to the court on what steps he has been able to take.

(d) Accommodation

8.10   Particulars of the accommodation in the home of the petitioner and the condition of the home.

(e) Members of the Petitioner's Household

8.11   Particulars of all members of the household of the petitioner and their relationship (if any) to the petitioner.

8.12   Paragraphs (d) and (e) are self-explanatory.

(f) Exclusion of One Spouse

8.13   Why in the case of a petition by one of two spouses the other spouse does not join in the petition. An adoption order may be made by one spouse if the court is satisfied that:

---

[30] Age of Legal Capacity (Scotland) Act 1991, s. 2(3).
[31] *A and A, Petitioners*, 1949 S.L.T. (Sh.Ct) 77.

(i) the other spouse cannot be found; or

(ii) the spouses have separated and are living apart and the separation is likely to be permanent; or

(iii) the other spouse is by reason of ill health, whether physical or mental, incapable of making an application for an adoption order.[32]

There have been no reported cases of this situation arising.

Although this paragraph of the report does not deal with the case of a **8.14** petition by a mother or father alone, it would appear to be an appropriate place in such a case to report on whether:

(i) the other parent is dead or cannot be found; or

(ii) there is some reason justifying the exclusion of the other parent[33]; or

(iii) in an adoption where a step-parent is married to the natural mother, the petition has been presented by the step-parent alone without the concurrence of the natural parent.[34]

(g) Means and Status of the Petitioners

Whether the means and status of the petitioners are such as to enable **8.15** them to maintain and bring up the child suitably. The circumstances of the petitioners may not be ideal. The curator *ad litem* should merely report the facts and give his opinion on them, but in the knowledge that the choice is generally not between the current adoption and some better adoption but between the current adoption and no adoption, and that in many households which do not come under the scrutiny of the court in an adoption process the parents are able (perforce) to bring up their children suitably on very limited means and that in unprepossessing houses and districts. In most cases it is sufficient to note the nature of the petitioner's employment—if he is employed—the income of the household which is available for bringing up the child, and the major outgoings, such as rent and local taxes or repayments of bond or mortgage or standard security interest. If any question arises the court can call for further information. There is less of a problem where the child—as in the case of a mother adopting her own child—has in fact been maintained suitably by the adopters for some time. In such cases even if the order were not granted the child would in all probability remain with the petitioners. Where there is competition between two households—such as that of the petitioners and that of the natural parent—the welfare of the child (including the material welfare) is a relevant consideration in a question whether the parent is withholding his or her agreement unreasonably.[35]

(h) Property of the Child

The purpose of this information is not so much to establish how well **8.16** provided the child is, but to guard against the adoption being used to acquire control or possession of the property of the child, or to balance the

---

[32] 1978 Act, s. 15(1)(b).

[33] 1978 Act, s. 15(3).

[34] 1978 Act, s. 15(1)(aa); see para. 1.22, above.

[35] *AB and CB v. X's Curator*, 1963 S.C. 124.

material welfare of the child in the event of the adoption order being granted. Thus, for example, substantial aliment payable by a natural parent might come to an end after adoption. Generally, in the absence of special provisions, when an adoption order is granted the adoptive parents become the guardians in relation to his estate[36] and on the child's death may become his heirs.[37] In the majority of cases the child has no estate of any significance. Such as there is, should be referred to—heritable property, shareholding or, more commonly, the amount at credit of any bank account. Insurances over the life of the child are dealt with below.[38]

(i) Petitioners' Understanding of Adoption

8.17   Whether the petitioners understand the nature and effect of an adoption order and, in particular, that the order, if made, will render them responsible for the maintenance and upbringing of the child. In most cases the petitioners will have a reasonable understanding of the effect of an adoption order on themselves and the child. The curator *ad litem* should ascertain that their understanding is correct, and explain to them that they will become—as far as is possible—the natural parents of the child to the exclusion of the real parents, and that the adoptive child will be equal with any natural children of theirs and that they will require to do all the things that any natural parent would do by feeding, clothing, educating and advising the child. If the petitioners have any reservations or lack of understanding of these matters the curator *ad litem* should report that fact to the court.

(j) Period of Care and Possession

8.18   When the mother of the child ceased to have care and possession of the child and to whom care and possession was transferred. The whole history of the child should be narrated briefly, but detailing the circumstances of the child leaving the natural mother, including her reasons for giving up the child and any period in care or in hospital or in a foster home. It should also be said whether the adoption arrangements were undertaken privately or by the intervention of an adoption agency, whose name and address should be included. The statutory requirements as to the duration of the period of care and possession have already been discussed.[39]

(k) Payments and Rewards

8.19   Whether any payment or other reward in consideration of the adoption has been received or agreed upon. Generally, it is not lawful to make or give to any person any payment or reward for or in consideration of:

    (a) the adoption by that person of a child;
    (b) the grant by that person of any agreement or consent required;

---

[36] Age of Legal Capacity (Scotland) Act 1991, s. 5(1).
[37] Wilkinson and Norrie, *The Law Relating to Parent and Child in Scotland* (1993, W. Green & Son Ltd), p. 522.
[38] See para. 8.29, below.
[39] See para 3.05, above.

(c) the transfer by that person of the care and possession of a child with a view to the adoption of the child;

(d) the making by that person of any arrangements for the adoption of a child.[40]

Any person who makes or gives or agrees or offers to make or give, **8.20** any such payment or reward, or who receives or agrees to receive or attempts to obtain any such payment or reward is liable on summary conviction to imprisonment for a term not exceeding three months or to a fine not exceeding level 5 on the standard scale (£5,000) or to both.[41] The court may still make an adoption order in relation to a child even where it found that the applicants have, as respects the child, contravened these provisions.[42] In addition, without prejudice to any power which the court has to make any other order in relation to the child as respects whom the offence was committed, it may order him to be removed to a place of safety until he can be restored to his parents or guardians or until other arrangements can be made for him.[43] There are exceptions in the case of certain payments made to an adoption society or a local authority or those made by the authority of the court.[44] Since 1977 the court must be satisfied in relation to a child that the petitioners have not contravened these provisions.[45] It is almost unheard of for such an offence to take place. Sometimes a mother who is about to adopt her own child along with her new husband will forgo her claim to arrears of aliment under her decree of divorce, but in most cases she does so because she realises that the prospect of payment is remote and because she wishes to wash her hands of her former marriage, not in consideration of her ex-husband giving his agreement to the adoption order.

Surrogacy Agreements "The making of a payment as part of a **8.21** surrogacy agreement becomes relevant to the question whether or not an order may be made for the child's adoption because of section 24(4) 'which prohibits the making of an adoption order unless the court is satisfied as respects the child that the applicant has not made an unlawful payment contrary to section 51'.[46] When regard is had as the first consideration to the need to safeguard and promote the welfare of the child throughout his childhood (now, 'throughout his life'[47]), the public policy objections resulting from the fact that the payment was made as part of a surrogacy arrangement is outweighed in this case."

---

[40] 1978 Act, s. 51(1).

[41] 1978 Act, s. 51(2).

[42] 1978 Act, s. 24(2) as substituted by the 1995 Act, s. 98(1), Sched. 2, para. 16: the prohibition does not apply to payments made to persons arranging adoptions who were outside the jurisdiction: *Re W (Adoption Application)* [1993] F.C.R. 988, *per* Brown J.

[43] 1978 Act, s. 51(2), (4).

[44] 1978 Act, s. 51(3).

[45] 1978 Act, s. 24(2).

[46] *C and C v. S* 1996 S.C.L.R. 837 at 850–851.

[47] 1978 Act, s. 6.

In other cases, the weight to be given to public policy grounds in assessing the welfare of the child was considered.[48] In some cases the arrangement has been that the prospective adopters have paid the actual expenses which the mother has incurred or have merely given the mother bed and board during the pregnancy.

8.22 Adoption Allowances The curator *ad litem* should report on these matters as his investigations indicate. The section does not strike at payments made in accordance with a scheme approved by the Secretary of State whereby an adoption agency makes payment to persons who have adopted or intend to adopt a child where the arrangements for the adoption were made or are to be made by that agency.[49] In Scotland all the adoption agencies which were in the pre-1995 local government areas had had their schemes approved by the Secretary of State. These local government areas have been replaced by councils constituted under the Local Government etc. (Scotland) Act 1994[50]; but none of the voluntary adoption societies has submitted such schemes for approval.[51] The Secretary of State may now make regulations as respects adoption allowances[52] and such regulations have been made.[53] The curator *ad litem* should report on whether any such payments have been made and, if so, he should report on:

(a) whether the scheme under which the payments purport to have been made have been approved by the Secretary of State;
(b) what the payments amount to;
(c) how long the payments will continue;
(d) why the payments have been made; and
(e) whether the payments were known to the petitioners and the child before the decision to adopt was made.

8.23   The report, however, should note not only whether the payments are lawful, but also whether or not they militate against the adoption: in relation to the petitioners in that the petitioners may have been more motivated by the prospect of gain than by genuine feelings for the child; and in relation to the child in that he may, on learning of the situation, doubt the motives of his adoptive parents in adopting him.[54] The curator *ad litem* should say, for example, whether he thinks that the petitioners would have adopted the child even if there had been no payment made or

---

[48] *D and D v. F*, 1994 S.C.L.R. 417 at 424; *Re Adoption Application AA 212/86 (Adoption Payment)* [1987] 2 F.L.R. 291, *per* Latey J.; *C (A Minor) (Adoption Application)* [1993] 1 F.L.R. 87, *per* Booth J.

[49] 1978 Act, s. 51(5).

[50] 1978 Act, s. 65(1) as amended by the Local Government etc. (Scotland) Act 1994, Sched. 13, para. 112(3).

[51] Information supplied to author by the Social Work Services Group, October 17, 1985 and March 13, 1998.

[52] 1978 Act, ss. 51A and 51B which came into force on April 1, 1998: Children (Scotland) Act 1996 (Commencement No. 3) Order 1996 (S.I. 1996 No. 3201) para. 3(7)(a).

[53] Adoption Allowance (Scotland) Regulations 1996 (S.I. 1996 No. 3257).

[54] Kilmarnock Sh.Ct. (D12/85), December 13, 1985, unreported.

in prospect, or whether the petitioners could not proceed to adoption because the fostering allowance would come to an end.[55]

(1) The Welfare of the Child

Whether the adoption of the child is likely to safeguard and promote **8.24** the welfare of the child throughout his life (formerly "throughout his childhood"). Also, the welfare of the child has now to be regarded as the paramount consideration, whereas, formerly, it was the first consideration.[56] The curator *ad litem* should deal with the welfare of the child, and the court in reaching its decision shall have regard to all the circumstances including the welfare of the child. In most cases the facts found by the curator *ad litem* in his report will make it self-evident that the welfare of the child is likely to be safeguarded. If the matter is in balance or if there is some special item of doubt the curator *ad litem* should narrate these matters and give his opinion as to the welfare of the child.

The welfare of the child was discussed at some length in a case in which **8.25** the petitioner was a single male who was living with another male in a homosexual relationship. The child was profoundly handicapped. The unmarried mother of the child had been out of the picture for some time (but her agreement to the making of the adoption order had not been given); and the petitioner was well suited to caring for the child. The petition was presented in the sheriff court, but the sheriff remitted the case (which was unopposed) at the earliest opportunity, because it seemed to the sheriff that it raised questions which were of national rather than local importance. The Lord Ordinary who dealt with the case was of the view that

> "there is a fundamental question of principle as to whether the statutory process of adoption should be sanctioned by the court in circumstances where it is expressly proposed by a single male prospective adopter that the child should be brought up jointly by himself and a third party with whom he cohabits in a homosexual relationship".

He refused to grant the prayer of the petition. The reclaiming motion of the petitioner was allowed. In the Inner House the Lord President said[57]:

> "In my opinion the short answer to the concerns which the Lord Ordinary has expressed on this point is that the present case raises no such fundamental question of principle. Section 6 of the 1978 Act states that, in reaching any decision relating to the adoption of a child, the court shall have regard to all the circumstances, first [now 'paramount'] consideration being given to the need to safeguard and

---

[55] *H, Petitioner*, Edinburgh Sheriff Court (E68/85), October 3, 1985, unreported; *cf. Adoption Application, Surrogacy, AA 212/86* [1987] Fam. 81, *per* Latey J.
[56] Both these alterations appear in the 1978 Act, s. 6 as substituted by the 1995 Act, s. 95. The earlier development of s. 6 is discussed in McNeill, *Adoption of Children in Scotland* (2nd ed.), para. 8.05(k).
[57] *T, Petitioner*, 1996 S.C.L.R. 897.

promote the welfare of the child throughout his childhood [now 'throughout his life'[58]]. There can be no more fundamental principle in adoption cases than that it is the duty of the court to safeguard and promote the welfare of the child. Issues relating to the sexual orientation, life style, race, religion or other characteristics of the parties involved must of course be taken into account as part of the circumstances. But they cannot be allowed to prevail over what is in the best interests of the child. The suggestion that it is a fundamental objection to an adoption that the proposed adopter is living with another in a homosexual relationship finds no expression in the language of the statute, and in my opinion it conflicts with the rule which is set out in section 6 of the Act."

Lord Wylie agreed with the words of the Lord President, and Lord Weir was also of the view that there was no fundamental question of principle.

8.26   Welfare can be defined as "benefit",[59] and includes material and non-material benefit.[60] Clearly, if the child were to be integrated into a materially better household or were to become financially better off as a result of an adoption order, these would be benefits for the child. In *AB and CB v. X's Curator*[61] it was held that in determining whether consent (now agreement) had been unreasonably withheld the sheriff-substitute ought to have taken into account all the circumstances of the case, including *inter alia* the welfare of the child.[62]

Benefit could also arise as a result of an adoption order if it would bring to an end fostering whereby the petitioners would be exposed to the changes of view of the local authority and the applications of the natural parents or bring the child into a normal family,[63] or add another brother or sister to the household,[64] or even in some cases would maintain the status quo and avoid uprooting the child,[65] or give the child at the beginning of a school life a name which is the same as that of the persons who to all in the locality would appear to be the child's mother and father,[66] or remove the stigma of illegitimacy[67] (it is doubtful if any general rule to the contrary can be drawn from an earlier sheriff court case[68]), or to avoid having in the same family some natural children and

---

[58] 1978 Act, s. 6 as substituted by the 1995 Act, s. 95.

[59] *cf. Re D* [1959] 1 Q.B. 229; *Re A* [1963] 1 W.L.R. 231.

[60] *Re Adoption Application 41/61 (No. 2)* [1964] Ch. 48 at 53, *per* Wilberforce J. and approved in the House of Lords in *J v. C* [1970] A.C. 668 at 713; *A v. B and C*, 1977 S.C. 27. In an uncontested case an adoption order was granted in favour of the child's own natural parents: there the child had been legitimated by the subsequent marriage of his parents; but the petitioners had opinion of counsel that the child could not benefit under a trust unless he had the status of an adopted child: *E and E, Petitioners*, Sheriff Smith, Cupar Sh.Ct. (AC11/93), November 29, 1993, unreported.

[61] 1963 S.C. 124.

[62] *cf. AB v. CD*, 1970 S.C. 268.

[63] *H and H, Petitioners*, 1976 S.L.T. 80 at 83; *Re R* [1967] 1 W.L.R. 34.

[64] *Re Adoption Application 41/61 (No. 2)* [1964] Ch. 48; *Re P (E)* [1968] 1 W.L.R. 1913.

[65] *AB and CB v. X's Curator*, 1963 S.C. 124 at 136, *per* Lord President Clyde, but *cf. A v. B and C*, 1971 S.C. (H.L.) 129 at 142, *per* Lord Reid.

[66] *H and H, Petitioners*, 1976 S.L.T. 80 at 83.

[67] *Re P (E)* [1968] 1 W.L.R. 1913; *W, Petitioners* (1915) 61 Sh.Ct. Rep. 130.

[68] *CD, Petitioners*, 1963 S.L.T. (Sh.Ct.) 7.

some stepchildren or give the child British nationality if that were to promote the welfare of the child throughout his childhood,[69] but in a single-judge decision "an accommodation adoption" was refused where the purpose was to acquire British nationality.[70] It has been said that the court should not treat as decisive benefits which were in substance the advantages of establishing a right of abode in the United Kingdom and thus infringe the public policy of not allowing an application for an adoption to be substituted for Immigration Act criteria and procedures. That was a case where the child was eight days short of his eighteenth birthday. The new criterion in section 6 of the Adoption (Scotland) Act 1978—"throughout his life"—might not have altered the view of the court, because it was agreed that the judge was entitled to take into account the benefits accruing to the child after the age of 18.[71]

Sometimes it is not possible for all brothers and sisters to be adopted by the same petitioners, as where the children of the one family had been brought up in different foster homes and the separate petitioners met the particular needs of each child. A relevant circumstance would include the effect that the adoption of one child of a family would have on another child of the same family.[72] An order was made where the petitioners were the mother and stepfather of the child which had been in their care for eight years, but where all three were of low intelligence. The family was happy but the house was not clean. The curator *ad litem* and the local authority reported that the granting of the order would be for the welfare of the child.[73] In an unreported case where the male petitioner who was a British subject and the female petitioner who was a Venezuelan national were seeking to adopt a Venezuelan child who was liable to be deported and the parties had another child of their own who was a British subject, the court took the view that an adoption order would keep the family together in Britain. Differences in colour between the child, foster parents and the potential adopters were considered in decisions in Scotland and England.[74]

On the other hand, in *Re D*,[75] Sir George Baker said that all too often adoption was sought "by the mother to disguise from her new neighbours on remarriage that she had been involved in a failed marriage; it cannot by itself be a ground for adoption or generally in the interests of the children": the criterion is the welfare of the child not the welfare of the parent. The payment by an adoption agency of an allowance before and after adoption which, if made in terms of the statute, is lawful may on the one hand be to the material benefit of the child, but on the other hand

---

[69] *W (A Minor) (Adoption: non-patrial)* [1986] Fam. 54; *Re A (An Infant)* [1963] 1 W.L.R. 231.

[70] cf. *Re A* [1963] 1 W.L.R. 231; *Re R* [1967] 1 W.L.R. 34; *Re H (A Minor) (Adoption: non-patrial)* (1982) 12 Fam. Law 121; *Re W* [1985] 3 All E.R. 449; *Re H* [1981] *Adoption and Fostering* 62.

[71] *Re K (A Minor) (Adoption Order: nationality)* [1995] Fam. 38.

[72] *Re E (A Minor)* [1988] C.L.Y. 2304; *The Guardian*, July 30, 1988, C.A.; *Re C (A Minor) (Contact with Sibling)* [1987] 2 F.L.R. 383

[73] *L and L, Petitioners*, Edinburgh Sh.Ct. (E98/84), unreported.

[74] *H and H v. S and S*, Lord Marnoch, March 10, 1995, unreported; *Re P (A Minor)* [1990] F.L.R. 96.

[75] [1973] Fam. 209 at 216.

may call in question the motives of the petitioners in seeking to adopt the child, and may then or later colour the view which the child may have of the motives of the petitioners.[76] It was unreasonable of a father to withhold his agreement merely to maintain his right of custody or access.[77]

8.27   Although a petition by a single parent is clearly competent[78] it may present difficulties. For example, in one case, an adoptive father was charged with having sexual intercourse with his adopted daughter then aged about 14.[79] Clearly, the court cannot guard against every wrong-doing by an adoptive parent towards an adoptive child, any more than between a natural parent and a natural child, but the likelihood of such wrongdoing is less where there are two adoptive parents. Some circum-stances may favour a single-parent adoption, as where a couple intended to adopt a child but one of them died before the petition was presented or in the course of the proceedings[80]; similarly, where the single petitioner is a relative or friend who has for some time before presenting the petition taken over the child on the death or default of the natural parents. In cases like that, the child has usually been with the petitioner for a considerable time without any problems arising; and in most cases the child is likely to remain with the petitioner whether the petition is granted or not, as with an unmarried woman of 38 adopting a boy of 14 who had been in her care for over a year.[81] On the other hand, where the single petitioner has had custody of the unrelated child for a short period, the welfare of the child would be less easy to demonstrate. However, as always, the whole circumstances of each particular case must be taken into account.

8.28   Since 1986 the court had to consider the question of custody as a preferred alternative to adoption; but this provision has been significantly modified.[82]

(m) Insurance on the Life of the Child

8.29   What insurance (if any) has been effected on the life of the child. This provision is not designed to ensure that the child is adequately covered by insurance, because generally a life policy, apart from questions of collateral, does not benefit the person whose life is covered, but the beneficiary who may be the petitioner. The paragraph is designed rather to enable the court to assess the probable effect of a substantial sum assured on the life of the child on the motives of the petitioner who may be the beneficiary under the policy or the heir of the child in the event of the adoption order being granted. A now repealed provision dealt with one

---

[76] 1978 Act, s. 51(5); see also para. 8.22, above.

[77] *AB, Petitioners*, Second Division, June 12, 1985, unreported; *A v. B and C*, Second Division, November 26, 1980, unreported.

[78] 1978 Act, s. 15(1).

[79] *H.M. Advocate v. RM*, 1969, J.C. 52.

[80] *H, Petitioner*, 1960 S.L.T. (Sh.Ct.) 3; *J, Petitioner*, Edinburgh Sh.Ct., March 22, 1985, unreported.

[81] *M, Petitioner*, Edinburgh Sh.Ct., January 21, 1985, unreported.

[82] See para. 1.14(f), above and para. 8.46, below.

situation where such a case might arise: a person who maintained a protected child[83] was deemed for the purposes of the Life Assurance Act 1774 to have no interest in the life of the child.[84] Policies of insurance other than life policies, if they are of a significant amount or value, may be regarded as assets; if so, they would no doubt be dealt with as part of the right or interests in property which the child has in terms of rule 2.26(2)(h). The rights and liabilities under a policy in respect of funeral expenses effected by the natural parent are by virtue of an adoption order transferred to the adoptive parents.[85]

(n) (i) *Interim Orders*

Whether it is desirable for the welfare of the child that the court should **8.30** be asked to make an interim order. The court has power in an application for an adoption order where the requirements of an adoption order relating to parental consent and duration of the placement are satisfied:

> (a) to postpone the determination of the application; and
>
> (b) to make an interim order giving parental responsibilities and parental rights to the petitioners for a period not exceeding two years by way of a probationary period on such terms as regards the provision for the maintenance and education and supervision of the welfare of the child and otherwise as the court may think fit.[86]

If the court were, in the opinion of the curator *ad litem* or on **8.31** information acquired otherwise, of a mind to grant an interim order, it would no doubt indicate to the petitioners that such a disposal was in issue, and give the parties an opportunity to be heard on the matter at interview or otherwise. An interim order would be appropriate where, for example, the petitioners appeared to be rather immature; or where for some similar reason the passage of time might resolve a difficulty other than testing the suitability of the applicants as adopters, for example, to see whether the child's best interests would be best served by a transfer to the natural father.[87] In *S v. Huddersfield Borough Council*, Buckley L.J. was of the opinion[88] that "probationary" imports a process investigation and experiment in relation to all the circumstances relevant to the proposed adoption and not merely to the suitability of the applicants. The probationary period may be up to two years, or for less than two years with extensions up to two years in all. An interim order is not an adoption order, and does not affect the status of the child nor nationality nor succession. The interlocutor granting the interim order requires to give parental responsibilities and parental rights to the petitioners and if appropriate directs that they aliment the child or ensure that he attends a particular school.[89] Towards the end of the probationary

---

[83] See para. 5.12, above.
[84] 1978 Act, s. 37(2); 1995 Act, s. 105(5), Sched. 5.
[85] 1978 Act, s. 43.
[86] 1978 Act, s. 25.
[87] *S v. Huddersfield Borough Council* [1975] 1 Fam. 113.
[88] *ibid.* at 124.
[89] See Append. 2.5.

period there should be a supplementary report from the curator *ad litem* which should indicate whether there has been a change in the circumstances of the petitioners in general and whether the matter which occasioned the interim order has been resolved. If there is to be supervision by another body such as the local authority, there should be a report from that body also. Since there is a maximum time-limit for the duration of an interim order, the interlocutor which makes the order should specify the date before which the supplementary reports are to be available—in any event in good time before the termination of the order. As has been indicated, there were separate provisions for England and Scotland whereby the court in an adoption process may in lieu of granting an adoption order direct that the application be treated as if it had been made for the custody of the child.[90]

(ii) *Particular Terms and Conditions*

8.32   Whether it is desirable for the welfare of the child that in making an adoption order the court should be asked to impose particular terms or conditions or to require the petitioner to make any particular order for the child and (if so) what provision. Recent decisions in England and Scotland have resolved the apparent difference which had arisen between the two jurisdictions. In the House of Lords, in an English case, the competency of the use of access after making an adoption order was affirmed[91]; and, in that case, in relation to the position in Scotland, Lord Fraser of Tullybelton said:

> "Our decision in this appeal that access can be regulated by an order in the adoption process, without the need for separate wardship proceedings, may remove one of the possible procedural differences between England and Scotland which was in the minds of the learned Judges in *A.B. v. C.B.*, 1985 SLT 514."[92]

The case in the Lords was itself also considered in a later Scottish case in the Inner House.[93] There, both parents of the child suffered from Huntington's disease and there was a 75 per cent chance that the child would develop that condition. The petitioners were aware of the benefits to the child of continuing to have access to the natural parents. The court was of the opinion that the sheriff had been right to make a condition to the adoption order in relation to these matters; but the court modified the terms of the condition. To meet the situation that in normal circumstances an adoption order once granted would be sealed up for 100 years, the court gave its authority to the sheriff to issue an extract of the adoption order (with its condition of access) to the petitioners, the child and each of

---

[90] 1975 Act, ss. 37, 53.

[91] *Re C (A Minor) (Adoption Order: conditions)* [1989] A.C. 1.

[92] In that case Lord Hunter was at one with the other judges when he said: "I do not consider it necessary to decide in the present case whether it is competent to adject to an adoption order a condition governing access. I wish distinctly to reserve my opinion on this point since I am not at present satisfied that the English cases cited to us justify such a course, particularly in view of what appear to be differing procedures in the two jurisdictions and the legal nature and consequences of an adoption order."

[93] *B and B, Petitioners*, 1996 S.C.L.R. 874.

the respondents. "This will provide them with a basis upon which they can return to the court for any further orders regarding access which may be required."[94] In the opinion of the court, it was said in relation to enactments which were the same in both countries, "it is appropriate that the Scottish courts should continue to look for guidance to English authority where this is available, so long as this is not in conflict with the Scottish authorities".[95] Without specifically approbating the words of Lord Fraser, the court accepted the unambiguous words of the statute but with a significant qualification: in a question of inserting in an adoption order a condition relating to access it was said:

> "We wish to emphasise, before parting with this case, that we consider it to be an exceptional one and that we should not like it to be thought that we are offering any encouragement to the court as a matter of course to add conditions about matters arising after the making of the adoption order, especially if they may require variation by the court. The guiding principle is that adoption provides complete security to the child by making the child part of the adopting parents' family. Conditions expressed in favour of third parties, which might make it necessary for the court to become involved in the making of further orders with a view to the child's welfare, will not be appropriate except in the very rare cases where the child's welfare might be prejudiced if a condition to that effect were not to be made. As Lord Ackner observed in *Re C*, in normal circumstances it is desirable that there should be a complete break from the child's natural family. But each case must be considered on its own facts and we are in no doubt that the highly unusual background to this case makes such a condition desirable in order to provide support and guidance to all those involved".[96]

In relation to access (now contact), Lord Ackner distinguished between **8.33** access sought by natural parents which may be inconsistent with the complete break which adoption normally creates, and access by others— such as brothers and sisters—whose rights have not been affected by the granting of the adoption order.[97] There is no reason to suppose that these considerations would apply equally to terms and conditions other than a condition of contact.

However, in the earlier case of *G and G, Petitioners*[98] the making of a **8.34** condition to an adoption order was held to be competent, but in very special circumstances. In a sheriff court case there was an agreement for access between the petitioners and the natural parent in the form of a joint minute. The court took the view that it was not necessarily bound by the agreement and requested the curator *ad litem* to consider the new situation

---

[94] *ibid.* at 880; *cf. S (A Minor) (Adoption Order: conditions)* [1995] A.C. 1.

[95] *B and B, Petitioners*, 1996 S.C.L.R. 874 at 880, following dicta of Lord President Clyde in *AB and CB v. X's Curator*, 1963 S.C. 123 at 135; see para. 1.04, above.

[96] *B and B, Petitioners*, 1996 S.C.L.R. 874 at 884, quoting Lord Ackner in *Re C (A Minor) (Adoption Order: conditions)* [1989] A.C. 1 at 17–18; *cf. FB and AB v. AC*, Second Division, July 10, 1998, unreported.

[97] *Re C (A Minor) (Adoption Order: conditions)* [1989] A.C. 1.

[98] First Division, July 19, 1985, unreported.

and report on the welfare of the child.[99] Thereafter, the court decided to interpone authority to the joint minute. Further, not only would the enforcement of any conditions be difficult—whether by proceedings for breach of an undertaking given by the petitioners in court, or by breach of caution—but the imposition of such sanctions could very well be detrimental to the family in which the child is. There is nothing in the legislation providing for any sanction for the enforcement of a condition attached to an adoption order.[1] Formerly, a parent could make the giving of his consent to the making of an adoption order conditional on the religious persuasion in which the child was to be brought up[2]: now, all that is required is that an adoption agency (but not the court) must in placing a child for adoption have regard (so far as is practicable) to any wishes of the child's parents and guardians as to the religious upbringing of the child,[3] but both the court and the adoption agency must have regard as far as practicable to the religious persuasion of the child.[4] In view of the terms of the statute—an adoption order may contain such terms and conditions as the court thinks fit[5]—it would be competent to impose a condition on the petitioners that the child be brought up in a particular religious persuasion.[6] Other conditions which might reasonably be imposed could include one that the child attend a particular school so that his education is not interrupted, or that he undergo necessary medical treatment. In a case where the petitioners were grandparents of the child whose inferior prospects of survival might prejudice the child financially, the sheriff granted the order subject to the undertaking of the natural father to pay a weekly sum into the hands of the children's officer for disbursement to the child in the event of need.[7] In cases where such conditions are imposed they require to be expressed in the order.

(o) Petitioners not Ordinarily Resident in the United Kingdom

8.35   If the petitioner is not ordinarily resident in the United Kingdom, whether a report has been obtained on the applicant's home and living conditions from a suitable agency in the country in which he is ordinarily resident. The former express provisions allowing adoption by persons who are not ordinarily resident in Great Britain[8] have been repealed and the requirements are now governed by the generality of section 13 of the 1978 Act whereby the child must have his home with the petitioners for one of three specified periods.[9] The place of the home is restricted by the

---

[99] Glasgow Sh.Ct., April 15, 1983, unreported.

[1] *Re G (TJ)* [1963] 2 Q.B. 73, a decision of the Court of Appeal under the 1958 Act.

[2] 1958 Act, s. 4(2); but this provision was repealed and has not been re-enacted in the 1975 Act.

[3] 1978 Act, s. 7.

[4] 1978 Act, s. 6(1)(b)(ii) as substituted by the 1995 Act, s. 95; see para. 8.38, below.

[5] 1978 Act, s. 12(6).

[6] See para. 8.32, above. As to adoption and religious persuasion, see para. 8.38, below.

[7] *GD, Petitioners*, 1950 S.L.T. (Sh.Ct.) 34.

[8] 1958 Act, s. 12(3); *Re W* [1962] Ch. 918. *Cf.* J. F. Josling and Allan Levy, *Adoption of Children* (10th ed.), p. 36. *Re Adoption Application AA, 121/1984* [1985] 7 C.L. 505a.

[9] See paras 3.05, 8.18, above.

requirement that the local authority (which includes English local authorities[10]) in a placement not by an adoption agency and the adoption agency in a non-relative adoption must be afforded sufficient opportunity to see the child with the petitioners together in the home environment.[11] It is for the court to decide if the local authority has had sufficient opportunity to see the child with the petitioners together in the home environment. In one exceptional case the petitioners' family was resident in the area of the local authority. The male petitioner, who was on military service in Germany and about to be posted to the Falkland Islands, was due to be in residence for certain periods during the three months before the granting of the petition. The petitioners' solicitors wrote and telephoned repeatedly to the appropriate social work office of the local authority in whose area the family had its home, telling them of these dates. The local authority did not acknowledge the letters and did not approach the family or the court. The court was satisfied that sufficient opportunities had been afforded to the local authority.[12]

It may be that in similar situations as, for example, where the petitioners had satisfied the requirements of domicile,[13] where the family has its home within a local authority area in Scotland, where the child is in the home environment with the petitioners, but the family is temporarily physically abroad in military, civil or commercial service or for pleasure, that the requirements of the legislation can still be satisfied by the petitioners. Clearly, the domicile of the petitioners will not be affected by temporary absence abroad. The child would need to be in Scotland at the time of presenting the petition. The child must have his home with the petitioners or one of them for, in most cases, at least 13 weeks,[14] but there is no requirement in that section that the care and possession need be in Scotland. In cases where the petitioner is a relative of the child or the child has been with the petitioners for at least 12 months, intimation must be given by the petitioners to the local authority within whose area they have their home of their intention to apply for an adoption order[15]: but the petitioners do not need to be in Scotland to do that, and in many cases it is done by solicitors. In terms of the legislation the local authority or the adoption agency must investigate and report to the court on the adoption. Both these bodies are juristic persons who can only do such acts through their servants or agents. The court will no doubt be satisfied that these bodies have had sufficient opportunities to see the child with the petitioners in their home environment if they entrust that aspect of the case to an agent such as a consular official, local social worker, or solicitor or military welfare officer.[16] Any matters required to be reported upon in terms of section 22 or 23 of the 1978 Act can also be dealt with by that agent; and in so far as the inquiry relates to the petitioners' home in Scotland, the local authority or adoption agency can investigate and

---

[10] 1978 Act, s. 65(1).
[11] 1978 Act, s. 13(3).
[12] *O and O, Petitioners*, Edinburgh Sh.Ct. (E90/84), January 1985, unreported.
[13] 1978 Act, ss. 14(2) and 15(2); see para. 2.04, above.
[14] 1978 Act, s. 13(1).
[15] 1978 Act, s. 22.
[16] 1978 Act, s. 13(3).

report in the normal way. Similarly, the report of the curator *ad litem* and, where appropriate, the reporting officer, would reflect the absence abroad of the family. If the court is not satisfied that the facts stated in the petition are supported by the documents or the reports of the curator *ad litem* and the reporting officer, it may make further inquiry by way of production of further documents or by hearing oral evidence.[17] If the child is not in the United Kingdom when the application is made, only the Court of Session has jurisdiction.[18]

8.36   If the petitioner is obviously ordinarily resident in the United Kingdom, the curator *ad litem* should merely state that fact: normally, this will be self-evident and will be stated in the petition. If the facts as seen by the curator *ad litem* appear to be otherwise, he will report that to the court which will decide on the question of residence. Where a foreign report is required, no doubt it can be provided by someone who is in use to provide such reports in that country or in the case of service personnel, someone with legal training.

(p) Petitioners' Reasons for Adopting[19]

8.37   Why the petitioner wishes to adopt the child. The information gleaned under this head will enable the court to learn something of the character of the petitioners and judge how responsibly they are approaching the problem of coping with a new child in the household. The usual reasons why petitioners wish to adopt are that they are unable to have children of their own either at all or without danger to the health of the female petitioner, that they wish to give the child the security of a family home, that they wish to add to their existing family, or that in the case of a mother adopting her own child on marriage or remarriage to the male petitioner the petitioners wish to give legal authority to a *de facto* situation which may have subsisted for years and which often becomes pressing when the child is about to go to school with a surname which is different from that of the male petitioner.[20] The motives of the petitioners might be affected by the receipt or the prospect of an allowance from an adoption agency under the 1978 Act.[21]

(q) Religious Persuasion (if any) of the Petitioners: Religious Persuasion (if any), Racial Origin and Cultural and Linguistic Background of the Child

8.38   The petitioner's religious persuasion, if any. Religion emerges in at least three ways in adoption law.

8.39   (i) Until 1975 the consent of any person to the making of an adoption order could be given subject to conditions with respect to the religious

---

[17] A.S. 1997, r. 2.11(4) (freeing) and r. 2.28(6) (adoption) (RCS, r. 67.6).
[18] 1978 Act, s. 56(3).
[19] The additional matters for investigation now contained in the present paragraphs (p), (q), (r) and (s) were introduced in 1966.
[20] *cf. H and H, Petitioners*, 1976 S.L.T. 80 at 83.
[21] See para. 8.19, above.

persuasion in which the child was proposed to be brought up.[22] Although
that power was repealed in the current legislation, as has been noted, it
would appear to be still competent for the court to impose a condition in the
adoption order that the child be brought up in a particular persuasion
under the general power to make such terms and conditions as it thinks fit.[23]

(ii) There is a statutory obligation imposed on an adoption agency, in **8.40**
placing a child for adoption to have regard (so far as practicable) to any
wishes of the child's parents and guardians as to the religious upbringing
of the child.[24] If the wishes of the parents or guardians were also before the
court, no doubt it would take them into account.

(iii) The religious persuasion and also the racial origin and cultural and **8.41**
linguistic background of the child is governed by the Adoption (Scotland)
Act 1978.[25] Information on the matter of religion will enable the court to
know whether there is likely to be a difference between the spouses on
these matters which might affect the welfare of the child. Most reports not
only state the religious persuasion of the petitioners but also the faith in
which the child is to be brought up. In *H and H, Petitioners*[26] the sheriff
granted an adoption order where Jewish petitioners sought to adopt a
Christian child and bring him up in the Jewish faith. In the 1970s at least
two other similar unreported cases were decided in the same way, and with
the greater population of non-Christian faiths now resident in Britain such
adoptions have become more common.

(iv) In terms of the rule, the curator *ad litem* is directed to establish the **8.42**
"racial origin and cultural and linguistic background of the child". These
attributes are not defined but the rules envisage that such a grouping of
people such as a race does exist, and that every child must possess a racial
origin. Presumably, the curator *ad litem* would have to come to a
conclusion as to the meaning of these terms; for example, whether he
is to regard as races the Scots, the English, the Welsh and the Irish. It
appears that if he did so, he would have satisfied the requirement
expressed in the rule if he merely reported (from his interview with the
family) that, for example, the child was born in Scotland of Scottish
parents, that he spoke English, that he is regarded by himself and his
parents as Scottish in race and cultural and linguistic background.
Perhaps race is intended to be applied to larger groups of peoples, such
as Asians, Africans and Europeans. No doubt, the curator *ad litem* would
have to ask similar questions about their racial origins and cultural and
linguistic background. In a case in the Inner House, also decided before
this provisions had come into force, it was said:

"Issues relating to the sexual orientation, lifestyle, race, religion or
other characteristics of the parties involved must of course be taken

[22] 1958 Act, s. 4(2) repealed by the 1975 Act, s. 108(1)(b) and Sched. 4, Pt IV.
[23] 1978 Act, s. 12(6); see para. 8.32, above.
[24] 1978 Act, s. 7.
[25] 1978 Act, s. 6(1)(b)(ii) as substituted by the 1995 Act, s. 95.
[26] 1949 S.L.T. (Sh.Ct.) 68.

into account as part of the circumstances. But they cannot be allowed to prevail over what is in the best interests of the child."[27]

(r) Age Difference between Petitioners and Child

8.43   The considerations arising from the difference in age between the petitioner and the child if such difference is greater or less than the normal difference in age between parents and their children. As has been indicated a petitioner must have attained the age of 21 or 18 if the petitioner is a parent of the child.[28] The present paragraph is directed to the situation where the petitioner may be too close in age to the child, or is too old to be a parent. Under adoption legislation now repealed, the applicant had to be, generally, at least 21 years older than the child.[29] Accordingly, the curator *ad litem* should deal with the matter by stating the ages of the petitioners and the child and whether it appears that there are any circumstances in that regard which would qualify the ability of the petitioners to look after the child properly, such as the fact that the character of the petitioner belies his or her age. Clearly, the court would be unlikely to consider granting an adoption order where the petitioners and the child were each anywhere near the statutory limits applying to them, namely, a 21-year-old petitioner and a 17-year-old child—a situation which could arise in the adoption of a stranger child. Where the petitioner is adopting her own child, it would be very difficult to envisage a situation where the court would regard the difference in ages between the petitioner and the child as being against the welfare of the child. If the suggestion is that the petitioner is too old, the court would wish to have the views of the curator *ad litem* on that aspect of the case and if he feels that it has a bearing on the welfare of the child, as where the petitioner is too old to cope with the child.

8.44   In one opposed sheriff court case the male petitioner was 63 years old and the child was four[30]; and in a recent English case the grandparents were in their middle 60s and the child was seven.[31] In both cases the adoption order was made.

(s) Suitability of the Petitioners

8.45   Such other matters, including an assessment of the petitioner's personality and, where appropriate, that of the child, as having a bearing on the mutual suitability of the petitioner and the child which affect the suitability of the petitioners and the child for the relationship created by adoption, and affect the ability of the petitioner to bring up the child. These matters are largely self-explanatory and the content and detail of the report will be governed by the circumstances of the case. Accordingly little guidance can be given. The curator *ad litem* is in a particularly

---

[27] *H and H v. S and S*, Lord Marnoch, March 10, 1995, unreported; *Re P (A Minor)* [1990] 1 F.L.R. 96.

[28] See para. 2.03, above.

[29] 1930 Act, s. 2(1)(b).

[30] *TF and HF, Petitioners*, 1949 S.L.T. (Sh.Ct.) 48.

[31] *Re W* [1980] Fam. 190; [1981] C.L.Y. 1751.

advantageous position in that he sees the family in its natural setting and is able to give an assessment of these matters which can seldom be achieved in the more anxious circumstances of a hearing or a proof before a judge.

(t) Whether to Make the Order or not[32]

Whether it would be better for the child that the court should make the **8.46** order than it should not. The present position is that in considering whether to make an adoption order under section 18(1), the court must have regard to the welfare of the child concerned as its paramount consideration and must not make the order in question unless it considers that it would be better for the child that it should do so than it should not.[33] The former provisions had a greater bias in favour of custody (now residence) rather than adoption.[34] In a case under the pre-existing provisions, it was held that if the choice between adoption or custody was evenly balanced, the court could not be satisfied that it would be better for the child's welfare to make a custodianship order.[35] Now, the curator *ad litem* should report on the possible disposals, adoption under section 6 of the Adoption (Scotland) Act 1978 or some other disposal (or even none) under section 11(7) of the Children (Scotland) Act 1995, but on substantially the same criterion, namely, that the welfare of the child is the paramount consideration.

> "The minimum intervention principle is of little strength in adoption and cannot be used to justify keeping the child in long-term fostering rather than being adopted, for the security given by the latter will always be a strong consideration and can easily outweigh the minimum intervention principle (see *C (A Minor) (Adoption Conditions), Re* [1998] A.C. 1 at 17 *per* Lord Ackner)."[36]

(u) Wishes of the Child to Express a View

Ascertain from the child whether he wishes to express a view and, where **8.47** the child wishes to express a view, ascertain that view. The corresponding paragraph in the 1984 Regulations was itself a new paragraph—although similar provisions have existed in previous legislation.[37] The 1995 rule, which follows upon the new formula introduced into the 1978 Act by the 1995 Act, provides that the court:

> "(a) shall have regard to all the circumstances, but shall regard the need to safeguard and promote the welfare of the child concerned throughout his life as the paramount consideration and shall have

---

[32] This provision in its present form was introduced in 1997 (A.S. 1997, r. 2.26(2)(t)): it is not based on the new s. 6A of the 1978 Act (introduced by the 1995 Act, s. 96) which only applies to adoption agencies. For residence (formerly custody) in adoption procedure, see para. 1.16, above.

[33] 1978 Act, s. 24(3).

[34] 1975 Act, s. 37 in England and Wales (repealed by the Children Act 1989) and s. 53(1) in Scotland (repealed by the 1995 Act; but that Act adds a new s. 51(5) which appears to refer to ss. 52 and 53 "of this Act").

[35] *Re LW (A Minor) (Adoption or Custodianship)* [1991] F.C.R. 867.

[36] Children (Scotland) Act 1995, annotated by K. McK. Norrie, *Green's Annotated Statutes* (1995), para. 36-209.

[37] Such as the Adoption of Children (Scotland) Act 1930, s. 3(b).

regard so far as practicable to his views (if he wishes to express them) taking into account his age and maturity".[38]

8.48   Formerly, the wishes and feelings of the child were those "regarding the decision", that is, the decision relating to the adoption of the child[39]; now, under the 1995 Act, the views of the child are not so qualified at all. But it is respectfully suggested that the better view is that "the new section 6(1) effects no substantive change, but the wording has been altered to consist with that used in ss. 6 and 16(2) of the present Act which themselves are designed to ensure that Scots law consists in this regard with Art. 12 of the UN Convention on the Rights of the Child".[40]

8.49   There are three situations in which the views of the child may be considered, according to his age and maturity:

> (i) if he has no understanding of these matters, the curator *ad litem* need only report that fact and the reason for the lack of understanding, such as non-age or mental inadequacy;
> (ii) if the child has sufficient understanding—and it is presumed that a child of 12 years or more shall be of sufficient age and maturity to form such a view[41]—the report should state what his views are; and
> (iii) if the child is of or over the age of 12, he must consent in writing[42] to the making of the adoption order, except that where the court is satisfied that the minor is incapable of giving his consent, when it may dispense with that consent. Otherwise, the adoption order cannot be made.[43] If a child has consented to the making of a freeing order, he still has to consent to the making of any subsequent adoption order. In England and Wales the consent of the child is not required.[44]

8.50   These provisions may raise difficult questions if the child has not been informed that he is about to be adopted by persons whom he has taken to be his natural parents, and if the petitioners are unwilling to let the child know the true position. It is not impracticable to take the child's views merely because it is inconvenient or unwelcome to the petitioners.[45] In relation to the manner of dealing with the wishes of the child it was said in *Re G (TJ)*:

---

[38] 1978 Act, s. 6 amended by the 1995 Act, s. 95.

[39] 1978 Act as unamended by the 1995 Act, s. 95.

[40] Children (Scotland) Act 1995, annotated by K. McK. Norrie, *Green's Annotated Statutes* (1995), para. 36-194, note to the 1995 Act, Sched. 2, para. 16.

[41] 1978 Act, s. 6(2).

[42] 1978 Act, s. 12(8) as substituted, from September 25, 1991, by the Age of Legal Capacity (Scotland) Act 1991, ss. 2(3) and 11(2).

[43] A.S. 1997, r. 2.23(1) (adoption) and r. 2.6(1) (freeing).

[44] 1978 Act, s. 12(8) (adoption) and s. 18(8) (freeing). Although in England and Wales the agreement of the child is not necessary, it is unlikely that if the child did not agree the order would be granted.

[45] *C and C, Petitioners*, Edinburgh Sh.Ct. (E5/85), March 9, 1985, unreported. A contrary view was expressed in a later case, *C, Petitioners*, 1993 S.C.L.R. 14, Sheriff Gow, Ayr Sh.Ct.: although the child was only six and may not have been of sufficient "age and understanding", that fact appears not to have been assessed and reported upon by the curator *ad litem*.

"The child was aged 12 at the time; and in such a case I think that, subject to what follows, the judge should satisfy himself about the child's understanding by speaking to the child himself. No doubt in most cases this would be best done in private. But where, as here, he has a very recent report by the child welfare officer of the local authority which tells him, inter alia, what the child's wishes are, I see no reason why the judge should not accept that report if he thinks it right to do so. If the report were some months old—as I gather it could be in some cases—he should, and I have no doubt would, verify for himself that the child's wishes remained the same, since the section does require, in my opinion, the ascertainment of those wishes as at the time of the hearing or near enough to that time to make no difference."[46]

The curator *ad litem* should in advance of visiting the home of the **8.51** petitioners make inquiries of the petitioners or their solicitors about the state of knowledge of the child and the attitude of the petitioners about the best time and the most propitious circumstances for broaching the matter with the child. Petitioners who are anxious about this aspect of the investigations of the curator *ad litem* can be reminded that if the child is not told not only will it be impossible in the case of a child of sufficient understanding for the adoption to be granted, but that it is almost inevitable that the child will be told of his status by third parties, perhaps in an undesirable way, and that the child will be entitled as of right to see the adoption process at the age of 16 and he will thereby see that he is adopted and learn the identity of his natural parents if they appear in the process. In *A, Petitioner*[47] in the course of an adoption, the court directed that a 19-year-old child who was the subject of an adoption process should be told the circumstances of his birth, his consent only being valid if given in the full knowledge of his parentage. If a child is not of the required age and maturity this fact should be reported on and the petitioners should be asked what their intentions are about informing the child later. Their refusal to do so is not decisive: the court must assess the advantages of adoption.[48] If they are unwilling to agree to inform the child—an attitude which sometimes arises out of a fear of hurting the child or, but less so nowadays, the unwillingness to reveal to the child that he was born out of wedlock—it may be appropriate for the sheriff to interview the petitioners on this matter with a view to getting the petitioners to undertake that they will inform the child that he is adopted, as soon as a convenient opportunity presents itself. In most cases it is desirable to inform the child as early as possible, so that when the emotional maturity of the child grows, the fact of the adoption will have little significance to him. Although the present provisions do not innovate on the old law in matters of substance, there has been a significant alteration in the procedure for bringing the views of the child to the sheriff. Similar rules apply

---

[46] [1963] 2 Q.B. 73 at 97, *per* Donovan L.J.
[47] 1936 S.C. 255.
[48] *Re S (A Minor) (Adoption by Step-parent)* [1988] 1 F.L.R. 418.

in freeing a child for adoption,[49] and also in procedures other than adoption which deal with children.[50]

8.52	The new rules allow for the views of the child to be conveyed to the sheriff alone in confidence.[51] Generally, where the child has indicated his wish to express his views, the sheriff may order such procedural steps to be taken as he considers appropriate to ascertain the views of the child. When the child has indicated his wish to express his views, the sheriff may not make an order for adoption unless an opportunity has been given for the views of the child to be obtained or heard. It is thought that the wish of the child would normally be expressed when the curator *ad litem* was conducting his investigations. But the wish of the child may also be expressed in other ways: the child or the parties may raise the wish of the child with the sheriff clerk or the sheriff. There are powers to make rules permitting a person who is not an advocate or a solicitor and who is not represented by an advocate or a solicitor to transmit, whether orally or in writing, the views of the child to the sheriff.[52] Howsoever the views of the child have been conveyed, if the views have been recorded in writing under this procedure or in the report of the curator *ad litem*,[53] the sheriff may direct that the written record shall be

(a) sealed in an envelope marked "Views of the child—confidential";
(b) be available to a sheriff only;
(c) not be opened by any person other than a sheriff; and
(d) not form a borrowable part of the process.[54]

8.53	It is difficult to conceive a situation where this very exceptional procedure should be adopted. It is expressly optional. If it were to be adopted, the effect would be to exclude from the parties' consideration material on which the court may make its decision without the parties having an opportunity to challenge the information which may be expressed in the views of the child. This may create difficulty since the paramount consideration for the court is the welfare of the child[55] and the court is bound to consider the interest and claims of the original parents, the adoptive parents and the child.[56] It is difficult to see how the court can make its decision to any extent on this information. The court could not mention it in its interlocutor, and if the parties were considering an appeal, they would be unable to learn the basis of the decision.

---

[49] A.S. 1997, rr. 2.9 and 2.17. There are presently no corresponding Rules of Court dealing with these matters.

[50] A.S. 1997, rr. 2.41 and 3.5.

[51] In a case decided before these provisions were in force, the court held that a sheriff was not in error in declining to interview a child of eight himself: *AB and CD v. EF*, June 5, 1991 *Adoption and Fostering*, Vol. 15, No. 4, p. 125.

[52] Sheriff Courts (Scotland) Act 1971, s. 32(1)(j) and Court of Session Act 1988, s. 5(ee): these powers were introduced by the 1995 Act, s. 105(3) and Sched. 4, paras 18, 45.

[53] A.S. 1997, r. 2.27(2).

[54] Since the written record remains part of the process, albeit not borrowable, it will form part of the process to be sealed up after the order has been granted: A.S. 1997, r. 2.33 (RCS, r. 67.32(2)).

[55] 1978 Act, s. 6.

[56] *A v. B and C*, 1971 S.C. (H.L.) 129 at 141, *per* Lord Reid.

Under the previous law, the curator *ad litem* reported to the court on **8.54**
all matters specified in the rules[57]; the current rules require the curator
ad litem to report similarly on all matters, except where the child
wishes to express a view. In relation to the wishes of the child there
appear to be the following possible courses open to the curator *ad
litem*:

> (a) the curator *ad litem* may ascertain that the child does not
> wish to express a view: he would report that fact as part of his
> report;
> (b) the curator *ad litem* may ascertain that the child does wish to
> express a view: he would ascertain that view; and
>> (i) if he considers it appropriate, convey that view to the sheriff
>> orally and not in his report; or
>> (ii) include it in his report in the normal way, and the sheriff
>> may or may not decide to impose the rules of confidentiality set
>> forth in rule 2.27[58];
> (c) it is possible that the child may wish to express a view,
> notwithstanding what the curator *ad litem* has reported on: the
> sheriff may use the curator *ad litem* as the person to ascertain the
> child's views.[59]

Quite apart from those provisions, the sheriff may, after considering the **8.55**
reports, feel that he should interview the child himself. However, this is
quite rare and in any event the sheriff would have to keep in mind the age
and understanding of the child before adopting such a course. A child may
instruct his own legal representative.[60]

(v) Report by Adoption Agency or Local Authority

Since there is a statutory obligation on the adoption agency[61] or the **8.56**
local authority[62] to report to the court on the suitability of the parents and
the welfare of the child, it seems appropriate that the curator *ad litem*
should go beyond the sundry paragraphs which are prescribed in the rules,
and report on whether he has been able to see the appropriate report and
to say whether he has any comments on it.

Modification in Report of Curator *ad Litem* in other Applications

Modification of the report of the curator *ad litem* is necessary in **8.57**
petitions other than the usual petition for adoption.

(a) In a petition to adopt a child abroad, the report should, in addition, **8.58**
deal with the special averments in the petition relating to the foreign

---

[57] A.S. (Adoption of Children) 1984 (S.I. 1984 No. 1013), para. 21(2).
[58] A.S. 1997, r. 2.27.
[59] *AB and CB v. DE*, 1990 S.C.L.R. 809; *AB and CD v. EF*, Inner House, June 5, 1991,
unreported; (1991) *Adoption & Fostering*, Vol. 15, No. 4, p. 124.
[60] Age of Legal Capacity (Scotland) Act, s. 2(4A).
[61] 1978 Act, s. 23.
[62] 1978 Act, s. 22.

element, such as the non-British domicile of the petitioners[63] and the law of the country in which it is intended to adopt the child.[64]

8.59   (b) In a petition for a Convention adoption order, the report should deal with the additional matters which relate principally to the foreign elements and which are specified in the rules.[65]

8.60   (c) In a petition for freeing a child for adoption, the report of the curator *ad litem* deals with more limited matters. The report should deal with[66]:

    (i)   the welfare of the child in terms of section 6 of the Adoption (Scotland) Act 1978;
    (ii) the truth of the facts stated in the petition;
    (iii) the consent of any minor child;
    (iv) the views (if any) of the child;
    (v) whether the freeing would promote the well-being of the child;
    (vi) whether it is better to make the order than not; and
    (vii) the current circumstances and care of the child.

In the Court of Session, the reporting officer also has to consider why the application is for a freeing order and not a full adoption order.[67]

8.61   (d) In a motion (or, in the Court of Session, a note), to revoke an order freeing a child for adoption there need only be the report of the curator *ad litem* dealing with the very limited matters of:

    (i)   the facts stated in the minute;
    (ii) the circumstances and care of the child with regard to his welfare; and
    (iii) the views (if any) of the child.[68]

Report of the Reporting Officer

8.62   The reporting officer may be appointed before the petition is presented in a petition to free a child for adoption or a petition for adoption in the sheriff court, and in a petition to free a child for adoption, or a petition for adoption in the Court of Session.[69]

8.63   In sheriff court petitions for adoption, the reporting officer must carry out the specified duties and report thereon.[70] These proceed on the basis that there has been no earlier order freeing the child for adoption, and

---

[63] 1978 Act, s. 49(1).
[64] A.S. 1997, r. 2.22 and Form 12 (RCS, r. 67.27).
[65] RCS, r. 67.35.
[66] A.S. 1997, r. 2.9(2)(a)–(g); sub-paras (d) and (f) were introduced by the 1997 Rules (RCS, r. 67.11(2), where the duties of the reporting officer are more limited.
[67] RCS, r. 67.11(2)(p).
[68] A.S. 1997, r. 2.16; sub-para. (c) was introduced by the 1997 Rules (RCS, r. 67.17(4), where the matters are set forth in greater detail, but are substantially to the same effect.
[69] 1978 Act, s. 58(3); A.S. 1997, rr. 2.7(3)2 and 25(4) (RCS, rr. 67.10(3) and 67.23(3)).
[70] A.S. 1997, r. 2.26(1) (RCS, r. 67.11).

accordingly the agreement of the natural parents is still outstanding. The statute provides that for the purpose of any application for an adoption order rules shall provide for the appointment in such cases as are prescribed of a reporting officer. In petitions for adoption where the child is free for adoption, a reporting officer shall not be appointed,[71] and there is no requirement in that case that there should be a hearing.[72] The fact that the child has already been freed for adoption may be vouched by production of an extract of an order freeing the child for adoption and the petitioner can refer to the date of the order and the name of the court which granted the order. In cases where the child has not been freed for adoption, if the parent does not co-operate with the reporting officer, he should report that fact to the court, and if the court is satisfied that all reasonable steps have been taken, it can proceed on that information. Such an uncooperative parent who has washed his hands of the child cannot thereby frustrate the whole process by declining to have anything to do with it.[73] The normal duties which the reporting officer has to carry out and report on are as follows.

(a) To witness any agreement executed by a parent or guardian (but not **8.64** the consent of a child) within the United Kingdom in a sheriff court case, and in Scotland only in a Court of Session case.[74] The reporting officer should lodge the agreement in process. Clearly, if the person whose agreement is required refuses to execute the agreement, or refuses to agree in any circumstances or cannot be found, the reporting officer should report that fact and state what efforts he has been able to take to ascertain the whereabouts of the parent. The style of report envisages that the parent will agree: there is no style for a parent not agreeing. Where the parent is outwith the United Kingdom, the agreement may be executed according to the statutory provisions which have already been dealt with.[75]

(b) To ascertain that each parent or guardian whose agreement is **8.65** required or may be dispensed with understands the effect of the adoption. The reporting officer should ascertain that that understanding is the correct one, namely that the effect of an adoption order would be to deprive the parent or guardian permanently of his parental rights and duties.[76]

(c) Where a parent or guardian whose agreement is required, or may **8.66** be dispensed with, can be found, to ascertain whether alternatives to

---

[71] A.S. 1997, r. 2.25(2): where the words "save for the purposes specified in rule 2.26(1)(a)" have been inserted in error.

[72] *ibid.* These additional words do not make sense, because by definition, the agreement of parents has already been disposed of in the earlier freeing proceedings, and there would be nothing further for a reporting officer to report on.

[73] 1978 Act, s. 59(2); A.S. 1997, r. 2.28(3) (RCS, r. 67.25 which envisages a hearing on receipt of the reports: but if reports have not been required under RCS, r. 67.23(1)(b) or (c), presumably there will be no need for a hearing, as s. 59(2) provides).

[74] A.S. 1997, r. 2.26(1)(a) and Form 13 (RCS, r. 67.24(1)(c) and Form 67.5-A).

[75] See para. 5.24, above.

[76] A.S. 1997, r. 2.26(1)(b) (RCS, r. 67.24(1)(f)).

adoption have been discussed with him. The main obvious alternative to adoption is residence (formerly custody). However, in most cases that alternative is not a realistic alternative because, for example, the parent has not kept up with the child while the child was with the adoption agency, or in the care of the local authority by virtue of an assumption of parental rights, or in the care of an adoption agency by virtue of an order freeing the child for adoption or in the care of the mother and her new husband who are the petitioners.[77]

8.67   (d) To ascertain whether there is any person other than those mentioned in the petition upon whom notice of the petition should be served.[78] This paragraph corresponds to the phrase in the crave of the petition, "and to order notice of this petition to be served on such persons, if any, as the court may think proper".[79] The court must also deal with intimation of a diet of hearing.[80] It is rare that there are any such persons. Where a parent who hitherto could not be found, or was thought to be dead or had been thought not to be a parent, emerged as a person whose agreement is required that would be a case for taking his agreement but hardly a case for giving him notice of the petition.

      (e) To ascertain whether the child is the subject of a supervision requirement.[81]

8.68   (f) To confirm that each parent or guardian whose agreement is required understands that he may withdraw his agreement at any time before the order is granted.[82]

Modifications in the Report of Reporting Officer in other Applications

8.69   In the case of a petition to free a child for adoption the report of the reporting officer should deal with (1) the consent of each parent or guardian to the making of the application for the order, and (2) their agreement to the making of an adoption order and the consequences of a freeing order,[83] and also deal with the four other matters which arise in a petition to free a child:

      (i) that the parent may withdraw his agreement at any time before the freeing order is made[84];
      (ii) that the parent may seek revocation of any order[85];
      (iii) that the parent may declare that he would prefer not to be involved in future questions concerning the adoption of the child[86]; and

---

[77] A.S. 1997, r. 2.26(1)(c) (RCS, r. 67.24(1)(i)).
[78] A.S. 1997, r. 2.26(1)(d) (RCS, r. 67.24(1)(g)).
[79] A.S. 1997, Form 11 (RCS, Form 67.22).
[80] See para. 5.34, above.
[81] A.S. 1997, r. 2.26(1)(e), a new provision introduced by the 1997 Rules.
[82] A.S. 1997, r. 2.26(1)(f) (RCS, r. 67.24(1)(j)).
[83] A.S. 1997, r. 2.8(1)(a)–(d) and (g) (RCS, r. 67.11(1)(c) and (d)).
[84] A.S. 1997, r. 2.8(1)(h) (RCS, r. 67.11(1)(s)).
[85] A.S. 1997, r. 2.8(1)(i) (RCS, r. 67.11(1)(n)).
[86] A.S. 1997, r. 2.8(1)(j) (RCS, r. 67.11(1)(o)).

(iv) in the case of a child whose father was not married to the mother the likelihood of any person claiming to be the father of the child

(1) applying for or being refused an order under section 11 of the 1995 Act (court orders relating to parental responsibilities); or

(2) entering into an agreement in terms of section 4(1) of the 1995 Act (agreement as to parental responsibilities).[87]

Reports under Sections 22 and 23

In cases where there is no dispute, these reports would indicate whether **8.70** from the point of view of the local authority or the adoption agency there was anything amiss. In adoption agency cases, the adoption agency will already know all about the case; and in most of the other cases the petitioner will be a mother adopting her own child. The report should begin with the name and designation of the author of the report, and should state that the source of the information is a visit to the home of the petitioners, or as the case may be. By statute the matters which require to be reported upon are:

(a) the suitability of the petitioners. The report should outline the occupations, the house and the members of the household, as well as the emotional and material ability of the petitioners to look after the child;

(b) any other matters relevant to the operation of section 6, which relates to the welfare of the child. The report should state that either the circumstances which have been noted make clear that the granting of the order is likely to safeguard and promote the welfare of the child throughout his life; or that it is not, for the reasons specified, for example, the character of the petitioners or the wishes of the child;

(c) in the case of a placement other than by an adoption agency, whether the child has been placed contrary to section 11, which relates to illegal placements. The report need only say that in the circumstances, for example, that the petitioner is a relative of the child, or that the child was placed by an adoption agency, or that the original placement of the child was for fostering and not for adoption and, accordingly, there has been no breach of section 11; or, there has or appears to have been a breach of section 11, in respect that someone other than an adoption agency or a relative purported to make arrangements for the adoption of the child or to place the child for adoption.

Elaborate rules provide for detailed information which is to be provided **8.71** in the reports under sections 22 and 23. To a considerable extent that information will be duplicated in the report of the reporting officer and the report of the curator *ad litem*.[88]

---

[87] A.S. 1997, r. 2.8(1)(k) (RCS, r. 67.11(1)(k)) but the statute provides that the court shall satisfy itself (not of the "likelihood" of the father applying) that he has "no intention" of applying for an order.

[88] RCS, r. 67.21.

Adoption Agency Reports

8.72   Parallel legislation which governs the functions of adoption agencies[89] puts a duty on the adoption agency where an application is made to the court:

>   (a) to free the child for adoption; or
>   (b) to adopt the child which has been placed by an adoption agency under the 1978 Act and the regulations

to provide a report to the court. The matters to be reported on (under these regulations) are:

>   (a) such information on the background and circumstances of the child, his family and (where appropriate) the petitioners, as the adoption agency has been able to discover in accordance with the regulations; and
>   (b) any other matters
>   (i) relative to the welfare of the child, or
>   (ii) by reiteration, as may be required by the court in accordance with section 23 of the 1978 Act. Section 23 only applies to adoptions.

8.73   In a petition to free a child for adoption, the very limited list of items which appeared in the statute has been greatly extended in the current rules.[90] Rule 2.5(2)(b)(x) has perpetuated the error that appeared in the Act of Sederunt of 1984[91] by referring to the "reputed" father, rather than the "person claiming to be the father"[92] and it is envisaged that the report of the adoption agency shall be lodged at the same time as the petition to free the child.[93]

8.74   The information which the adoption agency has been able to discover in accordance with the regulations refers to the matters which the adoption agency must obtain. These are set forth in the numbered particulars relating to the child, the natural parents, the guardian and the petitioners.[94]

Report by Children's Hearing[95]

8.75   Where a child is subject to a supervision requirement and the local authority for whose area the children's panel from which the hearing imposed the supervision requirement

---

[89] Adoption Agencies (Scotland) Regulations 1996 (S.I. 1996 No. 3266), reg. 22.

[90] A.S. 1997, r. 2.5(2)(b)(i)–(xii).

[91] Adoption of Children (S.I. 1984 No. 1013), para. 6(1)(j).

[92] A.S. 1997, r. 2.5(2)(b)(x).

[93] A.S. 1997, r. 2.5(2)(b). The differing provisions in the Rules of the Court of Session (RCS, r. 67.9(2)) are discussed at para. 5.08, above.

[94] Adoption Agencies (Scotland) Regulations 1996 (S.I. 1996 No. 3266), regs 8, 9 and Sched. 2, Pts I–IV.

[95] These provisions were introduced by the 1995 Act, s. 73.

(a) are satisfied that the best interests of the child would be served by applying for a freeing order or placing the child for adoption and they intend to place the child or apply for the order,[96] or

(b) where that local authority are aware that an application has been made and is pending, or is about to be made, in respect of such a child,[97]

then they must refer the case of the child to the principal reporter. The reporter must arrange for a children's hearing to review any supervision requirement.[98] When the supervision requirement is reviewed by the children's hearing, they may continue the review; or they may terminate, vary, insert a requirement or continue the requirement.[99] However, irrespective of what they do, they shall provide advice in respect of the proposed application for a freeing order or the prospective application for adoption for any court which may come to a decision in relation to the child[1]; and that court must consider the advice before coming to a decision in the matter.[2]

Procedure up to the Hearing

In most cases the reports under sections 22 or 23 of the 1978 Act will **8.76** be in process, along with the reports from the adoption agency in an application to free a child for adoption.[3] In some cases the report of the local authority under section 22 may not have been prepared, because the local authority will only have knowledge of the need for a report after the petitioners have given them notice of intention to adopt.[4] After the lodging of the petition the sheriff must appoint a curator *ad litem* and a reporting officer or reporting officers (where, for example, the parents live in different areas) and, where reasonably practicable, appoint the same person as curator *ad litem* and reporting officer in the same petition.[5] As indicated,[6] in all cases the reports must be made to the sheriff within four weeks from the date of the interlocutor appointing the curator *ad litem* and the reporting officer, or within such time as the sheriff in his discretion may allow.[7] A possible reason for allowing a longer time may be that the natural parent is outwith Scotland or outwith the United

---

[96] 1995 Act, s. 73(4).
[97] 1995 Act, s. 73(5).
[98] 1995 Act, s. 73(8).
[99] 1995 Act, s. 73(9).
[1] 1995 Act, s. 73(13).
[2] 1995 Act, s. 73(14); A.S. 1997, r. 2.11(5) (freeing) and r. 2.28(7) (adoption); (*cf.* RCS, r. 67.9(2) (freeing) where "the petition shall refer to a report or other documents produced which deal with" the enumerated items in the rule), r. 67.22 and Form 67.22 (adoption)).
[3] See para. 5.19, above.
[4] 1978 Act, s. 22(1).
[5] A.S. 1997, r. 2.25 (adoption), r. 2.8 (freeing) and r. 2.16 (revoking) (RCS, r. 67.25 envisages a hearing on receipt of the reports, but if the reports have not been required under r. 67.(1)(b) and (c), presumably there will be no need for a hearing); see para. 5.42, above.
[6] See para. 7.01, above.
[7] A.S. 1997, r. 2.8 (freeing), r. 2.16 (revocation) and r. 2.26 (adoption) (RCS, rr. 67.11(1)(u) and (2)(i), 67.14(4)(g) and 67.24(1)(l) and (2)(x) where the rules require preparation of the report within such period as the court may specify).

Kingdom: and a shorter period may be necessary if a parent who required
to be seen was about to go abroad or where the reporting officer or
curator *ad litem* is indisposed. When the reports of the curator *ad litem*
and the reporting officer have been received, the sheriff will normally
consider these reports and if the child is not free for adoption, instruct the
clerk of court (usually by a scroll instruction written on the report) to fix
the hearing[8] and prepare an interlocutor appointing the petitioners to
intimate the diet of hearing.

Different rules govern intimation in a petition to free a child for
adoption on the one hand and in a petition for adoption and a petition
to adopt a child abroad and a petition for a Convention adoption order on
the other.[9]

The sheriff has no express power to order intimation on anyone else
in a freeing application, whereas the Court of Session does.[10] In
petitions for adoption, in addition to the natural parents and the
minor children, as we have seen, a wider group of persons may also
receive intimation.[11]

THE HEARING

8.77 In every application to free a child for adoption and in every petition
for adoption where the child has not previously been freed, a hearing
must take place even where all the parties agree to the granting of the
adoption order. Where the child is free for adoption, the sheriff may fix
a diet of hearing. If no one entitled to appear at the hearing appears to
be heard, the sheriff may grant the adoption order on the motion of the
petitioner.[12] The motion is invariably oral and is moved by the
petitioner in person or by his solicitor or advocate. Strictly, appearance on behalf of the petitioner is not specified, but it is virtually
unavoidable if the petitioner is to learn whether there is to be an
appearance by any person entitled to appear. If the agreement of a
parent is to be dispensed with, and there is no appearance by that
parent, the court can usually proceed on the information in the process;
and if the natural parent compears and still declines to agree, matters
would presumably be required to be resolved by proof. If a person
entitled to appear does appear and wishes to be heard, the court may
hear him. A hearing on any matter of significance does not in practice
take place at this stage, because the petitioner and court have no prior
knowledge of the stance of the person entitled to appear. Obviously, if
that person is persisting in a refusal to agree to the making of the
adoption order, the petitioners could not be expected to be ready to go
to proof there and then, and the court could not reasonably be expected

---

[8] A.S. 1997, r. 2.11 (freeing), r. 2.18 (revocation) and r. 2.28 (adoption) (RCS, rr. 67.13,
67.15 and 67.25).

[9] See paras 5.43 and 5.44, above.

[10] RCS, r. 67.13(2)(b)(ii).

[11] See para. 5.43, above.

[12] A.S. 1997, r. 2.28(5) (adoption) and r. 2.11(3) (freeing). In the Court of Session the
provisions are more elaborate: RCS, r. 67.25 (adoption), r. 67.13 (freeing) and r. 67.15
(revoking).

to provide an immediate diet for such procedure. In that case, the rules provide that the court may order a further diet to be fixed at which evidence may be given in the presence of the petitioner or his solicitor.[13] In most cases this later diet would take the form of a proof and thereafter the court would proceed to a decision. If, at a hearing, an interim order is made, it would presumably be a matter of circumstances of each case whether it was necessary to have a further hearing to dispose of the matter at the end of the interim period.

---

[13] See para. 6.09, above.

CHAPTER 9

DECISION OF THE COURT

Preliminary Matters

9.01 In a petition for adoption where the child is not free for adoption, the court has to deal with the three aspects of the case—the preliminary matters, otherwise called "the conditions precedent", the agreements of the natural parents (along with the consent of the child) and the merits. In a petition for adoption where the child has been freed for adoption, the agreements are no longer in issue, and the court need only deal with the conditions precedent and the merits. In a petition to free a child for adoption, the merits are generally not in issue, and the court need only deal with the conditions precedent and the agreements.

9.02 When the court has before it all the information by way of productions, reports, interview (if any), hearing or proof, it will be able to deal with the averments in the petition and any other issues which have arisen. Some of the items (which are referred to as the conditions precedent) are straight-forward, such as the status and circumstances of the petitioners and the child, questions of domicile, jurisdiction, and the period of care and possession. No doubt, the court will confirm that the child mentioned in the extract of the entry in the Register of Births corresponds to the child mentioned in the petition and that the proposed new name for the child as set forth in the prayer of the petition corresponds with the name in the adoption order. There remain to be considered the merits of the proposed adoption and, in some cases, the question of dispensing with the agreement of a parent.

The Merits

9.03 In reaching any decision relating to the adoption of a child—of which the decision whether to grant an adoption order is one[1]—the court must have regard to all the circumstances, the paramount consideration being given to the need to safeguard and promote the welfare of the child throughout his life.[2] To regard as decisive one fact—such as that the

---

[1] As is a decision of the court to grant leave to serve a notice of intention not to allow a child to remain in foster parents' care under s. 30(2): *C (A Minor) (Adoption Notice to Local Authority), The Times*, June 28, 1994.

[2] 1978 Act, s. 6 as substituted by the 1995 Act, s. 95. For a detailed analysis of the making of s. 3, see Professor E. M. Clive, annotation to the Adoption (Scotland) Act 1978, s. 6, in Scottish *Current Law Statutes Annotated* (1978), Vol. 1, Chap. 28; McNeill, *Adoption of Children in Scotland* (2nd ed.), para. 9.02.

petitioners are the grandparents of the child[3] or that it is a step-parent adoption—would be contrary to the law: by statute the court must have regard to "all the circumstances".[4] Obviously, such a relationship is a circumstance among others to which the court must have regard, but in cases of these kinds, the court must balance the advantages from the point of view of the welfare of the child.[5] In addition, the court must have regard so far as practicable to the child's views (if he wishes to express them) taking account of his age and maturity.[6] In every case, the court will have to consider the welfare of the child, but the feelings of the child will only arise if the child is of an age at which they can be ascertained, and of all the circumstances other than these. The chief is whether the agreement of a parent who does not concur in the adoption order should be dispensed with by the court. The same three elements—the agreement of the parent, the welfare of the child, and the wishes of the child—were set forth in the earlier legislation but in a slightly different arrangement.[7] The welfare of the child and the feelings of the child have been discussed in relation to the report of the curator *ad litem*.[8] When each parent has given his or her agreement to the making of the adoption order, the merits of the case can be disposed of. In cases where the court is asked to dispense with the agreement of a parent that decision of the court is a question of fact.[9]

Dispensing with the Agreement of a Parent

Apart from the decision following on *Re D*.[10] the authorities are at one **9.04** in regarding the welfare of the child as relevant to the decision whether to dispense with the agreement of a parent in relation to the grounds to which it could apply, particularly the ground that the parent is withholding his agreement unreasonably.[11] The legislation provides that in "any decision relating to the adoption of a child" the court must have regard to all the circumstances including the welfare of the child.[12] There are dicta of the Court of Appeal to the effect that "any decision" does not apply to a decision to dispense with the agreement of a parent,[13] (which is different from a decision to find as fact that a ground for dispensing with the agreement of a parent has been established) but observations in the House of Lords to the contrary are more agreeable to the words of the Act:

> "As at present advised, I feel some reservation about accepting the construction put by the Court of Appeal (obiter, I think) on the

---

[3] *e.g. Re DX* [1949] Ch. 602.
[4] 1978 Act, s. 6; *Re W* [1971] A.C. 682 at 699, where Lord Hailsham referred to the "totality of the circumstances".
[5] *H and H, Petitioners*, 1976 S.L.T. 80; *T, Petitioner*, 1996 S.C.L.R. 897.
[6] 1978 Act, s. 6 as substituted by the 1995 Act, s. 95.
[7] 1958 Act, ss. 5 and 7(1)(b) and (2).
[8] See para. 8.24 *et seq.*, above.
[9] *Lothian Regional Council v. A*, 1992 S.L.T. 858 at 862.
[10] [1977] Fam. 25.
[11] *e.g. AB v. CD*, 1970 S.C. 268; *H and H, Petitioners*, 1976 S.L.T. 80 at 83; *A v. B and C*, 1971 S.C. (H.L.) 129 at 141, *per* Lord Reid.
[12] 1978 Act, s. 6.
[13] *Re D* [1977] Fam. 25.

Children Act. . . . Moreover, it is a strong thing in an Act of this sort to read 'any decision relating to the adoption of a child' in other than the ordinary and primary sense of those words."[14]

The correct approach which the court should apply in considering whether the agreement of a parent should be dispensed with has been the subject of recent decisions.

"The first point to be made is that, on a proper construction of s. 18(1)(*b*), it is necessary to approach the question whether the parents' agreement to an adoption order should be dispensed with in two stages. The first stage is to decide whether one or other of the grounds mentioned in s. 16(2) has been established by the evidence. This requires a decision to be taken on a question which is essentially one of fact, as can be seen clearly from an examination of the various grounds which are set out in s. 16(2). Questions as to whether the parent cannot be found or is incapable of agreement or has abandoned or neglected the child, for example, are all questions for determination upon the evidence and they do not require the exercise of a discretion by the court. There is no doubt that the ground mentioned in s. 16(2)(*b*) which is the only ground now in issue in this case raises broad questions of fact and degree, but it is important that it should be approached as a separate issue from that which must be decided at the second stage. This is because the question which must be addressed at this point is not whether the court thinks that agreement to an adoption order should be dispensed with but whether the parent is unreasonably withholding his consent. The second stage is to decide whether, if one or other of the grounds in s. 16(2) has been established, an order dispensing with the parent's agreement to an adoption order ought to be made. At this stage a discretion must be exercised by the court, and it is plain that the court must do what s. 6 of the Act requires, which is to have regard to all the circumstances, first consideration being given to the need to safeguard and promote the welfare of the child throughout his childhood [now, 'throughout his life'[15]]."[16]

Thus, if the court finds in fact that the ground is established, and if the court decides to dispense with the agreement of the parent, the final decision is whether to make the adoption order. Although these stages must be dealt with separately, it is inevitable that each stage will proceed on the whole evidence. The grounds for dispensing with agreement or consent are dealt with later.[17] In cases where the petition is opposed, the procedure becomes more complicated.

---

[14] *Re D* [1977] A.C. 602 at 641.
[15] 1978 Act, s. 6 as substituted by the 1995 Act, s. 95.
[16] *Lothian Regional Council v. A*, 1992 S.L.T. 858 at 862, approving *Central Regional Council v. L*, 1990 S.L.T. 818 at 821J.
[17] See para. 10.09, below.

CHAPTER 10

OPPOSED PETITIONS

MOST PETITIONS UNOPPOSED

The overwhelming majority of petitions for adoption proceed without **10.01** opposition. The court may grant the adoption order with or without conditions or make an interim order on such terms as the court may think fit. The court may refuse to grant the order; or the court may dismiss the petition; or allow it to be withdrawn; or in terms of the amended section 24(3) the court must not make the order unless it considers that it would be better for the child that it should do so than it should not.[1] If the court is satisfied that the necessary agreements and consents have been given or dispensed with, and if the other statutory requirements have been complied with—particularly that the court in reaching its decision has had regard to all the circumstances, the paramount consideration being given to the need to safeguard the welfare of the child throughout its childhood[2]—there seems to be no reason why the adoption order or order freeing the child for adoption should not be granted: certainly there is no need for there to be a "compelling reason" for granting the order.[3] Normally, the court will be satisfied with the verification of the statements in the petition provided by the documents and the reports— especially since the curator *ad litem* must "ascertain whether the facts stated in the petition are correct and if they are not establish the true facts".[4] Some courts feel, however, that in the case of adoption of a child who is not the child of either of the parties, the welfare of the child cannot be properly assessed without the court's interviewing the petitioners as well. In England, attendance before the court by the petitioners is obligatory except in a few cases.[5] In Scotland, the requirement of compulsory hearings may not necessitate the personal presence of the petitioners[6] although the practice in some courts is to have them attend in every case. In one unopposed petition, which had been remitted from the sheriff court to the Court of Session and in which the fact was that the petitioner was living with another male in the same household, the Lord Ordinary refused the petition. In the course of his opinion he said that he

---

[1] 1978 Act, s. 24(3) as substituted by the 1995 Act, s. 98(1) and Sched. 2, para. 16.
[2] 1978 Act, s. 6.
[3] *H and H, Petitioners*, 1976 S.L.T. 80; *T, Petitioner*, 1996 S.C.L.R. 897.
[4] A.S. 1997, r. 2.26(2)(c).
[5] *e.g.* Adoption Rules 1984 (S.I. 1984 No. 265), r. 23(4).
[6] A.S. 1997, r. 2.28 (RCS, r. 67.25(4)(a), "shall, if required by the court, appear and may be represented").

was "being asked to grant this petition without there having been any contradictor. As a result, the fundamental question of principle that I consider this case to raise has not been properly tested". The Inner House (which did not accept that there was a question of principle involved but regarded that situation as a circumstance to be taken into account), very unusually, and at the initiative of the Lord Advocate, appointed an *amicus curiae* who prepared extensive material, including published studies on the effect on a child of living in a homosexual relationship.[7]

OPPOSED PETITIONS

10.02 Because of the nature of procedure by petition there is no necessary contradictor. In adoption petitions a contradiction or defence to the prayer of the petition may arise where the agreement of a parent, or rarely the consent of a child, has not been given and it is sought to dispense with that agreement or consent. A contradiction could also arise where one of the persons upon whom the court in its discretion has ordained the petitioner to serve a notice of date of hearing in Form 7(8) seeks to enter the process. Such opposition is almost unheard of. The authority to dispense with the agreement of a parent is often craved in the prayer of the petition or, if the issue only arises later, by a separate motion. There is no place in adoption proceedings—other than a motion (or a note) to revoke a freeing order—for answers, even though in one case the court allowed fairly full answers for the respondent, and thereafter amendments for the parties.[8] Similarly, in *W v. C*[9] the natural mother who refused to consent to the making of the order lodged answers to the petition. However, in an unreported case dealing with the former analogous provisions decided by the Sheriff Principal of Lothian and Borders (Sir William Bryden) it was said:

> "The proper procedure was simply to ordain the Petitioners to serve on him a Notice in the form provided (Form C) informing him (1) of the date of the hearing, (2) of his right to 'appear and be heard,' and (3) that the court was being asked to dispense with his consent on the ground that he was withholding it unreasonably (See Act of Sederunt (Adoption of Children) 1959 as amended by Act of Sederunt (Adoption of Children Amendment) 1966)."

As has been noted, in the sheriff court there is no provision for answers but only a notice in terms of Form 7 which is of similar import to the previous Form C. In the Court of Session answers are expressly excluded,[10] whereas in a minute (or note) to revoke a freeing order, answers are expressly provided for.[11] In addition, there seems to be no reason why a parent, for example, should not be heard on an allegation that the proposed adoption would be detrimental to the welfare of the child, and

---

[7] *T, Petitioner*, 1996 S.C.L.R. 897 at 912E: the researches referred to in the case are preserved in two substantial black, lever arch binders and are in the process: *ex relatione* Mr M. Weir, Clerk to the First Division.

[8] A.S. 1997, r. 2.28(4)(d) (RCS, r. 67.25(2)(b)(ii)).

[9] (1939) 55 Sh.Ct. Rep. 261.

[10] See para. 5.36, above.

[11] A.S. 1997, r. 2.15(3) (RCS, r. 67.15(1)).

that whether or not he was agreeing to the making of the order such objectors—as with anyone else who had information that the petitioners were unsuitable—might be treated as witnesses or just sources of information which would put the court upon its inquiry and perhaps cause the court to seek comment or rebuttal from the petitioners. Contradiction might also arise where a person was seeking contact.[12] There have been cases where the respondent has challenged the relevancy of the petitioner's case; but in one case it was held that the particular averments were relevant since such a petition could not be dismissed unless the facts were patently insufficient in law.[13] If the petitioners do not pursue their action by keeping in touch with their solicitor, the respondents may seek to dismiss the petition. Since the welfare of the child is the first consideration, the court would be slow to grant such a motion until it was satisfied that the petitioners could not be found or that they had not answered an intimation to them to state whether they intended to proceed with the action. If the petition is dismissed, the petitioners can present a new petition. Where a mother who lived in Roumania, wrote to the reporting officer that she did not agree to the adoption of her child by the petitioner, the sheriff fixed a hearing sufficiently far ahead to enable the mother to take such advice as she thought fit on opposing the adoption procedure in court. In the note appended to his interlocutor, the sheriff set out briefly the procedure open to the mother.[14]

AGREEMENT OF PARENT OR GUARDIAN

Before an adoption order can be made the court must be satisfied that **10.03**

(a) the child is free for adoption by virtue of an order made in England and Wales under section 18 of the Adoption Act 1976 and not revoked, or made in Scotland under section 18 and not revoked, or

(b) (i) each parent or guardian freely, and with full understanding of what is involved, agrees unconditionally to the making of the adoption order (whether or not he knows the identity of the applicants), or

(ii) his agreement to the making of the adoption order should be dispensed with on certain grounds which are specified in the section.[15]

The form which the agreement should take has already been discussed.[16] Formerly, the consent was also required from the person or body with actual custody of the child, or who was liable to contribute to the support of the child.[17] Now these categories of persons are ones upon

---

[12] The question of contact in relation to adoption has already been discussed: see para. 8.46, above.

[13] *Z v. Z*, 1954 S.L.T. (Sh.Ct.) 57.

[14] Sheriff McNeill, Edinburgh Sh.Ct. (E73/92), January 26, 1993, unreported.

[15] 1978 Act, s. 16(1).

[16] See para. 5.24, above.

[17] Adoption of Children (Scotland) Act 1930, s. 2(3); 1950 Act, s. 2(4)(a).

whom the court may in its discretion ordain the petitioner to serve a notice in Form 7.[18] The natural parent's agreement must exist at the time of making the adoption order; accordingly, a parent can withdraw his agreement up to that time.[19] However, it was noted in the judgment of Ormrod L.J. in *Re H*,[20] with which the other judges agreed, that

> "it ought to be recognised by all concerned with adoption cases that once the formal consent has been given . . . or perhaps once the child has been placed with the adopters, time begins to run against the mother and, as time goes on, it gets progressively more and more difficult for her to show that the withdrawal of her consent is reasonable".

Where a mother withdrew her agreement at the last moment and a delay followed before a hearing, the test to be applied was whether a reasonable mother at the date of the hearing would give her agreement.[21]

Parent Defined

10.04   Parent is defined in the legislation. A parent means, irrespective of whether they are, or have been, married to each other

(a) the mother of the child, where she has parental responsibilities or parental rights in relation to him;
(b) the father of the child who has such responsibilities or rights; and
(c) both of his parents where both have such responsibilities or rights.[22]

There is no statutory provision which excludes from the category of person whose agreement is required a parent merely because he or she is also a petitioner: the statute refers to "every parent or guardian of the child."[23] Similarly, the petitioners must intimate the diet of hearing to every person whose agreement is required, even though one of these persons is one of the petitioners. Before the Children (Scotland) Act 1995, in the case of a natural parent adopting his own child along with the step-parent of the child, the effect of the adoption order was to deprive him permanently of his sole parental rights which would thereafter be shared with the other spouse. Since 1997 there are provisions[24] whereby, in step-adoptions, only the step-parent need seek the adoption order. The making of the adoption order in favour of the step-parent does not operate to extinguish the parental responsibilities and parental rights which immediately before the making of the order were vested in the natural parent to whom the adopter is married. These provisions are additional to the former provision where

---

[18] A.S. 1997, r. 2.28(4)(d) (RCS, r. 67.25(2)(b)(ii)).
[19] *e.g. AB, Petitioner*, 1976 S.L.T. (Sh.Ct.) 49
[20] [1977] 1 W.L.R. 471 at 472.
[21] *Re R (A Minor) (Adoption) (No. 2)* [1987] 1 F.L.R. 113, *per* Hollings J.
[22] 1978 Act, s. 65(1) as inserted by the 1995 Act, s. 98(1) and Sched. 2, para. 29(a)(v).
[23] 1978 Act, s. 16(1)(b).
[24] 1978 Act, s. 15(1)(aa).

the natural parent and the step-parent are joint petitioners: it seems that the two procedures are alternatives. There is a relaxation of other provisions, such as the necessity to have medical certificates as to the health of the child[25] in cases where the child was not placed by an adoption agency.

On the other hand "parent" for this purpose does not include—apart from the case of the unmarried father of a child who is a guardian of the child by virtue of a deed or will or certain statutes[26]—a natural father who was not married to the natural mother[27] unless he has parental responsibilities and parental rights in relation to the child. The reporting officer should never ask the unmarried father of a child if he is prepared to agree to a proposed adoption, unless he is a parent or he is a guardian, as these terms are defined in section 65(1) of the 1978 Act.[28] A parent who had an order for access (now contact) to the child would thus be a parent: a decision to the contrary[29] has been reversed by the current legislation. However, a father will become a parent whose agreement will be required if he acquires parental responsibilities or parental rights in relation to the child when he subsequently marries the mother of the child and thereby legitimates the child. This development occurred in one case during the currency of the litigation.[30] If a father is not a parent within the meaning of section 65(1) where he was not married to the natural mother, he does not become a parent merely because his name appears on or because he has adhibited his signature to the birth certificate of the child. Some courts nevertheless did serve a notice in Form C (now Form 7) on the unmarried father of the child. However, the father of a child who is not married to the mother is a "relative" for the purposes of the legislation.[31] The agreement of the husband of the natural mother, if he does not have parental responsibilities or parental rights in relation to the child is of no value. In legal aid applications for adoption therefore it would appear to be pointless to require the applicant to do more than state that the child's parents were not married to each other.

The position of the unmarried father of a child may be relevant in a petition to free the child for adoption: but that is of no moment, because in such cases only an adoption agency, not a natural parent, can be the petitioner.[32] (The unmarried father of a child is, however, a relative who may properly be a petitioner and, as such, the child may be placed without the intervention of an adoption agency[33]). In a decision of the European Court of Human Rights from the Republic of Ireland, it was said that the circumstances—namely, an unmarried father had lived with the mother for two years, had planned to have a child but had left before the child was born—amounted to a family life and he had a right to access to a court to

---

[25] A.S. 1997, r. 2.21(2)(c) (RCS, r. 67.22(2)(d)).

[26] Which are noted later: see para. 10.06; 1978 Act, s. 65(1).

[27] *A v. B*, 1953 S.C. 378; *A v. B and C*, 1971 S.C. (H.L.) 129.

[28] *A and B v. C*, 1991 G.W.D. 38-2298 (in Scotland); *Re L (A Minor) (Adoption Procedure)* [1991] 1 F.L.R. 171 (in England and Wales).

[29] *G and G, Petitioners*, First Division, July 19, 1985, unreported.

[30] *A v. B and C*, 1971 S.C. (H.L.) 129.

[31] 1978 Act, s. 65(1).

[32] 1978 Act, ss. 13(1) and 65(1).

[33] 1978 Act, s. 18(7).

challenge the placement of the child for adoption before the adoption took place.[34] The Scottish legislation does not specifically provide such a remedy; but it now puts a duty on the adoption agency to consider alternatives to adoption before making any arrangements for the adoption of a child.[35]

The Natural Mother

10.05   Where the natural mother is also a petitioner there is seldom any difficulty. However, where the natural mother is giving up her child for adoption, several problems may arise. In the case of a mother, but not in the case of a father, the agreement is ineffective if it is given by her less than six weeks after the birth of the child.[36] This provision takes into account the effect of childbirth on the mother's ability to make the best decision for herself and the child. In addition to the medical effects of the birth, a mother at any stage may be in emotional turmoil over the decision whether to deprive herself permanently of her parental rights over the child. In some cases, there may also be the personal reminder of illegitimacy or the fear of relatives learning of it. Although these considerations appear to bulk less large nowadays, care should be taken by the reporting officer and the solicitor for the petitioners in dealing with the mother, particularly when she may feel that the question of agreeing to the adoption order has been raised several times over a period of several months—when she is first asked about giving up the child, when she signs the form of agreement, when she confirms to the reporting officer that the effect of the adoption order would be to deprive her permanently of her parental rights, when she receives intimation of the hearing and when she attends the hearing, if she attends. Solicitors, reporting officers and curators *ad litem* should avoid distress in such cases by sending letters—if so requested—to the address selected by the mother, or by using plain envelopes or the like. It has been suggested that where the father of the child was not married to the mother and it is reasonably clear that the natural mother's husband is not the father the practice was not to serve on him.[37] Since the 1995 Act came into force, the criterion is whether the parent has or has not parental responsibilities or parental rights in relation to the child.

Pater Est Quem Nuptiae Demonstrant

10.06   In relation to the natural father, the presumption of paternity is expressed in the Latin brocard *pater est quem nuptiae demonstrant*, that is, he is the father of the child as is indicated by the marriage. Children

---

[34] *Keegan v. Ireland* (1994) 18 E.H.R.R. 342. The father was not seeking to overturn the adoption order, but he was awarded damages and expenses against the Irish Government. It is submitted, as was stated in the opinion of the Commission, that "the relationship between a natural father and a child born out of wedlock will differ in nature and degree": p. 355.

[35] 1978 Act, s. 6A.

[36] 1978 Act, s. 16(4).

[37] Dobie, *Sheriff Court Practice*, p. 547, citing *E, Petitioner* (1944) 60 Sh.Ct. Rep. 127 where the decision of the court proceeded on the inquiries made of the Registrar of Births as to the procedure adopted by him before registering a married woman's child as illegitimate: Registration of Births, Deaths and Marriages (Scotland) Act 1965, s. 18 as amended by the Law Reform (Parent and Child) (Scotland) Act 1986, s. 10 and Sched. 1, paras 8(2) and (3).

born in wedlock are presumed to be the legitimate children of the husband and wife.[38] Generally, as long as the marriage subsists until dissolved by death or divorce the presumption will apply and in the case of a petition for adoption of the child the agreement of the husband will be required because he is presumed to be the father of the child. It is, of course, possible to overcome the presumption with contrary evidence, such as non-access by the husband and at the time of conception—as where the husband was abroad or in prison (which fact is sometimes vouched by a letter from the prison authorities or an extract conviction from the appropriate court)—or where the husband is not capable of procreation. If the presumption has been displaced, then the husband is not the father. However, in addition to being a parent, the father must be one who has parental responsibilities or parental rights in relation to the child before his agreement is required to the making of an adoption order and he does not become a parent for the purpose of agreement to the making of an adoption order.

On the other hand, in a freeing application, the position of the unmarried father who does not have parental responsibilities or parental rights in relation to the child has to be considered[39] and he is a relative for the purposes of placing a child.[40] It is illogical and pointless for the husband of the natural mother who is not the father of the child to give his agreement to the making of the adoption order.[41] No doubt the circumstances of the case will determine whether the court is satisfied that the presumption has been overcome on the information contained in the reports, or whether additional evidence should be called for.[42] In one unreported case, there was a suggestion that the former husband of the natural mother who was also a petitioner was impotent or sterile and that the child was conceived as a result of artificial insemination in a foreign country by an unknown donor or donors. Had this been proved, it would have made it unnecessary to have the agreement of the husband. However, the court was not satisfied that the husband was unable to procreate or that he did not have access at the time of conception.

Guardian Defined

It is also necessary for the court to be satisfied that each guardian freely **10.07** agrees unconditionally to the making of the adoption order.[43] Guardian is defined as a person appointed by deed or will or by a court of competent jurisdiction to be the guardian of the child.[44]

Further, the appropriate parental rights and responsibilities relating **10.08** to any child which may be vested in a local authority under a parental

[38] Trayner, *Latin Maxims and Phrases* (4th ed., 1894, W. Green & Son Ltd, reprinted 1993); Gloag and Henderson, *Introduction to the Law of Scotland* (10th ed., 1995, W. Green & Son Ltd), para. 49.2, and the authorities therein cited.
[39] 1978 Act, s. 18(7).
[40] 1978 Act, ss. 11, 65(1).
[41] *E, Petitioner* (1944) 60 Sh.Ct. Rep. 127.
[42] A.S. 1997, r. 29 (RCS, r. 67.6).
[43] 1978 Act, s. 16(1)(b).
[44] 1978 Act, s. 65(1).

responsibilities order do not include the right to agree or decline to agree to the making of an adoption order, an order to adopt a child abroad or an order freeing a child for adoption.[45]

DISPENSING WITH AGREEMENT AND CONSENT

10.09 Once the identity of the parent or guardian has been established, the agreement of that person to the making of the order must be disposed of. If the parent or guardian has died—and that fact can be established by the production of the extract of an entry in the Register of Deaths or by other evidence—the difficulty has been overcome. If the person is not dead and does not agree to the making of the adoption order, or has withdrawn his agreement before the making of the order, the order cannot be made unless the court dispenses with the agreement on a ground specified in the Act. The grounds are set out in a systematic manner.[46]

10.10 Whatever were the former doubts or qualifications,[47] it is now established that all the grounds for dispensing with the agreement of a parent or guardian—including the ground that he is withholding his agreement unreasonably[48]—are questions of fact.[49] Obviously, whether a parent or guardian "cannot be found" is a simple question of fact; whereas, whether a parent or guardian is withholding his agreement unreasonably "raises broad questions of fact and degree".[50] As has been indicated,[51] the court must first decide whether it has been found in fact that the agreement of the parent has been withheld unreasonably; and then, if so, decide in its discretion whether the agreement should be dispensed with.

Grounds for Dispensing with Agreement or Consent

10.11 The grounds for dispensing with agreement or consent are discussed *seriatim*. The grounds are not mutually exclusive: for example, the parent who has persistently failed without reasonable cause to discharge his parental duties in relation to the child is very often also the parent who cannot be found.

---

[45] 1995 Act, s. 86(3).

[46] 1978 Act, s. 16(2).

[47] McNeill, *Adoption of Children in Scotland* (2nd ed.), para. 10.08; among the cases discussed *Re P* [1977] Fam. 25 was not followed in Scotland: *P v. Lothian Regional Council* (properly *Lothian Regional Council v. P*) 1989 S.L.T. 739.

[48] *P v. Lothian Regional Council* (properly *Lothian Regional Council v. P*), 1989 S.L.T. 739; *Lothian Regional Council v. A*, 1992 S.L.T. 858 at 862.

[49] *AB and CB v. X's Curator*, 1963 S.C. 124.

[50] *Lothian Regional Council v. A*, 1992 S.L.T. 858 at 862: this case is discussed more fully at para. 9.04, above.

[51] See para. 9.04, above.

(a) Is not Known, cannot be Found or is Incapable of Giving Agreement

(i) Is not known The first of these grounds was introduced by the **10.12** Children (Scotland) Act 1995, as was the conjunction of these three grounds. A parent may not be known where, for example, the child is a foundling.

(ii) Cannot be found This is one of the more common grounds; and is usually decided on the information contained in the reports and the productions. The reporting officer should state what steps he has been able to take in trying to trace the parent. Sometimes relatives of the natural parent are able to assist in providing an address or in forwarding communications to the parent. Failure to follow up such lines of inquiry have been commented upon and an appeal was allowed on the grounds that the petitioners had failed to take proper steps to serve notice of the proceedings on the natural mother.[52] In that case the petitioners

> "wrote or instructed their solicitors to write, to her last known address, and the letter was returned 'Gone away.' They caused advertisements to be inserted in the press, notifying her of the proposed proceedings. They caused inquiries to be made from the Post Office and other sources in an attempt to trace her whereabouts, but all those steps proved to be fruitless";

however, it was contended that petitioners "knew that the mother's father was in touch with the mother and that they knew his address" and that there was "one reasonable step which they omitted to take, and that was to get in touch with her father and ask him to tell the mother what they proposed". The court allowed the appeal and ordered a rehearing to give the mother a chance of being heard. The addresses which appear on the extract of an entry in the Register of Births or Register of Marriages or other productions may be the addresses of the party whose agreement is being sought or of his or her relatives. Government departments or employers may be prepared to pass on a communication to someone whose address they have but are unwilling to disclose to the petitioners. If a registered or recorded delivery letter is posted at the address of the natural father and the letter is taken in and nothing more is heard, or if it is returned marked "not known", "gone away" or "refused", the returned letter would be evidence that the natural father could not be found—at least at that address.

That fact may also be proved by other evidence. In a single-judge decision in England the phrase "cannot be found" was applied to the situation where the natural parents had returned to a hostile totalitarian state and there was no practical means of communicating with them.[53] If intimation of the hearing on a natural parent has been effected and he does not compear, it cannot be said that he cannot be found: some other ground would have to be established. It is for the petitioners to establish that the natural parent cannot be found. If there is doubt whether the

---

[52] *Re F (R)* [1970] 1 Q.B. 385.
[53] *Re R* [1966] 3 All E.R. 613; *cf. Re B* [1958] 1 Q.B. 12.

respondent is at home or is answering correspondence (for example, where the envelope was returned by the postal authorities marked "not at home"), it may be desirable to proceed by personal service.[54]

10.13 **(iii) Is incapable of giving agreement** This ground, which is less common, applies not only to the case of dispensing with the agreement of a parent or guardian but also to the case of dispensing with the consent of a minor child who is the subject of a petition for adoption.[55] Normally, the evidence of mental or physical incapacity would be that of a medical report on the condition of the person and the effect of that condition on his ability to understand what was required if he was asked to give his agreement or consent.[56] If the report is disputed, the matter would require to be resolved by proof. If the parent is of doubtful mental capacity, particularly if intimation of a hearing on the parent might be detrimental to the health of the parent, the court may *ex proprio motu* or on the motion of the solicitors for the parent, appoint a curator *ad litem* to the parent who can report to the court on his capacity. There may be cases where the petitioners know of the whereabouts of the natural parents and that they are in good health but because they are resident in a totalitarian country which is hostile to them to such an extent that they would not be capable of giving their agreement freely, the court will hold that they are incapable of giving their agreement.[57]

(b) Is Withholding his Agreement Unreasonably

10.14   This ground is frequently relied upon and has given rise to the greatest proportion of adoption cases in England and in Scotland, although the number of contested cases constitutes a very small part of the total number of adoption petitions. Whether the agreement is being withheld unreasonably is to be decided at the hearing[58] or proof. The test in deciding whether this ground exists is not the sincerity of the parent whose agreement is in question, but the reasonableness of his withholding the agreement.[59] In *B and B, Petitioners*[60] it was regarded as reasonable for the natural mother to see her child and meet the female petitioner before giving her consent; but it has been held by a court of seven judges (with one dissent) that disclosure to the natural parent of the identity of the proposed adopters was not an indispensable prerequisite of a valid consent.[61] In an appeal from the Court of Appeal, Lord Wilberforce narrated that the judges "said that a direction to dispense with consent should be given sparingly, and only in rare and exceptional cases: this was all the more so in cases such as *Re B* [1975] Fam 127 (as the present) where the adoption is desired by one natural parent and the other refuses

---

[54] *LRC v. S*, Glasgow Sh.Ct. (E24/91 and E25/91), May 27, 1991, unreported.

[55] 1978 Act, s. 12(8).

[56] *Lothian Regional Council, Petitioners*, Edinburgh Sh.Ct. (E83/85), October 3, 1985, unreported.

[57] *Re R* [1966] 3 All E.R. 613.

[58] *Re D* [1973] Fam. 209; *AB, Petitioner*, 1976 S.L.T. (Sh.Ct.) 49.

[59] *Re W (An Infant)* [1971] A.C. 682 at 698, 699.

[60] 1946 S.L.T. (Sh.Ct.) 36.

[61] *H and H, Petitioners*, 1944 S.C. 347.

consent" and said of these observations that "they contained and set forth no revolutionary or even new doctrine".[62] It is respectfully submitted that the use of the word "sparingly" suggests a mathematical approach to cases, whereas it is submitted that the correct approach must be that the court should give such a direction as the circumstances of the case then before it demand—irrespective of what had been decided in other cases. The effect of section 6 of the Adoption (Scotland) Act 1978 and the meaning of "welfare of the child" have been discussed.[63] The existence of this ground is a question of fact; and in such a situation no general rules can be laid down. Apart from a few exceptional cases where the parent, although not consenting to the making of the adoption order, did not appear in the process, almost all the reported cases have been ones in which there has been a live issue between the compearing parties—namely, whether the parental rights of the natural parent should yield to the welfare of the child which may result by the making of the adoption order. However, a significant consideration in deciding this question is whether the parent whose agreement is in issue is in reality a protesting parent or even a compearing parent.

As has been discussed earlier,[64] the existence of this ground, as of the other grounds specified in section 16, is a matter of fact and degree and is not "a decision relating to the adoption of a child" in terms of section 6, but no doubt, in making a finding in fact on this ground, the court would of necessity have to have regard to all the relevant circumstances of the case. If in an unopposed petition there is credible information such as would be contained in the reports and there is no challenge of it and no contrary information, the court can find in fact that the parent or guardian is withholding his agreement unreasonably and proceed to consider the motion of the petitioners at the hearing that that agreement should be dispensed with and, if appropriate, dispense with that agreement and proceed to deal with "the merits of the petition".[65] In that case the decision on dispensing with parental agreement was made much easier in that the parent was not only a non-protesting parent and a non-compearing parent but also a parent who had "washed his hands" of the child[66]; "and that he had accordingly persistently failed without reasonable cause to discharge his obligations" as a parent of the child. The court did not deal with the other ground for dispensing with the agreement of the parent—that it was unreasonably withheld—although that had been in issue in the sheriff court; but it seems that the same information would have justified upholding that ground also.

This and other cases can illustrate rather than define the meaning of the ground. Lord Wilberforce in *Re D*[67] said that the decision in *A v. B and C*[68] "shows how far the erosion of the natural parents' rights"

---

[62] *Re D* [1977] A.C. 602 at 627.

[63] See para. 8.24 *et seq.*, above.

[64] See para. 10.04, above.

[65] *H and H, Petitioners*, 1976 S.L.T. 80 at 83.

[66] This case was considered with approval in *T, Petitioner*, 1996 S.C.L.R. 897 at 902.

[67] [1971] A.C. 602 at 626.

[68] 1971 S.C. (H.L.) 129 (also cited as *O'Connor v. A and B* [1971] 1 W.L.R. 1227).

had gone; and in *A v. B and C*, Lord Guest pointed out[69] that: "No case was referred to in which the consent of the natural parents of a child to an adoption order was dispensed with when the parents had married"—but the marriage of the natural parents in that case took place during the currency of the litigation and after the natural father became free to marry. Nevertheless, "it has been said more than once that, other things being equal, it is in the best interests of a child to be with its natural parents."[70] It is trite law that what is to be considered in assessing the reasonableness of the natural parent in deciding whether he should give his agreement to the making of the order is "the totality of the circumstances".[71] The words of Lord Reid in the same case[72] provide a succinct statement of the position:

> "The test is an objective test—would a reasonable parent have withheld consent? I think that a reasonable parent, or indeed any other reasonable person, would have in mind the interests or claims of all three parties concerned—the child whose adoption is in question, the natural parents, and the adopting family. No doubt the child's interests come first, and in some cases they may be paramount. But I see no reason why the claims of the natural parents should be ignored. If the mother were deeply attached to the child and had only consented in the first place to adoption because of adverse circumstances, it would seem to me unjust that on a change of circumstances her affection for the child and her natural claim as a parent should be ignored. And the adopting family cannot be ignored either. If it was the mother's action which brought them in in the first place, they ought not to be displaced without good reason. So to balance these claims is no easy task. Often no ideal solution is possible. We are dealing largely with future probabilities, for the decision once made is irrevocable. So we cannot be certain what will be in the child's best interests in the long run. That seems to me to be an additional reason for giving considerable weight in proper cases to the claims of the natural parents and of the adopting family."[73]

10.15   That case followed *Re W*[74] in which the words of general import made by the Lord Chancellor (Hailsham) were referred to with approval. For completeness the whole paragraph is noted:

> "I only feel it necessary to add on this part of the case that I entirely agree with Russell L.J. when he said, in effect [1970] 2 Q.B. 589, 598,

---

[69] 1971 S.C. (H.L.) 129 at 143.

[70] *ibid. per* Lord Guest at 143.

[71] *ibid. per* Lord Simon at 147.

[72] *ibid.* at 141; *Re K* [1952] 2 All E.R. 877.

[73] "There is a trinity of interests involved—those of the child, those of the mother and those of the respondents": *A v. B and C*, Second Division, November 26, 1980, unreported.

[74] [1971] A.C. 682 at 700. It is respectfully suggested that this dictum has been expressed in a difficult phraseology: at first glance there is not a "band" of decisions, but only two decisions—to agree, or not to agree, to the making of the adoption order—on the facts and circumstances of the case. It appears that the last three sentences add nothing to the earlier words.

599, that it does not follow from the fact that the test is reasonableness that any court is entitled to substitute its own view for that of the parent. In my opinion, it should be extremely careful to guard against this error. Two reasonable parents can perfectly reasonably come to opposite conclusions on the same set of facts without forfeiting their right to be regarded as reasonable. The question in any given case is whether a parental veto comes within the band of possible reasonable decisions and not whether it is right or mistaken. Not every reasonable exercise of judgment is right, and not every mistaken exercise of judgment is unreasonable. There is a band of decisions within which no court should seek to replace the individual's judgment with his own."

In Scotland, the matter has been put thus:

"It is for the court to look at the whole matter afresh and to do so objectively in the knowledge that consent is being withheld by the parent. The question for the court is not whether it should allow an appeal against the parent's decision but whether a reasonable parent would in all the circumstances have withheld consent."[75]

The cases can do no more than emphasise the words of the statute that the **10.16** test is reasonableness. Indeed, the Court of Appeal has said "that the task of the court in determining an adoption application was to be performed not by applying a test based on other cases, but by having regard to all the statutory considerations".[76] There are cases which are examples of particular applications of that general rule. In deciding whether a parent who has more than one child is unreasonably withholding her agreement to an adoption order in respect of one of them, the court must consider what weight a parent should give to the effect that the adoption would have on another child of the family.[77] In one case of adoption of the children of a marriage after divorce and remarriage Cumming-Bruce J. said:

"I appreciate that in this case, as in many, it is strongly in the child's interest that he should be settled in the family life of the mother and her second husband; that he should form a close relationship with the father figure represented by that husband. I also appreciate that in this case, as in many, the fact that the child continues to have a relationship with his natural father is a source of practical inconvenience and irritation to the mother, who wishes to put her first husband out of her life as completely as possible. And, of course, the second husband may be expected to wish to keep the first husband completely out of their family life. Also, it is common experience that the emotional effect on the child of an attempt to maintain dual and frequently conflicting loyalties to both parents, and to the

---

[75] *D v. F*, 1994 S.C.L.R. 417 at 423, *per* Lord President Hope giving the opinion of the court.

[76] *H* (also cited as *A*) *(A Minor) (Adoption Application: non-patrial)* [1996] 4 All E.R. 600. Similarly, it was observed that a party focused too much on judgments in earlier proceedings and insufficiently upon the sheriff's judgment which was under review: *K and K, Petitioners*, Sheriff Principal Risk, Aberdeen Sh.Ct., February 8, 1994, unreported.

[77] *Re E (A Minor)* [1988] C.L.Y. 2304.

stepfather, is deeply disturbing and sometimes gravely destructive to the stable development of his personality. But the appropriate court to regulate and control these difficult problems is usually the court seised of the family problems of the first marriage. It may, on the facts of the present case, be wise to restrict or postpone access on the part of the father. The High Court and the county court are there to grapple with these problems. It is quite wrong to use the adoption law to extinguish the relationship between the protesting father and the child, unless there is some really serious factor which justifies the use of the statutory guillotine. The courts should not encourage the idea that after divorce the children of the family can be reshuffled and dealt out like a pack of cards in a second rubber of bridge. Often a parent who has remarried and has custody of the children from the first family is eager to achieve just that result, but such parents, often faced with very grave practical problems, are frequently blind to the real long-term interests of their children."[78]

10.17   The observations in that case "well and firmly though they were expressed . . . contained no revolutionary or even new doctrine".[79] *Re B*[80] was followed in a sheriff court case[81]; and a similar approach had been adopted earlier in *AB, Petitioners*.[82] In cases in which this ground is relied upon the claim of the natural parent looms larger than in other cases. The strictures in *Re B*[83] in favour of custody and against adoption as the proper method of securing the welfare of the child and the dicta to the effect that only where the welfare of the child "so overwhelmingly requires adoption" should a father be deprived of that status[84] can only have application where there is a protesting parent whose child is in the custody of the mother after divorce and is sought to be adopted by her and her new husband. In an unopposed case in Scotland the judgment of the court was that there was no need to show a "compelling reason" why adoption should be granted[85]:

> "The true question in all such cases which is relevant to both the merits of an application and to the motion to dispense with consent, is whether the making of an order or refusing to make it is more likely to enure to the welfare of the child (see *A. B. v. C. D.*, 1970 S.C. 268, the opinion of Lord President Clyde at p. 269)."

In a case where the sheriff erroneously proceeded on the view that the father's agreement and the children's best interests were distinct, the court was of the view that there was no need to remit to the sheriff: "We are in as good a position as the sheriff to reach a conclusion upon the issue in the light of the findings which the sheriff has made and the

---

[78] *Re B* [1975] Fam. 127 at 143.
[79] *Re D* [1971] A.C. 602, *per* Lord Wilberforce at 627.
[80] [1975] Fam. 127.
[81] *A and B v. C*, 1977 S.L.T. (Sh.Ct.) 55.
[82] 1959 S.L.T. (Sh.Ct.) 49.
[83] [1975] Fam. 127.
[84] *ibid.* at 140, 145; *cf. Re D* [1973] Fam. 209.
[85] *H and H, Petitioners*, 1976 S.L.T. 80 at 83.

reports which were before him." The court allowed the appeals, dispensed with the agreement of the respondent in each petition and granted the crave of each petition.[86]

(c) Has Persistently Failed Without Reasonable Cause to Fulfil one or other of the Following Parental Responsibilities in Relation to the Child

(i) The responsibility to safeguard and promote the child's health, development and welfare, or (ii) if the child is not living with him, the reponsibility to maintain personal relations and direct contact with the child on a regular basis This paragraph, which was introduced by the Children (Scotland) Act 1995,[87] is more elaborate than, but does not alter the substance of, the old paragraph. A parent has by reason of the relationship of parent and child the duty to aliment the child and guide the child in his upbringing. In England it has been said that parental duty also includes "the natural and moral duty of a parent to show affection, care and interest towards his child".[88] This would include adequate provision of housing, clothing and food, as well as ensuring that the needs of the child, such as education and medical treatment, were properly met. The commonest failure of a parent is in not providing aliment for the child—the majority of those cases is where there is a decree for payment of aliment either in the decree of divorce or in a separate decree or agreement associated with the decree of divorce and the former husband has not paid anything or has paid very little. If the failure is without reasonable cause, as where the parent is able to pay or even is able to earn a livelihood, the court may dispense with agreement on this ground. However, the whole circumstances should be considered, for example, whether the parent has kept up with the child by exercising any right of access, by writing letters or by sending cards or presents at Christmas or on birthdays. In *Re D*[89] it was held that the existence of the ground was a question of fact and degree; and where a father has temporarily withdrawn from the family during the period of the breakdown of the marriage and subsequent divorce and ancillary proceedings there was not such a degree of permanence as would deprive a father of his parental rights.

A different situation may arise if the petitioner has engineered the apparent indifference of the parent to the child by refusing him access or making its exercise virtually impossible or by rejecting his tender of aliment or the like.[90] Normally, the evidence in support of this failure would be the decree in which the aliment was fixed and the evidence of those who could speak to the non-payment of the aliment or to other circumstances. Although analogous grounds were to be found in the now repealed legislation which empowered a local authority to seek a parental responsibilities order,[91] these related to the fitness of a parent to have care of a child whereas "the question of adoption, however, is not concerned

10.18

---

[86] *cf. AB and CB, Petitioners*, 1990 S.C.L.R. 809.
[87] 1995 Act, s. 98(1) and Sched. 2, para. 10(a).
[88] *Re P* [1962] 3 All E.R. 789 at 794.
[89] [1973] Fam. 209.
[90] *A and B v. C*, 1977 S.L.T. (Sh.Ct.) 55; *Re B* [1975] Fam. 127.
[91] The current corresponding provisions are to be found in the 1995 Act, s. 86(2)(b)(ii) replacing the 1968 Act, s. 16.

with a parent's fitness to have care of the child sought to be adopted but of her right to refuse to agree to give up once and for all her parental rights and duties towards that child which is quite a different matter".[92]

(d) Has Seriously Ill-treated the Child, whose Reintegration into the same Household as the Parent or Guardian is, Because of the Serious Ill-treatment or for other Reasons, Unlikely

10.19   The conduct here may amount to only one incident as long as it is serious, such as one assault. The ground does not apply unless (because of the ill-treatment or for other reasons) the rehabilitation of the child within the household of the parent or guardian is unlikely. Proof of this would depend on medical and lay evidence and, if appropriate, any extract conviction of an offence by the parent against the child or the reports on the child by the social work department or the like. If the ground is established and the court decides to make the order sought in the petition it will do so by an interlocutor.

---

[92] *A and B, Petitioners*, Outer House, July 7, 1982, unreported.

CHAPTER 11

MAKING THE ORDER

INTERLOCUTOR

If the court is satisfied that all the statutory requirements such as **11.01** agreements, domicile, care and possession and the like have been complied with, and the court is satisfied that the granting of the order will safeguard and promote the welfare of the child throughout his life, then it will make the adoption order with or without conditions. The interlocutor may be in the form "Grants the prayer of the petition".[1] At the same time the court will make a certified copy of the adoption order for transmission to the Registrar General for Scotland,[2] the principal of which will remain with the process. In almost every case intimation of the adoption order to the Registrar General for Scotland is all that the petitioners require and, indeed, all that they have sought in the prayer of the petition.[3]

No extract of an adoption order may be issued except with the authority of the court which made the order.[4] This procedure is extremely rare.[5] An extract may be sought by lodging a petition setting forth the reasons for which an extract is required. If an extract is sought after the process has been sealed up, the petition should also crave authority to open up the process.[6] This rule only applies to adoption orders. An extract may be sought in the normal way in the case of other orders, such as an interim order which the petitioners would require to have for their purposes.[7] Presumably, for the same reasons, an extract of an order for adoption of a child abroad can be issued as in an ordinary action in court. In the case of a freeing order, an extract is issued by the sheriff clerk to the adoption agency.[8]

Where in a petition to free a child for adoption, a natural parent makes a declaration that he prefers not to be involved in future questions concerning the adoption of the child, such declaration must be recorded by the court.[9] Where some particular matter has been in issue and has

---

[1] *H and H, Petitioners*, 1976 S.L.T. 80 at 82.

[2] A.S. 1997, r. 2.31 (RCS, r. 67.30).

[3] See Append. 2.5.

[4] A.S. 1997, r. 2.32(2) (RCS, r. 67.31).

[5] *B and B, Petitioners*, 1996 S.C.L.R. 874.

[6] A.S. 1997, r. 2.32 (RCS, r. 67.31, by note when the petition is still depending before the court, and by petition when no petition is depending); Append. 2.17.

[7] See paras 1.09, 8.30, above.

[8] A.S. 1997, r. 2.14(1). This provision was introduced in the sheriff court in the 1997 Act of Sederunt: presumably the Court of Session would adopt a similar procedure.

[9] 1978 Act, s. 18(6); A.S. 1997, rr. 2.10(4) and 2.13. This provision was introduced in the sheriff court in the 1997 Act of Sederunt: presumably the Court of Session would adopt a similar procedure.

been resolved, usually by proof or some other form of inquiry beyond the verification contained in the reports, the court should make findings in fact on these matters, such as

> "(1) that the father of the child was married to the natural mother; (2) that the letters (Nos.　　　　of process) have been returned by the Post Office marked 'Gone away'; Therefore dispenses with the agreement of the natural father on the ground that he cannot be found in terms of the Adoption (Scotland) Act 1978, s. 16(2)(a)";

and if appropriate the sheriff should write a note setting forth the grounds on which he has proceeded.[10] Apart from the situations in which the court would as a matter of course insert in the interlocutor and order any particular terms or conditions, the court must in the case of an adoption by one person where one of the parents is excluded record the reason justifying that exclusion.[11]

In the case of an interim order the interlocutor should echo the words of the statute and postpone the determination of the adoption order until a specified date, appoint the curator *ad litem* to furnish a supplementary report on or before a date which is well before the date of postponement, make an interim order of custody of the child in favour of the petitioners for that period, and ordain them to aliment the child[12] generally or at a particular amount per week. The former provisions allowed the court to add such other conditions as to education and supervision of the welfare of the child and otherwise as the court thought fit.[13] These powers are implied in the order vesting parental responsibilities and parental rights, relating to the child, in the petitioners. Similarly, in the case of an order to adopt a child abroad the interlocutor should authorise the petitioners to remove the child from Great Britain immediately (or after a certain period) for the purpose of adopting the child under the law of the state of a particular country and vesting in them the parental responsibilities and parental rights relating to the child pending his adoption.[14]

Order not Granted

11.02　　(a) If the sheriff is not satisfied that the facts stated in the petition are supported by the documents lodged with the petition or by the reports of the curator *ad litem* and reporting officer, or

(b) if for any other reason the court considers it appropriate

he may order the production of further documents or that oral evidence be led.[15]

---

[10] Act of Sederunt (Sheriff Court Ordinary Cause Rules) 1993 (S.I. 1993 No. 1956), r. 12.2(3).

[11] 1978 Act, s. 15(3); see Append. 2.11.

[12] 1978 Act, s. 25; Append. 2.4.

[13] 1958 Act, s. 8(1); see Append. 2.5.

[14] 1978 Act, s. 49; see Append. 2.6.

[15] A.S. 1997, r. 2.29; *cf. T, Petitioner*, 1996 S.C.L.R. 897 at 906 where the corresponding but now replaced Rule of Court 2.29 was considered (RCS, r. 67.6).

One would expect that unless there was some fundamental and incurable impediment to the granting of the order, the party would be given an opportunity to amend his case or lead additional evidence[16]; and that in most unopposed cases the court would not require the personal attendance of the petitioners or the child—apart from the petitioner or his representatives being present at the hearing to move that the adoption order be granted.[17] In the case of refusal—with or without additional evidence—the interlocutor of the court would refuse the prayer of the petition and add a note setting forth the grounds of the refusal; and if appropriate the court may set forth findings in fact including negative findings.[18] The legislation, now repealed, envisaged that a petition can "lapse" or be withdrawn,[19] for example, where in the face of supervening opposition of a natural parent, the petitioners do not wish to proceed, or the petitioners realise that the petition is incompetent, as where one of the petitioners is under the age of 21. However, it is a question whether standing those powers relative to refusal, there is any statutory power in the court to dismiss the petition. In England there is a reference to the power to dismiss[20]: and in Scotland an inherent power to do so. Where the order is not granted certain results may follow. Where a previous application for a British adoption order has been refused, the court "shall not proceed to determine" an application by the same petitioners in relation to the same child unless

> (a) in refusing the previous application the court directed that this provision should not apply, or
> (b) it appears to the court that
>> (i) because of the change in circumstances, or
>> (ii) for any other reason

it is proper to proceed with the application.[21] A British adoption order means an adoption order granted in

> (a) Scotland under the Adoption (Scotland) Act 1978, s. 12,
> (b) England under the Adoption Act 1976, s. 12(1)
> (c) Northern Ireland,
> (d) the Channel Islands,
> (e) the Isle of Man,
> (f) a British colony, being a country designated for the purposes of that provision by an order of the Secretary of State or, if no country is so designated, any of those countries.[22]

---

[16] *cf. T, Petitioner*, 1996 S.C.L.R. 897 at 906.

[17] A.S. 1997, r. 2.11(3) (freeing) and r. 2.28(5) (adoption). There is no obligation on a petitioner to be present: 1978 Act, s. 59(2) and RCS, rr. 67.13(4) and 67.25(4) which empowers the court to require appearance.

[18] Lees, *Interlocutors*, p. 17; *cf. Brown and Lynn v. Western S.M.T.*, 1945 S.C. 31 at 46.

[19] *e.g.* 1978 Act, s. 32(4)(a).

[20] 1976 Act, s. 14(3).

[21] 1978 Act, s. 24(1).

[22] 1978 Act, s. 65(1).

Where the second adoption is at the instance of different persons, this section does not apply; but in most cases the court would want to know the history of the child. Also refusal by the court or withdrawal of the application or expiry of the period of an interim order without an adoption order having been made brings into operation the provisions whereby the child is returned to the adoption society or local authority which placed the child.[23]

REGISTRAR GENERAL FOR SCOTLAND

11.03 The communication to the Registrar General for Scotland of

(a) any adoption order,[24]
(b) amendment or revocation to an adoption order,[25] or
(c) cancellation of an adoption order on legitimation of the child[26]

to be made by the clerk of court, is effected by sending to the Registrar a certified copy of the order by recorded delivery post in an envelope marked "confidential", or by personal delivery by the clerk to the Registrar.[27] These provisions for transmission of a process do not apply to an interim order nor to an order for parental rights in relation to the child granted in lieu of an adoption order,[28] nor where the order is refused, dismissed or withdrawn, nor to a freeing order, nor to an order revoking a freeing order. But these observations do not affect requirements of confidentiality in relation to the process.[29] The principal order will remain with the process to be sealed up with it. It is usual for the clerk of court to delay sealing up the process until he has received acknowledgment from the Registrar that he has received the order. Further, since the parties are entitled to have open to them all documents lodged in process they should be entitled to have a sight of the process before it is sealed up, if only to check the interlocutor "at once" and in order to see if it correctly represents what the parties intended[30]—particularly that the proposed new names of the child as they appear in the prayer of the petition have been correctly transcribed in the order; or to decide what further action, such as an appeal, should be taken.

11.04 The adoption order contains a direction to the Registrar to make an entry regarding the adoption in the Adopted Children Register with the proposed forenames and surname of the child and to mark the original entry in the Register of Births with the word "Adopted".[31] Since these provisions remain unamended, it would seem that they would apply even

[23] 1978 Act, s. 30(3), (4).
[24] 1978 Act, s. 45 and Sched. 1, para. 1(7).
[25] 1978 Act, s. 45 and Sched. 1, para. 4(2).
[26] 1978 Act, s. 45 and Sched. 1, para. 6.
[27] A.S. 1997, r. 2.31 (RCS, r. 67.30: the mode of delivery is not specified; but presumably the clerk of court would follow the sheriff court provisions).
[28] 1978 Act, s. 24(3); see paras 1.09 *et seq.*, above.
[29] A.S. 1997, rr. 2.12 and 2.30 (RCS, r. 67.6); see para. 5.03, above.
[30] Lees, *Interlocutors*, pp. 1, 33.
[31] 1978 Act, s. 45 and Sched. 1, para. 1(5).

in the case of the new procedure whereby a step-parent who is married to the natural parent of the child presents a petition for adoption alone, without the concurrence of the natural parent[32]: the Adopted Children Register now records, "Details of persons who are parents by virtue of the Order".[33] Similarly, where an adopted child is adopted again the Registrar must mark the Adopted Children Register with the word "Re-adopted".[34] Where the child has been adopted or re-adopted in England, the Registrar must on notification from the English Registrar mark the entry with the words "Adopted (England)" or "Re-adopted (England)" as the case may be, and similarly with adoptions granted in Northern Ireland, the Isle of Man or any of the Channel Islands.

In the case of an adoption abroad, the Registrar must make an entry in the Register of Births consisting of the words "Proposed Foreign Adoption" or "Proposed Foreign Re-adoption" with the name of the country in which the order was made.[35] Clearly, where the birth of the child was registered outwith Scotland or where the child was never registered in any country (as was the case of a child found abandoned in Delhi), the Registrar's duty is limited to making an entry in the Adopted Children Register. For the sake of complete identification of a child born outwith the United Kingdom, the adoption order should, where possible, contain the date and place of birth of the child and details of the register in which the birth of the child was noted.

Once the entry is made in the Adopted Children Register, an extract can be obtained as in the case of any of the other registers. There is no question of the Registrar delaying to issue an extract until the days of appeal have expired.

Sealing the Process

In the case of an application to any court the process must immediately **11.05** after

(a) the communication to the Registrar General for Scotland of an adoption order, an amendment to an adoption order or a revocation of an adoption order being made, or

(b) the issue of an extract (if any)[36]

be enclosed by the clerk of court in a sealed envelope. The sealed envelope shall not be opened by the clerk of court, nor by any person having the control of the records of any court.[37]

Judgments in adoption cases, as with other civil judgments of the court, **11.06** will be recorded in the appropriate court books (that is, in the sheriff court, the act book, and in the Court of Session, the opinion department).

---

[32] See para. 2.02, above.
[33] Information from General Register Office, December 3, 1997.
[34] 1978 Act, s. 45 and Sched. 1, para. 1(6).
[35] 1978 Act, s. 45(3) and Sched. 1, para. 2(4).
[36] A.S. 1997, r. 2.32(2) (RCS, r. 76.31).
[37] A.S. 1997, r. 2.33(2) (RCS, r. 67.32 where the appropriate officer is clerk of court or the extractor).

They are public documents which are available for public inspection and copying in the same way as other judgments of the court. Accordingly, nothing which appears in the instance or the body of the judgments should enable the parties to be identified.[38] Generally, the more recent records are in the custody of the clerk of court, whereas the older records are transmitted from time to time to the Scottish Record Office and the custody of the Keeper of the Records of Scotland.[39] In terms of these provisions, only the officers mentioned have custody of the process. On a strict construction of the powers the sheriff or Lord Ordinary would have no locus to permit or refuse to open up the process. However, in practice, the clerk would discuss any doubtful application with the court. After the process has been transmitted from the court, in law, the court has no control over this aspect of the case, and in practice the Keeper of the Records of Scotland deals with transmitted Court of Session processes[40] unless the process is retransmitted to the Office of Court.[41] The process in a petition which was not granted does not require to be sealed up; and there is no provision to the effect that rules about confidentiality still apply in such a case. Certainly, where a second petition was presented, it would be very necessary to have the earlier process before the court in order to determine whether there had been "a change in circumstances".[42] Where an earlier petition has been withdrawn, it would be desirable to reveal the circumstances of that earlier petition in the later proceedings.

ACCESS TO ADOPTION RECORDS

11.07   At the age of 16, the adopted child may have access to three sets of records.

> (1) The legal process of the court (sheriff court or the Court of Session) which granted the adoption order. In a normal case, the process will contain the petition, and productions[43] including the extract of the entry in the Register of Births relating to the child (but not the extract of the entry in the Register of Marriages of the petitioners which is returned to the petitioners before the process is sealed), reports of the local authority (under section 22 of the 1978 Act) or the adoption agency (under section 23 of the 1978 Act) and reports of the curator *ad litem* and reporting officer. In a defended case, there will also be the typed shorthand notes, if they have been extended, and the interlocutor sheets which will include any judgments of the court. The more recent processes are in the custody of the court; and the older processes are transmitted to the custody of the Keeper of the Records in the Scottish Record Office.[44]

---

[38] See para. 5.03, above.
[39] Preservation of Sheriff Court Records Regulations 1969 (S.I. 1969 No. 1756), reg. 5; Public Records (Scotland) Act 1937, s. 2(1); Public Registers and Records (Scotland) Act 1948, s. 5.
[40] *cf.* RCS, r. 9.1.
[41] RCS, r. 9.2.
[42] See para. 3.13, above.
[43] See para. 5.19, above.
[44] See para. 11.09, below.

(2) The records of the Registrar General for Scotland which were created by him following the directions to him contained in the adoption order. Apart from the Adopted Children Register and indexes thereto (which are open to search on behalf of the public), the records include such other registers and books as may be necessary to link the entries in the Register of Births and the Adopted Children Register.[45] These records are kept by the Registrar General for Scotland in New Register House.

(3) The information which the adoption agency ("local authority or approved adoption agency") has relating to the child's adoption.[46] The nature and bulk of these case records (and indexes) will, no doubt, vary with the circumstances of each case. That information must be preserved for 75 years by the adoption agency or its successors.[47]

The child has an unqualified right to have access to the first two classes of records, but not to the last.

Access to the Process

After the process has been sealed in a sealed envelope, not only may it **11.08** not be opened by the person having control of the records of the court, but the process must not be made accessible to any person for 100 years after the date of the adoption order except in certain situations.[48] The process may be made available before the end of the 100-year period as follows.

(a) To an adopted child who has attained the age of 16 years, and to **11.09** whom the adoption process refers.[49] Once the child has been satisfactorily identified by the person having custody of the records of the court, he has an indefeasible right to have access to the process.[50] No formal application is required. In replying to a written request, the sheriff clerk would no doubt keep in mind that the applicant may not wish other members of his household to know that he is writing, and may be under some stress; and in these circumstances he may wish to use a plain envelope. It is desirable to ask the applicant to telephone and arrange a time to see the process and to tell the applicant to bring some means of identification. Most inquiries are done personally, but it is submitted that the custodier of the records might with propriety act on a request of an agent if he is satisfied that the identity of the child and that the authority of the agent are sufficiently

---

[45] 1978 Act, s. 45(5).

[46] Adoption Agencies (Scotland) Regulations 1996 (S.I. 1996 No. 3266), reg. 25.

[47] Adoption Agencies (Scotland) Regulations 1996 (S.I. 1996 No. 3266), regs 23 and 24.

[48] A.S. 1997, r. 2.33(2) (RCS, r. 67.32(2)).

[49] A.S. 1997, r. 2.33(2)(a) (RCS, r. 67.32(2)(a)).

[50] The child, subject to arranging to receive counselling, is also entitled to receive an extract of the entry relating to the adopted person in the register of births: 1978 Act, s. 45(7). However, in England, it is held that absolute right can be qualified by a real risk of a serious crime being committed or serious danger to a member of the public: *R. v. Registrar General, ex p. Smith* [1991] 2 Q.B. 393. It is respectfully suggested that that decision is unlikely to be followed in Scotland.

vouched, particularly if the child lives at a distance, and all the more so if the child lives abroad. Once the child knows the information he can tell whomsoever he likes; accordingly, there seems to be little objection to the child authorising an agent to seek out the information on his behalf. It is understood that the custodiers of these records adopt such an approach. In any event, bodies outwith the United Kingdom can petition the court for access to a process.[51] It may be desirable to have the agent give a written undertaking that he will only communicate the information to the child. The child should give ample notice in writing of his request so that the clerk of court can search out the process or discover whether it has been transmitted to Register House.

In some cases the information which the child may glean from the process may be unexpected and upsetting to the child; for example, the child may learn for the first time that his or her parents were not married. Accordingly, especially in the case of a teenage child it may be prudent for the custodier of the records to suggest that the child be accompanied by a relative or friend on the visit to the court or Register House. There are provisions for counselling of children who seek access to the records of the Registrar General for Scotland. If the process has been transmitted to Register House from the court which granted the adoption order, and if the application is made to the court, no doubt the Keeper of the Records can retransmit the process to the sheriff clerk there for the inspection of it by the child. There can be no objection to the child taking notes from the process or even having a copy made: no doubt the clerk of court would charge the appropriate fee for copying. It is submitted that where the process is in the custody of the Keeper of the Records the same rules as to inspection, copying and being given a copy would apply. It is also submitted that the legislation empowering the Keeper to issue extracts and certified copies of any records transmitted to him[52] does not preclude him from providing a simple uncertified copy of adoption processes, again subject to payment of the appropriate fee. The motives of the child in having access to the process do not matter; and there would appear to be no locus for the court to seek to counsel the child not to exercise his right.

11.10   (b) To the sheriff clerk (or deputy principal clerk or extractor) on an application to him by an adoption agency with the consent of the adopted person for the purpose of ascertaining the name of the agency, if any, responsible for the placement of that person, and informing the applicant of that name.[53]

11.11   (c) To a person, on an application made by him to the sheriff setting forth the reasons for which access is required.[54]

11.12   (d) To a court, public authority or administrative board (whether in the United Kingdom or not) having power to authorise an adoption, on petition by it to the court which granted the original order requesting that informa-

---

[51] See para. 11.09, below.
[52] Public Records (Scotland) 1937, s. 9.
[53] A.S. 1997, r. 233(2)(b) (RCS, r. 67.31(2)(c)).
[54] A.S. 1997, r. 2.33(2)(c) (RCS, r. 67.31(2)(e)).

tion be made available from the process for the purpose of discharging its duties in considering an application for adoption and specifying the precise reasons for which access to the process is required.[55] In an appeal before the First Division—a petition for the adoption of a child by a single male who was living with another male in a homosexual relationship—the court authorised the *amicus curiae* who had been appointed in the case to examine and extract information from processes where adoption orders had been made in the sheriff court.[56] In a case decided before the operation of the section 2 of the Succession (Scotland) Act 1964—which altered the rights of succession between an adopted child and his parent—an adopted child died intestate leaving estate. His adoptive parents did not know the identity of the natural parents of the child. They presented a petition to the court craving access to the process in order to ascertain the names of the natural parents: the petition was granted.[57] In another unreported case the adoptive parents and child were taking up permanent residence in Italy and the Italian authorities required an affidavit from the court narrating the circumstances of the adoption. There the court entertained a petition by the parents to open up the process to enable the clerk to make an affidavit in respect of those matters.

(e) To a person who is authorised in writing by the Secretary of State to **11.13** obtain information from the process for the purpose of such research as is designed to improve the working of adoption law and practice.[58] In several applications the Secretary of State for Scotland gave written authority to open up processes to enable the author of this book to check a step in procedure in a case where that information could not be got from the official report of the case or from the session papers and to those undertaking research on behalf of the Social Work Services Group of the Scottish Education Department.

Sometimes the authorisation is signed by the Secretary of State himself **11.14** and sometimes it is signed by a civil servant on his behalf.[59]

There is no express provision in the adoption legislation authorising the **11.15** opening up of the process when an appeal is marked. However, it is a necessary implication of the general provisions governing appeals that in order to transmit the process to the sheriff principal or to the principal clerk of session the sheriff clerk must open up the process and that all those connected with the appeal must have access to the process. Similarly, where an extract is sought after the process has been sealed up, it is necessarily implied that the court has power to open up the process; and rules provide for such a situation.[60]

---

[55] A.S. 1997, r. 2.33(2)(d) (RCS, r. 67.31(2)(d)).
[56] *T, Petitioner,* 1996 S.C.L.R. 897 at 911E.
[57] *B and B, Petitioners,* 1950 S.L.T. (Sh.Ct.) 34.
[58] A.S. 1997, r. 2.33(2)(e) (RCS, r. 67.31(2)(f)); see Append. 2.16.
[59] *Carltona v. Commissioners of Works* [1943] 2 All E.R. 560 at 563; *F v. Management Committee and Managers, Ravenscraig Hospital,* 1989 S.L.T. 49.
[60] A.S. 1997, r. 2.33(2)(c) (RCS, r. 67.32(2)(e)); *E and E, Petitioners,* Edinburgh Sh.Ct., July 24, 1985, unreported; see Append. 2.15.

11.16   Where there is a subsidiary petition, such as one to revoke a direction to
the Registrar General for Scotland or to amend an adoption order, it may
be necessary for the court to have access to the original process. It is the
practice to seal the subsidiary process and put it with the original process
and seal them in a single envelope.

11.17   Further, the child and anyone else having reasons therefor can at any
time petition the court by whom the adoption order was pronounced to
issue an extract.[61] However, such a course is not common.

Records of the Registrar General for Scotland

11.18   Once the Registrar General for Scotland has made an entry in the
Adopted Children Register, anyone is entitled to inspect the register and
be furnished with an extract of that entry, as soon as it has been made.[62] In
addition, an adopted child can, at the age of 16, have access to the
Adopted Children Register, and also to the index thereto and such other
necessary registers and books which are kept by the Registrar General for
Scotland.[63] When the Registrar General for Scotland gives the child such
information he must advise the child that counselling services are available.[64] This counselling is optional.

---

[61] A.S. 1997, r. 2.32(2) (RCS, r. 67.31).
[62] 1978 Act, s. 45(3).
[63] 1978 Act, s. 45(5).
[64] 1978 Act, s. 45(6).

CHAPTER 12

AMENDMENT AND REVOCATION

Scope of Amendment and Revocation

Amendment and revocation of adoption orders and rectification or **12.01**
cancellation of registers arise in four situations, apart from which the
provisions for altering other vital records are to be found in sections 42 to 44
of the Registration of Births, Deaths and Marriages (Scotland) Act 1965.[1]

(a) The court may on the application of the adopter or the adopted **12.02**
person amend the order by the correction of any error in the particulars
contained therein.[2] Unlike the situation in the next paragraph, the subject-
matter of the application and the time for raising it are not limited. It is
envisaged that the kind of situation where this provision would be resorted
to would be where the original order recorded the wrong particulars of the
child, as in the case of a foundling where the true original names and
the true date of birth emerged later, or where the court had to determine
the probable date of birth,[3] and the actual information came to light later.
It is submitted that this paragraph could not be used to correct a situation
created by the petitioners or their agents whereby they *per incuriam*
inserted the wrong name of the child in the prayer of the petition and
that was correctly incorporated in the order and in the Adopted Children
Register and failed to make an application under the next paragraph
within its time-limit of one year, because there was no error in the
particulars in the adoption order.

(b) The court may, if satisfied on the application of the adopter or the **12.03**
adopted person that within one year beginning with the date of the order
any new name has been given to the adopted person (whether in baptism
or otherwise), or taken by him, either in lieu of or in addition to the
name specified in the particulars required to be entered in the Adopted
Children Register in pursuance of the order, amend the order by
substituting or adding that name in those particulars, as the case may
require.[4] Normally, the petitioners state in the crave of the petition the
proposed new names of the child and the adoption order and the entry in
the Adopted Children Register will follow the crave. Nevertheless, this
provision permits alteration of these names if the giving or taking of the

---

[1] 1978 Act, s. 45(8).
[2] 1978 Act, s. 45(9) and Sched. 1, para. 4(1); Append. 2.20.
[3] 1978 Act, s. 45(9) and Sched. 1, para. 1(3).
[4] 1978 Act, s. 45(9) and Sched. 1, para. 4(1)(a).

new name is made within one year of the granting of the order.[5] There are separate provisions of an analogous nature, without prejudice to these provisions, applying to persons whose births are registered in Scotland and to persons in respect of whom there is an entry in the Adopted Children Register.[6]

12.04   (c) If satisfied on the application of any person concerned that a direction for the marking of an entry in

> (i) the Register of Births, or
> (ii) the Adopted Children Register

was wrongly so included, the court may revoke that direction.[7]

12.05   (d) Where any person adopted by his father or mother alone has subsequently become a legitimated person on the marriage of his father and mother, the court by which the adoption order was made may, on the application of any of the parties concerned, revoke that order and the clerk of court must cause the revocation to be communicated to the Registrar General for Scotland who will cause to be cancelled

> (i) the entry in the Adopted Children Register relating to the adopted person, and
> (ii) the marking with the word "Adopted" (or, as the case may be, with that word the word "(England)") or an entry relating to him in the Register of Births.[8]

12.06   Also, where a person adopted by his father or mother alone by virtue of a regulated adoption (which means an overseas adoption of a description designated under section 65(2) of the 1978 Act as that of an adoption regulated by the Convention) becomes legitimated on the marriage of his father and mother, the Court of Session may, upon an application under section 46(2) of the 1978 Act by the parties concerned, by order revoke the adoption.[9]

Procedure

12.07   Any application under these sections, apart from the first, is effected by petition to the court which pronounced the adoption order. The court may order the petitioner to intimate to such persons as to the sheriff shall seem appropriate.[10] Where appropriate the verification of the matters in the petition would depend on documentary evidence or the oral testimony of the petitioner or his witnesses who have knowledge of the matters. If the matter is in dispute, it may be necessary to have a more formal proof. As has been indicated, the manner of communication to the Registrar

---

[5] See Append. 2.19.
[6] Registration of Births, Deaths and Marriages (Scotland) Act 1965, s. 43.
[7] 1978 Act, s. 45(9) and Sched. 1, para. 4(1)(b); see Append. 2.20.
[8] 1978 Act, s. 45(9) and Sched. 1.
[9] 1978 Act, s. 46(2); see paras 1.14 and 1.15, above.
[10] A.S. 1997, r. 2.34 (RCS, r. 67.29).

General for Scotland of an amendment to an adoption order or of a revocation of an adoption order under these sections is the same as in the case of an adoption order.[11] Where an adoption order is quashed, or an appeal against an adoption order is allowed by any court, the court must give directions to the Registrar General for Scotland to cancel any entry in the Adopted Children Register.[12]

---

[11] A.S. 1997, r. 2.31 (RCS, r. 67.32); see para. 11.03, above.
[12] 1978 Act, s. 45(9) and Sched. 1, para. 4(3).

CHAPTER 13

APPEAL

Competency

13.01 The adoption legislation only mentions obliquely the right of appeal from the decision of a court of first instance.[1] However, the general provisions applicable to the sheriff court, namely sections 27 and 28 of the Sheriff Courts (Scotland) Act 1907, have been consistently adopted with regard to appeals from the sheriff to the sheriff principal[2]; or to the Court of Session[3]; and no doubt a further appeal from the sheriff principal to the Court of Session, and a reclaiming motion for review of the interlocutor granting an adoption order pronounced in the Outer House in a petition for adoption are also competent.[4] There is a subsequent appeal to the House of Lords.[5] "Every judgment of an inferior Court is subject to review, unless such review is excluded expressly or by necessary implication"[6] and "the presumption is that the ordinary forms of that Court are to be observed".[7] Appeals are almost always against the grant[8] or refusal of an adoption order[9] which are by their nature final interlocutors and presumably do not require leave to appeal or reclaim unless they are not "final judgments"[10] as, for example, where expenses have not been dealt with.[11] However, in one case the sheriff-substitute granted leave to appeal.[12] No doubt, an order freeing a child for adoption or an order revoking such an order, or an interim order is open to appeal in the same way. There appear to be no examples of appeals on incidental matters, but should such arise and require leave of the court[13] it is most unlikely that in

---

[1] *e.g.* 1978 Act, s. 45(9) and Sched. 1, para. 4(3).
[2] *A and B, Petitioners* (1931) 67 Sh.Ct. Rep. 255; 1932 S.L.T. (Sh.Ct.) 37; *C v. D,* 1968 S.L.T. (Sh.Ct.) 39.
[3] *e.g. K, Petitioner*, 1949 S.C. 140.
[4] RCS, r. 38.2.
[5] *e.g. A v. B and C*, 1971 S.C. (H.L.) 129, a case which was initiated before the sheriff-substitute.
[6] *Central Regional Council v. B*, 1985 S.L.T. 413; *Harper v. Inspector of Rutherglen* (1903) 6 F. 23, *per* Lord Trayner at 25, quoted with approval in *Acari v. Dumbartonshire County Council*, 1948 S.L.T. 438.
[7] *Magistrates of Portobello v. Magistrates of Edinburgh* (1882) 10 R. 130.
[8] *e.g. A v. B and C*, 1971 S.C. (H.L.) 129.
[9] *e.g. AB and CB v. X's Curator*, 1963 S.C. 124.
[10] Sheriff Courts (Scotland) Act 1907, s. 3(h).
[11] Macphail, *Sheriff Court Practice* (1988, W. Green & Son Ltd), para. 18-35 and cases cited therein. In a recent case, where expenses had not been dealt with in the sheriff court, parties and the appeal court appear not to have been alive to the need to have leave to appeal: *F v. D*, 1994 S.C.L.R. 417.
[12] *AB and CB v. X's Curator*, 1963 S.C. 124.
[13] Sheriff Courts (Scotland) Act 1907, ss. 27(f) and 28(d); RCS, r. 38.4b.

view of the need for expedition and the relative simplicity of a petition for adoption that leave would be readily granted. In the Court of Session the interlocutor of the Lord Ordinary appointing a reporting officer before presentation of the petition "shall be final".[14] The time for moving for leave to appeal in terms of the rules dealing with ordinary actions is seven days after the date of the interlocutor appealed against.[15] In an adoption process there is seldom any question of an extract being given out— as is normal in an ordinary action—accordingly the time for appealing will not be curtailed by an extract being given out during that time. In England where the petitioners made inadequate inquiry as to the whereabouts of the natural mother, the court allowed the appeal out of time.[16] It may be that an appeal out of time could be made before the sheriff principal or in the Court of Session under the discretionary power of the court to

> "relieve a party from the consequences of any failure to comply with the provisions of these Rules which is shown to be due to mistake, oversight or other excusable cause, on such conditions, if any, as the court thinks fit."[17]

Where the court relieves a party from the consequences of a failure to comply with a provision in the Rules under that paragraph, the court may pronounce such interlocutor as it thinks fit to enable the cause to proceed as if the failure to comply with that provision had not occurred.[18] It would be the appellate court, not the court of first instance, which would exercise this discretion.[19]

THE APPELLANT

Usually the parties in an appeal are the persons who were parties in the **13.02** court of first instance.[20] The term "party" is referred to in the legislation[21] but it is not defined. Presumably, anyone such as a person whose agreement was required but who did not compear because he was not aware of the proceedings in the court of first instance or of a diet in the proceedings could appeal. In England it has been held that where a natural parent, whether or not she was a party within the meaning of the Rules of Court, had her consent dispensed with while she was at a known address in Australia, the court had power to set the decision aside.[22] A similar situation arose where a natural mother was not a respondent in the lower court because the petitioners had not, in the view of the appeal court,

---

[14] RCS, r. 67.10(6) (freeing) and r. 67.23(6) (adoption).

[15] Act of Sederunt (Sheriff Court Ordinary Cause Rules) 1993 (S.I. 1993 No. 1956), r. 31.2; (RCS, r. 38.3).

[16] *Re F (R)* [1970] 1 Q.B. 385.

[17] RCS, r. 2.1(1).

[18] RCS, r. 2.1(2); *cf. Richardson v. Minister of Pensions*, 1945 S.C. 363; Act of Sederunt (Sheriff Court Ordinary Cause Rules) 1993 (S.I. 1993 No. 1956), r. 2.1, which applies to ordinary actions but would presumably be applied to adoption petitions also: see notes 6 and 7, above.

[19] *Hardy v. Robinson; Johnstone v. W. Y. Walker*, 1985 S.L.T. (Sh.Ct.) 40.

[20] *e.g. AB and CB v. X's Curator*, 1963 S.C. 124; *A v. B and C*, 1971 S.C. (H.L.) 129.

[21] *e.g.* 1978 Act, s. 46(1); A.S. 1997, r. 2.30 (RCS, r. 67.3).

[22] *Re B* [1958] 1 Q.B. 12.

made adequate inquiry into the whereabouts of the natural mother.[23] Beyond that, there is less certainty, for in procedure by petition, unlike procedure by summons or initial writ, there is no necessary contradictor who can become an appellant. It is a question whether other persons on whom notice of a hearing has been served,[24] but did not compear, or even persons on whom a notice could have been served but was not, could be treated as appellants. It would appear to be necessary in the interests of the child that the child or his curator *ad litem* who has the express duty of safeguarding these interests[25] should be able to appeal where, for example, the child's consent had not been given to the making of the adoption order. No doubt the decision of the court of first instance on incidental matters, such as an amendment of an adoption order, which are initiated by petition (or note) or the removal of a child from the custody of a petitioner, which is dealt with by a minute, can be reviewed at the instance of those seeking or resisting such motions.[26]

Procedure

13.03   When an appeal is marked in the court of first instance, the clerk of court will normally transmit the process to the appellate court according to the appropriate Rules of Court. If the sheriff has not appended a note to his interlocutor, the note of appeal must request that the sheriff write a note setting out his reasons for his decision.[27] It has been said that it would not be right for the court to proceed to review what purported to be the exercise of a discretion by a sheriff-substitute without knowing whether he exercised his discretion at all or whether he exercised it upon proper grounds.[28] In any event, the sheriff is bound to append a note setting forth the grounds upon which he has proceeded.[29] In addition, it is desirable that the reasons of a judge should be written with the least possible delay, lest the passage of time becomes a significant circumstance in the ultimate disposal of the case. In one case it was said in the judgment of the court:

> "It is essential, especially in a small court where judicial resources are already under pressure for other reasons, that the sheriff should be given at the outset a carefully considered forecast of the time which the proof is expected to take. With the benefit of that information arrangements can and should be made for the sheriff to be released from other duties so that he can give priority to the case without interruption and until it has been completed by the issuing of his interlocutor."[30]

---

[23] *Re F (R)* [1970] 1 Q.B. 385.
[24] A.S. 1997, r. 2.11 (freeing), r. 2.18 (revocation) and r. 2.28 (adoption) (RCS, rr. 67.13, 67.15 and 67.25).
[25] 1978 Act, s. 58(1)(a).
[26] A.S. 1997, rr. 2.34 and 2.35 (RCS, r. 67.29(1)(a) and (b)).
[27] Act of Sederunt (Sheriff Court Ordinary Cause Rules) 1993 (S.I. 1993 No. 1956), r. 31.4(2)(d).
[28] *Hoggan v. McKeachie*, 1960 S.L.T. (Notes) 64.
[29] Act of Sederunt (Sheriff Court Ordinary Cause Rules) 1993 (S.I. 1993 No. 1956), r. 12.2(3)(b).
[30] *Lothian Regional Council v. A*, 1992 S.L.T. 858 at 861–862.

No doubt the court can retain a copy or procure a copy of the process from the appeal court to enable the judge to write his note. Sheriffs have given their decision in the form of a Court of Session judgment[31] or in the form of findings in fact and in law with a note of the grounds on which they had proceeded, as was done by the sheriff in *AB and CB v. X's Curator*[32] and as is in conformity with rule 12.2(3)(b): this is the normal form now, and, it is submitted, the proper form.[33] Where the shorthand notes of the evidence at the proof are not available at the hearing of the appeal, the court may proceed on the basis of the findings in fact.[34]

Once the diet for the appeal has been fixed there are no specialities of procedure except that the hearing takes place behind closed doors and the rules of confidentiality apply equally in the appeal court as in the court of first instance.[35]

The granting of an adoption order and the making of an entry by the **13.04** Registrar General in the Adopted Children Register are not suspended or otherwise affected by the marking of an appeal in the adoption process: that would only arise if the adoption order were quashed on appeal and the court gave directions to the Registrar General to cancel any entry.[36] An adoption process usually ends with an order being made, a copy of which is transmitted to the Registrar General. However, unlike an ordinary action, an extract is not given out for the asking: accordingly, an appeal has no bearing on the issue of an extract as it would in an ordinary civil action. In a case where the appellant was appealing against an order freeing a child for adoption, it was held that the motion of the appellant to suspend the order was misconceived and the motion was refused.[37]

In the Court of Appeal, it was held that the court had no inherent power to **13.05** set aside an adoption order which had been made regularly with the proper procedure, on the ground that there had been a fundamental misapprehension that a Jewish baby was being placed with Jewish parents.[38] Similarly, pre-existing ill health of the child which only becomes apparent subsequently is not a ground for reduction of the adoption order[39]; and there is no statutory

---

[31] *A v. B and C*, 1971 S.C. (H.L.) 129 and Session Papers.

[32] 1963 S.C. 124.

[33] *Lothian Regional Council v. S*, Sheriff Principal Nicholson, Edinburgh Sh.Ct., February 14, 1991, unreported; *Strathclyde Regional Council v. C*, Sheriff Principal Caplan, Paisley Sh.Ct., December 20, 1987, unreported, where the opinion expressed in this paragraph—that the appropriate procedure is for the sheriff to issue findings in fact and in law—was approved.

[34] *A v. B and C*, Inner House, November 1, 1991, unreported; *Grampian Regional Council v. X*, Sheriff Principal Risk, Banff Sh.Ct., February 2, 1994, unreported on this point, reported at 1994 G.W.D. 10-579, 15-914; *M v. S*, Sheriff Principal Risk, Banff Sh.Ct., May 18, 1994, unreported; *K and K, Petitioners*, Sheriff Principal Risk, Aberdeen Sh.Ct., February 8, 1994, unreported.

[35] 1978 Act, s. 57.

[36] 1978 Act s. 45 and Sched. 1, para. 4(3).

[37] *Lothian Regional Council v. A*, 1991 G.W.D. 32-1887.

[38] *Re B (Adoption Order: jurisdiction to set aside)* [1995] Fam. 237.

[39] *J and J v. C's Tutor*, 1948 S.C. 636.

provision for cancellation of an adoption order.[40] It is doubtful whether an appeal against an adoption order should be granted on the ground that the child had not truly consented to the order being made if the facts nullifying the consent only came to light later.[41] A different and exceptional situation arose where a divorced father gave his agreement to an adoption order which had been granted in a petition by his former wife and her new husband. The father had not known that his former wife had been suffering from cancer (from which she died three months later). In addition the children wished to make their home with the father. The Court of Appeal took the view that ignorance of a salient fact can vitiate agreement to the making of an adoption on the ground of mistake, and the court set aside the adoption order.[42]

DISPOSAL OF THE APPEAL

13.06   The consistent unwillingness of the appellate courts to interfere with the decision of the courts of first instance is best illustrated by certain dicta in the House of Lords in English and Scottish decisions.

> "Adoption cases depend so much on general impression rather than the ascertainment of particular facts that, when the judge at first instance has seen the parties, an appeal court must be slow to reverse his decision unless he has misdirected himself as to the law or has otherwise clearly gone wrong."[43]

> "Parliament has entrusted the decision of this matter in the first instance to the county court and, for my part, I should be reluctant to disturb a decision reached without error of law upon a matter which must depend to a large extent upon the impression formed by the trial judge as to the character of the mother and other witnesses."[44]

> "Where there has been no misdirection in law it must be quite exceptional for an appellate court to be justified in interfering with the decision of such a matter by the instance tribunal."[45]

13.07   However, in a case where the sheriff had misdirected himself, the appeal court regarded itself as free to examine the merits and substitute its own discretion for that initially confided in the sheriff.[46] In a case where the

---

[40] *Skinner v. Carter* [1948] Ch. 387 at 395, *per* Lord Greene M.R.

[41] *X v. Y*, Temporary Sheriff Principal Coutts, Alloa Sh.Ct., May 20, 1993, unreported.

[42] *Re M (Minors) (Adoption)* [1991] 1 F.L.R. 458.

[43] *A v. B and C*, 1971 S.C. (H.L.) 129 at 141, *per* Lord Reid; *cf. P (Minors) (Adoption by step-parent)* 1988 F.C.R. 401 C.A.

[44] *Re W* [1971] A.C. 682 at 724, *per* Lord Guest and quoted with approval in *A v. B and C*, 1971 S.C. (H.L.) 129 at 147, *per* Lord Simon of Glaisdale.

[45] *Re D* [1977] A.C. 602 at 637, *per* Lord Simon of Glaisdale; *cf. Re P (Minors) (Adoption by step-parent)* [1988] F.C.R. 401; and *Re P (A Minor)* [1990] 1 F.L.R. 96 (where the appeal court did not interfere with the judge's conclusion which he had reached as to the racial interest of the child).

[46] *H and H, Petitioners*, 1976 S.L.T. 80. In a later case this procedure, adopted by the sheriff principal so that the children would not be exposed to further uncertainty, was approved: *Central Regional Council v. L* (reported as *L v. Central Regional Council*), 1990 S.L.T. 818; and in another case to avoid delay: *Central Regional Council v. M*, 1991 S.C.L.R. 300; *cf. Strathclyde Regional Council v. McL* (reported as *McL v. Strathclyde Regional Council*) 1992 G.W.D. 24-1355, *per* Sheriff Principal Hay.

appeal court found that the sheriff-substitute was wrong in law in not dispensing with the consent of the natural mother, it recalled the interlocutor refusing the adoption order and remitted the case back to the sheriff to review all the considerations,[47] and in other cases where the sheriff-substitute had proceeded by interview of the parties, the appeal court remitted the cause back to him to hold a proof.[48] In another case where it was not clear from his note whether the sheriff had all the relevant considerations in mind, the court remitted the cause back to him to report *quam primum*[49]; and in a case where it had not been established that it was likely that the child would be placed for adoption, and the sheriff had not made a finding on this point, the sheriff principal refused the appeal on other grounds. However, the sheriff principal observed that had the appeal been allowed on these other grounds he would have continued the appeal to allow the applicants, if so advised, to lead evidence as to the likelihood of the child being placed for adoption.[50] The Court of Session has not always issued written opinions in cases where a small point is in issue[51]; in two unreported appeals, the Inner House affirmed the decision of the sheriff without giving opinions[52] but in most other cases opinions have been given.[53]

CHANGE OF CIRCUMSTANCES

Recently there have been cases, in which perhaps because of delay, **13.08** circumstances have changed and the appeal court has sought up-to-date information. Thus, in one case, where there had been considerable delay throughout the course of the case to such an extent that additional evidence was essential, the sheriff principal continued the appeal for a short period for the hearing of further but limited evidence before him.[54] Following the continued appeal the sheriff principal made a few additional findings in fact, allowed the appeal and granted the order.[55] In another case, also with some delay, where the alcohol dependency of a mother was in issue, her current position was raised in an appeal before the sheriff principal: the sheriff principal remitted consideration of the two up-to-date reports to the sheriff to enable him to report back to him.[56] The

---

[47] *AB and CB v. X's Curator*, 1963 S.C. 124 at 136 and 138.

[48] *AB v. CD*, 1970 S.C. 268; *K, Petitioner*, 1949 S.C. 140; *C v. D*, 1968 S.L.T. (Sh.Ct.) 30.

[49] *A v. B and C*, 1977 S.C. 27 at 32; *Strathclyde Regional Council v. A*, 1993 G.W.D. 9-585, where again there was significant delay and the sheriff was required to hear further evidence as to the change of circumstances and make further findings in fact.

[50] *Grampian Regional Council v. X*, 1994 G.W.D. 10-579 and 15-914.

[51] *A, Petitioner*, 1936 S.C. 255; *B and B, Petitioners*, 1936 S.C. 256; *C and C, Petitioners*, 1936 S.C. 257; *D, Petitioner*, 1938 S.C. 223.

[52] Second Division, Glasgow Sh.Ct. (3B/115/1978), January 23, 1981, unreported; *A and A v. A*, Second Division, March 16, 1983, unreported.

[53] *e.g. A and B v. C*, 1977 S.C. 27; *AB v. CB*, 1985 S.L.T. 514.

[54] *Lothian Regional Council v. S*, Sheriff Principal Nicholson, Edinburgh Sh.Ct., February 14, 1991, unreported: the sheriff cannot *ex proprio motu* allow or order further proof: Macphail, *Sheriff Court Practice* (1988, W. Green & Son Ltd), para. 18-79.

[55] *Lothian Regional Council v. S*, Sheriff Principal Nicholson, Edinburgh Sh.Ct., March 26, 1991, unreported.

[56] *Lothian Regional Council v. R*, Sheriff Principal O'Brien, Linlithgow Sh.Ct., February 3, 1987, unreported; 1987 G.W.D. 8-242; 1987 S.C.L.R. 362.

sheriff reported that he would not have reached a different decision if all the reports had previously been available. After hearing parties on the report the sheriff principal then refused the appeal.[57] However, elsewhere, it was observed in an appeal before the sheriff principal, that a report produced by the respondents at the appeal had not been read because of the dangers in introducing into an appeal unrestricted information not before the sheriff.[58]

---

[57] *W v. Lothian Regional Council* (properly, *Lothian Regional Council v. R*), Sheriff Principal O'Brien, Linlithgow Sh.Ct., February 25, and March 17, 1987; 1987 G.W.D. 13-440.

[58] *Lothian Regional Council v. M*, Sheriff Principal O'Brien, Linlithgow Sh.Ct., November 4, 1987; 1988 G.W.D. 39-1600; *cf. G v. G* [1985] 1 W.L.R. 647.

CHAPTER 14

EXPENSES

Apart from the common law right inherent in every civil court to award **14.01**
expenses in any cause that comes before it,[1] a court of first instance in an
adoption process may make such order with regard to the expenses, the
expenses of a reporting officer and a curator *ad litem* or any other person
who attended the hearing, of an application under the chapter of the rules
which deals with adoptions as it thinks fit and may modify such expenses
or direct them to be taxed on such scale as he may determine.[2] In a petition
for adoption, there is a crave for expenses.[3] In the normal unopposed
petition the petitioners will pay their own expenses including court dues,[4]
the account of their solicitor and, usually included in that account, the fee
and expenses of the curator *ad litem* and the reporting officer. In an
opposed petition if expenses are not dealt with, the judgment will not be
final and leave to appeal will be necessary.[5]

Since 1984, every local authority council must in certain cases[6]: **14.02**

(a) defray the expenses incurred by a member of a panel of curators
ad litem and reporting officers established in their area, and
(b) pay to him such fees and allowances as they think fit.

The effect of the regulations is that from 1986, the local authority must
pay these sums in all cases where the curator *ad litem* and reporting officer
are appointed from the panel.[7] However, there is a significant and unusual
exception: the local authority are not empowered to pay the fees of the
curator *ad litem* or reporting officer if

---

[1] MacLaren, *Expenses*, 3.

[2] A.S. 1997, r. 2.2. Before 1984 the corresponding rule narrated similar specific items; and
after 1984 the corresponding rule referred to "the expenses" without such specification. It is
submitted that the enumeration of the particular items does not detract from the generality of
"the expenses" and that all matters of expenses are for the court to decide (RCS, r. 67.7 where
particular but different items are enumerated).

[3] A.S. 1997, r. 2.21(1) Form 11 (RCS, r. 67.22 and Form 67.22).

[4] Sheriff Court Fees Order 1997 (S.I. 1997 No. 687), paras 2(1), 3 and Sched. 1, para. 6;
Court of Session etc. Fees Order 1997 (S.I. 1997 No. 688), para. 4 and Sched. 1, para. 1.

[5] Macphail, *Sheriff Court Practice* (1988, W. Green & Son Ltd), para. 18-35.

[6] See para. 7.04, above.

[7] Curators *ad litem* and Reporting Officers (Panels) (Scotland) Regulations 1984
(S.I. 1984 No. 566), reg. 10 (as amended by Curators *ad litem* and Reporting Officers
(Panels) (Scotland) Amendment Regulations 1985 (S.I. 1985 No. 1556), reg. 4).

(a) the child was not placed by an adoption agency; and

(b) the adoption order, or the order to adopt a child abroad is not granted by the court.[8]

In the cases where there is a liability on them, the local authorities have agreed among themselves on a scale of fees both for normal and for extraordinary cases. Normally, a curator *ad litem* or a reporting officer who was drawn from the panel and who had been required to undertake additional work or to resolve unusual problems would render an account in respect of his extra work to the local authority. Usually the curator *ad litem* or the reporting officer would ask the court to approve the additional remuneration either informally or by means of a formal interlocutor. These provisions do not affect the power of the court to deal with the expenses of the whole petition wherein an account of expenses and fee of the curator *ad litem* and the reporting officer would form only a part. Indeed, the provisions[9] only identify who should pay these sums; they do not detract from the power of the court to make any order with regard to expenses.[10] If the court, on the motion of the curator *ad litem* or the reporting officer, made an order assessing his fee at a sum greater than the local authorities had agreed to pay, no doubt the petitioners would be liable to pay the excess. It is thought, however, that the local authority would respect the court's determination in this matter.

14.03   In addition to these local authority panels, there are in most sheriff courts persons who are not on the local authority panels who (as envisaged in the legislation[11]) may be appointed by the sheriff to act as curators *ad litem* and reporting officers. Courts will no doubt prefer not to use the local authority panel in cases where the child was not placed by an adoption agency because there is no certainty of payment and because liability will only arise if the order is granted.[12] Sometimes the natural parent, whose agreement has to be taken, lives in a local authority area different from the area of the sheriff court dealing with the petition. Then the court may appoint a member of the panel within its area who would travel to the other area and look to his own local authority for payment; or the court may appoint a member of the panel in the other area who would look to that local authority for payment. No doubt considerations of economy would determine which course was adopted. Delay in paying the fee of the curator *ad litem* became a problem in some courts and has been met by indicating to the solicitors at the time of lodging the petition that the court would expect that payment should normally be made as soon as the report had been lodged and suggesting that in cases where the petitioners were not assisted persons they should put the solicitors in funds at least to the extent of the fee in cases where the petitioners (and not the

---

[8] See para. 7.04, above.

[9] Assuming that they are *intra vires*.

[10] See para. 14.01, above.

[11] 1995 Act, s. 101(1)(a), (b); see para. 7.04, above.

[12] See para. 7.04, above.

local authority) are liable to pay the fee. In cases where the local authority are liable to pay, arrangements should be made whereby the curator *ad litem* and the reporting officer intimate to the local authority that the reports have been lodged. When the reports have been lodged and the curator *ad litem* or the reporting officer intimates that fact, then fees should be paid within a matter of days. Although the report is not called for by the petitioner, but by the court, he may be in the first instance responsible for the fees and expenses of the reports.[13] If no explanation for delay in payment were forthcoming the court could make him personally liable. The style of petition includes in the prayer the words "and to pronounce such other or further orders or directions upon such matters, including the expenses of this petition, as the court may think fit".[14] Even in the event of opposition, the question of expenses is seldom raised and each side is liable for his own expenses. In a case where the question of expenses was raised, an unsuccessful respondent might be liable for such additional expenses as were occasioned by his intervention, or an unsuccessful petitioner might be liable for all or part of the expenses depending on the nature of the circumstances. In one appeal which appeared to have little merit the Court of Session found the unsuccessful appellant liable in the expenses of the appeal but his liability was modified at nil.[15]

---

[13] A.S. 1997, r. 2.2 (RCS, r. 67.7). It is submitted that these general provisions would be wide enough to cover such an arrangement as is provided for in the ordinary rules: Act of Sederunt (Sheriff Court Ordinary Cause Rules) 1993 (S.I. 1993 No. 1956), r. 33.21 (RCS, r. 42.15).

[14] A.S. 1997, Form 2.10 and Form 5 (RCS, r. 67.12 and Form 67.12).

[15] Glasgow Adoption, Second Division, (3B/115/1978), January 23, 1981, unreported. As to legal aid see para. 5.10, above.

ADOPTION (SCOTLAND) ACT 1978

(1978 c. 28)

ARRANGEMENT OF SECTIONS

PART I

THE ADOPTION SERVICE

The Adoption Service

PART II

ADOPTION ORDERS

The making of adoption orders

PART III

CARE AND PROTECTION OF CHILDREN AWAITING ADOTION

Restrictions on removal of children

Protected children

PART IV

STATUS OF ADOPTED CHILDREN

PART V

REGISTRATION AND REVOCATION OF ADOPTION ORDERS AND CONVENTION ADOPTIONS

PART VI

MISCELLANEOUS AND SUPPLEMENTAL

An Act to consolidate the enactments relating to adoption in Scotland with amendments to give effect to recommendations of the Scottish Law Commission.

[July 20, 1978]

PART I

THE ADOPTION SERVICE

The Adoption Service

Establishment of Adoption Service

1.—(1) It is the duty of every local authority to establish and maintain within their area a service designed to meet the needs, in relation to adoption, of—

(a) children who have been or may be adopted;

(b) parents and guardians of such children; and

(c) persons who have adopted or may adopt a child;

and for that purpose to provide the requisite facilities, or secure that they are provided by approved adoption societies.

(2) The facilities to be provided as part of the service maintained under subsection (1) include—

(a) [*Repealed by the Children (Scotland) Act 1995 (c. 36), ss.98(1) 105(5), Sched. 2, para. 2 and Sched. 5*];

(b) arrangements for assessing children and prospective adopters, and placing children for adoption;

(bb) counselling and assistance (but, without prejudice to sections 51 to 51B, not assistance in cash) to children who have been adopted and to persons who have adopted a child; and

(c) counselling for other persons if they have problems relating to adoption.

(3) The facilities of the service maintained under subsection (1) shall be provided in conjunction with the local authority's other social services and with approved adoption societies in their area, so that help may be given in a co-ordinated manner without duplication, omission or avoidable delay.

(4) The services maintained by local authorities under subsection (1) may be collectively referred to as "the Scottish Adoption Service", and a local authority or approved adoption society may be referred to as an adoption agency.

Local authorities' social work

2. The social services referred to in section 1(3) are the functions of a local authority under any of the enactments mentioned in subsection (1B) of section 5 of the Social Work (Scotland) Act 1968 (power of Secretary of State to issue directions to local authorities in respect of their functions under certain enactments), including, in particular but without prejudice to the generality of the foregoing, a local authority's functions relating to—

(a) the promotion of the welfare of children by diminishing the need to receive children into care or keep them in care, including (in exceptional circumstances) the giving of assistance in cash;

(b) the welfare of children in the care of a local authority;

(c) the welfare of children who are foster children within the meaning of the Foster Children (Scotland) Act 1984;

(d) [*Repealed by the Children (Scotland) Act 1995 (c. 36), s.105(5) and Sched. 5*];

(e) the provision of residential accommodation for expectant mothers and young children and of day-care facilities;

(f) the regulation and inspection of nurseries and child minders;

(g) care and other treatment of children through court proceedings and children's hearings.

Adoption societies

Approval of adoption societies

3.—(1) Subject to any regulations made under section 9(1), a body which is a voluntary organisation may apply to the Secretary of State for his approval to its acting, or as the case may be continuing to act, as an adoption society, whether functioning generally or in relation to some service maintained, or to be maintained, as part of the Scottish Adoption Service and specified in the application (the service so specified being in this section and in section 4 referred to as the body's "specified service").

(1A) Application under subsection (1) shall be in such manner as may be specified in regulations made by the Secretary of State under this section.

(2) In considering an application under subsection (1), the Secretary of State shall take into account the matters relating to the applicant specified in subsections (3) to (5) and any other matters which appear to him to be relevant; and if, but only if, he is satisfied that, as the case may be, the applicant is likely to make, or is making, an effective contribution to the Scottish Adoption Service or to the applicant's specified service, he shall by notice to the applicant give the approval sought.

(2A) Approval under subsection (2) shall operate from such date as may be specified in the notice or, in the case of a renewal of approval, from the date of the notice.

(3) In considering the application, the Secretary of State shall have regard, in relation to the period for which approval is sought, to the following—
  (a) the applicant's adoption programme,
  (aa) the procedures in accordance with which the applicant deals with, or as the case may be proposes to deal with, complaints arising in relation to its exercise of its functions and, where the applicant is already an approved adoption society, the manner in which it deals with particular complaints,
  (b) the number and qualifications of its staff,
  (c) its financial resources, and
  (d) the organisation and control of its operations.

(4) Where it appears to the Secretary of State that the applicant is likely to operate extensively within the area of a particular local authority he shall ask the authority whether they support the application, and shall take account of any views about it put to him by the authority.

(5) Where the applicant is already an approved adoption society or, whether before or after the passing of this Act, previously acted as an adoption society, the Secretary of State, in considering the application, shall also have regard to the record and reputation of the applicant in the adoption field, and the geographical areas within which, the services as respects which and the scale on which it is currently operating or has operated in the past.

(6) If after considering the application the Secretary of State is not satisfied that the applicant is likely to make or, as the case may be, is making an effective contribution to the Scottish Adoption Service, or as the case may be to the applicant's specified service, the Secretary of State shall, subject to section 5(1) and (2), by notice inform the applicant that its application is refused.

(7) If not withdrawn earlier under section 4, approval given under this section shall last for such period not exceeding three years from the date on which it becomes operative, and shall then expire or, in the case of an approved adoption society whose further application for approval is pending at that time, shall expire on the date that application is granted or, as the case may be, refused.

Withdrawal of approval

4.—(1) If, while approval of a body under section 3 is operative, it appears to the Secretary of State that the body is not making an effective contribution to the Scottish Adoption Service or, as the case may be for the body's specified service, he shall, subject to section 5(3) and (4), by notice to the body withdraw the approval from a date specified in the notice.

(2) If an approved adoption society fails to provide the Secretary of State with information required by him for the purposes of carrying out his functions under subsection (1), or fails to verify such information in the manner required by him, he may by notice to the society withdraw the approval from a day specified in the notice.

(3) Where approval is withdrawn under subsection (1) or (2) or expires the Secretary of State may direct the body concerned to make such

arrangements as to children who are in its care and other transitional matters as seem to him expedient.

Procedure on refusal to approve, or withdrawal of approval from, adoption societies

5.—(1) Before notifying a body which has applied for approval that the application is refused in accordance with section 3(6) the Secretary of State shall serve on the applicant a notice—

    (a) setting out the reasons why he proposes to refuse the application;

    (b) informing the applicant that it may make representations in writing to the Secretary of State within 28 days of the date of service of the notice.

(2) If any representations are made by the applicant in accordance with subsection (1), the Secretary of State shall give further consideration to the application taking into account those representations.

(3) The Secretary of State shall, before withdrawing approval of an adoption society in accordance with section 4(1), serve on the society a notice—

    (a) setting out the reasons why he proposes to withdraw the approval; and

    (b) informing the society that it may make representations in writing to the Secretary of State within 28 days of the date of service of the notice.

(4) If any representations are made by the society in accordance with subsection (3), the Secretary of State shall give further consideration to the withdrawal of approval under section 4(1) taking into account those representations.

(5) This section does not apply where the Secretary of State, after having considered any representations made by the applicant in accordance with this section, proposes to refuse approval or, as the case may be, to withdraw approval for reasons which have already been communicated to the applicant in a notice under this section.

Welfare of children

Duty to promote welfare of child

6.—(1) Without prejudice to sections 12(8) and 18(8), in reaching any decision relating to the adoption of a child, a court or adoption agency shall have regard to all the circumstances but—

    (a) shall regard the need to safeguard and promote the welfare of the child concerned throughout his life as the paramount consideration; and

    (b) shall have regard so far as practicable—

        (i) to his views (if he wishes to express them) taking account of his age and maturity; and

        (ii) to his religious persuasion, racial origin and cultural and linguistic background.

(2) Without prejudice to the generality of paragraph (b) of subsection (1), a child twelve years of age or more shall be presumed to be of sufficient age and maturity to form a view for the purposes of that paragraph.

Duty to consider alternatives to adoption

6A. In complying with its duties under section 6 of this Act, an adoption agency shall, before making any arrangements for the adoption of a child, consider whether adoption is likely best to meet the needs of that child or whether for him there is some better, practicable, alternative; and if it concludes that there is such an alternative it shall not proceed to make those arrangements.

Religious upbringing of adopted child

7. An adoption agency shall in placing a child for adoption have regard (so far as is practicable) to any wishes of the child's parents and guardians as to the religious upbringing of the child.

Supplemental

Inactive or defunct adoption societies

8. [*Repealed by the Children (Scotland) Act 1995 (c. 36), ss.98(1), 105(5), Sched. 2, para. 4 and Sched. 5.*]

Regulation of adoption agencies

9.—(1) The Secretary of State may by regulations prohibit unincorporated bodies from applying for approval under section 3; and he shall not approve any unincorporated body whose application is contrary to regulations made under this subsection.

(2) The Secretary of State may make regulations for any purpose relating to the exercise of its functions by an approved adoption society including, without prejudice to the generality of this subsection, regulations as to procedures for dealing with complaints arising in relation to such exercise.

(3) The Secretary of State may make regulations with respect to the exercise by local authorities of their functions of making or participating in arrangements for the adoption of children.

(3A) Regulations under this section may make provision—

(a) as to the determination by an adoption agency of whether, as regards a child for whose adoption it proposes to make arrangements, any such agreement as mentioned in sections 16(1)(b)(i) and 18(1)(a) is likely to be forthcoming and as to a period by the end of which, if they have determined that the agreement is unlikely to be forthcoming and if no application has been made for an adoption order in relation to the child, application for an order under section 18(1) shall require to be made in relation to him; and

(b) where the case of a child for whose adoption an adoption agency proposes to make arrangements is referred under section 73(4)(c)(ii) or (iii) of the Children (Scotland) Act 1995 to the Principal Reporter (within the meaning of Part II of that Act), as to circumstances in which and, on the occurrence of such circumstances, a period by the end of which, if no application has been made for an adoption order in relation to the child, application for an order under section 18(1) shall require to be made in relation to him.

(4) Any person who contravenes or fails to comply with regulations made under subsection (2) shall be guilty of an offence and liable on summary conviction to a fine not exceeding level 5 on the standard scale.

(5) Regulations under this section may make different provisions in relation to different cases or classes of cases and may exclude certain cases or classes of cases.

10. [*Repealed by the Health and Social Services and Social Security Adjudications Act 1983 (c. 41), Sched. 2, para. 39 and Sched. 10.*]

Restriction on arranging adoptions and placing of children

11.—(1) A person other than an adoption agency shall not make arrangements for the adoption of a child, or place a child for adoption, unless the proposed adopter is a relative of the child.

(2) An adoption society which is—

(a) approved as respects England and Wales under section 3 of the Adoption Act 1976; or

(b) registered as respects Northern Ireland under Article 4 of the Adoption (Northern Ireland) Order 1987,

but which is not approved under section 3 of this Act, shall not act as an adoption society in Scotland except to the extent that the society considers it necessary to do so in the interests of a person mentioned in section 1 of that Act or, as the case may be, Article 3 of that Order.

(3) A person who—

(a) takes part in the management or control of a body of persons which exists wholly or partly for the purpose of making arrangements for the adoption of children and which is not an approved adoption society or a local authority; or

(b) contravenes subsection (1); or

(c) both receives a child placed with him in contravention of subsection (1) and knows that the placement is with a view to his adopting the child,

shall be guilty of an offence and liable on summary conviction to imprisonment for a term not exceeding three months or to a fine not exceeding level 5 on the standard scale or to both.

(4) In any proceedings for an offence under paragraph (a) of subsection (3), proof of things done or of words written, spoken or published (whether or not in the presence of any party to the proceedings) by any person taking part in the management or control of a body of persons, or in making arrangements for the adoption of children on behalf of the body, shall be sufficient evidence of the purpose for which that body exists.

(5) Section 26 shall apply where a person is convicted of a contravention of subsection (1) as it applies where an application for an adoption order is refused.

PART II

ADOPTION ORDERS

12.—(1) An adoption order is an order vesting the parental responsibilities and parental rights in relation to a child in the adopters, made on their application by an authorised court; except that an adoption order may be made in relation to a person who has attained the age of 18 years if the application for it was made before such attainment.

(2) Subject to subsection (3A) the order does not affect the parental responsibilities and parental rights so far as they relate to any period before the making of the order.

(3) The making of an adoption order operates to extinguish—

(a) any parental responsibility or parental right relating to the child which immediately before the making of the order was vested in a person (not being one of the adopters) who was—

    (i) a parent of the child, or

    (ii) a guardian of the child appointed by a deed or by the order of a court;

(b) any duty owed to the child—

    (i) to pay or provide aliment in respect of any period occurring after the making of the order;

    (ii) to make any payment arising out of parental responsibilities and parental rights in respect of such a period.

(3A) Where the adoption order is made by virtue of section 15(1)(aa), its making shall not operate to extinguish the parental responsibilities and parental rights which immediately before the making of the order were vested in the natural parent to whom the adopter is married.

(4) Nothing in subsection (3) shall extinguish any duty arising under a deed or agreement which constitutes a trust or which expressly provides that the duty is not to be extinguished by the making of an adoption order;

(5) An adoption order may not be made in relation to a child who is or has been married.

(6) An adoption order may contain such terms and conditions as the court thinks fit.

(7) An adoption order may be made notwithstanding that the child is already an adopted child.

(8) An adoption order shall not be made in relation to a child of or over the age of 12 years unless with the child's consent; except that, where the court is satisfied that the child is incapable of giving his consent to the making of the order, it may dispense with that consent.

(9) Where a court making an adoption order in relation to a child who is subject to a supervision requirement is satisfied that, in consequence of its doing so, compulsory measures of supervision in respect of the child are no longer necessary, it may determine that the child shall forthwith cease to be subject to that requirement.

Child to live with adopters before order made

13.—(1) Where the applicant, or one of the applicants, is a parent, step-parent or relative of the child, or the child was placed with the applicants by an adoption agency, an adoption order shall not be made unless the child is at least nineteen weeks old and at all times during the preceding thirteen weeks had his home with the applicants or one of them.

(2) Where subsection (1) does not apply, an adoption order shall not be made unless the child is at least twelve months old and at all times during the preceding twelve months had his home with the applicants or one of them.

(3) An adoption order shall not be made unless the court is satisfied that sufficient opportunities to see the child with the applicant, or in the case of an application by a married couple, both applicants together in the home environment have been afforded—

    (a) where the child was placed with the applicant by an adoption agency, to that agency, or

    (b) in any other case, to the local authority within whose area the home is.

Adoption by married couple

14.—(1) An adoption order shall not be made on the application of more than one person except in the circumstances specified in subsections (1A) and (1B).

(1A) An adoption order may be made on the application of a married couple where both the husband and the wife have attained the age of 21 years.

(1B) An adoption order may be made on the application of a married couple where—

    (a) the husband or the wife—

        (i) is the father or mother of the child; and

        (ii) has attained the age of 18 years; and

    (b) his or her spouse has attained the age of 21 years.

(2) An adoption order shall not be made on the application of a married couple unless—

    (a) at least one of them is domiciled in a part of the United Kingdom, or in the Channel Islands or the Isle of Man, or

    (b) the application is for a Convention adoption order and section 17 is complied with, or

    (c) both of them were habitually resident in any of the places mentioned in paragraph (a) above throughout the period of one year which ends with the date of their application.

Adoption by one person

15.—(1) An adoption order may be made on the application of one person where he has attained the age of twenty-one years and—

    (a) is not married, or

   (aa) not being a person who may make application by virtue of paragraph (b) below, is married to a person—

        (i) who is the natural parent of the child concerned; and

        (ii) in whom are vested parental responsibilities and parental rights in relation to the child,

    (b) not being a person who may make application by virtue of paragraph (aa) above, is married and the court is satisfied that—

        (i) his spouse cannot be found, or

        (ii) the spouses have separated and are living apart, and the separation is likely to be permanent, or

       (iii) his spouse is by reason of ill-health, whether physical or mental, incapable of making an application for an adoption order.

(2) An adoption order shall not be made on the application of one person unless—

    (a) he is domiciled in a part of the United Kingdom, or in the Channel Islands or the Isle of Man, or

    (b) the application is for a Convention adoption order and section 17 is complied with, or

    (c) he was habitually resident in any of the places mentioned in paragraph (a) above throughout the period of one year which ends with the date of his application.

(3) An adoption order shall not be made on the application of the mother or father of the child alone unless the court is satisfied that—

    (a) the other parent is dead or cannot be found or, by virtue of section 28 of the Human Fertilisation and Embryology Act 1990, there is no other parent, or

    (b) there is some other reason justifying the exclusion of the other parent,

and where such an order is made the reason justifying the exclusion of the other parent shall be recorded by the court.

Parental agreement

16.—(1) An adoption order shall not be made unless—

    (a) the child is free for adoption by virtue of an order made

        (i) in Scotland under section 18;

        (ii) in England and Wales under section 18 of the Adoption Act 1976; or

        (iii) in Northern Ireland under Article 17(1) or 18(1) of the Adoption (Northern Ireland) Order 1987,

        and not revoked; or

    (b) in the case of each parent or guardian of the child the court is satisfied that—

        (i) he freely, and with full understanding of what is involved, agrees unconditionally to the making of an adoption order (whether or not he knows the identity of the applicants), or

        (ii) his agreement to the making of the adoption order should be dispensed with on a ground specified in subsection (2).

(2) The grounds mentioned in subsection (1)(b)(ii) are, that the parent or guardian—

    (a) is not known, cannot be found or is incapable of giving agreement;

    (b) is withholding agreement unreasonably;

    (c) has persistently failed, without reasonable cause, to fulfil one or other of the following parental responsibilities in relation to the child—

        (i) the responsibility to safeguard and promote the child's health, development and welfare; or

        (ii) if the child is not living with him, the responsibility to maintain personal relations and direct contact with the child on a regular basis;

    (d) has seriously ill-treated the child, whose reintegration into the same household as the parent or guardian is, because of the serious ill-treatment or for other reasons, unlikely.

(3) Subsection (1) does not apply in any case where the child is not a United Kingdom national and the application for the adoption order is for a Convention adoption order.

(4) Agreement is ineffective for the purposes of subsection (1)(b)(i) if given by the mother less than six weeks after the child's birth.

(5) [*Repealed by the Children (Scotland) Act 1995 (c. 36), ss.98(1), 105(5), Sched. 2, para. 10 and Sched. 5.*]

Convention adoption order

17.—(1) An adoption order shall be made as a Convention adoption order if the application is for a Convention adoption order and the following conditions are satisfied both at the time of the application and when the order is made.

(2) The child—

(a) must be a United Kingdom national or a national of a Convention country, and

(b) must habitually reside in British territory or a Convention country, and

(c) must not be, or have been, married.

(3) The applicant or applicants and the child must not all be United Kingdom nationals living in British territory.

(4) If the application is by a married couple, either—

(a) each must be a United Kingdom national or a national of a Convention country, and both must habitually reside in Great Britain, or

(b) both must be United Kingdom nationals, and each must habitually reside in British territory or a Convention country,

and if the applicants are nationals of the same Convention country the adoption must not be prohibited by a specified provision (as defined in subsection (8)) of the internal law of that country.

(5) If the application is by one person, either—

(a) he must be a United Kingdom national or a national of a Convention country, and must habitually reside in Great Britain, or

(b) he must be a United Kingdom national and must habitually reside in British territory or a Convention country,

and if he is a national of a Convention country the adoption must not be prohibited by a specified provision (as defined in subsection (8)) of the internal law of that country.

(6) If the child is not a United Kingdom national the order shall not be made—

(a) except in accordance with the provisions, if any, relating to consents and consultations of the internal law relating to adoption of the Convention country of which the child is a national, and

(b) unless the court is satisfied that each person who consents to the order in accordance with that internal law does so with full understanding of what is involved.

(7) The reference to consents and consultations in subsection (6) does not include a reference to consent by and consultation with the applicant and members of the applicant's family (including his or her spouse), and for the purposes of subsection (6) consents may be proved in the manner prescribed by act of sederunt and the court shall be treated as the authority by whom, under the law mentioned in

subsection (6), consents may be dispensed with and the adoption in question may be effected; and where the provisions there mentioned require the attendance before that authority of any person who does not reside in Great Britain, that requirement shall be treated as satisfied for the purposes of subsection (6) if—

(a) that person has been given a reasonable opportunity of communicating his opinion on the adoption in question to the proper officer or clerk of the court, or to an appropriate authority of the country in question, for transmission to the court; and

(b) where he has availed himself of that opportunity, his opinion has been transmitted to the court.

(8) In subsections (4) and (5) "specified provision" means a provision specified in an order of the Secretary of State as one notified to the Government of the United Kingdom in pursuance of the provisions of the Convention which relate to prohibitions on an adoption contained in the national law of the Convention country in question.

Freeing for adoption

Freeing child for adoption

18.—(1) Where, on an application by an adoption agency which is a local authority, an authorised court is satisfied in the case of each parent or guardian of the child that—

(a) he freely, and with full understanding of what is involved, agrees generally and unconditionally to the making of an adoption order, or

(b) his agreement to the making of an adoption order should be dispensed with on a ground specified in section 16(2),

the court shall, subject to subsection (8), make an order declaring the child free for adoption.

(2) No application shall be made under subsection (1) unless—

(a) it is made with the consent of a parent or guardian of a child, or

(b) the adoption agency is applying for dispensation under subsection (1)(b) of the agreement of each parent or guardian of the child, and the child is in the care of the adoption agency.

(3) No agreement required under subsection (1)(a) shall be dispensed with under subsection (1)(b) unless the child is already placed for adoption or the court is satisfied that it is likely that the child will be placed for adoption.

(4) An agreement by the mother of the child is ineffective for the purposes of this section if given less than six weeks after the child's birth.

(5) On the making of an order under this section, the parental responsibilities and parental rights in relation to the child are transferred to the adoption agency.

(6) Before making an order under this section, the court shall satisfy itself, in relation to each parent or guardian of the child who can be found, that he has been given an opportunity of making, if he so wishes, a declaration that he prefers not to be involved in future questions concerning the adoption of the child; and any such declaration shall be recorded by the court.

(7) Before making an order under this section in the case of a child whose father is not, and has not been, married to the mother and does not have any parental responsibilities or parental rights in relation to the child, the court shall satisfy itself in relation to any person claiming to be the father that—

    (a) he has no intention of applying for, or, if he did so apply, it is likely that he would be refused, an order under section 11 of the Children (Scotland) Act 1995 (orders in relation to parental responsibilities and parental rights); and

    (b) he has no intention of entering into an agreement with the mother under section 4(1) of that Act (acquisition by natural father by agreement of such responsibilities and rights), or, if he has such an intention, that no agreement under that subsection is likely to be made.

(8) An order under this section shall not be made in relation to a child of or over the age of 12 years unless with the child's consent; except that where the court is satisfied that the child is incapable of giving his consent to the making of the order, it may dispense with that consent.

(9) Where a court making an order under this section in relation to a child who is subject to a supervision requirement is satisfied that, in consequence of its doing so, compulsory measures of supervision in respect of the child are no longer necessary, it may determine that the child shall forthwith cease to be subject to that requirement.

Progress reports to former parent

19.—(1) This section and section 20 apply to any person (in this section and in section 20 referred to as the "relevant parent") who was required to be given an opportunity of making a declaration under section 18(6) but either—

    (a) did not do so; or

    (b) having done so, subsequently by written notice under this subsection by the adoption agency to which the parental responsibilities and parental rights have been transferred, has withdrawn such declaration.

(2) Within the fourteen days following the date twelve months after the making of the order under section 18, the adoption agency to which the parental responsibilities and parental rights were transferred on the making of the order, unless it has previously by notice to the relevant parent informed him that an adoption order has been made in respect of the child, shall by notice to the relevant parent inform him—

    (a) whether an adoption order has been made in respect of the child, and (if not)

    (b) whether the child has his home with a person with whom he has been placed for adoption.

(3) If at the time when the relevant parent is given notice under subsection (2) an adoption order has not been made in respect of the child, it is thereafter the duty of the adoption agency to give notice to the relevant parent of the making of an adoption order (if and when made), and meanwhile to give the relevant parent notice whenever the child is placed for adoption or ceases to be placed with a person with a view to his being adopted by that person.

(4) If at any time the relevant parent by notice makes a declaration to the adoption agency that he prefers not to be involved in future questions concerning the adoption of the child—

(a) the agency shall secure that the declaration is recorded by the court which made the order under section 18, and

(b) the agency is released from the duty of complying further with subsection (3) as respects that relevant parent,

but a declaration under this subsection may be withdrawn in the same way as may a declaration under subsection (6) of section 18, in which event the agency shall no longer be so released.

Revocation of s.18 order

20.—(1) The relevant parent, at any time more than 12 months after the making of the order under section 18 when—

(a) no adoption order has been made in respect of the child, and

(b) the child does not have his home with a person with whom he has been placed for adoption.

may apply to the court which made the order for a further order revoking it on the ground that he wishes to resume the parental responsibilities and parental rights.

(1A) The adoption agency, at any time after the making of the order under section 18 when the conditions mentioned in paragraphs (a) and (b) of subsection (1) above are satisfied, may apply to the court which made the order for a further order revoking it.

(2) While an application under subsection (1) or (1A) is pending the adoption agency having the parental responsibilities and parental rights shall not place the child for adoption without the leave of the court.

(3) Where an order freeing a child for adoption is revoked under this section, the court shall, by an order under section 11 of the Children (Scotland) Act 1995 determine on whom are to be imposed the parental responsibilities, and to whom are to be given the parental rights, in relation to the child.

(4) Subject to subsection (5), if an application under subsection (1) is dismissed on the ground that to allow it would contravene the principle embodied in section 6—

(a) the relevant parent who made the application shall not be entitled to make any further application under subsection (1) in respect of the child, and

(b) the adoption agency is released from the duty of complying further with section 19(3) as respects that parent.

(5) Subsection (4)(a) shall not apply where the court which dismissed the application gives leave to the relevant parent to make a further application under subsection (1), but such leave shall not be given unless it appears to the court that because of a change in circumstances or for any other reason it is proper to allow the application to be made.

Variation of s. 18 order so as to substitute one adoption agency for another

21.—(1) On an application to which this section applies an authorised court may vary an order under section 18 so as to transfer the parental responsibilities and parental rights relating to the child from the adoption agency to which they are transferred by virtue of the order ("the existing agency") to another adoption agency ("the substitute agency").

(2) This section applies to any application made jointly by the existing agency and the would-be substitute agency.

(3) Where an order under section 18 is varied under this section, section 19 shall apply as if the parental responsibilities and parental rights relating to the child had been transferred to the substitute agency on the making of the order.

Supplemental

Notification to local authority of adoption application

22.—(1) An adoption order shall not be made in respect of a child who was not placed with the applicant by an adoption agency unless the applicant has, at least three months before the date of the order, given notice to the local authority within whose area he has his home of his intention to apply for the adoption order.

(2) On receipt of such a notice the local authority shall investigate the matter and submit to the court a report of their investigation.

(3) Under subsection (2), the local authority shall in particular investigate,—

(a) so far as is practicable, the suitability of the applicant, and any other matters relevant to the operation of section 6 in relation to the application; and

(b) whether the child was placed with the applicant in contravention of section 11.

(4) A local authority which receive notice under subsection (1) in respect of a child whom the authority know to be in the care of another local authority shall, not more than seven days after the receipt of the notice, inform that other local authority in writing that they have received the notice.

Children subject to supervision requirements

22A.—(1) An approved adoption society shall refer the case of a child who is subject to a supervision requirement to the Principal Reporter where it is satisfied that the best interests of the child would be served by its placing the child for adoption and it intends so to place him.

(2) On a case being referred to him under subsection (1), the Principal Reporter shall arrange for a children's hearing to review the supervision requirement in question and shall make any arrangements incidental to that review.

(3) Subsections (9), (13) and (14) of section 73 of the Children (Scotland) Act 1995 (which provide, respectively, for acting on the review of a supervision requirement, a report by a children's hearing and consideration of that report) shall apply in relation to a children's hearing arranged under this section as those subsections apply in relation to one arranged by virtue of subsection (4)(c)(iii) of that section.

(4) In this section "Principal Reporter" has the same meaning as in Part II of the Children (Scotland) Act 1995.

Reports where child placed by agency

23. Where an application for an adoption order relates to a child placed by an adoption agency, the agency shall submit to the court a report on the suitability of the applicants and any other matters relevant to the operation of section 6, and shall assist the court in any manner the court may direct.

Restrictions on making adoption orders

24.—(1) The court shall not proceed to determine an adoption for an adoption order in relation to a child where a previous application for a British adoption order made in relation to the child by the same persons was refused by any court unless—

(a) in refusing the previous application the court directed that this subsection should not apply, or

(b) it appears to the court that because of a change in circumstances or for any other reason it is proper to proceed with the application.

(2) The court may make an adoption order in relation to a child even where it is found that the applicants have, as respects the child, contravened section 51.

(3) In considering whether to make an adoption order or an order under section 18(1), the court shall regard the welfare of the child concerned as its paramount consideration and shall not make the order in question unless it considers that it would be better for the child that it should do so than that it should not.

Interim orders

25.—(1) Where on an application for an adoption order the requirements—

(a) of section 16(1); and

(b) in a case where the child was not placed with the applicant by an adoption agency, of section 22(1),

are complied with the court may postpone the determination of the application and make an order giving parental responsibilities and parental rights to the applicants for a probationary period not exceeding two years upon such terms for the aliment of the child and otherwise as the court thinks fit.

(2) Where the probationary period specified in an order under subsection (1) is less than two years, the court may by a further order extend the period to a duration not exceeding two years in all.

Timetable for resolving question as to whether agreement to adoption orders etc. should be dispensed with

25A. In proceedings in which the question arises as to whether the court is satisfied as is mentioned in section 16(1)(b)(ii) or 18(1)(b), the court shall, with a view to determining the question without delay—

(a) draw up a timetable specifying periods within which certain steps must be taken in relation to those proceedings; and

(b) give such directions as it considers appropriate for the purpose of ensuring, so far as is reasonably practicable, that the timetable is adhered to.

Care etc. of child on refusal of adoption order

26. [*Repealed by the Children (Scotland) Act 1995 (c. 36), s.105(5) and Sched. 5.*]

PART III

CARE AND PROTECTION OF CHILDREN AWAITNG ADOPTION

Restrictions on removal of children

Restrictions on removal where adoption agreed or application made under s.18

27.—(1) Where—
(a) an adoption agency has placed a child with a person with a view to his being adopted by the person; and
(b) the consent of each parent or guardian of the child has been duly obtained to that placement (whether or not in knowledge of the identity of the person),

any such parent or guardian shall not be entitled to remove the child from the care and possession of the person without the leave either of the adoption agency or of the court.

(2) The reference in subsection (1) to consent having been duly obtained is to its having been obtained in accordance with such regulations as may be made by the Secretary of State for the purposes of this section.

(3) Any person who removes a child in contravention of subsection (1) shall be guilty of an offence and liable on summary conviction to imprisonment for a term not exceeding three months or a fine not exceeding level 5 on the standard scale or both.

(4), (5) [*Repealed by Health and Social Services and Social Security Adjudications Act 1983 (c. 41), Sched. 2, para. 42, and Sched. 10.*]

Restrictions on removal where applicant has provided home for five years

28.—(1) While an application for an adoption order in respect of a child made by the person with whom the child has had his home for the five years preceding the application is pending, no person is entitled, against the will of the applicant, to remove the child from the applicant's care and possession except with the leave of the court or under the authority conferred by any enactment or on the arrest of the child.

(2) Where a person ("the prospective adopter") gives notice to the local authority within whose area he has his home that he intends to apply for an adoption order in respect of a child who for the preceding five years has had his home with the prospective adopter, no person is entitled, against the will of the prospective adopter, to remove the child from the prospective adopter's care and possession, except with the leave of the court or under authority conferred by an enactment or on the arrest of the child, before—

    (a) the prospective adopter applies for the adoption order, or

    (b) the period of three months from the receipt of the notice by the
        local authority expires,

whichever occurs first.

    (3) In any case where subsection (1) or (2) applies and—

    (a) the child was in the care of a local authority before he began to
        have his home with the applicant or, as the case may be, the
        prospective adopter, and

    (b) the child remains in the care of a local authority,

the authority in whose care the child is shall not remove the child from the
care and possession of the applicant or of the prospective adopter except
in accordance with section 30 or 31 or with leave of a court.

    (4) Subsection (3) does not apply where the removal of the child is
authorised under or by virtue of Chapter 2 or 3 of Part II of the Children
(Scotland) Act 1995.

    (5) A local authority which receives such notice as is mentioned in
subsection (2) in respect of a child whom the authority know to be in the
care of another local authority, shall, not more than seven days after the
receipt of the notice, inform that other authority in writing that they have
received the notice.

    (6) Subsection (2) does not apply to any further notice served by the
prospective adopter on any local authority in respect of the same child
during the period referred to in paragraph (b) of that subsection or within
28 days after its expiry.

    (7) Any person who contravenes subsection (1) or (2) shall be guilty of
an offence and liable on summary conviction to imprisonment for a term
not exceeding three months or a fine not exceeding level 5 on the standard
scale or both.

    (8), (9) [*Repealed by Health and Social Services and Social Security
Adjudications Act 1983 (c. 41), Sched. 2, para. 42, and Sched. 10.*]

    (10) The Secretary of State may by order amend subsection (1) or (2) to
substitute a different period for the period of five years mentioned in that
subsection (or the period which by a previous order under this subsection,
was substituted for that period).

    (11) In subsections (2) and (3) "a court" means a court having
jurisdiction to make adoption orders.

Return of child taken away in breach of s.27 or 28

    29.—(1) An authorised court may on the application of a person
from whose care and possession of a child has been removed in breach
of section 27 or 28, or section 27 or 28 of the Adoption Act 1976 or
Article 28 or 29 of the Adoption (Northern Ireland) Order 1987 order
the person who has so removed the child to return the child to the
applicant.

    (2) An authorised court may on the application of a person who has
reasonable grounds for believing that another person is intending to
remove the child from the applicant's care and possession in breach of
section 27 or 28, or section 27 or 28 of the Adoption Act 1976 or Article 28
or 29 of the Adoption (Northern Ireland) Order 1987 by order direct that
other person not to remove the child from the applicant's care and

possession in breach of section 27 or 28, or section 27 or 28 of the Adoption Act 1976 or Article 28 or 29 of the Adoption (Northern Ireland) Order 1987.

Return of children placed for adoption by adoption agencies

30.—(1) Subject to subsection (2), at any time after a child has been delivered into the care and possession of any person in pursuance of arrangements made by an approved adoption society or local authority for the adoption of the child by that person, and before an adoption order has been made on the application of that person in respect of the child—

(a) that person may give notice in writing to the society or authority of his intention not to retain the care and possession of the child; or

(b) the society or authority may cause notice in writing to be given to that person of their intention not to allow the child to remain in his care and possession.

(2) No notice under paragraph (b) of subsection (1) shall be given in respect of a child in relation to whom an application has been made for an adoption order except with the leave of the court to which the application has been made.

(3) Where a notice is given to an adoption society or local authority by any person, or by such a society or authority to any person, under subsection (1), or where an application for an adoption order made by any person in respect of a child placed in his care and possession by such a society or authority is refused by the court or withdrawn, that person shall, within seven days after the date on which notice was given or the application refused or withdrawn, as the case may be, cause the child to be returned to the society or authority, who shall receive the child.

(4) Where the period specified in an interim order made under section 25 (whether as originally made or as extended under subsection (2) of that section) expires without an adoption order having been made in respect of the child, subsection (3) shall apply as if the application for an adoption order upon which the interim order was made had been refused at the expiration of that period.

(5) It shall be sufficient compliance with the requirements of subsection (3) if the child is delivered to, and is received by, a suitable person nominated for the purpose by the adoption society or local authority.

(6) Where an application for an adoption order is refused the court may, if it thinks fit at any time before the expiry of the period of seven days mentioned in subsection (3), order that period to be extended to a duration, not exceeding six weeks, specified in the order.

(7) Any person who contravenes the provisions of this section shall be guilty of an offence and liable on summary conviction to imprisonment for a term not exceeding three months or to a fine not exceeding level 5 on the standard scale or to both; and the court by which the offender is convicted may order the child in respect of whom the offence is committed to be returned to his parent or guardian or to the adoption society or local authority which made the arrangements referred to in subsection (1).

Application of s.30 where child not placed for adoption

31.—(1) Where a person gives notice in pursuance of section 22(1) to the local authority within whose area he has his home of his intention to apply for an adoption order in respect of a child who is for the time being in the care of a local authority, not being a child who was delivered into the care and possession of that person in pursuance of such arrangements as are mentioned in section 30(1), that section shall apply as if the child had been so delivered, except that where the application is refused by the court or withdrawn the child need not be returned to the local authority in whose care he is unless that authority so require.

(2) Where notice of intention is given as aforesaid in respect of any child who is for the time being in the care of a local authority then, until the application for an adoption order has been made and disposed of, any right of the local authority to require the child to be returned to them otherwise than in pursuance of section 30 shall be suspended.

(3) While the child remains in the care and possession of the person by whom the notice is given no contribution shall by payable (whether under a contribution order or otherwise) in respect of the child by any person liable under section 78 of the Social Work (Scotland) Act 1968 to make contributions in respect of him (but without prejudice to the recovery of any sum due at the time the notice is given), unless twelve weeks have elapsed since the giving of the notice without the application being made or the application has been refused by the court or withdrawn.

Protected children

Meaning of "protected child"

32.–37. [*Repealed by the Children (Scotland) Act 1995 (c. 36), ss.98(1), 105(5), Sched. 2, para. 21 and Sched. 5.*]

Part IV

Status of Adopted Children

Meaning of "adoption order" in part iv

38.—(1) In this Part "adoption order" means—
(a) an adoption order within the meaning of section 65(1);
(b) an adoption order under the Children Act 1975, the Adoption Act 1958, the Adoption Act 1950 or any enactment repealed by the Adoption Act 1950;
(c) an order effecting an adoption made in England, Wales, Northern Ireland, the Isle of Man or any of the Channel Islands;
(d) an "overseas adoption" within the meaning of section 65(2); or
(e) any other adoption recognised by the law of Scotland;
and cognate expressions shall be construed accordingly.

(2) The definition of adoption order includes, where the context admits, an adoption order which took effect before the commencement of the Children Act 1975.

Status conferred by adoption

39.—(1) A child who is the subject of an adoption order shall be treated in law—
  (a) where the adopters are a married couple, as if—
      (i) he had been born as a legitimate child of the marriage (whether or not he was in fact born after the marriage was constituted); and
      (ii) he were not the child of any person other than the adopters;
  (b) where the adoption order is made by virtue of section 15(1)(aa) as if—
      (i) he had been born as a legitimate child of the marriage between the adopter and the natural parent to whom the adopter is married (whether or not he was in fact born after the marriage was constituted); and
      (ii) he were not the child of any person other than the adopter and that natural parent; and
  (c) in any other case, as if—
      (i) he had been born as a legitimate child of the adopter; and
      (ii) he were not the child of any person other than the adopter.

(2) Where a child has been adopted by one of his natural parents as sole adoptive parent and the adopter thereafter marries the other natural parent, subsection (1) shall not affect any enactment or rule of law whereby, by virtue of the marriage, the child is rendered the legitimate child of both natural parents.

(3) This section has effect—
  (a) in the case of an adoption before 1st January 1976, from that date, and
  (b) in the case of any other adoption, from the date of the adoption.

(4) Subject to the provisions of this Part, this section—
  (a) applies for the construction of enactments or instruments passed or made before or after the commencement of this Act so far as the context admits; and
  (b) does not affect things done or events occurring before the adoption or, where the adoption took place before 1st January 1976, before that date.

(5) This section has effect subject to the provision of section 44.

40. [*Repealed by the British Nationality Act 1981 (c. 61), Sched. 9.*]

Miscellaneous enactments

41.—(1) Section 39 does not apply in determining the forbidden degrees of consanguinity and affinity in respect of the law relating to marriage or in respect of the crime of incest, except that, on the making of an adoption order, the adopter and the child shall be deemed, for all time coming, to be within the said forbidden degrees in respect of the law relating to marriage and incest.

(2) Section 39 does not apply for the purposes of any provision of—
  (a) the British Nationality Act 1981,
  (b) the Immigration Act 1971,
  (c) any instrument having effect under an enactment within paragraph (a) or (b), or

(d) any other law for the time being in force which determines British citizenship, British Dependent Territories citizenship, the status of a British National (Overseas) or British Overseas citizenship.

(3), (4), (5) [*Repealed by the Social Security Act 1988 (c. 7), Sched. 5.*]

Pensions

42. Section 39(1) does not affect entitlement to a pension which is payable to or for the benefit of a child and is in payment at the time of his adoption.

Insurance

43. Where a child is adopted whose natural parent has effected an insurance with a friendly society or a collecting society or an industrial insurance company for the payment on the death of the child of money or funeral expenses, the rights and liabilities under the policy shall by virtue of the adoption be transferred to the adoptive parents who shall for the purposes of the enactments relating to such societies and companies be treated as the person who took out the policy.

Effect of s.39 on succession and *inter vivos* deed

44. Section 39 (status conferred by adoption) does not affect the existing law relating to adopted persons in respect of—
  (a) the succession to a deceased person (whether testate or intestate), and
  (b) the disposal of property by virtue of any *inter vivos* deed.

PART V

REGISTRATION AND REVOCATION OF ADOPTION ORDERS AND CONVENTION ADOPTIONS

Adopted children register

45.—(1) The Registrar General for Scotland shall maintain at the General Register Office a register, to be called the Adopted Children Register, in which shall be made such entries as may be directed to be made therein by adoption orders, but no other entries.

(2) An extract of any entry in the Adopted Children Register maintained under this section, if purporting to be sealed or stamped with the seal of the General Register Office, shall, without any further or other proof of that entry, be received as evidence of the adoption to which it relates and, where the entry contains a record of the date of birth or the country of the birth of the adopted person, shall also be received as aforesaid as evidence of that date or country.

(3) The Registrar General for Scotland shall cause an index of the Adopted Children Register maintained under this section to be made and kept in the General Register Office; and the Registrar General for Scotland shall—
  (a) cause a search to be made of that index on behalf of any person or permit that person to search the index himself, and

(b) issue to any person an extract of any entry in that register which that person may require,

in all respects upon and subject to the same terms, conditions and regulations as to payment of fees and otherwise as are applicable under the Registration of Births, Deaths and Marriages (Scotland) Act 1965 in respect of searches in other indexes kept in the General Register Office and in respect of the supply from that office of extracts of entries in the registers of births, deaths and marriages.

(4) The Registrar General for Scotland shall, in addition to the Adopted Children Register and the index thereto, keep such other registers and books, and make such entries therein, as may be necessary to record and make traceable the connection between any entry in the register of births which has been marked "Adopted" pursuant to paragraph 1 of Schedule 1 or any enactment at the time in force and any corresponding entry in the Adopted Children Register maintained under this section.

(5) The registers and books kept under subsection (4) shall not be, nor shall any index thereof be, open to public inspection or search, nor, except under an order of the Court of Session or a sheriff, shall the Registrar General for Scotland furnish any information contained in or any copy or extract from any such registers or books to any person other than an adopted person who has attained the age of 16 years and to whom that information, copy or extract relates or a local authority Board or adoption society falling within subsection (6) which is providing counselling for that adopted person.

(6) Where the Registrar General for Scotland furnishes an adopted person with information under subsection (5), he shall advise that person that counselling services are available—

(a) if the person is in Scotland—
  (i) from the local authority in whose area he is living;
  (ii) where the adoption order relating to him was made in Scotland, from the local authority in whose area the court which made the order sat; or
  (iii) from any other local authority in Scotland;
(b) if the person is in England and Wales—
  (i) from the local authority in whose area he is living;
  (ii) where the adoption order relating to him was made in England and Wales, from the local authority in whose area the court which made the order sat; or
  (iii) from any other local authority in England and Wales;
(c) if the person is in Northern Ireland—
  (i) from the Board in whose area he is living;
  (ii) where the adoption order relating to him was made in Northern Ireland, from the Board in whose area the court which made the order sat; or
  (iii) from any other Board;
(d) if the person is in the United Kingdom and his adoption was arranged by an adoption society—
  (i) approved under section 3;
  (ii) approved under section 3 of the Adoption Act 1976; or
  (iii) registered under Article 4 of the Adoption (Northern Ireland) Order 1987,

from that society.

(6A) Where an adopted person who is in Scotland—

(a) is furnished with information under subsection (5); or

(b) applies for information under—

(i) section 51(1) of the Adoption Act 1976; or

(ii) Article 54 of the Adoption (Northern Ireland) Order 1987,

any body mentioned in subsection (6B) to which the adopted person applies for counselling shall have a duty to provide counselling for him.

(6B) The bodies referred to in subsection (6A) are—

(a) any local authority falling within subsection (6)(a); and

(b) any adoption society falling within subsection (6)(d) so far as it is acting as an adoption society in Scotland.

(7) Where an adopted person has arranged to receive counselling from a local authority, Board or adoption society falling within subsection (6), the Registrar General for Scotland shall, on receipt of a request from the local authority, Board or adoption society, and on payment of the appropriate fee, send to the authority Board or society an extract of the entry relating to the adopted person in the register of births.

(8) The provisions of the Registration of Births, Deaths and Marriages (Scotland) Act 1965 with regard to the correction of errors in entries shall apply to the Adopted Children Register maintained by the Registrar General for Scotland and to registration therein in like manner as they apply to any register of births and to registration therein.

(9) Schedule 1 to this Act, which, among other things, provides for the registration of adoptions and the amendment of adoption orders, shall have effect.

(10) In this section—

"Board" means a Health and Social Services Board established under Article 16 of the Health and Personal Social Services (Northern Ireland) Order 1972; and

"local authority", in relation to England and Wales, means the council of a county (other than a metropolitan county), a metropolitan district, a London borough or the Common Council of the City of London.

Revocation of adoptions on legitimation

46.—(1) Where the natural parents of a child, one of whom has adopted him in Scotland, have subsequently married each other, the court by which the adoption order was made may, on the application of any of the parties concerned, revoke that order.

(2) Where a person adopted by his father or mother alone by virtue of a regulated adoption has subsequently become a legitimated person on the marriage of his father and mother, the Court of Session may, upon an application under this subsection by the parties concerned, by order revoke the adoption.

Annulment etc. of overseas adoptions

47.—(1) The Court of Session may, upon an application under this subsection, by order annul a regulated adoption or an adoption effected by a Convention adoption order—

(a) on the ground that at the relevant time the adoption was prohibited by a notified provision, if under the internal law then in force in the country of which the adopter was then a national or the adopters were then nationals the adoption could have been impugned on that ground;

(b) on the ground that at the relevant time the adoption contravened provisions relating to consents of the internal law relating to adoption of the country of which the adopted person was then a national, if under that law the adoption could then have been impugned on that ground;

(c) on any other ground on which the adoption can be impugned under the law for the time being in force in the country in which the adoption was effected.

(2) The Court of Session may, upon an application under this subsection—

(a) order that an overseas adoption or a determination shall cease to be valid in Great Britain on the ground that the adoption or determination is contrary to public policy or that the authority which purported to authorise the adoption or make the determination was not competent to entertain the case;

(b) decide the extent, if any, to which a determination has been affected by a subsequent determination.

(3) Any court in Great Britain may, in any proceedings in that court, decide that an overseas adoption or a determination shall, for the purposes of those proceedings, be treated as invalid in Great Britain on either of the grounds mentioned in subsection (2).

(4) An order or decision of the High Court on an application under subsection (2) of section 53 of the Adoption Act 1976 shall be recognised and have effect as if it were an order or decision of the Court of Session on an application under subsection (2) of this section.

(5) Except as provided by this section and section 46(2) the validity of an overseas adoption or a determination shall not be impugned in Scotland in proceedings in any court.

Provisions supplementary to ss.46(2) and 47

48.—(1) Any application for an order under section 46(2) or 47 or a decision under section 47(2)(b) shall be made in the prescribed manner and within such period, if any, as may be prescribed.

(2) No application shall be made under section 46(2) or 47(1) in respect of an adoption unless immediately before the application is made the person adopted or the adopter habitually resides in Scotland or, as the case may be, both adopters habitually reside there.

(3) In deciding in pursuance of section 47 whether such an authority as is mentioned in section 53 was competent to entertain a particular case, a court shall be bound by any finding of fact made by the authority and stated by the authority to be so made for the purpose of determining whether the authority was competent to entertain the case.

(4) In section 47—

"determination" means such a determination as is mentioned in section 53;

"notified provision" means a provision specified in an order of the Secretary of State as one in respect of which a notification to or by the Government of the United Kingdom was in force at the relevant time in pursuance of the provisions of the Convention relating to prohibitions contained in the national law of the adopter; and

"relevant time" means the time when the adoption in question purported to take effect under the law of the country in which it purports to have been affected.

PART VI

MISCELLANEOUS AND SUPPLEMENTAL

Adoption of child abroad

49.—(1) Where on an application made in relation to a child by a person who is not domiciled in England and Wales or Scotland or Northern Ireland an authorised court is satisfied that he intends to adopt the child under the law of or within the country in which the applicant is domiciled, the court may, subject to the following provisions of this section, make an order transferring to him the parental responsibilities and parental rights in relation to the child.

(2) The provisions of Part II relating to adoption orders, except sections 12(1), 14(2), 15(2), 17 to 21 and 25, shall apply in relation to orders under this section as they apply in relation to adoption orders subject to the modification that in section 13(1) for "nineteen" and "thirteen" there are substituted "thirty-two" and "twenty-six" respectively.

(3) Section 45 and paragraphs 1 and 2(1) and (3) of Schedule 1 shall apply in relation to an order under this section as they apply in relation to an adoption order except that any entry in the register of births or the Adopted Children Register which is required to be marked in consequence of the making of an order under this section shall, in lieu of being marked with the word "Adopted" or "Re-adopted" (with or without the addition of the words "(England)" or "(Northern Ireland)"), be marked with the words "Proposed foreign adoption" or "Proposed foreign re-adoption", as the case may require.

(4) [*Repealed by the Children Act 1989 (c. 41), Sched. 15.*]

Restriction on removal of children for adoption outside Great Britain

50.—(1) Except under the authority of an order under section 49, or under section 55 of the Adoption Act 1976 or Article 57 of the Adoption (Northern Ireland) Order 1987, it shall not be lawful for any person to take or send a child who is a British subject or a citizen of the Republic of Ireland out of Great Britain to any place outside the United Kingdom, the Channel Islands and the Isle of Man with a view to the adoption of the child by any person not being a parent or guardian or relative of the child; and any person who takes or sends a child out of Great Britain to any place in contravention of this subsection, or makes or takes part in any arrangements for transferring the care and possession of a child to any person for that purpose, shall be guilty of an offence and liable on summary conviction to imprisonment for a term not exceeding three months or to a fine not exceeding level 5 on the standard scale or to both.

(2) In any proceedings under this section, a report by a British consular officer or a deposition made before a British consular officer and authenticated under the signature of that officer shall, upon proof that the officer or the deponent cannot be found in the United Kingdom, be sufficient evidence of the matters stated therein, and it shall not be necessary to prove the signature or official character of the person who appears to have signed any such report or deposition.

(3) A person shall be deemed to take part in arrangements for transferring the care and possession of a child to a person for the purpose referred to in subsection (1) if—

    (a) he facilitates the placing of the child in the care and possession of that person; or

    (b) he initiates or takes part in any negotiations of which the purpose or effect is the conclusion of any agreement or the making of any arrangement therefor, or if he causes another person to do so.

Prohibition on certain payments

51.—(1) Subject to the provisions of this section and of section 51A(3), it shall not be lawful to make or give to any person any payment or reward for or in consideration of—

    (a) the adoption by that person of a child;

    (b) the grant by that person of any agreement or consent required in connection with the adoption of a child;

    (c) the transfer by that person of the care and possession of a child with a view to the adoption of the child; or

    (d) the making by that person of any arrangements for the adoption of a child.

(2) Any person who makes or gives, or agrees or offers to make or give, any payment or reward prohibited by this section, or who receives or agrees to receive or attempts to obtain any such payment or reward, shall be guilty of an offence and liable on summary conviction to imprisonment for a term not exceeding three months or to a fine not exceeding level 5 on the standard scale or to both; and without prejudice to any power which the court has to make any other order in relation to the child as respects whom the offence was committed, it may order him to be removed to a place of safety until he can be restored to his parents or guardian or until other arrangements can be made for him.

(3) This section does not apply to any payment made to an adoption agency by a parent or guardian of a child or by a person who adopts or proposes to adopt a child, being a payment in respect of expenses reasonably incurred by the agency in connection with the adoption of the child, or to any payment or reward authorised by the court to which an application for an adoption order in respect of a child is made.

(4) This section does not apply to—

    (a) any payment made by an adoption agency to a person who has applied or proposes to apply to a court for an adoption order or an order under section 49, being a payment of or towards any legal or medical expenses incurred or to be incurred by that person in connection with the application; or

(b) any payment made by an adoption agency to another adoption agency in consideration of the placing of a child in the care and possession of any person with a view to the child's adoption; or

(c) any payment made by an adoption agency to a voluntary organisation for the time being approved for the purposes of this paragraph by the Secretary of State as a fee for the services of that organisation in putting that adoption agency into contact with another adoption agency with a view to the making of arrangements between the adoption agencies for the adoption of a child.

(5) Subject to section 51B, if an adoption agency submits to the Secretary of State a scheme for the payment by the agency of allowances to persons who have adopted or intend to adopt a child where arrangements for the adoption were made, or are to be made, by that agency, and the Secretary of State approves the scheme, this section shall not apply to any payment made in accordance with the scheme (including any such payment made by virtue of section 51B).

(6) The Secretary of State, in the case of a scheme approved by him under subsection (5), may at any time—

(a) [*Repealed by the Children (Scotland) Act 1995 (c. 36), ss.98(1), 105(5), Sched. 2, para. 24 and Sched. 5.*]

(b) revoke the scheme.

(7) [*Repealed by the Children (Scotland) Act 1995 (c. 36), ss.98(1), 105(5), Sched. 2, para. 24 and Sched. 5.*]

(8) [Repealed by S.I. 1989 No. 194.]

(9)–(11) [*Repealed by the Children (Scotland) Act 1995 (c. 36), ss.98(1), 105(5), Sched. 2, para. 24 and Sched. 5.*]

Adoption allowances schemes

51A.—(1) Subject to subsection (2), an adoption agency which is—

(a) a local authority shall, within such period after the coming into force of this section as the Secretary of State may by order direct;

(b) an approved adoption society may,

prepare a scheme (in this section and in section 51B referred to as an "adoption allowances scheme") for the payment by the agency of allowances to any person who has adopted, or intends to adopt, a child in any case where arrangements for the adoption were made, or as the case may be are to be made, by the agency.

(2) The Secretary of State may make regulations as respects adoption allowances schemes; and without prejudice to the generality of this subsection such regulations may in particular make provision as to—

(a) the procedure to be followed by an agency in determining the amount of an allowance;

(b) the circumstances in which an allowance may be paid;

(c) the factors to be taken into account in determining the amount of an allowance;

(d) the procedure for review, variation and termination of allowances;

(e) the information about allowances which is to be supplied by an agency to a person who intends to adopt a child; and

(f) the procedure to be followed by an agency in drawing up, in making alterations to, or in revoking and replacing, an adoption allowances scheme.

(3) Section 51(1) shall not apply to any payment made in accordance with an adoption allowances scheme (including any such payment made by virtue of section 51B).

Transitional provisions as respects adoption allowances

51B. After the coming into force of section 51A—
(a) no scheme for the payment of allowances shall be submissible under subsection (5) of section 51 and
(b) a scheme which has been approved under that subsection of that section shall forthwith be revoked under subsection (6)(b) of that section, so however that where a person was before its revocation receiving payments made in accordance with that scheme he may continue to receive payments so made which, had there been no revocation, would have fallen to be made to him or he may agree to receive, instead of the continued payments, payments made in accordance with an adoption allowances scheme.

Restriction on advertisements

52.—(1) It shall not be lawful for any advertisement to be published indicating—
(a) that the parent or guardian of a child desires to cause a child to be adopted; or
(b) that a person desires to adopt a child; or
(c) that any person (not being an adoption agency) is willing to make arrangements for the adoption of a child.

(2) Any person who causes to be published or knowingly publishes an advertisement in contravention of the provisions of this section shall be guilty of an offence and liable on summary conviction to a fine not exceeding level 5 on the standard scale.

Effect of determination and orders made in England and Wales and overseas in adoption proceedings

53.—(1) Where an authority of a Convention country or any British territory other than the United Kingdom having power under the law of that country or territory—
(a) to authorise or review the authorisation of a regulated adoption or a specified order; or
(b) to give or review a decision revoking or annulling a regulated adoption, a specified order or a Convention adoption order,
makes a determination in the exercise of that power, then, subject to sections 46(2) and 47 and any subsequent determination having effect under this subsection, the determination shall have effect in Scotland for the purpose of effecting, confirming or terminating the adoption in question or confirming its termination, as the case may be.

(2) Subsections (2) to (4) of section 12 shall apply in relation to an order freeing a child for adoption (other than an order under section 18) as if it were an adoption order; and on the revocation in England and Wales or Northern Ireland of an order freeing a child for adoption subsection (3) of section 20 shall apply as if the order had been revoked under that section.

(3) Sections 12(3) and (4) and 43 apply in relation to a child who is the subject of an order which is similar to an order under section 49 and is made (whether before or after this Act has effect) in England and Wales, Northern Ireland, the Isle of Man or any of the Channel Islands, as they apply in relation to a child who is the subject of an adoption order.

Evidence of adoption in England, Wales and Northern Ireland

54. Any document which is receivable as evidence of any matter—
- (a) in England and Wales under section 50(2) of the Adoption Act 1976; or
- (b) in Northern Ireland under Article 63(1) of the Adoption (Northern Ireland) Order 1987,

shall also be so receivable in Scotland.

Evidence of agreement and consent

55.—(1) Any agreement or consent which is required by this Act to be given to the making of an order or application for an order (other than an order to which section 17(6) applies) may be given in writing, and, if the document signifying the agreement or consent is witnessed in accordance with rules, it shall be sufficient evidence without further proof of the signature of the person by whom it was executed.

(2) A document signifying such agreement or consent which purports to be witnessed in accordance with rules, shall be presumed to be so witnessed, and to have been executed and witnessed on the date and at the place specified in the document, unless the contrary is proved.

56.—(1) In this Act, "authorised court", as respects an application for an order relating to a child, shall be construed as follows.

(2) Subject to subsections (4) and (5), if the child is in Scotland when the application is made, the following are authorised courts—
- (a) the Court of Session;
- (b) the sheriff court of the sheriffdom within which the child is.

(3) If, in the case of an application for an adoption order or for an order freeing a child for adoption, the child is not in Great Britain when the application is made, the Court of Session is the authorised court.

(4) In the case of an application for a Convention adoption order, paragraph (b) of subsection (2) does not apply.

(5) Subsection (2) does not apply in the case of an application under section 29 but for the purposes of such an application the following are authorised courts—
- (a) if there is pending in respect of the child an application for an adoption order or an order freeing him for adoption, the court in which that application is pending;
- (b) in any other case—
  - (i) the Court of Session;
  - (ii) the sheriff court of the sheriffdom within which the applicant resides.

Proceedings to be in private

57. All proceedings before the court under Part II, section 29 or section 49 shall be heard and determined in private unless the court otherwise directs.

Curators *ad litem* and reporting officers

58.—(1) For the purpose of any application for an adoption order or an order freeing a child for adoption or an order under section 20 or 49, rules shall provide for the appointment, in such cases as are prescribed—

   (a) of a person to act as curator *ad litem* of the child upon the hearing of the application, with the duty of safeguarding the interests of the child in the prescribed manner;

   (b) of a person to act as reporting officer for the purpose of witnessing agreements to adoption and performing such other duties as the rules may prescribe.

(2) A person who is employed—

   (a) in the case of an application for an adoption order, by the adoption agency by whom the child was placed; or

   (b) in the case of an application for an order freeing a child for adoption, by the adoption agency by whom the applicant was made; or

   (c) in the case of an application under section 20, by the adoption agency with the parental responsibilities and parental rights in relation to the child,

shall not be appointed to act as curator *ad litem* or reporting officer for the purposes of the application but, subject to that, the same person may if the court thinks fit be both curator *ad litem* and reporting officer.

(3) Rules may provide for the reporting officer to be appointed before the application is made.

Rules of procedure

59.—(1) Subject to subsection (4), provision shall be made by act of sederunt with regard to any matter to be prescribed under this Act and generally with regard to all matters of procedure and incidental matters arising out of this Act and for carrying this Act into effect.

(2) In the case of—

   (a) an application for an adoption order in relation to a child who is not free for adoption;

   (b) an application for an order freeing a child for adoption,

rules shall require every person who can be found and whose agreement or consent to the making of the order is required to be given or dispensed with under this Act to be notified of a date and place where he may be heard on the application and of the fact that, unless he wishes or the court requires, he need not attend.

(3) In the case of an application under section 49, rules shall require every person who can be found, and whose agreement to the making of the order would be required if the application were for an adoption order (other than a Convention adoption order), to be notified as aforesaid.

(4) This section does not apply to sections 9, 10 and 11.

Orders, rules and regulations

60.—(1) Any power to make orders or regulations conferred by this Act on the Secretary of State or the Registrar General for Scotland shall be exercisable by statutory instrument.

(2) A statutory instrument containing regulations made under any provision of this Act, except section 3(1), shall be subject to annulment in pursuance of a resolution of either House of Parliament.

(3) An order under section 28(10) shall not be made unless a draft of the order has been approved by resolution of each House of Parliament.

(4) An order made under any provision of this Act may be revoked or varied by a subsequent order under that provision.

(5) Any order, rule or regulation made under this Act may make different provision for different circumstances and may contain such incidental and transitional provisions as the authority making the order or regulation considers expedient.

(6) The Registrar General for Scotland shall not make regulations under paragraph 1(1) of Schedule 1 except with the approval of the Secretary of State.

(7) The Statutory Instruments Act 1946 shall apply to a statutory instrument containing regulations made for the purposes of this Act by the Registrar General for Scotland as if the regulations had been made by a Minister of the Crown.

Offences by bodies corporate

61. Where an offence under this Act committed by a body corporate is proved to have been committed with the consent or connivance of or to be attributable to any neglect on the part of, any director, manager, member of the committee, secretary or other officer of the body, he as well as the body shall be deemed to be guilty of that offence and shall be liable to be proceeded against and punished accordingly.

Service of notices etc.

62. Any notice or information required to be given under this Act may be given by post.

Nationality

63.—(1) If the Secretary of State by order declares that a description of persons specified in the order has, in pursuance of the Convention, been notified to the Government of the United Kingdom as the description of persons who are deemed to possess the nationality of a particular Convention country, persons of that description shall, subject to the following provisions of this section, be treated for the purposes of this Act as nationals of that country.

(2) Subject to section 48(3) and subsection (3) of this section, where it appears to the court in any proceedings under this Act, or to any court by which a decision in pursuance of section 47(3) falls to be given, that a person is or was at a particular time a national of two or more countries, then—

(a) if it appears to the said court that he is or was then a United Kingdom national, he shall be treated for the purposes of those proceedings or that decision as if he were or had then been a United Kingdom national only;

(b) if, in a case not falling within paragraph (a), it appears to the said court that one only of those countries is or was then a Convention country, he shall be treated for those purposes as if he were or had then been a national of that country only;

(c) if, in a case not falling within paragraph (a), it appears to the said court that two or more of those countries are or were then Convention countries, he shall be treated for those purposes as if he were or had then been a national of such one only of those Convention countries as the said court considers is the country with which he is or was then most closely connected;

(d) in any other case, he shall be treated for those purposes as if he were or had then been a national of such only of those countries as the said court considers is the country with which he is or was then most closely connected.

(3) A court in which proceedings are brought in pursuance of section 17, 46(2) or 47 shall be entitled to disregard the provisions of subsection (2) in so far as it appears to that court appropriate to do so for the purposes of those proceedings; but nothing in this subsection shall be construed as prejudicing the provisions of section 48(3).

(4) Where, after such inquiries as the court in question considers appropriate, it appears to the court in any proceedings under this Act, or to any court by which such a decision as aforesaid falls to be given, that a person has no nationality or no ascertainable nationality, he shall be treated for the purposes of those proceedings or that decision as a national of the country in which he resides or, where that country is one of two or more countries having the same law of nationality, as a national of those countries.

Internal law of a country

64.—(1) In this Act "internal law" in relation to any country means the law applicable in a case where no question arises as to the law in force in any other country.

(2) In any case where the internal law of a country falls to be ascertained for the purposes of this Act by any court and there are in force in that country two or more systems of internal law, the relevant system shall be ascertained in accordance with any rule in force throughout that country indicating which of the systems is relevant in the case in question or, if there is no such rule, shall be the system appearing to that court to be most closely connected with the case.

Interpretation

65.—(1) In this Act, unless the context otherwise requires—

"adoption agency" in sections 11, 13, 18 to 23 and 27 includes an adoption agency within the meaning of section 1 of the Adoption Act 1976 (adoption agencies in England and Wales) and an adoption agency within the meaning of Article 3 of the Adoption (Northern Ireland) Order 1987 (adoption agencies in Northern Ireland);

"adoption order"—

(a) means an order under section 12(1); and

(b) in sections 12(3) and (4), 18 to 20, 27, 28, 30 and 31 and in the definition of "British adoption order" in this subsection includes an order under section 12 of the Adoption Act 1976 and Article 12 of the Adoption (Northern Ireland) Order 1987 (adoption orders in England and Wales and Northern Ireland respectively); and

(c) in sections 27, 28, 30 and 31 includes an order under section 49, section 55 of the Adoption Act 1976 and Article 57 of the Adoption (Northern Ireland) Order 1987 (orders in relation to children being adopted abroad);

"adoption society" means a body of persons whose functions consist of or include the making of arrangements for, or in connection with, the adoption of children;

"approved adoption society" means an adoption society approved under Part I and, in sections 30 and 45, includes an adoption society approved under Part I of the Adoption Act 1976;

"authorised court" shall be construed in accordance with section 56;

"body of persons" means any body of persons, whether incorporated or unincorporated;

"British adoption order" means—

(a) an adoption order as defined in this subsection; and

(b) an order under any provision for the adoption of a child effected under the law of any British territory outside the United Kingdom;

"British territory" means, for the purposes of any provision of this Act, any of the following countries, that is to say, Great Britain, Northern Ireland, the Channel Islands, the Isle of Man and a colony, being a country designated for the purposes of that provision by order of the Secretary of State or, if no country is so designated, any of those countries;

"child", except where used to express a relationship, means a person who has not attained the age of eighteen years;

"compulsory measures of supervision" has the same meaning as in Part II of the Children (Scotland) Act 1995;

"the Convention" means the Convention relating to the adoption of children concluded at The Hague on 15th November 1965 and signed on behalf of the United Kingdom on that date;

"Convention adoption order" means an adoption order made in accordance with section 17(1);

"Convention country" means any country outside British territory, being a country for the time being designated by an order of the Secretary of State as a country in which, in his opinion, the Convention is in force;

"England" includes Wales;

"guardian" means—

(a) a person appointed by deed or will or by a court of competent jurisdiction to be the guardian of the child, and

(b) [*Repealed by the Children (Scotland) Act 1995 (c. 36), ss.98(1), 105(5), Sched. 2, para. 29 and Sched. 5.*]

"internal law" has the meaning assigned by section 64;

"local authority" means a council constituted under section 2 of the Local Government etc. (Scotland) Act 1994 and, in sections 13, 22, 28, 30, 31 and 45, includes the council of a county (other than a metropolitan county), a metropolitan district, a London borough or the Common Council of the City of London;

"notice" means a notice in writing;

"order freeing a child for adoption" means an order under section 18 and, in sections 27(2) and 53 includes an order under—

(a) section 18 of the Adoption Act 1976; and

(b) Article 17 or 18 of the Adoption (Northern Ireland) Order 1987;

"overseas adoption" has the meaning assigned by Secretary of State (2);

"parent" means, irrespective of whether or not they are, or have been, married to each other—

(a) the mother of the child, where she has parental responsibilities or parental rights in relation to him;

(b) the father of the child where he has such responsibilities or rights; and

(c) both of his parents, where both have such responsibilities or rights;

"parental responsibilities" and "parental rights" have the meanings respectively given by sections 1(3) and 2(4) of the Children (Scotland) Act 1995 (analogous expressions being construed accordingly);

"place of safety" means any residential or other establishment provided by a local authority, a police station, or any hospital, surgery or other suitable place the occupier of which is willing temporarily to receive a child;

"prescribed" means prescribed by act of sederunt;

"Registrar General for Scotland" means the Registrar General of Births, Deaths and Marriages for Scotland;

"regulated adoption" means an overseas adoption of a description designated by an order under subsection (2) as that of an adoption regulated by the Convention;

"relative" in relation to a child means a grandparent, brother, sister, uncle or aunt, whether of the full blood or half-blood or by affinity and includes, where the child is illegitimate, the father of the child where he is not a parent within the meaning of this Act, and any person who would be a relative within the meaning of this definition if the father were such a parent;

"rules" means rules made by act of sederunt;

"specified order" means any provision for the adoption of a child effected under enactments similar to sections 12(1) and 17 in force in Northern Ireland or any British territory outside the United Kingdom;

"supervision requirement" has the same meaning as in Part II of the Children (Scotland) Act 1995;

"United Kingdom national" means, for the purposes of any provision of this Act, a citizen of the United Kingdom and Colonies satisfying such conditions, if any, as the Secretary of State may by order specify for the purposes of that provision;

"voluntary organisation" means a body, other than a public or local authority, the activities of which are not carried on for profit.

(2) In this Act "overseas adoption" means an adoption of such a description as the Secretary of State may by order specify, being a

description of adoptions of children appearing to him to be effected under the law of any country outside Great Britain; and an order under this subsection may contain provision as to the manner in which evidence of an overseas adoption may be given.

(3) For the purposes of this Act, a person shall be deemed to make arrangements for the adoption of a child if he enters into or makes any agreement or arrangement for, or for facilitating the adoption of the child by any other person, whether the adoption is effected, or is intended to be effected, in Great Britain or elsewhere, or if he initiates or takes part in any negotiations of which the purpose or effect is the conclusion of any agreement or the making of any arrangement therefor, or if he causes another person to do so, but the making,under section 70 of the Children (Scotland) Act 1995, by a children's hearing of a supervision requirement which, in respect that it provides as to where he is to reside, facilitates his being placed for adoption by an adoption agency, shall not constitute the making of such arrangements.

(4) Except so far as the context otherwise requires, any reference in this Act to an enactment shall be construed as a reference to that enactment as amended by or under any other enactment, including this Act.

(5) In this Act, except where otherwise indicated—
  (a) a reference to a numbered Part, section or Schedule is a reference to the Part or section of, or the Schedule to, this Act so numbered, and
  (b) a reference in a section to a numbered subsection is a reference to the subsection of that section so numbered, and
  (c) a reference in a section, subsection or Schedule to a numbered paragraph is a reference to the paragraph of that section, subsection or Schedule so numbered.

(6) Any reference in this Act to a child being in, received into or kept in, care (whether or not such care is expressed as being the care of a local authority and except where the context otherwise requires) shall be taken to be a reference to his being looked after by a local authority and shall be construed in accordance with section 17(6) of the Children (Scotland) Act 1995; and any reference to the authority in whose care a child is, shall be construed accordingly.

Transitional provisions, amendments and repeals

66.—(1) The transitional provisions contained in Schedule 2 shall have effect.

(2) The enactments specified in Schedule 3 shall have effect subject to the amendments specified in that Schedule, being amendments consequential upon the provisions of this Act.

(3) The enactments specified in Schedule 4 are hereby repealed to the extent specified in column 3 of that Schedule.

Short title, commencement and extent

67.—(1) This Act may be cited as the Adoption (Scotland) Act 1978.

(2) This Act shall come into force on such date as the Secretary of State may by order appoint and different dates may be appointed for different provisions.

(3) Until the date appointed under subsection (2) for sections 3, 4, 5 and 8, in this Act and in the Adoption Act 1958 "adoption agency" means a local authority or a registered adoption society within the meaning of the said Act of 1958.

(4) This Act shall extend to Scotland only.

SCHEDULES

Section 45   SCHEDULE 1

REGISTRATION OF ADOPTIONS

Registration of adoption orders

1.—(1) Every adoption order shall contain a direction to the Registrar General for Scotland to make in the Adopted Children Register maintained by him an entry recording the adoption in such form as the Registrar General for Scotland may by regulations specify.

(2) The direction contained in a Convention adoption order in pursuance of this paragraph shall include an instruction that the entry made in that register in consequence of the order shall be marked with the words "Convention order".

(3) For the purposes of compliance with the requirements of subparagraph (1)—

(a) where the precise date of the child's birth is not proved to the satisfaction of the court, the court shall determine the probable date of his birth and the date so determined shall be specified in the order as the date of his birth;

(b) where the country of birth of the child is not proved to the satisfaction of the court, then, if it appears probable that the child was born within the United Kingdom, the Channel Islands or the Isle of Man, he shall be treated as having been born in Scotland, and in any other case the particulars of the country of birth may be omitted from the order and from the entry in the Adopted Children Register;

and the names to be specified in the order as the name and surname of the child shall be the name or names and surname stated in that behalf in the application for the adoption order, or, if no name or surname is so stated, the original name or names of the child and the surname of the applicant.

(4) There shall be produced with every application for an adoption order in respect of a child whose birth has been registered under the Registration of Births, Deaths and Marriages (Scotland) Act 1965 or under any enactment repealed by that Act an extract of the entry of the birth.

(5) Where on an application to a court for an adoption order in respect of a child (not being a child who has previously been the subject of an adoption order made by a court in Scotland under this Act or any enactment at the time in force) there is proved to the satisfaction of the court the identity of the child with a child to whom an entry in the register of births relates, any adoption order made in pursuance of the application shall contain a direction to the Registrar General for Scotland to cause the entry in that register to be marked with the word "Adopted".

(6) Where an adoption order is made in respect of a child who has previously been the subject of an adoption order made by a court in Scotland under this Act or any enactment at the time in force, the order shall contain a direction to the Registrar General for Scotland to cause the previous entry in the Adopted Children Register to be marked with the word "Re-adopted".

(7) Where an adoption order is made, the clerk of the court which made the order shall cause the order to be communicated to the Registrar General for Scotland and upon receipt of the communication the Registrar General for Scotland shall cause compliance to be made with the directions contained in the order.

Registration of adoptions in England, Northern Ireland, the Isle of Man and the Channel Islands

2.—(1) Where the Registrar General for Scotland is notified by the Registrar General that an adoption order has been made by a court in England in respect of a child to whom an entry in the register of births or the Adopted Children Register relates, the Registrar General for Scotland shall cause the entry to be marked "Adopted (England)" or, as the case may be, "Re-adopted (England)".

(2) Where the Registrar General for Scotland is notified by the authority maintaining a

register of adoptions in Northern Ireland, the Isle of Man or any of the Channel Islands that an order has been made in that country authorising the adoption of a child to whom an entry in the register of births or the Adopted Children Register relates, he shall cause the entry to be marked "Adopted" or "Re-adopted", as the case may be, followed by the name in brackets of the country in which the order was made.

(3) Where, after an entry has been marked under the foregoing provisions of this paragraph, the Registrar General for Scotland is notified as aforesaid that the order has been quashed, that an appeal against the order has been allowed or that the order has been revoked, he shall cause the marking to be cancelled; and an extract of an entry in any register, being an entry the marking of which is cancelled under this sub-paragraph, shall be deemed to be accurate if and only if both the marking and the cancellation are omitted therefrom.

(4) The foregoing provisions of this paragraph shall apply in relation to orders corresponding to orders under section 49 as they apply in relation to orders authorising the adoption of a child; but any marking of an entry required by virtue of this sub-paragraph shall consist of the words "proposed foreign adoption" or, as the case may require, "proposed foreign re-adoption" followed by the name in brackets of the country in which the order was made.

Registration of overseas adoptions

3. If the Registrar General for Scotland is satisfied that an entry in the register of births relates to a person adopted under an overseas adoption and that he has sufficient particulars relating to that person to enable an entry, in the form specified for the purposes of this paragraph in regulations made under paragraph 1(1), to be made in the Adopted Children Register in respect of that person, he shall—
  (a) make such an entry in the Adopted Children Register; and
  (b) if there is a previous entry in respect of that person in that register, mark the entry (or if there is more than one such entry the last of them) with the word "Re-adopted" followed by the name in brackets of the country in which the adoption was effected; and
  (c) unless the entry in the register of births is already marked with the word "Adopted" (whether or not followed by other words), mark the entry with that word followed by the name in brackets of the country aforesaid.

Amendment of orders and rectification of registers

4.—(1) The court by which an adoption order has been made may, on the application of the adopter or of the adopted person, amend the order by the correction of any error in the particulars contained therein, and may—
  (a) if satisfied on the application of the adopter or the adopted person that within one year beginning with the date of the order any new name has been given to the adopted person (whether in baptism or otherwise), or taken by him, either in lieu of or in addition to a name specified in the particulars required to be entered in the Adopted Children Register in pursuance of the order, amend the order by substituting or adding that name in those particulars, as the case may require;
  (b) if satisfied on the application of any person concerned that a direction for the marking of an entry in the register of births or the Adopted Children Register included in the order in pursuance of sub-paragraph (5) or (6) of paragraph 1 was wrongly so included, revoke that direction.

(2) Where an adoption order is amended or a direction revoked under sub-paragraph (1), the clerk of the court shall cause the amendment to be communicated in the prescribed manner to the Registrar General for Scotland who shall as the case may require—
  (a) cause the entry in the Adopted Children Register to be amended accordingly; or
  (b) cause the marking of the entry in the register of births or the Adopted Children Register to be cancelled.

(3) Where an adoption order is quashed or an appeal against an adoption order allowed by any court, the court shall give directions to the Registrar General for Scotland to cancel any entry in the Adopted Children Register, and any marking of an entry in that Register, or the register of births as the case may be, which was effected in pursuance of the order.

(4) If the Registrar General for Scotland is satisfied—
  (a) that a Convention adoption order or an overseas adoption has ceased to have effect, whether on annulment or otherwise; or
  (b) that any entry or mark was erroneously made in pursuance of paragraph 3 in any register mentioned in that paragraph,

he may cause such alterations to be made in any such register as he considers are required in consequence of the cesser or to correct the error; and where an entry in such a register is amended in pursuance of this sub-paragraph, an extract to the entry shall be deemed to be accurate if and only if it shows the entry as amended but without indicating that it has been amended.

Marking of entries on re-registration of birth

5. Without prejudice to any other provision of this Act where, after an entry in the register of births has been marked in accordance with paragraph 2 or 3, the birth is re-registered under section 20(1) of the Registration of Births, Deaths and Marriages (Scotland) Act 1965 (re-registration of birth in certain cases), the entry made on re-registration shall be marked in the like manner.

Cancellations in registers on legitimation

6. Where an adoption order is revoked under section 46(1) the clerk of the court shall cause the revocation to be communicated in the prescribed manner to the Registrar General for Scotland who shall cause to be cancelled—

(a) the entry in the Adopted Children Register relating to the adopted person; and

(b) the marking with the word "Adopted" (or, as the case may be, with that word and the word "(England)") or any entry relating to him in the register of births;

and an extract of an entry in any register, being an entry the marking of which is cancelled under this paragraph shall be deemed to be accurate if and only if both the marking and the cancellation are omitted therefrom.

7. In this Schedule, "Registrar General" means the Registrar General for England and Wales.

Section 66   SCHEDULE 2

Transitional Provisions and Savings

General

1. In so far as anything done under an enactment repealed by this Act could have been done under a corresponding provision of this Act it shall not be invalidated by the repeal but shall have effect as if done under that provision.

2. Where any period of time specified in an enactment repealed by this Act is current at the commencement of this Act, this Act shall have effect as if the corresponding provision thereof had been in force when that period began to run.

3. Nothing in this Act shall affect the enactments repealed by this Act in their operation in relation to offences committed before the commencement of this Act.

4. Any reference in any enactment or document, whether express or implied, to an enactment repealed by this Act shall, unless the context otherwise requires, be construed as a reference to the corresponding enactment in this Act.

Existing adoption orders

5.—(1) Without prejudice to paragraph 1, an adoption order made under an enactment at any time before this Act comes into force shall not cease to have effect by virtue only of a repeal effected by this Act.

(2) Paragraph 4(1) and (2) of Schedule 1 shall apply in relation to an adoption order made before this Act came into force as if the order had been made under section 12, but as if, in sub-paragraph (1)(b) of the said paragraph 4, there were substituted for the reference to paragraph 1(5) and (6) a reference—

(a) in the case of an order under the Adoption Act 1950, to section 20(4) and (5) of that Act,

(b) in the case of an order under the Adoption Act 1958, to section 23(4) and (5) of that Act.

(3) The power of the court under the said paragraph 4(1) to amend an order includes power in relation to an order made before 1st April 1959, to make on the application of the adopter or adopted person any such amendment of the particulars contained in the order as appears to be required to bring the order into the form in which it would have been made if paragraph 1 of Schedule 1 had applied to the order.

(4) Section 46(1) and paragraph 6 of Schedule 1 shall apply in relation to an adoption order made under an enactment at any time before this Act came into force as they apply in relation to an adoption order made under this Act.

Payments relating to adoptions

6. Section 51(8), (9) and (10) shall not have effect if, immediately before section 51 comes into force, there is in force in Scotland an order under section 50(8) of the Adoption Act 1958.

Registers of adoptions

7. Any register or index to a register kept under the Adoption Act 1958, or any register or index deemed to be part of such a register, shall be deemed to be part of the register or index kept under section 45.

Commencement of act

8. An order under section 67(2) may make such transitional provision as appears to the Secretary of State to be necessary or expedient in connection with the provisions thereby brought into force, including such adaptations of those provisions or any provision of this Act then in force or any provision of the Adoption Act 1958 or the Children Act 1975 as appear to him to be necessary or expedient in consequence of the partial operation of this Act.

Section 66   SCHEDULE 3

CONSEQUENTIAL AMENDMENSTS

.   .   .   .   .   .

Section 66   SCHEDULE 4

REPEALS

.   .   .   .   .   .

ACT OF SEDERUNT (RULES OF THE COURT OF SESSION 1994) 1994

(S.I. 1994 No. 1443)

[May 31, 1994]

· · · · · ·

CHAPTER 67

APPLICATIONS UNDER THE ADOPTION (SCOTLAND) ACT 1978

PART I

GENERAL PROVISIONS

Application and interpretation of this chapter

67.1.—(1) This Chapter applies to applications under the Adoption (Scotland) Act 1978.

(2) In this Chapter, unless the context otherwise requires—

"the Act of 1978" means the Adoption (Scotland) Act 1978;

"the Act of 1978" means the Children (Scotland) Act 1995;

"freeing for adoption order" means an order made in accordance with section 18(1) of that Act;

"Her Majesty's Forces" means the Royal Navy, the regular armed forces as defined in section 225 of the Army Act 1955, the regular air force as defined in section 223 of the Air Force Act 1955 and the Queen Alexandra's Royal Naval Nursing Services;

"parental responsibilities" has the meaning given by section 2(4) of that Act;

"section 49 order" means an order made in accordance with section 49(1) of the Act of 1978.

Disapplication of certain rules to this chapter

67.2. Unless otherwise provided in this Chapter, the following rules shall not apply to a petition or note to which this Chapter applies:—

rule 14.5 (first order in petitions),

rule 14.6(1)(d) (period of notice for lodging answers where service by advertisement),

rule 14.7 (intimation and service of petitions),

rule 14.8 (procedure where answers lodged),

rule 14.9 (unopposed petitions).

Confidentiality of documents in process

67.3. Unless the court otherwise directs, in any cause to which this Chapter applies—

(a) any document lodged in process, including a report by a local authority, an adoption agency, a reporting officer or a curator *ad litem*, shall be treated as confidential and open only to the court, the parties, the reporting officer and the curator *ad litem*; and

(b) a reporting officer or curator *ad litem* shall treat any information obtained by him in relation to the cause as confidential, and shall not disclose any such information to any person unless it is necessary for the proper execution of his duties.

Selection of reporting officer or curator ad litem

67.4. Where the court appoints a reporting officer or a curator *ad litem* and there is an established panel of persons from whom the appointment may be made, the reporting officer or curator *ad litem* shall be selected from that panel unless the court considers that it would be appropriate to appoint a person who is not on the panel.

Timetable for resolving question as to whether agreement to adoption order etc. should be dispensed with

67.4A.—(1) A timetable shall be drawn up forthwith under section 25A of the Act of 1978 by the court when any of the following occurs—

(a) there is presented to it a petition with a crave for an agreement of the parent or guardian of a child to be dispensed with on a ground specified in section 16(2) of that Act;

(b) it appears to the court, from the report of an adoption agency, local authority or reporting officer that the question of dispensing with such agreement on a ground so specified arises; or

(c) such agreement (being agreement which, if not given, it would be competent to dispense with on a ground so specified) is given but is afterwards withdrawn.

(2) To ensure, so far as is reasonably practicable, that the timetable is adhered to, the court shall give such directions as it considers appropriate.

Form of agreements and consents

67.5.—(1) An agreement by a parent or guardian—

(a) for the purposes of section 16(1)(b) of the Act of 1978 (agreement to adoption), shall be in Form 67.5–A unless the applicant for the adoption order is such person as is mentioned in section 15(1)(aa) of that Act, in which case it shall be in Form 67.5–F;

(b) for the purposes of section 16(1)(b), by virtue of section 49 of that Act (adoption of child abroad), shall be in Form 67.5–A; or

(c) for the purposes of section 18(1)(a) of that Act (agreement to freeing for adoption), shall be in Form 67.5–B.

(2) A consent—

(a) by a child for the purposes of section 12(8) of the Act of 1978 (consent to adoption), shall be in Form 67.5–C;

(b) by a parent or guardian for the purposes of section 18(2)(a) of that Act (consent to application for freeing for adoption), shall be in Form 67.5–D; or

(c) by a child for the purposes of section 18(8) of that Act (consent to freeing for adoption), shall be in Form 67.5–E.

(3) An agreement or consent referred to in this rule which is executed furth of Scotland shall be witnessed—

(a) where it is executed in England, Wales or Northern Ireland, by a justice of the peace or commissioner for oaths;

(b) where it is executed furth of the United Kingdom—

    (i) in the case of a parent or guardian serving in Her Majesty's Forces, by an officer holding a commission in those forces; or

   (ii) by a British consular official or any person authorised, by the law of the country where the agreement or consent is executed, to administer an oath for any legal purpose.

Consideration of views of child and of certain reports

67.5A. In a cause to which this Chapter applies, the court shall not adopt an adoption order or grant or revoke an order freeing a child for adoption—

   (a) where the child has indicated to the court, or his curator *ad litem* if one has been appointed under this Chapter, a wish to express views on a matter affecting the child unless—

      (i) an opportunity has been given for those views to be obtained or heard (the court ordering such steps to be taken in that regard as it considers appropriate); and

     (ii) due weight has been given by the court to such views as the child does express (account being taken of his age and maturity); and

   (b) where a report has been received in relation to the child by virtue of section 73(13) of the Act of 1995 (report of children's hearing where child subject to supervision requirement), unless the court has first considered the report.

Orders for evidence

67.6.—(1) In a cause to which this Chapter applies, the court may, before determining the cause, order—

   (a) production of further documents (including affidavits); or

   (b) parole evidence.

(2) A party may apply by motion for the evidence of a person to be received in evidence by affidavit; and the court may make such order as it thinks fit.

Children who may require compulsory measures of supervision

67.6A. Where, under subsection (1) of section 54 of the Act of 1995 (question arising as to whether compulsory measures of supervision are necessary) a matter is referred to the Principal Reporter, the clerk of court shall give him written intimation of the court's decision, which shall include a certified copy of the interlocutor, and shall specify in the intimation which of the conditions referred to in that subsection it appears to the court has been satisfied.

Expenses

67.7. In a cause to which this Chapter applies, the court may make such order as to expenses, including the expenses of a local authority or an adoption agency which prepared a report, a reporting officer, a curator *ad litem*, or any other person who attended a hearing, as it thinks fit.

PART II

FREEING FOR ADOPTION

Interpretation of this part

67.8. In this Part, "petition" means the petition referred to in rule 67.9(1).

Applications for freeing for adoption order

67.9.—(1) An application under section 18(1) of the Act of 1978 (freeing child for adoption) shall be made by petition.

(2) The petition shall include averments in relation to, or refer to a report or other documents produced which deal with—

(a) whether the petition is presented with the consent of a parent or guardian;

(b) whether the petition is applying for dispensation with the agreement of a parent or guardian under section 18(2)(b) of the Act of 1978 (agreement to freeing for adoption) and the ground on which dispensation is sought;

(c) how the needs of the child came to the notice of the petitioner;

(d) any relevant family circumstances of the child;

(e) a description of the physical and mental health of the child (including any special needs) and his emotional, behavioural and educational development;

(f) the discussion by the petitioner with the parents or guardians of the child and, if appropriate, with the child about their wishes and the alternatives to adoption;

(g) the knowledge of the petitioner of the position of other relatives or persons likely to be involved;

(h) the search by the petitioner for any parent or guardian who cannot be found;

(i) the likelihood of placement of the child for adoption and whether a petition for an adoption order is likely in the near future;

(j) the arrangements of the petitioner for the care of the child in the event of the granting of the prayer of the petition;

(k) whether the petitioner has given each parent or guardian who can be found an opportunity to make a declaration for the purposes of section 18(6) of the Act of 1978 (declaration of preference not to be involved in future questions concerning the adoption);

(l) whether the petitioner has considered the position of any person claiming to be the child's father (being a person who is not married to the mother); and

(m) whether the petitioner intends to give notice to a relevant parent under section 19(2) and (3) of that Act (progress reports).

(3) On presentation of the petition, there shall be lodged in process as a production—

(a) an extract or a certified copy of any entry in the register of births relating to the child; and

(b) any consent of a parent or guardian required by section 18(2)(a) of the Act of 1978 (consent to freeing for adoption).

Appointment of reporting officer and curator ad litem

67.10.—(1) On presentation of the petition, the court shall pronounce an interlocutor—

(a) appointing a reporting officer; and

(b) appointing a curator *ad litem* where it appears desirable in order to safeguard the interests of the child.

(2) Where a curator *ad litem* is appointed, the court may order—

(a) the petitioner,

(b) a local authority, or

(c) the reporting officer,

to make available to the curator *ad litem* any report or information in relation to the child and the natural father and mother of the child.

(3) A person may, before presenting the petition, apply by letter to the Deputy Principal Clerk for the appointment of a reporting officer.

(4) An application under paragraph (3) shall—

(a) set out the reasons for which the appointment is sought;

(b) not require to be intimated to any person;

(c) be accompanied by an interlocutor sheet; and

(d) be placed by the Deputy Principal Clerk before the Lord Ordinary for his decision.

(5) The Deputy Principal Clerk shall give written intimation to the applicant under paragraph (3) of the decision of the Lord Ordinary.

(6) The decision of the Lord Ordinary on an application under paragraph (3) shall be final and not subject to review.

(7) The letter and the interlocutor sheet in an application under paragraph (3) shall be kept in the Petition Department and subsequently placed in the process of the petition.

Duties of reporting officer and curator ad litem

67.11.—(1) A reporting officer appointed under rule 67.10 shall—

(a) inquire into the facts and circumstances averred in the petition;

(b) ascertain the whereabouts of each parent or guardian and, if practicable, meet him;

(c) witness any execution in Scotland of any agreement in Form 67.5–B by a parent or guardian under section 18(1)(a) of the Act of 1978 (agreement to freeing for adoption) and investigate whether the agreement is given freely, unconditionally and with full understanding of what is involved and, where the reporting officer has been appointed before the petition has been presented, any consent in Form 67.5–D by a parent or guardian under section 18(2)(a) of that Act (consent to freeing for adoption);

(d) where a parent or guardian is furth of Scotland, confirm his views in writing, ensure that any agreement under section 18(1) of the Act of 1978 is witnessed in accordance with rule 67.5(3) and investigate whether the agreement is given freely, unconditionally and with full understanding of what is involved;

(e) ensure that each parent or guardian who can be found and who has executed an agreement for the purposes of section 18(1)(a) of the Act of 1978 understands that he may renounce that agreement at any time before a freeing for adoption order is made;

(f) witness any execution in Scotland of a consent of a child in Form

67.5–E under section 18(8) of the Act of 1978 (consent to freeing for adoption) and ensure that he understands the consequences of that consent;

(g) where a child in respect of whom a consent under section 18(8) of the Act of 1978 is required is furth of Scotland, confirm his consent in writing and ensure that the consent is witnesses in accordance with rule 67.5(3);

(h) consider whether the petitioner has made every reasonable effort to find every person whose agreement is required;

(i) investigate whether there are any other persons with a relevant interest and whether they should be informed of the petition;

(j) ascertain whether the petitioner has considered the position of any person claiming to be the child's father (being a person who is not married to the mother);

(k) where such a person so claiming does not have parental responsibilities or parental rights in relation to the child, ascertain the likelihood of that person—

  (i) applying for an order under section 11(1) of the Act of 1995 (orders relating to parental responsibilities etc.);

  (ii) being refused such an order if he does so apply; or

  (iii) entering into an agreement with the mother under section 4(1) of that Act (natural father's acquisition of parental responsibilities etc. by agreement);

(l) discuss alternatives to adoption with each parent or guardian who can be found;

(m) explain the consequences of a freeing for adoption order to each parent or guardian who can be found;

(n) ensure that each parent or guardian who can be found understands he may be able to apply under section 20 of the Act of 1978 and rule 67.14 for revocation of a freeing for adoption order, and the procedure for making such an application;

(o) ensure that each parent or guardian who can be found has been given an opportunity to make a declaration under section 18(6) of the Act of 1978 that he prefers not to be involved in future questions concerning the adoption of the child;

(p) consider why the application is for a freeing for adoption order and not a full adoption order;

(q) consider whether the account by the petitioner of the likelihood of arranging adoption after a freeing for adoption order is correct;

(r) consider whether any payment or reward prohibited by section 51 of the Act of 1978 (prohibition on certain payments) has been received or agreed upon;

(s) ensure that each parent or guardian who can be found is aware of the date (if known) of the hearing to determine the application if he wishes to appear, and confirm that such person whose agreement is required and has not been dispensed with understands that he may withdraw his agreement at any time before the freeing for adoption order is made;

(ss) ascertain whether the child is subject to a supervision requirement;

(t) draw to the attention of the court any matter which may be of assistance; and

(u) prepare a report in relation to the exercise of his duties within such period as the court may specify.

(2) A curator *ad litem* appointed under rule 67.10(1)(b) shall—

(a) safeguard generally the interests of the child;

(b) inquire, so far as he considers necessary, into the facts and circumstances averred in the petition;

(bb) ascertain from the child whether he wishes to express any views as respects the petition;

(bc) ascertain whether it would be better for the child that an order were made under section 18(1) of the Act of 1978 than that it were not made;

(c) confirm any consent by a child under section 18(8) of the Act of 1978 (consent to freeing for adoption);

(d) inquire into any matters not averred in the petition which appear to him to be relevant to the making of a freeing for adoption order;

(e) ascertain the current circumstances and care of the child;

(f) where the agreement or consent of a parent or guardian or the consent of a child is sought to be dispensed with, consider whether the ground of dispensation has been made out;

(g) consider whether, in his opinion, the child should be present at the hearing to determine the petition;

(h) perform such other duties as appear to him to be necessary or as the court may require; and

(hh) in performing his duties under this paragraph, regard the need to safeguard and promote the welfare of the child throughout the child's life as the paramount consideration; and

(i) prepare a report in relation to the exercise of his duties within such period as the court may specify.

(3) The reporting officer shall, on completion of his report, send to the Deputy Principal Clerk—

(a) the report and a copy of it for each party;

(b) any agreement for the purposes of section 18(1)(a) of the Act of 1978 (agreement of parent or guardian to freeing for adoption);

(c) any declaration for the purposes of section 18(6) of the Act of 1978 (declaration of preference not to be involved in future questions concerning adoption); and

(d) any consent under section 18(8) of the Act of 1978 (consent of child to freeing for adoption).

(4) The curator *ad litem* shall, on completion of his report, send the report, and a copy of it for each party, to the Deputy Principal Clerk.

Declaration of preference not to be involved

67.12.—(1) A declaration under section 18(6) or 19(4) of the Act of 1978 (declaration of preference not to be involved in future questions concerning adoption) shall be in Form 67.12–A; and any withdrawal of either such declaration shall be in Form 67.12–B.

(2) A declaration referred to in paragraph (1) which is executed furth of Scotland shall be witnessed in accordance with rule 67.5(3).

(3) The making of a declaration referred to in paragraph (1) shall be recorded in an interlocutor pronounced by the court.

(4) For the purposes of section 19(4)(a) of the Act of 1978, the adoption agency shall—

(a) lodge the declaration, and

(b) apply to the court by motion,

in the process of the petition to which the declaration relates to have that declaration recorded.

(5) Where a withdrawal such as is referred to in paragraph (1) is lodged, it shall be recorded in an interlocutor pronounced by the court and then intimated forthwith to the adoption agency by the clerk of court.

Hearing of freeing for adoption petition

67.13.—(1) On receipt of the reports mentioned in rule 67.11(3) and (4), the Deputy Principal Clerk shall—

(a) cause the reports and any other documents to be lodged in process;

(b) give written intimation to each party of the lodging of those documents and make them available to each party; and

(c) within seven days thereafter, cause—

    (i) the petition to be put out on the By Order Roll before the Lord Ordinary; and

    (ii) written intimation of the date of the hearing on the By Order Roll to be given to each party.

(2) At the hearing on the By Order Roll, the court—

(a) shall pronounce an interlocutor appointing the petition to a hearing to determine the petition; and

(b) may, in such interlocutor—

    (i) order any person whose agreement or consent is required to be given or dispensed with to attend the hearing;

    (ii) order intimation of the date of the hearing to any person not mentioned in paragraph (3)(a), (aa), (b) or (c); and

    (iii) order the reporting officer or curator *ad litem*, as the case may be, to perform any additional duties to assist the court in determining the petition.

(3) The petitioner shall intimate the date of the hearing ordered under paragraph (2)(a) in Form 67.13 to—

(a) every person whose whereabouts are known to him and whose agreement or consent is required to be given or dispensed with;

(aa) where the child's mother is not married to his father, any person whose whereabouts are so known and who, being a person who claims to be the child's father, is neither the child's guardian nor a person with regard to whom an order in relation to parental responsibilities as respects the child has been made under section 11(1) of the Act of 1995;

(b) the reporting officer appointed under rule 67.10(1)(a);

(c) any curator *ad litem* appointed under rule 67.10(1)(b); and

(d) any person on whom intimation was ordered under paragraph (2)(b)(ii) of this rule.

(4) At the hearing ordered under paragraph (2)(a)—

(a) the petitioner, the reporting officer and, where one has been appointed, the curator *ad litem* shall, if required by the court, appear and may be represented;

(b) any person required by the court to attend the hearing shall appear and may be represented; and

(c) any other person to whom intimation was made under paragraph (3)(a), (aa) or (d) may appear or be represented.

Intimation of making of order freeing a child for adoption where he is subject to a supervision requirement
67.13A. Where on making an order under section 18 of the Act of 1978 in relation to a child who is subject to a supervision requirement the court makes a determination under subsection (9) of that section (that is to say, a determination that the child shall forthwith cease to be subject to that requirement), the clerk of court shall intimate the determination to the Principal Reporter.

Applications for revocation of freeing for adoption order
67.14.—(1) An application under section 20(1) or (1A) of the Act of 1978 (application for revocation of freeing for adoption order) shall be made by note.

(2) On presentation of a note under paragraph (1), the court shall pronounce an interlocutor—

(a) ordering service of the note on—

(i) the relevant parent if the application is under section 20(1A);

(ii) any person who appeared who was represented at the hearing for the freeing for adoption order except a parent or guardian who has made a declaration under section 18(6) or 19(4) of the Act of 1978 (declaration of preference not to be involved in future questions concerning adoption); and

(iii) the adoption agency (or any substitute adoption agency) having the parental responsibilities and parental rights in relation to the child if the application is under section 20(1); and

(b) where it appears desirable in order to safeguard the interests of the child, appointing a curator *ad litem*.

(3) A note under paragraph (1) shall not be intimated on the walls of the court or advertised.

(4) Where a curator *ad litem* is appointed under paragraph (2)(b), the court may order—

(a) the adoption agency,

(b) a local authority, or

(c) the reporting officer appointed in the petition,

to make available to the curator *ad litem* any report or information in relation to the child and the natural father and mother of the child.

(5) A curator *ad litem* appointed under paragraph (2)(b) shall—

(a) inquire into the facts and circumstances averred in the note;

(aa) ascertain from the child whether he wishes to express any views as respects the application;

(b) ascertain whether 12 months have elapsed between the making of the freeing for adoption order and the date of presentation of the note;

(c) where the application is under—

(i) subsection (1) of section 20 of the Act of 1978 and a previous application under that subsection was refused; or

(ii) subsection (1A) of that section and a previous application under that subsection was refused,

inquire whether there has been any change of circumstances, or there is any other reason for the current application, of which the court should be aware in determining the note;
  (d) inquire into any other matter which appears to him to be relevant for determination of the note;
  (e) consider whether, in his opinion, the child should be present at the hearing to determine the note;
  (f) perform such other duties as appear to him to be necessary or as the court may require; and
  (ff) in performing his duties under this paragraph, regard the need to safeguard and promote the welfare of the child throughout the child's life as the paramount consideration;
  (g) prepare a report in relation to the exercise of his duties within such period as the court may specify.
  (6) The curator *ad litem* shall, on completion of his report, send the report, and a copy of it for each party, to the Deputy Principal Clerk.

Hearing of application for revocation of freeing for adoption order
  67.15.—(1) Where no curator *ad litem* has been appointed under rule 67.14(2)(b), the note shall, within seven days after the expiry of the period of notice for lodging answers, apply by motion for a hearing to determine the note.
  (2) Where a curator *ad litem* has been appointed under rule 67.14(2)(b)—
  (a) the Deputy Principal Clerk shall—
    (i) cause the report sent to him under rule 67.14(5) to be lodged in process; and
    (ii) give written intimation of the lodging of the report to the note and any person on whom service was executed by virtue of rule 67.14(2)(a) and make that report available to them; and
  (b) within seven days after receipt of a copy of the intimation under sub-paragraph (a)(ii), the note shall apply by motion for a hearing to determine the note.
  (3) Where a noter has previously made an application under section 20(1) of the Act of 1978 (application for revocation of freeing for adoption order) which has been refused by any court, he shall, in his motion under paragraph (1) or (2), seek leave under section 20(5) of that Act to allow the note to proceed.
  (4) On a date being fixed for a hearing to determine the note, the noter shall intimate the date of the hearing in Form 67.15 to any person to whom intimation was given by virtue of rule 67.14(2).
  (5) At the hearing to determine the note, the noter and any person who received intimation under paragraph (4) shall appear and may be represented.

Parental responsibilities and parental rights when orders freeing a child for adoption is revoked
  67.15A. The court, on revoking an order freeing a child for adoption shall, by order under section 11(1) of the Act of 1995, specify on whom are to be imposed the parental responsibilities, and to whom are to be given the parental rights, in relation to the child; and the clerk of court shall give written intimation accordingly to any person so specified.

Applications to place a child for adoption

67.16. An application under section 20(2) of the Act of 1978 (application by adoption agency for leave to place a child) shall be made by motion.

Applications for transfer of parental rights and duties between adoption agencies

67.17. An application under section 21 of the Act of 1978 (variation of order under section 18 of that Act so as to substitute one adoption agency for another) shall be made by note.

Applications relating to return, removal or prohibition of removal of child

67.18. An application under section 29 of the Act of 1978 (order to return a child to, or not to remove a child from, the care of the applicant)—

    (a) in relation to a breach of section 27(1) of the Act of 1978 (restrictions on removal of child where application for freeing for adoption order pending), an application under section 29 of that Act, or

    (b) an application for leave under section 27(1) of that Act (leave to remove a child where application for freeing for adoption order pending),

shall be made by note.

PART III

ADOPTION

Interpretation of this part

67.19. In this Part, unless the context otherwise requires, "the petition" means the petition referred to in rule 67.22(1).

Protection of identity of petitioner

67.20.—(1) Where a person, who seeks to apply for an adoption order, wishes to prevent his identity being disclosed to any person whose agreement is required under section 16(1)(b) of the Act of 1978 (agreement of parent or guardian to adoption), he may, before presenting a petition, apply by letter to the Deputy Principal Clerk for a serial number to be assigned to him.

(2) On receipt of such a letter, the Deputy Principal Clerk shall assign a serial number to the applicant and shall enter a note of it opposite the name of the applicant in a register of serial numbers.

(3) Where a serial number has been assigned under paragraph (2)—

    (a) the record of the serial number and the person to whom it applies shall be treated as confidential and disclosed only to the court;

    (b) any agreement under section 16(1)(b) of the Act of 1978 shall not name or design the petitioner but shall refer to him by means of the serial number;

    (c) it shall be used to name or design the petitioner for all purposes connected with the petition.

Reports by local authority or adoption agency

67.21.—(1) A report by a local authority under section 22(2), or by an adoption agency under section 23, of the Act of 1978 shall include the following matters:—

(a) information about how the needs of the child came to the notice of the local authority or the adoption agency;

(b) the family circumstances of the child;

(c) where the child was placed for adoption by an adoption agency, a description of the physical and mental health of the child (including any special needs) and his emotional, behavioural and educational development;

(d) where the child is not subject to a freeing for adoption order, an account of the discussion with the parents or guardians of the child about their wishes and the alternatives to adoption;

(e) where appropriate, an account of the discussion with the child about his wishes and, if the child is of or over the age of 12 years, his capability to decide to consent to the making of the adoption order;

(f) the position of other relatives or persons likely to be involved;

(g) an account of the search for a parent or guardian who cannot be found;

(h) information about the mutual suitability of the petitioner and the child for the relationship created by adoption and the ability of the petitioner to bring up the child including an assessment of the personality of the petitioner and, where appropriate, that of the child;

(i) particulars of all members of the household of the petitioner and their relationship to the petitioner;

(j) a description of the accommodation in the home of the petitioner;

(k) where a sole petitioner is married, why the other spouse has not joined in the petition;

(l) whether the petitioner understands the nature and effect of an adoption order and in particular that the order, if made, will make the petitioner responsible for the maintenance and upbringing of the child;

(m) whether the means and standing of the petitioner are such as to enable him to maintain and bring up the child suitability;

(n) what right or interest in property the child has;

(o) whether any payment or reward prohibited by section 51 of the Act of 1978 (prohibition on certain payments) has been received or agreed upon;

(p) whether the life of the child has been insured and for what sum;

(q) information about the religious persuasion, (if any), racial origin and cultural and linguistic background both of the child and of the petitioner;

(r) considerations arising from the difference in age between the petitioner and the child if this is more or less than the normal difference in age between parents and children;

(s) whether adoption is likely to safeguard and promote the welfare of the child throughout its life; and

(ss) whether arrangements for the adoption of the child have been made in contravention of section 11 of the Act of 1978 or the child has been placed for adoption in contravention of that section; and

(t) any other information which may be of assistance to the court.

(2) On completion of the report referred to in paragraph (1), the local

authority or the adoption agency, as the case may be, shall send the report, and a copy of it for each party, to the Deputy Principal Clerk.

(3) On receipt of the report referred to in paragraph (2), the Deputy Principal Clerk shall—

(a) where the petition has been presented, cause the report to be lodged in process; and

(b) where the petition has not yet been presented, cause the report to be retained in the Petition Department for lodging in process when the petition is presented.

Applications for adoption order

67.22.—(1) An application for an adoption order shall be made by petition in Form 67.22.

(2) On presentation of the petition, there shall be lodged in process as productions—

(a) an extract or a certified copy of any entry in the register of births relating to the birth of the child;

(b) an extract or a certified copy of an entry in the register of births relating to the birth of the petitioner;

(c) where the petition is by a married couple, an extract or a certified copy of the entry in the register of marriages relating to their marriage;

(d) where the child was not placed for adoption with the applicant by an adoption agency, a medical report showing the physical and mental health of the child (including any special needs) and his emotional, behavioural and educational development;

(e) a medical certificate of the health of the petitioner except where the petitioner is a parent of the child; and

(f) where the child has been freed for adoption, a certified copy of the interlocutor granting the freeing for adoption order in respect of that child.

Notice of petition and appointment of reporting officer and curator ad litem

67.23.—(1) On the presentation of the petition, the court shall pronounce an interlocutor—

(a) requiring the petitioner to serve a notice in Form 67.23—

(i) where the child has been placed for adoption, on the adoption agency which placed the child; and

(ii) where the child has not been placed for adoption, on the local authority within whose area the petitioner has his home;

(b) appointing a reporting officer unless the child is free for adoption and is under the age of 12 years; and

(c) appointing a curator *ad litem* where it appears desirable in order to safeguard the interests of the child.

(2) Where a curator *ad litem* is appointed under paragraph (1), the court may order—

(a) the adoption agency,

(b) the local authority, or

(c) the reporting officer,

to make available to the curator *ad litem* any report or information in relation to the child and the natural father and mother of the child.

(3) A person may, before presenting the petition, apply by letter to the Deputy Principal Clerk for the appointment of a reporting officer.

(4) An application under paragraph (3) shall—

(a) set out the reasons for which the appointment is sought;

(b) not require to be intimated to any person;

(c) be accompanied by an interlocutory sheet; and

(d) be placed by the Deputy Principal Clerk before the Lord Ordinary for his decision.

(5) The Deputy Principal Clerk shall give written intimation to the applicant under paragraph (3) of the decision of the Lord Ordinary.

(6) The decision of the Lord Ordinary on an application under paragraph (3) shall be final and not subject to review.

(7) The letter and the interlocutor sheet in an application under paragraph (3) shall be kept in the Petition Department and subsequently placed in the process of the petition.

Duties of reporting officer and curator ad litem

67.24.—(1) A reporting officer appointed under rule 67.23(1)(b) shall, where appropriate—

(a) inquire into the facts and circumstances averred in the petition and the report of the local authority or adoption agency;

(b) where the child is not free for adoption, ascertain the whereabouts of each parent or guardian and, if practicable, meet him;

(c) witness any execution in Scotland of any agreement in Form 67.5–A or 67.5 by a parent or guardian under section 16(1)(b) of the Act of 1978 (agreement to adoption), and investigate whether the agreement is given freely, unconditionally and with full understanding of what is involved;

(d) where a parent or guardian is furth of Scotland, confirm his views in writings, ensure that any agreement under section 16(1)(b) of the Act of 1978 is witnessed in accordance with rule 67.5(3) and investigate whether the agreement is given freely; unconditionally and with full understanding of what is involved;

(e) witness any consent of a child in Form 67.5–C under section 12(8) of the Act of 1978 (consent to adoption) and ensure that he understands the consequences of that consent;

(f) ensure that each parent or guardian whose agreement is required understands that in agreeing to the adoption he is (except where the adoption order falls to be made by virtue of section 15(1)(aa) of the Act of 1978) giving up all future claims to the child and that all parental responsibilities and parental rights will (with that exception) be transferred to and will vest in the adopter;

(g) where the child is not free for adoption, consider whether the local authority or adoption agency has made every reasonable effort to find every person whose agreement is required;

(h) investigate whether there are any other persons with a relevant interest and whether they should be informed of the petition;

(i) ascertain from any parent or guardian who can be found whether alternatives to adoption have been discussed with him;

(j) ensure that each parent or guardian whose agreement is required or may be dispensed with is aware of the date (if known) of the hearing to determine the application if he wishes to appear, and confirm that such person whose agreement is required and has not been dispensed with understands that he may withdraw his agreement at any time before the adoption order is made;

(jj) ascertain whether the child is subject to a supervision requirement;

(k) draw to the attention of the court any matter which may be of assistance; and

(l) prepare a report in relation to the exercise of his duties within such period as the court may specify.

(2) A curator *ad litem* appointed under rule 67.23(1)(c) shall—

(a) safeguard generally the interests of the child;

(b) inquire, so far as he considers necessary, into the facts and circumstances averred in the petition;

(bb) ascertain from the child whether he wishes to express any views as respects the petition;

(bc) ascertain whether it would be better for the child that an adoption order were made than that it were not made.

(c) ascertain particulars of the condition of, and accommodation in, the home of the petitioner;

(d) ascertain particulars of all members of the household of the petitioner and their relationship to the petitioner;

(e) where a sole petitioner is married, ascertain why the other spouse has not joined in the petition;

(f) ascertain whether the means and status of the petitioner are sufficient to enable him to maintain and bring up the child suitably;

(g) ascertain any rights or interests in property of the child;

(h) ascertain whether a payment or reward prohibited by section 51 of the Act of 1978 (prohibition on certain payments) has been received or agreed upon;

(i) establish that the petitioner understands that the nature and effect of an adoption order is to transfer the parental responsibilities and parental rights in relation to the child to the petitioner and make him responsible for the maintenance and upbringing of the child;

(j) where applicable, ascertain when the mother of the child ceased to have the care and possession of the child and to whom care and possession were transferred;

(k) ascertain whether the proposed adoption is likely to safeguard and promote the welfare of the child throughout his life;

(l) ascertain whether the life of the child has been insured and for what sum;

(m) ascertain whether it may be in the interests of the child that the court should pronounce an interlocutor making an order under section 25 of the Act of 1978 (interim orders), or making an adoption order subject to particular conditions including the making of special provision for the child, or whether an order such as is mentioned in section 11(2)(b) of the Act of 1995 (imposing parental responsibilities or giving parental rights) should be made;

(n) where the petitioner is not ordinarily resident in the United Kingdom, ascertain whether a report has been obtained on the house and living conditions of the petitioner from a reliable agency in the country of his ordinary residence;

(o) ascertain the reasons why the petitioner wishes to adopt the child;
(p) ascertain the religious persuasion (if any), social origin and cultural and linguistic background both of the child and the petitioner;
(q) where the difference in age between the petitioner and the child is greater or less than the normal difference between parent and child, assess the implications of that difference in relation to the petition;
(r) consider any other matter, including the personality of the petitioner and where appropriate, that of the child which might affect the suitability of the petitioner to be a parent bringing up the child;
(s) ascertain, so far as practicable, the wishes and feelings of the child regarding the proposed adoption;
(t) ascertain, where the father of the child does not have parental rights, the likelihood of the father gaining any such parental rights, whether by marriage or as the result of any order by any court;
(u) where the agreement of a parent or guardian or the consent of a child is sought to be dispensed with, consider whether the ground of dispensation has been made out;
(v) consider whether, in his opinion, the child should be present at the hearing to determine the petition;
(w) perform such other duties as appear to him to be necessary or as the court may require; and
(ww) in performing his duties under this paragraph, regard the need to safeguard and promote the welfare of the child throughout the child's life as the paramount consideration; and
(x) prepare a report in relation to the exercise of his duties within such period as the court may specify.

(3) The reporting officer shall, on completion of his report, send to the Deputy Principal Clerk—
(a) the report and a copy of it for each party;
(b) any agreement for the purposes of section 16(1)(b) of the Act of 1978 (agreement of parent or guardian to adoption); and
(c) any consent under section 12(8) of the Act of 1978 (consent of child to adoption).

(4) The curator *ad litem* shall, on completion of his report, send the report, and a copy of it for each party, to the Deputy Principal Clerk.

Hearing of adoption petition
67.25.—(1) On receipt of the reports referred to in rules 67.21 and 67.24, the Deputy Principal Clerk shall—
(a) cause the reports and any other documents to be lodged in process;
(b) give written intimation to each party of the lodging of those documents and make them available to each party; and
(c) within seven days thereafter, cause—
   (i) the petition to be put out on the By Order Roll before the Lord Ordinary; and
   (ii) written intimation of the date of the hearing on the By Order Roll to be given to each party.

(2) At the hearing on the By Order Roll, the court—
(a) shall pronounce an interlocutor appointing the petition to a hearing to determine the petition; and
(b) may, in such interlocutor—

    (i) order any person whose agreement or consent is required to be given or dispensed with to attend the hearing;

    (ii) order intimation of the date of the hearing to any person not mentioned in paragraph (3)(a) to (dc);

    (iii) order the reporting officer or curator *ad litem* to perform additional duties to assist the court in determining the petition.

(3) The petitioner shall intimate the date of the hearing ordered under paragraph (2)(a) in Form 67.25 to—

    (a) every person whose whereabouts are known to him and whose agreement or consent is required to be given or dispensed with;

    (b) the reporting officer appointed under rule 67.23(1)(b);

    (c) any curator *ad litem* appointed under rule 67.23(1)(c);

    (d) the local authority or adoption agency referred to in rule 67.21;

    (da) any person keeping the child by virtue of a child protection order, of a supervision requirement or of a warrant granted by a children's hearing;

    (db) any person to whom the parental responsibilities and parental rights in relation to the child have been transferred by a parental responsibilities order or an order under section 11 of the Act of 1995;

    (dc) any person having parental responsibility (within the meaning of the Children Act 1989) for the child by virtue of section 5 of that act or of a care order or residence order within the meaning of that Act; and

    (e) any person on whom intimation has been ordered under paragraph (2)(b)(ii).

(4) At the hearing ordered under paragraph (2)(a)—

    (a) the petitioner, the adoption agency, the reporting officer and, where one has been appointed, the curator *ad litem* shall, if required by the court, appear and may be represented;

    (b) any person required by the court to attend the hearing shall appear and may be represented;

    (c) any other person to whom intimation was made under paragraph (3)(a) or (e) may appear or be represented.

Intimation of making of adoption order where child subject to supervision requirement

67.25A. Where on making an adoption order in relation to a child who is subject to a supervision requirement the court makes a determination under section 12(9) of the Act of 1978 (that is to say, a determination that the child shall forthwith cease to be subject to that requirement), the clerk of court shall intimate the determination to the Principal Reporter.

    67.26. [*Revoked by S.I. 1997 No. 853.*]

Applications under section 49(1) of the Act of 1978

67.27.—(1) An application under section 49(1) of the Act of 1978 (application to adopt a child abroad) shall be made by petition.

(2) The provisions of this Part shall, with the necessary modifications,

apply to an application under section 49(1) of the Act of 1978 as they apply to an application for an adoption order.

(3) Evidence that the child in respect of whom the application is made may be adopted under the law of or in the country in which the petitioner is domiciled may be given by a signed statement by a person qualified in the law of that country.

Applications for return, removal or prohibition of removal of child

67.28.—(1) An application under section 29 of the Act of 1978 (order to return a child to, or not to remove a child from, the care of the applicant) shall be made—

(a) in relation to a breach of section 27(1) or 28(1) of that Act (restrictions on removal of child where application for adoption order pending), by note in the process of the petition for an adoption order or a section 49 order to which it relates; or

(b) in relation to a breach of section 28(3) (restriction on removal where child was or is in care of the local authority) of that Act, by petition.

(2) An application for leave—

(a) under section 27(1) or 28 of the Act of 1978 (leave to remove a child) shall be made by note in the process of the petition for an adoption order or a section 49 order to which it relates;

(b) under section 30(2) of that Act (leave to adoption agency to give notice of intention to remove a child) shall be made by note in the process of the petition for an adoption order or a section 49 order to which it relates.

(3) Subject to paragraph (4), rule 67.2 (disapplication of certain rules to this Chapter) shall not apply to an application mentioned in paragraph (1) or (2) of this rule.

(4) An application mentioned in paragraph (1) or (2) shall not be intimated on the walls of the court or advertised.

Applications to amend or revoke a direction in, or revoke, an adoption order

67.29.—(1) An application—

(a) under paragraph 4(1) of Schedule 1 to the Act of 1978 (amendment, or revocation of a direction in, and adoption order), or

(b) under section 46 of that Act (revocation of an adoption order on legitimation),

shall be made by petition.

(2) Subject to paragraph (3), rule 67.2 (disapplication of certain rules to this Chapter) shall not apply to an application mentioned in paragraph (1) of this rule.

(3) An application mentioned in paragraph (1) shall not be intimated on the walls of the court or advertised.

Registration of certified copy interlocutor

67.30. On the court pronouncing an interlocutor making—

(a) an adoption order,

(b) an amendment to, or a revocation of a direction in, an adoption order,

(c) a revocation of an adoption order,

(d) a section 49 order, or

(e) a Convention adoption order,

the clerk of court shall forthwith send a certified copy of that interlocutor to the Registrar General for Scotland in a sealed envelope marked "confidential".

Extract of order

67.31. An extract of an adoption order or a section 49 order shall not be issued except by order of the court on an application to it—

(a) where there is a petition for the adoption order or the section 49 order, as the case may be, depending before the court, by motion; or

(b) where there is no such petition depending before the court, by petition.

Procedure after intimation to Registrar General or issue of extract

67.32.—(1) After a certified copy of an interlocutor mentioned in rule 67.30 has been sent to the Registrar General for Scotland, the clerk of court or the Extractor, as the case may be, shall—

(a) place the whole process in an envelope bearing only—

  (i) the name of the petitioner;

  (ii) the full name of the child to whom the process relates; and

  (iii) the date of the order; and

(b) seal the envelope and mark it "confidential".

(2) No person shall open a process referred to in paragraph (1) or inspect its contents within 100 years after the date of the adoption order or the section 49 order, as the case may be, except—

(a) the person adopted under the order after he has reached the age of 16 years;

(b) any other person or body entitled under section 45(5) of the Act of 1978 to access to the registers and books kept under section 45(4) of that Act, with the written authority of the adopted person;

(c) the Deputy Principal Clerk or Extractor, as the case may be, on the written application to him by an adoption agency with the written agreement of the adopted person for the purpose of ascertaining the name of the adoption agency responsible for the placement of that person for adoption;

(d) by order of the court on an application made by petition presented by another court or authority (whether within the United Kingdom or not) having the power to authorise an adoption for the purpose of obtaining information in connection with an application to it for adoption;

(e) by order of the court on an application made by petition presented by any person; and

(f) a person who is authorised in writing by the Secretary of State to obtain information from the process for the purpose of research designed to improve the working of adoption law and practice.

PART IV

CONVENTION ADOPTION ORDERS

Interpretation of this part
67.33.—(1) In this Part—
"Convention country" has the meaning assigned in section 65(1) of the Act of 1978;
"the petition" means the petition referred to in rule 67.35 or 67.41, as the case may be.
(2) Any reference in this Part to the nationality of a person who is not solely a United Kingdom national means the nationality of that person as determined in accordance with section 63 of the Act of 1978.

Application of Part III to this part
67.34. Part III (adoption), except the following rules, shall apply to the petition:—
rule 67.19 (interpretation of Part III),
rule 67.20 (protection of identity of petitioner),
rule 67.27 (applications under section 49(1) of the Act of 1978),
rule 67.29 (applications to amend or revoke a direction in, or revoke, an adoption order).

Applications for Convention adoption order
67.35.—(1) An application for a Convention adoption order shall be made by petition in Form 67.22.
(2) The petition shall include averments in relation to—
(a) the nationality of the petitioner;
(b) the nationality of the child;
(c) the place and the country where the petitioner habitually resides;
(d) the place and the country where the child habitually resides;
(e) whether the child is, or has been, married;
(f) where the petitioner is a national of a Convention country, or where both petitioners are nationals of the same Convention country, whether there is a specified provision within the meaning of section 17(8) of the Act of 1978 in respect of that country which prohibits the adoption; and
(g) where the child is not a United Kingdom national, any provision relating to consents and consultations, of the internal law with respect to adoption of the Convention country of which the child is a national.
(3) The prayer of the petition shall include a crave that the court direct the Registrar General for Scotland—
(a) to insert the words "Convention Order" in the entry to be made by him in the Adopted Children Register regarding the adoption;
(b) to intimate the terms of the order to the appropriate authorities referred to in rule 67.39(2) or (3) or 67.41(5)(b) (designated authorities of Convention country), as the case may be.

Investigations by curator ad litem
67.36.—(1) The curator *ad litem* appointed under rule 67.23(1)(b) by virtue of rule 67.34 (application of Part III to this Part) shall also

investigate the averments referred to in rule 67.35(2) and shall include the results of his investigations in his report.

(2) Where in the course of his investigations, the curator *ad litem* requires a report from any authority outside Great Britain, he shall request the local authority to request that other authority to provide that report.

Evidence of nationality

67.37. There shall be lodged in process as productions—

(a) any document relied on as evidence of the nationality of the petitioner or that of the child; and

(b) where the nationality of the petitioner or that of the child is of a Convention country, a signed statement by a person qualified in the law of that country confirming such nationality under that law.

Petition in respect of a non-U.K. child

67.38.—(1) This rule applies to a petition where the child is not a United Kingdom national.

(2) On presentation of the petition, there shall be lodged in process as a production a signed statement by a person qualified in the law of the Convention country of which the child is a national setting out the consent or consultation required by the internal law of that country with respect to adoption.

(3) A consent referred to in section 17(7) of the Act of 1978 shall be in a form which complies with any requirement of the internal law with respect to adoption of the Convention country of which the child is a national, but where the court is not satisfied that such consent has been made with full understanding of what is involved, it may call for further evidence.

(4) A document mentioned in paragraph (2) or (3) may be received in evidence without being spoken to.

(5) Where a consent or consultation referred to in paragraph (2) or (3) could properly be dispensed with under the internal law of the country concerned, the court may dispense with that consent or consultation in accordance with the provisions of that law.

(6) Where the court pronounces an interlocutor appointing the petition to a hearing under rule 67.25(2)(a) by virtue of rule 67.34 (application of Part III to this Part), the requirements of rule 67.25(3) (intimation of date of hearing to certain persons) shall include a requirement to intimate the date of the hearing in Form 67.25 to—

(a) any person whose consent is referred to in section 17(7) of the Act of 1978 but who has not given such consent;

(b) any person who, in accordance with the internal law with respect to adoption of the Convention country of which the child is a national, has to be consulted, but does not have to consent to, the adoption.

(7) For the purposes of section 17(7)(a) of the Act of 1978, the proper officer of the court shall be the Deputy Principal Clerk.

Additional notice to Registrar General

67.39.—(1) The Deputy Principal Clerk shall send to the Registrar General for Scotland—

(a) with any Convention adoption order, a notice specifying the authorities mentioned in paragraph (2) and requesting him to inform them of the terms of the order;

(b) with any order made under section 46(2) of the Act of 1978 revoking a Convention adoption order, a notice specifying the authorities mentioned in paragraph (3) of this rule and requesting him to inform them of the terms of the order under that section.

(2) The authorities referred to in paragraph (1)(a) are the designated authorities of any Convention country—

(a) of which the child is a national;

(b) in which the child was born;

(c) in which a petitioner habitually resides; or

(d) of which a petitioner is a national.

(3) The authorities referred to in paragraph (1)(b) are the designated authorities of any Convention country—

(a) of which the adopted person is a national; or

(b) in which the adopted person was born.

Interim orders

67.40. Where the petitioner is a national, or both petitioners are nationals, of a Convention country, the court shall take account of any specified provision (as defined in section 17(8) of the Act of 1978) of the internal law of that country before making any order under section 25 of that Act (interim orders).

Revocation or annulment of regulated adoptions

67.41.—(1) This rule applies to an application for an order under section 46(2) (revocation of regulated adoption), or section 47 (annulment etc, of regulated adoption, Convention adoption order or overseas adoption), of the Act of 1978.

(2) An application mentioned in paragraph (1) shall be made by petition.

(3) An application under section 47(1) of the Act of 1978 (annulment) shall not, except with the leave of the court, be made later than two years after the date of the regulated adoption to which it relates.

(4) Where the adopted person is under the age of 18 years on the date of the presentation of a petition under this rule, the court shall appoint a curator *ad litem* with the duties mentioned in rule 67.24(2).

(5) On the court pronouncing an interlocutor making an order referred to in paragraph (1), the Deputy Principal Clerk shall—

(a) send a notice of the order to the Registrar General for Scotland specifying—

(i) the date of the adoption;

(ii) the name and address of the authority which granted the adoption;

(iii) the names of the adopter or adopters and of the adopted person as given in that petition;

(iv) the country in which the adoption was granted;

(v) the country of which the adopted person is a national; and

(vi) the country in which the adopted person was born; and

(b) where any such country is a Convention country, request the Registrar General for Scotland to inform the designated authorities of that country of the terms of the order.

ACT OF SEDERUNT (CHILD CARE AND MAINTENANCE RULES) 1997

(S.I. 1997 No. 291)

[April 1, 1997]

The Lords of Council and Session, under and by virtue of the powers conferred on them by sections 17, 20, 22, 23, 24 and 28(1) of the Maintenance Orders Act 1950, sections 2(4)(c), 2A(1) and 21(1) of the Maintenance Orders Act 1958, section 32 of the Sheriff Courts (Scotland) Act 1971, section 59 of the Adoption (Scotland) Act 1978 (as modified and applied in relation to parental orders under section 30 of the Human Fertilisation and Embryology Act 1990 and applications for such orders by paragraph 15 of Schedule 1 to the Parental Orders (Human Fertilisation and Embryology) (Scotland) Regulations 1994, section 48 of the Civil Jurisdiction and Judgments Act 1982, sections 27(2), 28(1) and 42(1) of the Family Law Act 1986 and section 91 of the Children (Scotland) Act 1995 and of all other powers enabling them in that behalf, having approved, with modifications, draft rules submitted to them by the Sheriff Court Rules Council in accordance with section 34 of the Sheriff Courts (Scotland) Act 1971, do hereby enact and declare:

CHAPTER 1

PRELIMINARY

Citation and commencement
1.1—(1) This Act of Sederunt may be cited as the Act of Sederunt (Child Care and Maintenance Rules) 1997 and shall come into force on 1st April 1997.

(2) This Act of Sederunt shall be inserted in the Books of Sederunt.

Interpretation
1.2—(1) In this Act of Sederunt, unless the context otherwise requires—
   "Ordinary Cause Rules" means the First Schedule to the Sheriff Courts (Scotland) Act 1907;
   "Principal Reporter" has the same meaning as in section 93(1) of the Children (Scotland) Act 1995;
   "sheriff clerk" includes the sheriff clerk depute.

(2) Unless the context otherwise requires, any reference in this Act of Sederunt to a specified Chapter, Part or rule shall be construed as a reference to the Chapter, Part or rule bearing that number in this Act of Sederunt, and a reference to a specified paragraph, sub-paragraph or head shall be construed as a reference to the paragraph, sub-paragraph or head so numbered or lettered in the provision in which that reference occurs.

(3) Any reference in this Act of Sederunt to a numbered Form shall be construed as a reference to the Form so numbered in Schedule 1 to this Act of Sederunt and includes a form substantially to the same effect with such variation as circumstances may require.

Affidavits
1.3 An affidavit required in terms of any provision of this Act of Sederunt may be emitted—
  (a) in the United Kingdom, before an notary public or any other competent authority;
  (b) outwith the United Kingdom, before a British diplomatic or consular officer, or any person authorised to administer an oath or affirmation under the law of the place where the oath or affirmation is made.

Revocations and transitional provisions
1.4—(1) Subject to paragraphs (2) and (3), the Acts of Sederunt mentioned in column (1) of Schedule 2 to this Act of Sederunt are revoked to the extent specified in column (3) of that Schedule.

(2) Nothing in paragraph (1) or in Chapter 2 shall affect any cause which has been commenced before 1st April 1997 and to which that Chapter would otherwise apply, and such a cause shall proceed according to the law and practice in force immediately before that date.

(3) Nothing in paragraph (1) shall affect any cause to which paragraph 8(1) of Schedule 3 to the Children (Scotland) Act applies, and such a cause shall proceed according to the law and practice in force immediately before 1st April 1997.

CHAPTER 2

ADOPTION OF CHILDREN

PART I

GENERAL

Interpretation
2.1 In this Chapter, unless the context otherwise requires—
  "the Act" means the Adoption (Scotland) Act 1978;
  "the 1995 Act" means the Children (Scotland) Act 1995;
  "adoption agency" means a local authority or an approved adoption society;
  "Her Majesty's Forces" means the Royal Navy, the regular forces as defined by section 225 of the Army Act 1955, the regular air force

as defined by section 223 of the Air Force Act 1955, the Queen Alexandra's Royal Naval Nursing Service and the Women's Royal Naval Service; and

"Registrar General" means the Registrar General of Births, Deaths and Marriages for Scotland.

Expenses

2.2 The sheriff may make such an order with regard to the expenses, including the expenses of a reporting officer and a curator *ad litem* or any other person who attended a hearing, of an application under this Chapter as he thinks fit and may modify such expenses or direct them to be taxed on such scale as he may determine.

Intimation to Principal Reporter

2.3 Where in such proceedings as are referred to in subsection (2)(c) of section 54 of the 1995 Act (reference to the Principal Reporter by court) a matter is referred by the sheriff to the Principal Reporter under that section, the interlocutor making the reference shall be intimated by the sheriff clerk forthwith to the Principal Reporter; and that intimation shall specify which of the conditions in paragraph (2)(a) to (h), (j), (k) or (l) of section 52 of the 1995 Act it appears to the sheriff has been satisfied.

Timetables under section 25A of the Act

2.4 In proceedings in which such a timetable as is referred to in section 25A(a) of the Act (timetable for resolving question) is required, the court shall draw up the timetable forthwith where—

(a) there is presented a petition with a crave for the agreement of a parent or guardian to be dispensed with;

(b) it appears to the court from a report by an adoption agency, local authority or reporting officer that a question as to dispensing with such agreement arises; or

(c) such agreement previously given is withdrawn.

PART II

APPLICATION FOR AN ORDER DECLARING A CHILD FREE FOR ADOPTION

Petition

2.5—(1) An application under section 18(1) of the Act (freeing child for adoption) for an order declaring a child free for adoption shall be made by petition in Form 1.

(2) There shall be lodged in process at the same time as the lodging of a petition under paragraph (1)—

(a) an extract of the entry in the Register of Births relating to the child who is the subject of the application;

(b) a report of the adoption agency which deals with the following matters—

(i) how the needs of the child came to the notice of the petitioner;

(ii) any relevant family circumstances of the child;

(iii) a description of the physical and mental health of the child (including any special needs) and his emotional, behavioural and educational development;

   (iv) an account of the discussion by the petitioner with the parents or guardians of the child and, if appropriate, with the child about their wishes and the alternatives to adoption;

   (v) the knowledge of the petitioner of the petition of other relatives or persons likely to be involved;

   (vi) an account of the search by the petitioner for any parent or guardian who cannot be found;

   (vii) the likelihood of placement of the child for adoption and whether a petition for an adoption order is likely in the near future;

   (viii) the arrangements of the petitioner to care for the child after the granting of the prayer of the petition for an order freeing the child for adoption;

   (ix) whether the petitioner has given each parent or guardian who can be found an opportunity to make a declaration under section 18(6) of the Act that he prefers not to be involved in future questions concerning the adoption of the child;

   (x) an account of the enquiries by the petitioner into the circumstances of any reputed father;

   (xi) the intentions of the petitioner about giving notice to a former parent or guardian under section 19(2) and (3) of the Act (progress reports to former parent); and

   (xii) any other information which may be of assistance to the Court; and

  (c) any other document founded upon by the petitioner in support of the terms of the petition.

(3) Where an adoption agency which proposes to apply under paragraph (1) wishes to prevent the address of the child being disclosed to any person whose agreement or consent is required by section 18(1)(a) or (2) of the Act respectively, the agency may apply to the sheriff clerk for a serial number to be assigned for that purpose.

Agreement and consents to order freeing child for adoption

2.6—(1) An agreement required by section 18(1)(a), or a consent required by section 18(2) or 18(8) of the Act, if given in writing shall be in Form 2, 3 or 4 as appropriate and such form, duly executed, shall be sufficient evidence of such agreement or consent.

(2) A form of agreement or of consent executed outwith the United Kingdom shall be sufficient evidence of such agreement or consent if it is witnessed—

  (a) where the person who executes the form is serving in Her Majesty's Forces, by an officer holding a commission in any of those forces; or

  (b) in any other case, by a British consular official, or by any person for the time being authorised by the law of the country in which the form is executed to administer an oath for any judicial or legal purpose.

Appointment of curator ad litem *and reporting officer*

2.7—(1) The sheriff shall, after the lodging of a petition under rule 2.5(1), appoint a curator *ad litem* and reporting officer and the same person may be appointed as curator *ad litem* and reporting officer in the same petition, if the sheriff considers that doing so is appropriate in the circumstances.

(2) The sheriff may appoint a person who is not a member of a panel established under regulations made by virtue of section 101 of the 1995 Act to be a curator *ad litem* or a reporting officer.

(3) The sheriff may, on cause shown, appoint a reporting officer prior to the lodging of a petition.

(4) An application for an appointment under paragraph (3) shall be made by letter addressed to the sheriff clerk specifying the reasons for the appointment, and shall not require to be intimated to any other person.

Duties of reporting officer and curator ad litem

2.8—(1) a reporting officer appointed under this Part shall—
  (a) witness any consent to the making of an application for an order freeing a child for adoption executed within the United Kingdom by a parent or guardian of the child and shall lodge the consent in process;
  (b) witness any agreement executed within the United Kingdom by a parent or guardian of a child to the making of an adoption order in respect of the child and lodge the agreement in process;
  (c) ascertain that each parent or guardian who can be found understands that the effect of an adoption order would be to extinguish his parental responsibilities and rights;
  (d) ascertain from any parent or guardian who can be found, whether alternatives to adoption have been discussed with him;
  (e) ascertain whether there is any person other than those mentioned in the petition upon whom notice of the petition should be served;
  (f) ascertain whether the child is subject to a supervision requirement;
  (g) confirm that each parent or guardian who can be found understands the implications of an order freeing the child for adoption;
  (h) confirm that each parent or guardian who has given his agreement and can be found understands that he may withdraw his agreement at any time before an order under section 18(1) of the Act is made;
  (i) confirm that each parent or guardian who can be found is aware that he may in the circumstances set forth in section 20 of the Act (revocation of section 18 order) apply to the court for revocation of any order under section 18(1) of the Act and of the appropriate procedure for such an application;
  (j) confirm that each parent or guardian who can be found has been given an opportunity to make a declaration in terms of section 18(6) of the Act and, where the parent or guardian elects to make such declaration, shall comply with rule 2.10; and
  (k) in the case of a child whose father is not married to the mother, consider the likelihood of any person claiming to be the father of the child—
      (i) applying for or being refused an order under section 11 of the 1995 Act (court orders relating to parental responsibilities); or
      (ii) entering into an agreement in terms of section 4(1) of that Act (agreement as to parental responsibilities and rights),
and shall report in writing thereon to the sheriff within 4 weeks from the

date of the interlocutor appointing the reporting officer, or within such other period as the sheriff in his discretion may allow.

(2) A curator *ad litem* appointed under this Part shall have regard to the welfare of the child as his paramount duty and shall further—

- (a) generally safeguard the interests of the child who is the subject of the petition and ensure that consideration has been given to the interests of the child for the purposes of section 6 of the Act (duty to promote welfare of child);
- (b) ascertain whether the facts stated in the petition are correct except where investigation of such facts falls within the duties of the reporting officer;
- (c) where the child who is sought to be freed for adoption is over the age of 12 years, witness any consent to the order executed by him in the United Kingdom and lodge the consent in process;
- (d) ascertain from the child whether he wishes to express a view and where a child indicates his wish to express a view, ascertain that view;
- (e) ascertain whether an order freeing the child for adoption would safeguard and throughout his life promote the welfare of the child;
- (f) ascertain whether it would be better for the child that the court should make the order than it should not make such order; and
- (g) report on the current circumstances and care of the child,

and, subject to paragraph (3), shall report in writing thereon to the sheriff within 4 weeks from the date of the interlocutor appointing the curator, or within such other period as the sheriff in his discretion may allow.

(3) Subject to any order made by the sheriff under rule 2.9(1)(a), the views of the child ascertained in terms of paragraph (2)(d) may, if the curator *ad litem* considers appropriate, be conveyed to the sheriff orally.

Procedure where child wishes to express a view

2.9—(1) Where a child has indicated his wish to express his views the sheriff, without prejudice to rule 2.8(2)(d)—

- (a) may order such procedural steps to be taken as he considers appropriate to ascertain the views of that child; and
- (b) shall not make an order under this Part unless an opportunity has been given for the views of that child to be obtained or heard.

(2) Where the views of a child, whether obtained under this rule or under rule 2.8(2)(d), have been recorded in writing, the sheriff may direct that such a written record shall—

- (a) be sealed in an envelope marked "Views of the child—confidential";
- (b) be available to a sheriff only;
- (c) not be opened by any person other than a sheriff; and
- (d) not form a borrowable part of the process.

Declaration made under section 18(6) of the Act

2.10—(1) A declaration made under section 18(6) of the Act (declaration of preference not to be involved in future questions concerning the adoption of the child) shall be in Form 5, be signed by each parent or guardian of the child and shall, subject to paragraph (3), be witnessed by the reporting officer.

(2) The reporting officer shall provide a copy of the form of declaration to each parent or guardian of the child for signature and shall explain to him the consequences of signing the declaration and of the terms of section 19 of the Act (progress reports to former parents).

(3) A declaration executed outwith the United Kingdom shall be witnessed in the manner prescribed by rule 2.6(2)(a) or (b).

(4) The reporting officer shall submit the executed declaration to the sheriff clerk who shall thereafter record the declaration in the manner prescribed in rule 2.13.

(5) A withdrawal of a declaration made under section 18(6) of the Act may be made at any time and shall be made by notice in writing in Form 6 to the sheriff clerk who shall forthwith record the withdrawal in the manner prescribed in rule 2.13 and intimate the withdrawal to the adoption agency.

Hearing

2.11—(1) When the reports of the reporting officer and the curator *ad litem* have been received by the court, the sheriff shall order a diet of hearing to be fixed.

(2) The petitioner shall intimate the diet of hearing in accordance with Form 7—

(a) to every person, whose whereabouts are known to him and whose agreement or consent in terms of section 18 of the Act is required or must be dispensed with; and

(b) in the case of a child whose father is not married to the mother, to any person whose whereabouts are known to him and who claims to be the father of the child but who is not his guardian and in respect of whom no order relating to parental responsibilities has been made.

(3) Subject to paragraph (5), if no person entitled to appear appears and wishes to be heard, the sheriff may make an order freeing the child for adoption on the motion of the petitioner.

(4) Subject to paragraph (5), if a person entitled to appear appears and wishes to be heard, the sheriff may hear him or may order a further diet to be fixed at which he may be heard and evidence given at any such diet shall be given in the presence of the petitioner or his solicitor.

(5) Before making an order, the sheriff shall consider any report received by him in terms of section 73(14) of the 1995 Act (report by children's hearing).

Confidentiality

2.12—(1) Unless the sheriff otherwise directs, all documents lodged in process including the reports by the curator *ad litem* and the reporting officer shall be available only to the sheriff, the curator *ad litem*, the reporting officer and the parties; and such documents shall be treated as confidential by any persons involved in, or a party to, the proceedings and by the sheriff clerk.

(2) The reporting officer and curator *ad litem* shall treat all information obtained in the exercise of their duties as confidential and shall not disclose any such information to any person unless disclosure of such information is necessary for the proper discharge of their duties.

(3) This rule is subject to rule 2.9(2).

Adoption register

2.13—(1) The sheriff clerk shall maintain a register known as "the Adoption Register".

(2) The sheriff clerk shall enter in the Adoption Register any declaration made under section 18(6) of the Act submitted to him by the reporting officer and any withdrawal made in terms of rule 2.10(5).

(3) A declaration under section 19(4) of the Act (declaration by former parent not to be involved in future questions concerning the adoption) shall be made in Form 5 and the adoption agency shall submit the declaration to the sheriff clerk who shall enter it in the Adoption Register.

Final procedure

2.14—(1) Where an order under this Part has been granted the sheriff clerk shall—

(a) after the expiry of 14 days from the date of, or date of confirmation of, the order without appeal having been taken, issue an extract of the order to the petitioner and thereafter seal the process in an envelope marked "Confidential"; and

(b) where that order includes a determination under section 18(9) of the Act (cancellation of supervision requirement), intimate the making of that determination to the Principal Reporter.

(2) The envelope referred to in paragraph (1)(a) shall not be unsealed by the sheriff clerk or any other person having control of the records of that or any court, and the process shall not be made accessible to any person, for one hundred years after the date of the granting of the order except—

(a) to the person freed for adoption by the order once he has attained the age of sixteen years;

(b) to the sheriff clerk, on an application made to him by an adoption agency, with the consent of the person to whom the process relates, for the purpose only of ascertaining the name of the agency, if any, responsible for the placement of that person and informing the applicant of that name;

(c) to a person, on an application made by him to the sheriff setting forth the reasons for which access to the process is required;

(d) to a court, public authority or administrative board (whether in the United Kingdom or not) having power to authorise an adoption, on petition by it to the court which granted the original order requesting that information be made available from the process for the purpose of discharging its duties in considering an application for adoption and specifying the precise reasons for which access to the process is required; or

(e) to a person who is authorised by the Secretary of State to obtain information from the process for the purposes of such research as is intended to improve the working of adoption law and practice.

PART III

REVOCATION ORDERS, ETC.

Application for revocation

2.15—(1) An application under section 20(1) of the Act for revocation of an order freeing a child for adoption shall be made by minute in Form 8 in the process of the original application and shall specify detailed proposals for the future well-being of the child.

(2) On the lodging of a minute under paragraph (1), the sheriff shall order the applicant to intimate the minute to the petitioner in the original application and to such other person as shall to the sheriff seem appropriate.

(3) Any person to whom intimation has been made under paragraph (2) may, within 14 days after the date on which intimation is made, lodge answers to the minute.

Appointment of curator ad litem

2.16—(1) On the lodging of a minute under rule 2.15(1), the sheriff may appoint a curator *ad litem* who shall have regard to the welfare of the child as his paramount duty and shall further—

(a) investigate the facts contained in the minute;

(b) investigate the circumstances and care of the child with regard to the promotion of his welfare throughout his life; and

(c) ascertain from the child whether he wishes to express a view and where a child indicates his wish to express a view, ascertain that view,

and, subject to paragraph (2), shall report in writing thereon to the sheriff within 4 weeks from the date of the interlocutor appointing the curator, or within such other period as the sheriff in his discretion may allow.

(2) Subject to any order made by the sheriff under rule 2.17(1)(a), the views of the child ascertained in terms of paragraph (1)(c) may, if the curator *ad litem* considers appropriate, be conveyed to the sheriff orally.

Procedure where child wishes to express a view

2.17—(1) Where a child has indicated his wish to express his views the sheriff, without prejudice to rule 2.16(1)(c)—

(a) may order such procedural steps to be taken as he considers appropriate to ascertain the views of that child; and

(b) shall not make an order under this Part unless an opportunity has been given for the views of that child to be obtained or heard.

(2) Where the views of a child, whether obtained under this rule or under rule 2.16(1)(c), have been recorded in writing, the sheriff may direct that such a written record shall—

(a) be sealed in an envelope marked "Views of the child—confidential";

(b) be available to a sheriff only;

(c) not be opened by any person other than a sheriff; and

(d) not form a borrowable part of the process.

Hearing

2.18—(1) Where answers have been lodged under rule 2.15(3), the sheriff shall order a diet of hearing to be fixed.

(2) Where no answers to the minute under rule 2.15(1) have been lodged the sheriff may—

(a) order the relevant adoption agency to submit a report to him;

(b) order a diet of hearing to be fixed; or

(c) order both such a report and such a diet of hearing.

(3) An order made under this Part shall specify the person—

(a) to whom parental rights are given in consequence of the making of the order; and

(b) on whom parental responsibilities are imposed in consequence of the making of the order,

and intimation shall be given to such a person on the making of such an order.

Application to place a child

2.19—(1) An application by an adoption agency under section 20(2) of the Act (leave of court to place a child) shall be made by minute in Form 9 in the original process.

(2) A minute under paragraph (1) shall be intimated by the applicant to such persons as shall to the sheriff seem appropriate.

Further application with leave of the court

2.20 A further application made with leave of the sheriff in terms of section 20(5) of the Act (further application by former parent with leave of the court) shall be made by minute in Form 10 in the original process and the provisions of rules 2.15(2) and (3), 2.16 and 2.17 shall apply to such a further application.

PART IV

ADOPTION ORDERS

Application for adoption order

2.21—(1) An application for an adoption order, or for an order vesting parental responsibilities and rights relating to a child under section 49(1) of the Act (adoption of children abroad), shall be made by petition in Form 11 or 12 as appropriate.

(2) There shall be lodged in process along with the petition—

(a) an extract of the entry in the Register of Births relating to the child who is the subject of the application;

(b) in the case of a joint petition by a married couple, an extract of the entry in the Register of Marriages relating to their marriage;

(c) where the child was not placed for adoption with the applicant by an adoption agency, three copies of a medical report showing the physical and mental health of the child (including any special needs) and his emotional, behavioural and educational development;

(d) any report by the local authority required by section 22(2) of the Act (investigation by local authority on receipt of notice of intention to apply for adoption order);

(e) any report by an adoption agency required by section 23 of the Act (report on the suitability of the applicants);

(f) where appropriate, an extract of the order freeing the child for adoption; and

(g) any other document founded upon by the petitioner in support of the terms of his petition.

(3) A report by a local authority under section 22(2), or an adoption agency under section 23, of the Act shall include the following matters—

(a) information about how the needs of the child came to the notice of the agency;

(b) the family circumstances of the child;

(c) where the child was placed for adoption by an adoption agency, a description of the physical and mental health of the child (including any special needs) and his emotional, behavioural and educational development;

(d) an account of the discussion with the parents or guardians of the child and, if appropriate, with the child about their wishes and the alternatives to adoption;

(e) the position of other relatives or persons likely to be involved;

(f) an account of the search for a parent or guardian who cannot be found;

(g) information about the mutual suitability of the petitioner and the child for the relationship created by adoption and the ability of the petitioner to bring up the child including an assessment of the personality of the petitioner and, where appropriate, that of the child;

(h) particulars of all members of the household of the petitioner and their relationship to the petitioner;

(i) a description of the accommodation in the home of the petitioner;

(j) in a petition by one of two spouses, why the other spouse has not joined in the petition;

(k) whether the petitioner understands the nature and effect of an adoption order and in particular that the order, if made, will make the petitioner responsible for the maintenance and upbringing of the child;

(l) whether the means and standing of the petitioner are such as to enable him to maintain and bring up the child suitably, and what right or interest in property the child has;

(m) whether any payment or other reward in consideration of the adoption, other than an approved adoption allowance, has been received or agreed upon;

(n) what insurance has been offered on the life of the child;

(o) the religious persuasion, if any, of the petitioner and the religious persuasion, if any, racial origin and cultural and linguistic background of the child;

(p) considerations arising from the difference in age between the petitioner and the child if this is more or less than the normal difference in age between parents and children;

(q) whether adoption is likely to safeguard and promote the welfare of the child throughout its life; and

(r) any other information which may be of assistance to the court.

(4) A report by a local authority under section 22(2) of the Act shall also specify whether the child was placed with the applicant in contravention of section 11 of the Act (restriction on arranging adoptions).

(5) If no report by an adoption agency or local authority under paragraph (2)(d) or (e) is available to be lodged along with the petition, the sheriff shall pronounce an interlocutor requiring the adoption

agency or local authority concerned to prepare and lodge such a report in court within 4 weeks from the date of the interlocutor, or within such other period as the sheriff in his discretion may allow.

Additional requirements where child to be adopted abroad

2.22—(1) In a petition for an order under section 49(1) of the Act, the petitioner shall, in addition to complying with rule 2.21, adduce evidence of the law of adoption in the country in which he is domiciled.

(2) The evidence of the law of adoption required under paragraph (1) may be in the form of an affidavit by a person who is conversant with the law of adoption of that country and who practises or has practised law in that country or is a duly accredited representative of the government of that country in the United Kingdom.

Consents and agreements to adoption orders

2.23—(1) A consent to an order required by section 12(8) of the Act (need for child's consent), or an agreement required by section 16(1) of the Act (parental agreement), or such an agreement where the application is made by a person to whom section 15(1)(aa) of the Act (adoption by one person) applies, if given in writing shall be in Form 4, 13 or 14 as appropriate and such form duly executed shall be sufficient evidence of such consent or agreement.

(2) A form of consent or agreement executed outwith the United Kingdom shall be sufficient evidence of such consent or agreement if it is witnessed—

(a) where the person who executes the form is serving in Her Majesty's Forces, by an officer holding a commission in any of those forces; or

(b) in any other case, a British diplomatic or consular officer, or any person authorised to administer an oath or affirmation under the law of the place where the consent or agreement is executed.

Protection of identity of petitioner

2.24—(1) When any person who proposes to apply under rule 2.21 wishes to prevent his identity being disclosed to any person whose agreement to the order is required, he may, before presenting the petition, apply to the sheriff clerk for a serial number to be assigned to him for all purposes connected with the petition.

(2) On receipt of an application for a serial number, the sheriff clerk shall assign such a number to the applicant and shall enter a note of it opposite the name of the applicant in a register of such serial numbers.

(3) The contents of the register of serial numbers and the names of the persons to whom each number relates shall be treated as confidential by the sheriff clerk and shall not be disclosed to any person other than the sheriff.

(4) Where a serial number has been assigned to an applicant in terms of paragraph (2), any form of agreement to an adoption order which is required shall not contain the name or designation of the petitioner but shall refer to him by means of the serial number assigned to him and shall specify the year in which, and by which court, the serial number has been assigned.

Appointment of curator ad litem *and reporting officer*

2.25—(1) Subject to paragraph (2) the sheriff shall, after the lodging of a petition under rule 2.21, appoint a curator *ad litem* and reporting officer and the same person may be appointed as curator *ad litem* and reporting officer in the same petition, if the sheriff considers that doing so is appropriate in the circumstances.

(2) Where an order freeing the child for adoption has been made, the sheriff shall not appoint a reporting officer save for the purpose specified in rule 2.26(1)(a).

(3) The sheriff may appoint a person who is not a member of a panel established under regulations made by virtue of section 101 of the 1995 Act to be curator *ad litem* or a reporting officer.

(4) The sheriff may, on cause shown, appoint a reporting officer prior to the lodging of such a petition.

(5) An application for an appointment under paragraph (4) shall be made by letter addressed to the sheriff clerk specifying the reasons for the appointment, and shall not require to be intimated to any other person.

Duties of reporting office and curator ad litem

2.26—(1) Subject to rule 2.25(2), a reporting officer appointed under this Part shall—

(a) witness any agreement executed within the United Kingdom by a parent or guardian of a child to the making of an adoption order in respect of the child and lodge the agreement in process;

(b) ascertain that each parent or guardian who is not a petitioner and whose agreement is required or may be dispensed with understands the effect of the adoption order;

(c) where a parent or guardian whose agreement is required or may be dispensed with can be found, ascertain whether alternatives to adoption have been discussed with him;

(d) ascertain whether there is any person other than those mentioned in the petition upon whom notice of the petition should be served;

(e) ascertain whether the child is subject to a supervision requirement; and

(f) confirm that each parent or guardian whose agreement is required understands that he may withdraw his agreement at any time before an order is made,

and shall report in writing thereon to the sheriff within 4 weeks from the date of the interlocutor appointing the reporting officer, or within such other period as the sheriff in his discretion may allow.

(2) A curator *ad litem* appointed under this Part shall have regard to the welfare of the child as his paramount duty and shall further—

(a) generally safeguard the interests of the child whose adoption is the subject of the petition;

(b) where the child in respect of whom an adoption order is sought is over the age of 12 years, witness any consent to the order executed by him in the United Kingdom and lodge the consent in process;

(c) ascertain whether the facts stated in the petition are correct and if they are not establish the true facts;

(d) obtain particulars of accommodation in the home of the petitioner and the condition of the home;

(e) obtain particulars of all members of the household of the petitioner and their relationship to the petitioner;

(f) in the case of a petition by only one of two spouses, ascertain the reason of the other spouse for not joining in the application;

(g) ascertain whether the means and status of the petitioner are sufficient to enable him to maintain and bring up the child suitably;

(h) ascertain what rights or interests in property the child has;

(i) establish that the petitioner understands the nature and effect of an adoption order and in particular that the making of the order will render him responsible for the maintenance and upbringing of the child;

(j) where appropriate, ascertain when the mother of the child ceased to have the care and possession of the child and to whom care and possession was then transferred;

(k) ascertain whether any payment or other reward in consideration of the adoption has been given or agreed upon;

(l) establish whether the adoption is likely to safeguard and promote the welfare of the child throughout his life;

(m) ascertain whether the life of the child has been insured and if so for what sum;

(n) ascertain whether it may be in the interests of the welfare of the child that the sheriff should make any interim order or make the adoption order subject to particular terms and conditions or require the petitioner to make special provision for the child and if so what provision;

(o) where the petitioner is not ordinarily resident in the United Kingdom, establish whether a report has been obtained on the home and living conditions of the petitioner from a suitable agency in the country in which he is ordinarily resident;

(p) establish the reasons of the petitioner for wishing to adopt the child;

(q) establish to which religion, if any, the petitioner subscribes and the religious persuasion, if any, racial origin and cultural and linguistic background of the child;

(r) assess the considerations which might arise where the difference in ages as between the petitioner and the child is greater or less than the normal difference in age between parents and their children;

(s) consider such other matters, including the personality of the petitioner and, where appropriate, that of the child, which might affect the suitability of the petitioner and the child for the relationship created by adoption and affect the ability of the petitioner to bring up the child;

(t) ascertain whether it would be better for the child that the court should not make the order; and

(u) ascertain from the child whether he wishes to express a view and where a child indicates his wish to express a view, ascertain that view,

and, subject to paragraph (3), shall report in writing thereon to the sheriff within 4 weeks from the date of the interlocutor appointing the curator, or within such other period as the sheriff in his discretion may allow.

(3) Subject to any order made by the sheriff under rule 2.27(1)(a), the views of the child ascertained in terms of paragraph (2)(u) may, if the curator *ad litem* considers appropriate, be conveyed to the sheriff orally.

Procedure where child wishes to express a view
2.27—(1) Where a child has indicated his wish to express his views the sheriff, without prejudice to rule 2.26(2)(u)—
   (a) may order such procedural steps to be taken as he considers appropriate to ascertain the views of that child; and
   (b) shall not make an order under this Part unless an opportunity has been given for the views of that child to be obtained or heard.

(2) Where the views of a child, whether obtained under this rule or under rule 2.26(2)(u), have been recorded in writing, the sheriff may direct that such a written record shall—
   (a) be sealed in an envelope marked "Views of the child—confidential";
   (b) be available to a sheriff only;
   (c) not be opened by any person other than a sheriff; and
   (d) not form a borrowable part of the process.

Hearing
2.28—(1) On receipt of the reports of the reporting officer and the curator *ad litem* in respect of a child who is not free for adoption, the sheriff shall fix a diet of hearing.

(2) On receipt of the report of the curator *ad litem* in respect of a child who is free for adoption, the sheriff may fix a diet of hearing.

(3) The petitioner shall intimate in Form 7 the diet of hearing referred to in paragraphs (1) and (2) to—
   (a) in a petition for an adoption order, every person who can be found and whose agreement or consent to the making of such an order is required to be given or dispensed with; or
   (b) in a petition for an order under section 49(1) of the Act, every person who can be found and whose agreement to the making of such an order would be required if the application were for an adoption order.

(4) The sheriff may, if he considers it appropriate, ordain the petitioner to serve notice of the date of the hearing in Form 7 on—
   (a) any person or body having the rights and powers of a parent of the child or having the custody or care of the child or a local authority having the child committed to its care by virtue of sections 11, 54 or 86 of the 1995 Act or sections 5, 8 or 31 of the Children Act 1989;
   (b) any person liable by virtue of any order or agreement to contribute to the maintenance of the child;
   (c) the local authority to whom the petitioner has given notice of his intention to apply for an adoption order;
   (d) any other person or body who in the opinion of the sheriff ought to be served with notice of the hearing.

(5) Subject to paragraph (7), if no person entitled to appear at such a hearing appears to be heard, the sheriff may grant an adoption order on the motion of the petitioner.

(6) Subject to paragraph (7), if a person entitled to appear appears and

wishes to be heard, the sheriff may hear him or may order a further diet to be fixed at which he may be heard and evidence given at such a diet shall be given in the presence of the petitioner or his solicitor.

(7) Before making an order, the sheriff shall consider any report received by him in terms of section 73(14) of the 1995 Act.

Insufficient evidence

2.29 If the sheriff is not satisfied that the facts stated in the petition are supported by the documents lodged with it or by the reports of the curator *ad litem* and reporting officer, or if for any other reason he considers it appropriate he may order the production of further documents or that oral evidence be led.

Confidentiality

2.30—(1) Unless the sheriff otherwise directs, all documents lodged in process including the reports by the curator *ad litem* and the reporting officer shall be available only to the sheriff, the curator *ad litem*, the reporting officer and the parties; and such documents shall be treated as confidential by all persons involved in, or party to, the proceedings and by the sheriff clerk.

(2) The reporting officer and curator *ad litem* shall treat all information obtained in the exercise of their duties as confidential and shall not disclose any such information to any person unless disclosure of such information is necessary for the proper discharge of their duties.

(3) This rule is subject to rule 2.27(2).

Communications to the Registrar General

2.31 The communication to the Registrar General of an adoption order or order for the revocation of an adoption order required to be made by the sheriff clerk shall be made by sending a certified copy of the order to the Registrar General either by recorded delivery post in an envelope marked "Confidential", or by personal delivery by the sheriff clerk in a sealed envelope marked "Confidential".

Adoption orders

2.32—(1) An adoption order granted by the sheriff shall specify the name and address of the adoption agency, if any, which has taken part in the arrangements for placing the child in the care of the petitioner.

(2) No extract of an adoption order shall be issued except with the authority of the sheriff who made the order or, in that sheriff's absence, of the sheriff principal.

(3) The authority required by paragraph (2) shall be obtained by lodging a petition setting forth the reasons for which the extract is required.

Final procedure

2.33—(1) After the granting of an order under this Part the court process shall, immediately upon the communication under rule 2.31 being made or, in the event of an extract of the order being issued under rule 2.32, immediately upon the issue of such extract, be sealed by the sheriff clerk in an envelope marked "Confidential".

(2) The envelope referred to in paragraph (1) shall not be unsealed by the sheriff clerk or any other person having control of the records of that or any court, and the process shall not be made accessible to any person, for one hundred years after the date of the granting of the adoption order except—

(a) to an adopted child who has attained the age of sixteen years and to whose adoption the process refers;

(b) to the sheriff clerk, on an application made to him by an adoption agency and with the consent of the adopted person for the purpose only of ascertaining the name of the agency, if any, responsible for the placement of that person and informing the applicant of that name;

(c) to a person, on an application made by him to the sheriff setting forth the reasons for which access to the process is required;

(d) to a court, public authority or administrative board (whether in the United Kingdom or not) having power to authorise an adoption, on petition by it to the court which granted the original order requesting that information be made available from the process for the purpose of discharging its duties in considering an application for adoption and specifying the precise reasons for which access to the process is required; or

(e) to a person who is authorised by the Secretary of State to obtain information from the process for the purposes of such research as is intended to improve the working of adoption law and practice.

(3) The sheriff clerk shall—

(a) where an adoption order includes a determination under section 12(9) of the Act, intimate the making of that determination to the Principal Reporter; and

(b) where appropriate, intimate the making of an adoption order to the court by which an order freeing the child for adoption was made.

Amendment of adoption order

2.34—(1) An application under paragraph 4(1) of Schedule 1 to the Act (amendment of orders and rectification of registers) shall be by petition to the court which pronounced the adoption order.

(2) The sheriff may order the petitioner to intimate the petition to such persons as to the sheriff may seem appropriate.

Revocation of adoption order

2.35—(1) An application under section 46(1) of the Act (revocation of adoption order where adoptive parent marries other parent) shall be by petition to the court which pronounced the adoption order.

(2) On lodging of a petition under this rule, the sheriff shall order such service as he considers appropriate.

Application for removal of child pending adoption

2.36—(1) An application under section 27(1) (restrictions on removal where adoption agreed or application made under section 18(1)), section 28 (restrictions on removal where applicant has provided home for five years), section 29 (return of child taken away in breach of section 27 or 28) or section 30(2) (return of children placed for adoption) of the Act shall be made by minute lodged in the process of the original adoption petition.

(2) A minute under paragraph (1) shall set forth the relevant facts and the crave which the minuter wishes to make.

(3) On receipt of the minute the sheriff shall order a diet of hearing to be fixed and shall ordain the minuter to send a notice of such hearing in Form 15 together with a copy of the minute by registered post or by recorded delivery letter to the petitioner in the original petition, to the curator *ad litem* in the original petition, to any person who may have care and possession of the child and to such other persons as the sheriff may deem appropriate.

APPENDIX 2

STYLES AND INTERLOCUTORS

1. Oath of Curator *ad Litem* and Reporting Officer (*to be Administered at the Time of Appointment*)

(a) Edinburgh,   1986. In presence of AB sheriff
of   at
Compeared CD who declared his acceptance of the office of
curator *ad litem* and reporting officer in such cases as are remitted
to him by the sheriff for the purpose of investigating and reporting to
the court in terms of the Adoption (Scotland) Act 1978. (*To be
signed by the curator* ad litem *and reporting officer and witnessed by
the sheriff.*)

(b) Edinburgh,   1986. In presence of AB sheriff
of   at
Compeared CD who took an oath in the following terms: I, CD swear
by almighty God (*or affirms*) that I will faithfully perform the duties of
the office of curator *ad litem* and reporting officer in all matters under
the Adoption (Scotland) Act 1978 in which I may be appointed by the
sheriff of   at   to act as curator *ad litem* and
reporting officer. (*To be signed by the curator* ad litem *and reporting
officer and witnessed by the sheriff.*)

2. Interlocutor Nominating a Curator *ad Litem* and Reporting Officer[1]

Edinburgh,   1986. The sheriff having considered the cause
Appoints CD to be curator *ad litem* and reporting officer in the petition
for the purpose of investigating and reporting to the court in terms of
the Adoption (Scotland) Act 1978 and Act of Sederunt (Child Care and
Maintenance Rules) 1997 on or before four weeks from the date of this
interlocutor (*or within such period as the sheriff in his discretion may
allow*).

3. Interlocutor Freeing a Child for Adoption[2]

Edinburgh,   1986. The sheriff having resumed consideration
of the cause, Makes an order declaring the child AB free for adoption as
craved.

---

[1] See para. 7.01.
[2] *Lothian Regional Council v. A*, 1992 S.L.T. 858.

4. Interlocutor Making an Interim Order[3]

Edinburgh,   1986. The sheriff having resumed consideration of the cause, postpones the determination of the cause until (*being a date not exceeding two years*); appoints the curator *ad litem* to furnish a supplementary report on or before (*being a date about eight weeks before the end of the interim order*), makes an order giving the parental responsibilities and parental rights to the petitioners during the period of postponement, ordains the petitioners jointly and severally to aliment the child (*and add such other conditions as to education and supervision of the child as the court thinks fit*), appoints the clerk of court to send a copy of this interlocutor to the curator *ad litem*.

5. Adoption Order[4]

SHERIFFDOM OF LOTHIAN AND BORDERS AT EDINBURGH
Adoption
Order

Under the Adoption (Scotland) Act 1978

ADOPTION ORDER

in

PETITION

[of]

AB (*name and designation*) and CB (*name and designation*)

for

AUTHORITY TO ADOPT

DB (*name as in birth certificate or name by which
the child is ordinarily known*) residing with the petitioners

Edinburgh,   1986. The sheriff authorises the petitioners AB and CB to adopt the male (*or* female) child DB who was born in Scotland (*or such other country as may be*) on September 17, 1980 and is identical with DB to whom an entry numbered 123 was made on November 1, 1980 in the Register of Births for the registration district of Johnstone in the County of Renfrew relates, in terms of the Adoption (Scotland) Act 1978 (*if any conditions, insert them; if no conditions, insert* "No conditions"); directs the Registrar General for Scotland to make an entry regarding the said adoption in the Adopted Children Register in the form prescribed by him, giving the name R as the forename, and B as the surname of the child in that form, and to include the above-mentioned date and country of birth in the entry recording the adoption; and directs the Registrar General for Scotland to cause the entry of the birth of the child in the Register of Births to be marked with the word "adopted".

(1) Relationship of the petitioners to the child: The female petitioner is the mother of the child (*or as the case may be; if there is no relationship, insert* "None").

---

[3] See paras 1.09, 8.30.
[4] See para. 11.01.

(2) Adoption Agency which has taken part in the arrangements for placing the child in the care of the petitioners: (*insert name and address of adoption agency*; *if none, insert* "None").

6. Order to Adopt Child Abroad[5]

SHERIFFDOM OF LOTHIAN AND BORDERS AT EDINBURGH
Order to adopt a child abroad

Under the Adoption (Scotland) Act 1978

ORDER UNDER SECTION 49

in

PETITION

[of]

AB (*name and designation*) and CB (*name and designation*)

for

AUTHORITY TO ADOPT ABROAD

DB (*name as in birth certificate or name by which
the child is ordinarily known*) residing with the petitioners

Edinburgh,   1986. The sheriff makes an adoption order in favour of the petitioners under the Adoption (Scotland) Act 1978, section 49, vesting in the petitioners the parental responsibilities and parental rights in relation to the child (*if any conditions, insert them; if no conditions, insert* "Without any Conditions"); authorises the petitioners AB and CB to remove the male child DB who was born in Scotland (*or such other country as may be*) on September 17, 1980 and is identical with DB to whom an entry numbered 123 was made on November 1, 1980 in the Register of Births for the registration district of Johnstone in the County of Renfrew from Great Britain for the purpose of adopting the child under the law of the State of   in the Country of   ; directs the Registrar General for Scotland to make an entry regarding the provisional adoption in the Adopted Children Register in the form prescribed by him, giving the name R as the forename, and B as the surname of the child in that form, and to include the above-mentioned date and country of birth in the entry recording the provisional adoption; and directs the Registrar General for Scotland to cause the entry of the birth of the child (*or* the Adopted Children Register) to be marked with the words "proposed foreign adoption" (*or* "proposed foreign re-adoption") provisionally adopted.

(1) Relationship, etc. (*as in style 5.*)

7. Freeing Order

Edinburgh,   1986. The sheriff makes an order freeing for adoption the child AB who was born at   on   and who is identical with   to whom an entry numbered   was made

---

[5] See paras 1.10, 11.01.

on   in the Register of Births for the registration district of the county of   (*or as the case may be*), in terms of the Adoption (Scotland) Act 1978, section 18.

8. Interlocutor Appointing Statutory Hearing

Edinburgh,   1986. The sheriff having resumed consideration of the cause, Assigns (*date, time and place*) as diet of hearing in terms of Act of Sederunt (Child Care and Maintenance Rules) 1997, paragraph 2.11 (*petition to free a child for adoption*), or paragraph 2.28 (*petition for adoption*), appoints the petitioners to intimate the diet of hearing in terms of Form 7 to the natural parents of the child (*or other persons as the case may be*).

9. Interlocutor Appointing a Hearing on a Particular Point[6]

Edinburgh,   1986. The sheriff appoints the petitioners and their solicitors (or the solicitors of the petitioners) to be heard on the question of the care and possession of the child (*or whatever other matter*) and appoints (*time and place*) as a diet therefor.

10. Interlocutor Appointing a Proof[7]

Edinburgh,   1986. The sheriff on motion of parties (*or ex proprio motu*) allows parties a proof and appoints (*time and place*) as a diet therefor.

11. Interlocutor Making an Adoption Order Justifying the Exclusion of one Parent[8]

Edinburgh,   1986. The sheriff having resumed consideration of the cause and in particular the letter of the natural father (No.   of Process) finds that the natural father does not wish to take part in the adoption at the instance of the natural mother; therefore finds that there is reason justifying the exclusion of the natural father in terms of the Adoption (Scotland) Act 1978, section 15(3).

12. Declaration in Terms of Section 18[9]

(a) I, MN (*design*), the mother of the child, declare that I prefer not to be involved in future questions concerning the adoption of the child AB (*to be witnessed in the presence of the reporting officer*).

(b) The foregoing declaration was received at the office of the sheriff clerk on   and has been recorded in the adoption register of the court.

---

[6] See paras 5.20, 11.01.
[7] See para. 6.09.
[8] See para. 11.01.
[9] See paras 5.20, 11.01.

13. Revocation Order

Edinburgh,   1986. The sheriff having considered the foregoing minute and having seen the freeing application E63/89 in relation to the child AB, born on   and the order freeing the child for adoption granted on   , Revokes the same; Appoints intimation of this order to

(a) CD (*being the person to whom parental rights are given in consequence of the making of the revocation order*) and

(b) EF (*being the person on whom parental responsibilities are imposed in consequence of the making of the revocation order*) in terms of the Act of Sederunt (Child Care and Maintenance Rules) 1997, rule 2.18.

14. Interlocutor where Child Seeks Access to the Process (Assuming that the Court has a Locus in the Matter[10])

Edinburgh,   1986. The sheriff having considered the letter of AB dated   , having seen the sealed envelope containing the process of register or serial number 1234 (relating to the adoption of the child AB at the instance of CB and DB) which was granted on   and being satisfied that AB is the person to whom the adoption relates, and that he is now 16 years of age, authorises the sheriff clerk to make available to AB for inspection the process upon proof of his identity to the satisfaction of the clerk of court, all in terms of the Act of Sederunt (Child Care and Maintenance Rules) 1997, rule 2.33(2)(a); and thereafter to reseal the process. (*In any event the clerk of court should make a minute narrating that the process was opened up and a similar note on the outside of the envelope.*)

15. Petition for Access to the Process[11]

XY for the petitioner states to the court that:

(1) On   an adoption order with register or serial number of 1234 was granted in Edinburgh Sheriff Court.

(2) On   AB appeared on petition in that court charged at the instance of the present petitioner with *inter alia* perjury in respect that on   at Edinburgh Sheriff Court in a proof in the proceedings to which the process relates he deponed falsely on oath that (*take in the false statement*) whereas the truth as he well knew was (*take in true statement*).

(3) The petitioner is of the opinion that it is necessary for the purposes of his investigation for him to have access to the process (*or other reason as the case may be*).

Therefore the petitioner craves the court to ordain the clerk of court or other person having control of the records of the court to open up the process to furnish the petitioner with the process or a certified copy thereof in terms of the Act of Sederunt (Child Care and Maintenance Rules) 1997, rule 2.33(2)(c).

---

[10] See para. 11.07.

[11] *cf. B and B*, 1950 S.L.T. (Sh.Ct.) 34.

16. Letter to the Secretary of State Seeking Information from a Process[12]

CONFIDENTIAL: ADOPTIONS

Dear Sir

Adoption of children: Rules of Court, Rule 67.32(2)(f);
A v B, 1955 S.C. 378

I am presently engaged in writing a textbook on adoption in Scotland. It is not clear from the law report of this case (1955 S.C. 378) or from the Session Papers (which only relate to the custody aspect of the case) under what power the associated sheriff court case was transmitted to the Court of Session: I feel it would be necessary to see the motion sheet and interlocutor sheets to find this out. I understand that the process in its sealed state will now have been transmitted to the Keeper of the Records of Scotland.

In terms of rule 67.32(2)(f) it is necessary to have your authority in writing to open up the process and make it accessible to me so that I may obtain this information from the process. I would submit that the writing of such a textbook falls within the terms of the rule, *viz.*, "for the purpose of such research as is designed to improve the working of adoption law and practice". I have, of course, no interest at all in the identity of any of the parties to the petition.

If you are agreeable to my request, please let me know where and when the process may be seen.

17. Petition for Extract of an Adoption Order[13]

XY for the petitioners states to the court that:

(1) On   an adoption order with register or serial number 1234 was granted in Edinburgh Sheriff Court in favour of the petitioners.

(2) The petitioners and their family including the adopted child intend to emigrate to   and take up the nationality of that country.

(3) The immigration authorities there require an extract of the adoption order relating to the adopted child as appears from their letter which is produced (*or other reason as the case may be*).

> Therefore the petitioners crave the court to authorise the clerk of court or other person having control of the records to open up the process and give out an extract of the adoption order and transmit the extract to the petitioners on payment of the dues thereof; in terms of the Act of Sederunt (Child Care and Maintenance Rules) 1997, rule 2.32.

18(a). Petition to Correct an Error in Adoption Order[14]

XY for the petitioners states to the court that:

(1) On   an adoption order with register or serial number 1234 was granted in Edinburgh Sheriff Court in favour of the petitioners.

---

[12] See para. 11.13.
[13] See para. 11.01; *E and E, Petitioners*, Edinburgh Sh.Ct. (E197/74), July 24, 1985, unreported.
[14] See para. 12.02; *K and K, Petitioners*, Edinburgh Sh.Ct., October 3, 1985, unreported.

(2) It was stated in the petition for the adoption order and incorporated in the adoption order that the date of birth of the child was March 15, 1970 whereas the correct date of birth of the child is August 29, 1969 (*or other reason as the case may be*).

Therefore the petitioners crave the court to open up the process and to amend the adoption order dated   by altering the date of birth of the child from March 15, 1970 to August 29, 1969; and direct the Registrar General for Scotland to cause the entry in the Adopted Children Register to be amended accordingly, in terms of the Adoption (Scotland) Act 1978, Schedule 1, paragraph 4(1) and Act of Sederunt (Child Care and Maintenance Rules) 1997, rule 2.34; and thereafter to re-seal the process.

(b). Interlocutor Following Thereon

Edinburgh,   1986. The sheriff having resumed consideration of the cause, grants the prayer of the petition; directs the Registrar General for Scotland, to cause the entry relating to the child AB to be amended by deleting to the date of birth as March 15, 1970, and substituting therefor August 29, 1969, in terms of the Adoption (Scotland) Act 1978, Schedule 1, paragraph 4(1) and Act of Sederunt (Child Care and Maintenance Rules) 1997, rule 2.34.

19(a). Petition to Alter the Name of an Adopted Child[15]

XY for the petitioners states to the court that:

(1) On   an adoption order with register or serial number 1234 was granted in Edinburgh Sheriff Court in favour of the petitioners in which the name of the child by which he was to be known was specified in the prayer of the petition as John Smith.

(2) The petitioners are desirous that the child should be known as James Smith.

(3) Less than a year has elapsed since the granting of the order and the child being given this new name.

Therefore the petitioners crave the court to open up the process and to amend the adoption order dated   by altering the name of the child from John Smith to James Smith; and direct the Registrar General for Scotland to cause the entry in the Adopted Children Register to be amended accordingly, in terms of the Adoption (Scotland) Act 1978, Schedule 1, paragraph 4(1) and Act of Sederunt (Child Care and Maintenance Rules) 1997, rule 2.34; and thereafter to re-seal the process.

(b). Interlocutor Following Thereon

Edinburgh,   1986. The sheriff having resumed consideration of the cause, grants the prayer of the petition; directs the Registrar General for Scotland, to cause the entry relating to the child John Smith to be amended by deleting the forename "John" and substituting therefor the forename "James"; appoints the clerk of court to send a certified copy of

---

[15] See para. 12.03.

the amended order to the Registrar General for Scotland in terms of the Adoption (Scotland) Act 1978, Schedule 1, paragraph 4(1) and Act of Sederunt (Child Care and Maintenance Rules) 1997, rule 2.35 and thereafter to re-seal the process.

20. Petition to Revoke a Direction Wrongly Included in an Adoption Order

XY for the petitioners states to the court that:

(1) On   an adoption order with register or serial number 1234 was granted in Edinburgh Sheriff Court in favour of the petitioners.

(2) The adoption order wrongly included the name of the child as John Smith whereas the correct name of the child as was specified in the prayer of the petition is James Smith.

(3) The Registrar General for Scotland has in conformity with the adoption order made an entry in the Adopted Children Register in the name of John Smith.

(4) The error only came to the notice of the petitioners when they procured an extract of an entry in the Adopted Children Register relative to the child.

Therefore the petitioners crave the court to open up the process and to amend the adoption order dated   by substituting for the name "John Smith" the name "James Smith", and direct the Registrar General for Scotland to cause the entry in the Adopted Children Register to be amended accordingly, in terms of the Adoption (Scotland) Act 1978, Schedule 1, paragraph 4(1) and Act of Sederunt (Child Care and Maintenance Rules) 1997, rule 2.35; and thereafter to re-seal the process.

21. Petition to Revoke an Adoption Order on the Marriage of the Parents of the Child[16]

XY for the petitioners states to the court that:

(1) On   an adoption order to which register or serial number 1234 had been assigned was made in Edinburgh Sheriff Court whereby the first petitioner adopted the child DB who was born at   on   .

(2) The child was the illegitimate child of the petitioners.

(3) The petitioners were married to each other on   and the child was thereby legitimated.

(4) The petitioners wish that the adoption order be revoked in terms of the Adoption (Scotland) Act 1978, section 46.

Therefore the petitioners crave the court to revoke the adoption order of register or serial number 1234 dated   direct the Registrar General for Scotland to cancel the entry in the Adopted Children Register relating to the child DB and also the marking with the word "adopted" (*or, as the case may be, with that word and the word* "Scotland" *or* "(England)") of any entry relating to him in the Register of Births.

---

[16] See paras 1.23, 12.05.

22. Minute for Leave to Remove a Child from Custody of a Person with whom the Child has his Home[17]

XY for the minuter states to the court that:

(1) On   a petition for adoption (*or* to free a child for adoption) with register or serial number 1234 was presented and is presently pending in respect of the child AB.

(2) The minuter is the mother of the child.

(3) On or about   the minuter gave her agreement to the making of the adoption order at a time when she felt that she was unable to look after the child properly.

(4) The minuter now believes that she can give a good home to the child and she wishes to withdraw her agreement and take the child back into her custody.

> Therefore the minuter craves the court to fix a date for the hearing of the minute and ordains the minuter to serve notice in Form 15 together with a copy of the minute by registered post or recorded delivery to the petitioners, the curator *ad litem*, to any other person who may have the care and possession of the child and to such other person or persons as the sheriff shall deem appropriate (if any) in terms of the Adoption (Scotland) Act 1978, section 27(1) (*or* section 27(2)) and Act of Sederunt (Child Care and Maintenance Rules) 1997, paragraph 2.36.

23. Minute for Leave to Remove a Child where the Applicant has Provided a Home for Five Years[18]

(*Adapt style 22 as required by the Adoption (Scotland) Act 1978, section 28.*)[19]

24. Minute for Return of a Child taken away in Breach of Section 27 or Section 28 of the 1978 Act[20]

(*Adapt style 22 as required by the Adoption (Scotland) Act 1978, section 28.*)

25. Minute by an Adoption Agency for Return of Child Placed for Adoption[21]

XY for the minuters states to the court that:

(1) On   the child was delivered into the care and possession of the petitioners in pursuance of arrangements made by the minuters for adoption of the child.

(2) No adoption order has been made in respect of the child.

(3) The minuters are apprehensive about the safety of the child while in the care and possession of the petitioners, in respect that (*state the circumstances*).

---

[17] See para. 5.12.
[18] See para. 5.12.
[19] See para. 5.12.
[20] See para. 5.12.
[21] See para. 5.12.

(4) The minuters wish to give notice in writing of their intention not to allow the child to remain in the care and possession of the petitioners.

Therefore the minuters crave the court to fix a date for hearing of the minute, etc. (*as in style 22*) in terms of the Adoption (Scotland) Act 1978, section 30(2) and Act of Sederunt (Child Care and Maintenance Rules) 1997, paragraph 2.36.

APPENDIX 3

FORMS OF REPORTS[1]

Preamble

It is desirable for the clerk of court to make available to curators *ad litem*, reporting officers and others, information about their duties, as follows:

(1) The curator *ad litem* or the reporting officer should not take up this appointment if he is employed by, or has been recently employed by:

    (a) the adoption agency which placed the child for adoption;

    (b) the adoption agency which are the petitioners in a freeing for adoption;

    (c) the adoption agency, which in a minute to revoke, have the parental rights and duties in relation to the child;

    (d) the local authority which must report to the court under section 22 of the 1978 Act; or

    (e) a solicitor acting in the case;

but should be in touch with the clerk of court.

(2) The fees of the curator *ad litem* and the reporting officer become due when the report is lodged with the sheriff clerk, and are the responsibility of the solicitor for the petitioners *or*, if the petitioners have no solicitor, the petitioners themselves *or* the local authority in terms of Statutory Instrument 1984 No. 566, paragraph 10 (*delete which is inapplicable*).

(3) Where the report is called for by the court, the report should begin with the interlocutor of the court at the top of the first page. In all cases, the instance and register or serial number should be on the first page, with the report proper beginning on a fresh page: that second page should be headed by the register number or serial number only. In the report itself, no reference should be made to the child or the parties by name, or in any other way whereby they may be identified. The style of the **first page** is as follows.

---

[1] See Chap. 8.

SHERIFFDOM OF LOTHIAN AND BORDERS AT EDINBURGH

Edinburgh, January 1986. The sheriff [*take in interlocutor appointing curator* ad litem *or the reporting officer or both*]

REPORT

NM (*design*)
Curator *ad litem* (*or reporting officer*)

in

PETITION

of

AB and CB (*design*)

PETITIONERS

To free for adoption (*or* to adopt) the child, CD (*design*)
(which petition has assigned to it serial number SN 222/85 (if any)
and

register number E999/85)

A. PETITION TO FREE CHILD FOR ADOPTION

1. Report of Reporting Officer[2]

REPORT

of Reporting Officer

in

Petition which has assigned to it serial number SN 222/85 (if any)
and
register number E999/85

(a) The natural mother (*or* natural father) gave consent to the making of this application and wishes the child to be adopted.

(b) I have witnessed the agreement of the mother and the father to the making of an adoption order.

(c) The natural mother (*or* father) understands that the effect of the adoption order will be to extinguish her (*or* his) responsibilities and rights, *or* the natural mother or father cannot be found (*narrate the efforts to trace the parent*).

(d) The natural mother and father told me that alternatives to adoption had been discussed with them.

(e) There is no person other than those mentioned in the petition

---

[2] A.S. 1997, r. 2.8(1) (RCS, r. 67.11(1)); see paras 8.62 *et seq.*

upon whom notice of the petition should be served (in the Court of Session, "should be informed of the petition": R.C. 67.11(1)(h) and 67.24(1)(h)).

(f) The child is not the subject of a supervision order, *or* is the subject of a supervision order made at   on   .

(g) Each parent understands the implications of the order freeing the child for adoption (*or as the case may be*).

(h) Each parent who has given his agreement understands that he may withdraw his agreement at any time before the order under section 18(1) is made.

(i) Each parent who has given his agreement understands that he may in the circumstances set forth in section 20 of the 1978 Act apply for revocation of the freeing order and is aware of the appropriate procedure for such an application: the declaration under section 18(1) has been signed by the parent and witnessed by me; I have given a copy of the form of declaration to the parent; and I have explained to him the consequences of signing the declaration in terms of section 19 of the 1978 Act on progress reports to former parents.

(j) Each parent has been given an opportunity to make a declaration in terms of section 18(6) of the 1978 Act on progress reports to the former parents.

(k) The father of the child was not married to the mother of the child. XY claims to be the father of the child; but the mother denies that he is. XY is married and lives with his wife and their two children at   ; he is unemployed. He has shown no interest in the child or the mother or in the present process. In these circumstances there is little likelihood of XY (a) applying for an order under section 11 of the 1995 Act, or (b) entering into a agreement in terms of section 4(1) of the 1995 Act (*or as the case may be*).

"NM"
Reporting Officer

2. Report of Curator *ad Litem*[3]

REPORT

of curator *ad litem*

in

Petition which has assigned to it serial number SN 222/85 (if any)
and
register number E999/85

(a) In the opinion of the curator *ad litem* the interests of the child have been safeguarded. In the circumstances narrated in this report the curator

---

[3] A.S. 1997, r. 2.8(2) (RCS, r. 67.11(2)).

is of the opinion that the freeing of the child for adoption is likely to safeguard and promote the welfare of the child throughout his life *or* the curator is of the opinion that the freeing of the child for adoption would not safeguard and promote the welfare of the child: particular reference is made to paragraphs   and   (*or as the case may be*).

(b) Apart from the facts which fall within the duties of the reporting officer, the facts stated in the petition are correct, except (*state any exceptions*).

(c) The child who is over the age of 12 has consented to the order. The form of consent has been signed by the child and witnessed by me and is lodged in process, *or* the child is incapable of giving his consent because he is suffering from mental illness. A medical reported dated   is produced.

(d) The child wishes to express a view and that view is (*take in the view of the child*), *or* the child does not wish to express a view.

(e) In my view the freeing of the child for adoption would safeguard and, throughout his life, promote the welfare of the child.

(f) In my view it would be better for the child that the court should make the order than that it should not make the order (*or as the case may be*)

(g) The child is presently in the care of   (*describe briefly the care and the circumstances*).

"NM"

Curator *ad litem*

3. Report of Adoption Agency[4]

This report has been prepared by NM, an officer of the   Agency from information that the Agency has been able to discover in accordance with the Adoption Agencies (Scotland) Regulations 1996, reg. 22.

(a) The needs of the child came to the notice of the petitioners (*take in the circumstances*).

(b) The family circumstances of the child are (*take in the circumstances*).

(c) The child's physical and mental health are good; he has no special needs; his emotional, behavioural and educational development is appropriate to his years (*or as the case may be*).

(d) At meetings with them the petitioners have discussed with the parents and the child (who is 12 years old) their wishes and the alternatives to adoption, *or* the petitioners have been unable to trace the parents (*or as the case may be*).

---

[4] This form is based on the sheriff court rules where the report is to be lodged in process at the same time as the lodging of the petition: (A.S. 1997, r. 2.52). In the Court of Session the petition "shall include averments in relation to, or refer to a report or other documents produced which deal with" the matters enumerated in the rule which are substantially the same as are set out in the sheriff court rules: RCS, r. 67.9(2); see paras 5.19, 8.70.

(e) To the knowledge of the petitioners, AB, the grandmother of the child and DE, a friend of the mother of the child are likely to be involved in the child as persons who cared for the child (*or as the case may be*).

(f) The petitioners have asked the mother of the child about the identity and whereabouts of GH, the parent (*or* guardian) of the child, but she has no knowledge of this (*or as the case may be*).

(g) There is every likelihood that the child will be placed for adoption; and the adoption petition is likely in the near future (*or as the case may be*).

(h) In the event of the order freeing the child for adoption being granted the petitioners propose that the child will be in the care of foster parents (*or as the case may be*).

(i) The petitioners have discussed at length with the parents whether they wish to make a declaration under section 18(6) of the 1978 Act and they prefer not to be involved in future questions concerning the adoption of the child (*or as the case may be*).

(j) The petitioners have seen XY who claims to be the father of the child but whom the mother denies is the father. XY is married and lives with his wife and their two children at   ; he is unemployed. He has shown no interest in the child or the mother or in the present process. In these circumstances there is little likelihood of XY (a) applying for an order under section 11 of the 1995 Act or (b) entering into an agreement in terms of section 4(1) of the 1995 Act (*or as the case may be*).

(k) The petitioners intend in giving notice under section 19(2) and (3) to the former parent to (*take in their intention*).

(l) The petitioners have no further information to report (*or as the case may be*).

"NM"
(*designation*)

B. MINUTE TO REVOKE A FREEING ORDER

4. Report of Curator *ad Litem*[5]

(a) The curator *ad litem* has investigated the facts contained in the minute and found them to be correct, except (*take in any exceptions and state the true facts*).

(b) The child is   years old, and having been born on   at   . The child was in the care and possession of the natural mother until when he was transferred to the care of   .

(c) Since the order freeing the child for adoption was made on   the child has been in the care of   at   .

(d) In the opinion of the curator *ad litem* the welfare of the child throughout his life would be best achieved by refusing (*or granting*) this application because (*state briefly the reasons*).

---

[5] A.S. 1997, r. 2.8 (RCS, r. 67.11); see paras 5.35, 8.61.

(e) The child is   years old and is not of sufficient age and maturity to form a view, *or* The child is aged 12 and wishes to express a view and that view is that he wishes to remain with   *or* he wishes to be returned to the care of his mother (*or as the case may be*), *or* the child does not wish to express a view.

"NM"
Curator *ad litem*

C. PETITION FOR ADOPTION

5. Report by Reporting Officer[6]

(a) The reporting officer has witnessed the agreement to the making of an adoption order in respect of the child in the petition by the natural mother. The agreement is lodged in process, *or* she declines to give her agreement, *or* the reporting officer has been unable to trace the natural mother (*state efforts to trace the natural mother and produce copy letters or returned postal packets, or, as the case may be. Similarly, in relation to the natural father*).

(b) The natural mother (*or* the natural father) understands that the effect of the adoption order would be to deprive her (*or* him permanently of her (*or* his) parental rights.

(c) The reporting officer has ascertained that alternatives to adoption have been discussed with the natural mother (*or* the natural father).

(d) There is no person other than those mentioned in the petition upon whom the notice of the petition should be served; *or* notice of the petition should be served on (*take in names*).

(e) The natural mother (*or* natural father) understands that she (*or* he) may withdraw the agreement at any time before the order sought is made. (*This paragraph will require to be adapted depending on the circumstances*).

"NM"
Reporting Officer

6. Report of Curator *ad Litem*[7]

(a) In the opinion of the curator *ad litem* the interests of the child have been safeguarded.

(b) It is impracticable in the view of the age of the child to ascertain his wishes and feelings, but the petitioners intend to inform the child that he is adopted as soon as possible when a suitable moment arises, *or* The child who is over the age of 12 has consented to the order. The form of consent has been signed by the child and witnessed by me and is lodged in process, *or* The child is incapable of giving his consent because he is suffering from mental illness. A medical report dated   is produced.

---

[6] A.S. 1997, r. 2.26(1) (RCS, r. 67.11(1)); see para. 8.62.
[7] A.S. 1997, r. 21.2 (RCS, r. 67.11(2)); see para. 8.07.

The statements in the petition have been investigated and it appears that they are correct, except (*state any exceptions*) and the true facts are (*state the true facts*).

(d) The petitioners are joint owners of a semi-detached villa of four (*or as the case may be*) apartments with kitchen and bathroom in the   district of the city. The house is well furnished and maintained.

(e) The household consists of the petitioners, the child and the father of the female petitioner. The petitioners are related to the child in that the female petitioner is the mother of the child, *or* the petitioners are not related to the child. The other members of the household are   and their relationship to the petitioners is   .

(f) This is a joint petition; and both petitioners confirmed that they wish to adopt the child, *or* one spouse is not a petitioner because that spouse cannot be found (*or other reason specified in section 15(1)(b) of the 1978 Act*), *or* the petitioner is married to the natural parent of the child in whom are vested parental responsibilities and parental rights in relation to the child.

(g) The male petitioner is a   and earns £   per week; the female petitioner is a housewife and has no separate income apart from child benefit of £   per week. The petitioners have a building society loan over their house in respect of which the monthly repayments are £   ; they also pay council tax of £   . It appears that their means are sufficient to enable them to maintain and bring up the child suitably.

(h) The child has no right to, or interest in, any property; *or* the child is the owner of (*take in a brief description of the property*).

(i) The petitioners understand the nature and effect of an adoption order and in particular that the order, if granted, will render them responsible for the maintenance and upbringing of the child.

(j) The child is   years of age having been born on   at   . The child was in the care and possession of the natural mother from birth until about six weeks thereafter, when she left the child in the care of the petitioners who have had the care and possession of the child since then; *or* the child has been in the care and possession of the female petitioner since birth and in the joint care and possession of the petitioners since their marriage. The adoption arrangements were undertaken privately, *or* were undertaken by the   Adoption Society (*take in address*).

(k) No payment or other reward appears to have been given or agreed upon in consideration of the adoption; except that the adoption agency has resolved to pay an adoption allowance to the petitioners of £   per week in respect of the child, in terms of their scheme which has been approved by the Secretary of State, beginning on   (*or as the case may be*).

(l) In the circumstances narrated in this report the curator is of the opinion that the adoption is likely to safeguard and promote the welfare of the child throughout his life.

(m) No insurance appears to have been effected over the life of the child; *or* life policy number   for £   has been effected over the life of the child by the petitioners and the premiums are kept up by them.

(n) The curator is of the opinion that there is no need to make an interim order or to impose any particular terms and conditions in making the order; *or* to make special provision for the child (*such as medical treatment*); *or*, in view of the obvious immaturity of the petitioners, the curator feels that the court may wish to proceed in the first instance by way of an interim order of one (*or* two) years.

(o) The petitioners are ordinarily resident in the United Kingdom, and are of   nationality; *or* the male petitioner is ordinarily resident in Germany and a report is produced on his home and living conditions there from the local authority there.

(p) The petitioners wish to adopt the child so that both of them may have full parental rights over the child, *or* because the female petitioner is unable to have children herself (*or as the case may be*).

(q) The petitioners are members of the Church of Scotland and intend to bring up the child in that persuasion (*or as the case may be*). The child was born in Scotland of Scottish parents and has lived all his life in Scotland: his origin and cultural and linguistic background are Scottish.

(r) The male petitioner is   years old and the female petitioner is   and the child is   : the curator is of the opinion that the petitioners are within the normally accepted age range of parenthood; *or* notwithstanding the age of the female petitioner, she is very active and has already coped well with the child for almost a year (*or as the case may be*).

(s) (*The contents of this paragraph must be so peculiar to the circumstances of each case that it would be of little value to do more than enumerate the matters set forth in the Act of Sederunt, para. 2.26(2)(s), viz. such other questions or matters, including an assessment of the personalities of the petitioners and (where appropriate) the child, as having a bearing on (i) the mutual suitability of the petitioners and the child for the relationship created by adoption, and (ii) the ability of the petitioners to bring up the child.*)

(t) The welfare of the child would be better safeguarded and promoted by the making of an adoption order, than it would be by not making the order.

(u) The child is   years old and is not of sufficient age and maturity to form a view; *or* the child is aged 12 and wishes to express a view and that view is that he wishes to remain with   *or* he wishes to be returned to the care of his mother (*or as the case may be*) or the child does not wish to express a view.

(v) The curator *ad litem* has been able to consider the report of the local authority (under section 22) *or* of the adoption agency (under section 23) and has no observations to make (*or as the case may be*); *or* the curator *ad litem* has not been able to see the report of the local authority (under section 22) *or* of the Adoption Agency (under section 23) and is unable to make any observations on it.

"NM"
Curator *ad litem*

7. Report of Adoption Agency (under *Section 22 or 23*)

This report under section 22 was prepared by NM, an officer of the   Council, from visits to the home of the petitioners (*or as the case may be*), *or* This report under section 23 has been prepared by NM, an officer of the   Agency from information that the Agency has been able to discover in accordance with the Adoption Agencies (Scotland) Regulations 1996, regulation 22.

(a) The needs of the child came to the notice of the agency in the following way (*state the circumstances*).

(b) The family circumstances are (*state the circumstances*).

(c) The child was (*or* was not) placed by an adoption agency. The physical and mental health of the child is good (*or as the case may be*); the child has no special needs (*or as the case may be*); and his emotional, behavioural and educational development is appropriate to his years (*or as the case may be*).

(d) At meetings with them the petitioners have discussed with the parents and the child (who is 12 years old) their wishes and the alternatives to adoption, *or* the petitioners have been unable to trace the parents (*or as the case may be*).

(e) To the knowledge of the petitioners, AB, the grandmother of the child and DE, a friend of the mother of the child, are likely to be involved in the child as persons who cared for the child (*or as the case may be*).

(f) The petitioners have asked the mother of the child about the identity and whereabouts of GH, the parent (*or* guardian) of the child but she has no knowledge of this (*or as the case may be*).

(g) The petitioners and the child have lived together for   and are mutually suitable for the relationship created by adoption and the petitioners, who have two children of their own, are well able to bring up the child (*or as the case may be*). The personality of the petitioners is (*take in*). The personality of the child is (*take in*).

(h) The household consists of the petitioners, the child and the father of the female petitioner. The petitioners are related to the child in that the female petitioner is the mother of the child; *or* the petitioners are not related to the child. The other members of the household are   and their relationship to the petitioners is   (*or as the case may be*).

---

[8] A.S. 1997, r. 2.21(3) (RCS, r. 67.21(1)); see para. 8.07.

(i) The petitioners are joint owners of a semi-detached villa *or* flat of   apartments (*or as the case may be*) with kitchen and bathroom in the   district of the city. The house is well furnished and maintained.

(j) This is a joint petition; and both petitioners confirmed that they wish to adopt the child, *or* one spouse is not a petitioner because that spouse cannot be found (*or other reason specified in section 15(1)(b) of the 1978 Act*) *or* the petitioner is married to the natural parent of the child in whom are vested parental responsibilities and parental rights in relation to the child.

(k) The petitioners understand the nature and effect of an adoption order and in particular that the order, if granted, will render them responsible for the maintenance and upbringing of the child.

(l) The male petitioner is a   and earns £   per week; the female petitioner is a housewife and has no separate income apart from child benefit of £   per week. The petitioners have a building society loan over their house in respect of which the monthly repayments are £   ; they also pay council tax of £   . It appears that their means are sufficient to enable them to maintain and bring up the child suitably.

(m) No payment or other reward appears to have been given or agreed upon in consideration of the adoption; except that the adoption agency has resolved to pay an adoption allowance to the petitioners of £   per week in respect of the child, in terms of their scheme which has been approved by the Secretary of State, beginning on

.

(n) No insurance appears to have been affected over the life of the child; *or* life policy number   for £   has been effected over the life of the child by the petitioners and the premiums are kept up by them.

(o) The petitioners are members of the Church of Scotland and intend to bring up the child in that persuasion (*or as the case may be*). The child was born in Scotland of Scottish parents and has lived all his life in Scotland: his origin and cultural and linguistic background are Scottish.

(p) The male petitioner is   years old and the female petitioner is   and the child is   : it appears that the petitioners are within the normally accepted age range of parenthood; *or* notwithstanding the age of the female petitioner, she is very active and has already coped well with the child for almost a year (*or as the case may be*).

(q) In the circumstances narrated in this report the adoption is likely to safeguard and promote the welfare of the child throughout his life.

(r) There is no further information to report (*or as the case may be*).

(s) (*In a report by a local authority under section 22(2) only*) The proposed adopter is the mother (*or* other relative) of the child, and accordingly the child was placed in accordance with section 11 of the 1978 Act.

"NM"
(*designation*)

APPENDIX 4

OVERSEAS REGISTERS[1]

The countries in the list which follows are those in respect of which orders in council have been made under Evidence (Foreign, Dominion and Colonial Documents) Act 1933 and Oaths and Evidence (Overseas Authorities and Countries) Act 1963 whereby an official copy of an entry in the public registers of those countries is admissible in the courts in the United Kingdom in so far as it conforms with the terms of the order. After each country is the year and number of the statutory instrument which incorporates the order in council relating to that country.

Aden 1965/1527
Australia (Commonwealth) 1938/739
Antigua 1965/312
Bahamas 1961/2041
Barbados........................... 1962/641
Basutoland........................ 1965/1719
Bechuanaland 1965/1720
Belgium 1933/383
Belize. *See* British Honduras, below.
Bermuda 1961/2042
Botswana. *See* Bechuanaland, above.
British Antarctic Territory 1962/2605
British Guiana 1961/2043
British Honduras................. 1961/2044
British Indian Ocean Territory ... 1984/857
Canada............................ 1962/2606
Cayman Islands.................... 1965/313
Denmark........................... 1969/144
Dominica 1961/2045
Falkland Islands 1962/2607
Fiji................................ 1961/2046
France............................ 1937/515
Germany (Federal Republic) 1970/819
Gibraltar.......................... 1961/2047
Grenada............................ 1966/82

Guyana. *See* British Guiana, above.
Hong Kong........................ 1962/642
Ireland (Republic) 1969/1059
Italy 1969/145
Jamaica 1962/643
Kenya 1965/1712
Lesotho. *See* Basutoland, above.
Luxembourg....................... 1972/116
Mauritius 1961/2048
Montserrat........................ 1962/644
Netherlands....................... 1970/284
New Zealand 1959/1306
St. Helena 1961/2049
St. Lucia 1965/1722
Sarawak........................... 1961/2050
Seychelles 1962/2608
Sierra Leone...................... 1962/2609
Swaziland 1965/1865
Tanganyika 1961/2051
Tanzania. *See* Tanganyika, above and Zanzibar, below.
Turks and Caicos Islands........... 1966/83
Uganda 1961/2052
U.S.A............................. 1969/146
Zanzibar 1961/2053

---

[1] See para. 5.22.

INDEX

[References are to paragraph numbers of the text or to the appendices]

257

Hearing, *cont.*
should if appropriate have notice of,
7.03
statutory, 6.01, 8.77
appearance or representation of
parties, 5.15, 10.02
court must order, after reports of
curator *ad litem* and reporting
officer have been lodged, 6.04
deals with agreements of parents and
consents of children, 5.43
disposal of agreements, 10.11
interlocutor ordering, Append. 2.8
intimation of, 5.43. *See also*
Intimation.
introduced in 1984, 5.43, 6.04
mode of appearance or
representation, 8.77
must be ordered,
even if parties are not in dispute, 6.04
in adoption of child abroad, 5.43
in adoption, where child is not free
for adoption, 8.77
in freeing order, 8.77
not necessary in petition for
adoption, if child has been freed
for adoption, 6.05
notice on all parents, even if also a
petitioner, 10.04
opposed petitions, court normally
appoints a proof, 6.05, 8.77
personal appearance of petitioners
not required, 10.02
petitioners to lodge execution of
service of notice, 6.06
procedure, 8.77
unopposed petition, court usually
grants order at, 6.04, 8.77
Home environment, adoption agency or
local authority to be afforded an
opportunity to see child with
petitioners in, 3.05
Homosexual petitioner, a circumstance to
be considered, 8.25 *et seq.*

Interim order, 1.09, 8.30, Append. 2.4
duration to be stated, 8.31, 11.01
extract of, petitioners have a right to,
11.01
interlocutor, 11.01
intimation to curator *ad litem*, 8.31
limited effect of, 1.09
may be for up to two years, 8.30
nature of, 8.30, Append. 2.4
parental responsibilities and parental
rights, 1.09
subject to appeal, 13.01
supplementary report of curator *ad
litem* before end of, 8.31, 11.01,
Append. 2.4
Interlocutors, 5.27, Append. 2
adopting a child abroad, Append. 2.6

Interlocutors, *cont.*
allowing access to process by child at
16, 11.09, Append. 2.14
altering name of child, 12.02
appointing a hearing, 5.27, 11.01,
Append. 2.8
proof, 6.09, Append. 2.10
service in terms of Form 7, 5.27
appointing curator *ad litem* and
reporting officer, 5.27, 7.01,
Append. 2.2
excluding one spouse, 11.01, Append. 2.11
final, 11.01, *cf.* Append. 2.5
freeing child for adoption, *cf.* Append.
2.5
granting adoption order, 11.01, *cf.*
Append. 2.5
granting interim order, 8.30, 11.01, *cf.*
Append. 2.4
granting order adopting child abroad,
1.10, *cf.* Append. 2.6
pronounced as situation demands, 5.27
records each step in procedure, 5.27
revoking a freeing order, Append. 2.13
Interview by the court, 6.03
generally not required where facts not
in dispute, 6.04
in camera, 6.04
judge may examine witnesses, 6.04
on oath, 6.04
signs interlocutor thereafter, 6.04
solicitor may be present, and examine
witnesses, 6.04
witnesses usually seen separately, 6.04
Intimation of hearing
every person whose agreement or
consent is required, 5.43, 5.44, 8.76
judicial intimation under Citation
Amendment (Scotland) Act 1882,
s. 3, 5.19
persons on whom, may be made. *See
also* **Hearing**
Intimation of petition, not provided for,
5.43, 5.44, 8.76
Isle of Man, 1.35

Judgment, form of, 13.03
Judgments, public documents open to
inspection, 11.06
**Judgments should not mention parties by
name,** 11.06
Jurisdiction
child outwith Great Britain, Court of
Session has private jurisdiction, 5.09
Convention adoption order, Court of
Session has privative jurisdiction,
5.09
EEC/E.U. rules of, not applicable to
adoption procedure, 2.06
freeing for adoption, 5.08
prorogation not competent, 2.06
See also **Authorised court.**

Law reports, should not mention parties by name, 5.03
Lay person, other than a party,
not entitled to appear in court, 5.11, 5.18
not entitled to present papers in court offices, 5.11, 5.18
Legal aid
application need not be concerned with unmarried father of child, 14,01
assessment under s. 2(6)(e), 14.01
availability, 5.15
certificate to be lodged in process, 5.19
liability of unsuccessful assisted party, 5.15
Legislation governing adoption, 1.02 *et seq.*
Legitimation
citizenship and, 1.29
following adoption order, 1.22
following on marriage of parents makes revocation competent, 1.23
former procedure, 1.01
of child, revocation of adoption order, 12.05(d), Append. 2.21
Local authority
adoption agency includes, 4.12
defined, 4.12, 5.13
elected members may see reports, 5.03
English, included in definition of adoption agency, 5.13
may make arrangements for adoption of child, 4.12
notice to, of intention to adopt, 3.05 *et seq.*
proved by production of acknowledgment, 5.23
to be produced in process, 5.19

Male petitioner, alone adopting female child, 3.04
Marriage
certificate of petitioners, to be produced, 5.19
child who is or has been married, cannot be adopted, 3.02
Married couple as petitioners, 2.01, 2.02
Medical report
no prescribed style in sheriff court, 5.19
Medical evidence
health of petitioner, 2.08
ill-treatment of child, 2.08
inability to give consent or agreement, 2.08, 10.13
not to be called on self-evident matters, 5.06
Medical report
capacity of parent to give agreement to adoption order, 10.13
health of child
necessary, where child not placed by adoption agency, 5.19
reasonably up to date, 5.19
style, 5.19

Merits
adoption, dealt with, whether or not child is free for adoption, 9.01
no one fact to be decisive, 9.03
"totality of circumstances" to be considered, 9.03
Minute, 13.02
for leave to give notice not to allow child to remain in care and possession, 5.13, Append. 2.25
for leave to remove child, 5.13, Append. 2.23
for return of child, 5.13, Append. 2.24
(or note) to revoke freeing order, 5.17

Name of child, alteration, 12.03, Append. 2.19
Nationality, 1.29
of child in Convention adoption order, 3.09
Natural mother, minor, generally need not have curator *ad litem*, 7.02
Natural parents, best interests of child to be with, 10.17
Note to revoke freeing order. *See* **Minute.**

Offences
making arrangements for adoption, not being an approved adoption society or local authority, 4.13
making or giving a payment or reward in consideration of adoption, etc., 8.20
removal of child from care and possession, 5.13
taking a child out of Great Britain with a view to adoption, 1.10
Opposed petitions, 10.01
most petitions unopposed, 10.01
Order freeing child for adoption to be produced in subsequent petition for adoption, 5.19
Order not granted
court refuses the prayer of petition, 11.02
petition withdrawn, 11.02
refusal
competent without further documents or evidence, 11.02
court may not make new order unless change in circumstances, 11.02
or withdrawal, disposal of child, 11.02
Ordinary residence, 2.06
adoption of child abroad, 1.10, Append. 2.6
affidavit on foreign law to be produced, 5.09
Outer House, petitions presented to, 5.09